SPONSOR OF THE PUBLICATION

iΣN SNf STAVROS NIARCHOS FOUNDATION

Great Moments in

GREEK ARCHAEOLOGY

© 2007 Kapon Editions, Athens, Greece
23-27 Makriyanni Str. Athens 117 42, Greece
e-mail: kapon_ed@otenet.gr   www.kaponeditions.gr

English translation © 2007 Kapon Editions
First published in Greek and English by Kapon Editions

Second printing

At Kapon Editions
Rachel Misdrachi-Kapon, *Designer*
Moses Kapon, *Artistic Consultant*
Dora Dialeti-Komini, Zeta Livieratou, George Diamantis, *Copy Editors*
Eleni Valma, Matina Vroulou, Ioannis Alekou, *DTP*
Stelios Anastasiou, Michalis Janetakis, *Processor of Illustrations*
D. Plessas, Michailides Brothers, Toxo, *Colour separations*

Printed by Magna Print Ltd
Bound by Moutsis Brothers
Printed on Magno Satin, 150 gsm

Published in English in the United States of America in 2007 by
The J. Paul Getty Museum, Los Angeles

Getty Publications
1200 Getty Center Drive, Suite 500
Los Angeles, California 90049-1682
www.getty.edu

At Getty Publications
Gregory M. Britton, *Publisher*
Mark Greenberg, *Editor in Chief*
Ann Lucke, *Managing Editor*
Cynthia Newman Bohn, *Copy Editor*

Library of Congress Cataloging-in-Publication Data

Great moments in Greek archaeology /Panos Valavanis,
Vasileios Petrakos, Angelos Delivorrias
p. cm.
ISBN 978-0-89236-910-2 (hardcover)
1. Greece—Antiquities. 2 Excavations (Archaeology)—Greece. I. Title.
DF77.P48 2007
938-dc22
                               2007016609
Printed in Greece

Great Moments in
GREEK ARCHAEOLOGY

Academic Coordinator: **PANOS VALAVANIS**   *Translated by* **Dr. DAVID HARDY**   *Foreword by* **ANGELOS DELIVORRIAS**

Essays by

GEORGE F. BASS / ALBERTO G. BENVENUTI / GEORGE CH. CHOURMOUZIADIS / CHRISTOS DOUMAS

STELLA DROUGOU / SPYROS IAKOVIDES / EVANGELOS CH. KAKAVOYIANNIS / VASSOS KARAGEORGHIS

SUSAN WOMER KATZEV / HELMUT KYRIELEIS / COLIN F. MACDONALD / FANI MALLOUCHOU-TUFANO

DOMINIQUE MULLIEZ / WOLF-DIETRICH NIEMEIER / VASILEIOS PETRAKOS / ALIKI SAMARA-KAUFFMANN

MARINA SOPHRONIDOU / GEORGIOS STEINHAUER / JUTTA STROSZECK / HARRY E. TZALAS / PANOS VALAVANIS

The J. Paul Getty Museum

Los Angeles

Acknowledgments

We are very grateful to the Stavros Niarchos Foundation for its generous donation, thanks to which we were able to respond to the unusually great demands of this complex volume, and also to ensure the high quality we believe to be a feature of the publication.

The publication of this book owes much to the authors, who not only wrote the individual chapters but also contributed to the illustration of it by providing material from their archives. We would also like particularly to thank Angeliki Kokkou for her contribution at every stage of the publication, and also for the photographs she made available to us. Special thanks, too, go to Yannis Papaioannou for the valuable advice and information he provided.

We wish also to thank the museums and foundations, collectors, friends and colleagues, both in Greece and abroad, who gave us permission publish objects from their collections, and assisted us in our long efforts to assemble the illustrative material. Their names appear in the list that follows:

Yanis Bitsakis, Elpida Cheri, Michelle Chmelar, Calliopi Christofi, George David, Ekaterini Dellaporta, Nota Demopoulou-Rethemiotaki, Tania Devetzi, Georgios Fafalis, Nikos Fintikakis, Marianne Hamiaux, Eleni Hatzaki, Clio Karageorghis, Natassa Kastriti, Manolis Korres, Dimitra Koukiou, Eleni Kourinou, Michael Krumme, Nelly Kyriazi, Marie-France Lemoine-Molimard, Stelios Lydakis, Vicky Maniati, Niki Markasioti, Craig A. Mauzy, Socrates Mavrommatis, Ioannis K. Mazarakis-Ainian, Jasen Messic, Eleni Morati, Ioanna Ninou, Kiki Orphanou, Clairy Palyvou, Panagiota Panariti, Eleni Papazoglou, Sara Paton, Ingo Pini, Kalliopi Preka, Rosa Proskynitopoulou, Elisavet Stasinopoulou, Ilaria Symiakaki, Thodoros Theodorou, Pitsa Tsakona, George Vozikis, Gudrun Walter, Diana Zafiropoulou.

MUSEUMS – ARCHIVES – COLLECTIONS
Croatia: Archaeological Museum in Zadar. **Cyprus:** Cyprus Museum, Municipality of Aghia Napa. **Denmark:** Det kongelige Bibliotek, Kunstakademiets Bibliotek, Statens Museum for Kunst. **France:** École Nationale Supérieure des Beaux-Arts, Louvre Museum, Musée de l' Ephèbe (Agde). **Germany:** Akademie der Wissenschaften und der Literatur–Corpus der minoischen und mykenischen Siegel CMS, Dietmar Siegert Collection (Munich), Staatliche Museen zu Berlin–Museum für Vor- und Frühgeschichte. **Great Britain:** The Ashmolean Museum of Art and Archaeology (Oxford), The British Museum. **Greece:** Acropolis Museum, Archaeological Museum of Delphi, Archaeological Museum of Herakleion, Archaeological Museum of Kerameikos, Archaeological Museum of Olympia, Archaeological Museum of Piraeus, Archaeological Museum of Samos, Archaeological Museum of Volos, Archaeological Receipts Fund, Archaeological Society at Athens, Archives of the Excavations at Akrotiri (Thera), Archive of the newspaper 'Kathimerini', A.S. Maïlis Collection, Benaki Museum, Committee for the Conservation of the Acropolis Monuments, 1st Ephorate of Prehistoric and Classical Antiquities, 3rd Ephorate of Prehistoric and Classical Antiquities, Ephorate of Underwater Antiquities, Epigraphical Museum, French School of Athens, G. David Collection, GEOMET Ltd., German Archaeological Institute, Hellenic Institute for the Preservation of Nautical Tradition, Italian Archaeological School at Athens, Melina Merkouri Foundation, Municipal Art Gallery of Athens, Museum of the City of Athens (Vouros-Eutaxias Foundation), Museum of the History of the Ancient Olympic Games, Museum of Prehistoric Thera, National Archaeological Museum, National Historical Museum, Numismatic Museum, Prefectorial Administration of Kastoria, P. Venieris Collection, Shelter for the Protection of the Royal Tombs (Vergina), The American School of Classical Studies at Athens, The Antikythera Mechanism Research Project, The Thera Foundation – Petros M. Nomikos, Th. Theodorou Collection. **Italy:** Archaeological Museum of Ravenna, National Museum of Reggio di Calabria. **Russia:** Pushkin Museum. **Turkey:** Archaeological Museum of Smyrna (Izmir), The Bodrum Museum of Underwater Archaeology. **USA:** Institute of Nautical Archaeology (INA), N. Catsimpoolas Collection (Boston), The J. Paul Getty Museum.

Publisher's note

Beneath the deposits of our own truth
the realities of other times
pass on their secret way.

Beneath today's experiences
memories of other souls that went before grow silent
countless layers of ash and oblivion.

Only through cracks in time
can we commune with the unseen
which in its own way lends profundity to our life.

Kerameikos, *from the collection* Passage *by Yiannis Ch. Papaioannou*

It was the words of this poem that convinced us that the time had come to put into practice an idea of our good friend Panos Valavanis and publish a book devoted not to archaeological finds or an important archaeological site, but to the story of how they were discovered.

The present book could not have been published without a generous grant from the Stavros Niarchos Foundation, for which we are very grateful.

The history of Kapon Editions so far represents a modest endeavour to promote the ancient –and later– heritage of Greece. Ever since we were children we have been enchanted by the creations of people of earlier ages. It is not just their aesthetic value that moves us, but also the patina of time which, though a sign of decay, gives these works an added value, a further dimension. The material remains of our culture are channels of communication with the past and delineate the chronological sequence of the periods of history. As we touch them, we feel the warmth of the hands that made and used them. As we gaze at them, we learn to see the world with the eyes of people who viewed life differently from the way we do today. We often call these finds 'treasures', not so much for the valuable material of which they are made, or for their rarity and excellence as artworks, but because they bear witness to the inexhaustible imagination of creative man.

We often felt that we could detect the special feeling engendered by contact with archaeological ruins in the eyes of the archaeologists with whom we collaborated from time to time in the course of our work. We like to believe that we have been good students and have learned from them how to track down and enjoy archaeological finds. We look upon this book as a repayment, a tribute to those people who uncovered ancient places and became the great masters of Greek archaeology. The writers of the various chapters have recorded the works of men and the great moments of their contribution to scholarship with knowledge and sensitivity, and we owe them our heartfelt thanks. We would also like to express our gratitude to Professor Angelos Delivorrias who wrote the introduction. It was a great pleasure for us to collaborate with the J. Paul Getty Museum on the English language edition. This has made it possible for a volume of great importance for Greek archaeology to appear abroad as well as in Greece, so that the story of the discovery of these unique finds will become very widely known. We know the Getty shares our passion for the ancient heritage of Greece and an admiration of those who work to uncover it.

In *Great Moments in Greek Archaeology* we have tried to record the significance and emotion of discovering remains and artworks that attest to historical continuity in Greece. The wealth of photographs that capture the unique moments of archaeological discovery and the texts, written by scholars in a professional yet elegant style, enable readers to follow the story of the great discoveries and share in the feelings of those who were the first to gaze upon the masterpieces as they emerged from the bowels of the earth or the depths of the sea. Every trench dug in the soil by the archaeologist's spade is, we believe, a 'crack in time', through which we can discern our roots and, in the words of the poem, *commune with the unseen which in its own way lends profundity to our life.*

MOSES and RACHEL KAPON

7

Contents

GREAT MOMENTS IN GREEK ARCHAEOLOGY

GREAT MOMENTS IN MARINE ARCHAEOLOGY

MASTERPIECES OF GREEK SCULPTURE SEE THE LIGHT OF DAY

Foreword

Kapon Editions continues to enrich the bibliography relating to the history and art of ancient times and succeeding periods of Greek civilisation and has made a systematic effort to transmit the messages of this civilisation to the rest of the world. The present volume, however, is outstanding not because it diverts their publishing policy in a different direction, but because it summarises their beliefs in exemplary fashion, at the same time redefining the ideological reference point of their overall contribution to the world of Greek books.

I shall begin with what seems to me most important: the conscious choice of readership from a world in which experts and those who have no specialist knowledge are represented equally, the basic criteria being competency in the field of knowledge and a wide range of general interests. I refer, in other words, to the rare virtue of "popularisation": the facility, by no means common, to summarise even the most intricate scientific questions and set them forth in a completely comprehensible manner. This ability is shared by all those who have collaborated on this publication, without betraying their authority as scholars and without blunting the significance of their research achievements. Without, that is, restricting the scope of the exciting discoveries with which they are dealing, and thereby alienating the appropriate receivers from the legitimate broadcasters. In addition to the evident academic ethos of the authors, I believe we can detect the contribution of Panos Valavanis in coordinating, or rather animating, the publication.

Through the pages of this volume, the various texts and wonderful illustrations, readers are called upon to walk along the exciting pathways of a scintillating story of investigation: a journey that will enable them to follow actively the most important stages in the discovery of the ancient Greek world, and to experience retrospectively the truly *Great Moments in Greek Archaeology*. On this journey, no better guide could be found than the informative chronicle written by Vasilis Petrakos. Not so much because his observations throw into relief the decisive contribution made by Greek archaeologists, through study and publication, to the liberation of the remains of the past from the vast volumes of earth heaped upon them by time, oblivion, and the misfortunes of the site; but because his text provides the guidelines around which the other, individual narratives are articulated; these, moreover, give rise to a highly stimulating feeling: that the achievements of Greek archaeology, as of any other academic discipline, can only be understood as the product of a fruitful dialogue among several voices. It would in any case be strange if the Greek heritage, a priceless treasure for all humankind, were not served by a dynamic army of comrades-in-arms that also included scholars from the rest of the world, from the appropriate state services and scientific centres, and from university foundations and related organisations: if in this case, that is, we did not learn the lesson taught by famous symphony orchestras as they interpret the supreme musical creations.

If I read its internal rationale correctly, *Great Moments in Greek Archaeology* is not concerned with recounting individual episodes of the epic of Greek excavation, which continues to reveal the ancient Greek miracle to us, but with throwing into relief the components of a single, unified cultural reserve. Viewed in this way, the findings of the excavations that have been conducted or are still ongoing at Sesklo, Dimini and Dispilio, at Poliochni, Knossos and Akrotiri, at Mycenae and Salamis on Cyprus, on the Acropolis and in the Agora and Kerameikos in Athens, at Delos and Delphi, Olympia and Vergina, are not unconnected with each other. Just as the apparently independent conclusions drawn for each site as a result of minute examination, weaving the coherent canvas of an attractive narrative, are not unconnected with each other. When taken together, the crumbs of information added on each occasion broaden our knowledge of the ancient Greek people and their lives, their social consciousness and their political maturity, their beliefs and their art, forming a constantly increasing store of testimonies from remains devoured by the earth or swallowed by the sea over the course of the centuries: whether these be unique creations of architecture and revolutionary innovations in urban design, impressive theatres and grandiose sanctuaries, or the countless masterpieces discovered on Samos and at Merenda, at Piraeus and on Melos and Samothrace, in the Aegean and Ionian seas, at Livadostra, on Antikythera and at Marathon, at Artemision and on Kalymnos. Even more valuable, however, are the less spectacular but equally interesting aspects of public and private life, of the darker sides of history, and of economy, trade and seafaring, as retrieved from apparently insignificant fragments, vases, coins and inscriptions.

I shall not name any of the authors of this volume individually, but would like to express my sincere thanks to them all.

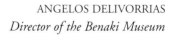

ANGELOS DELIVORRIAS
Director of the Benaki Museum

Introduction

History is the record of continuity, of the constant, eternal progress of mankind and the events that shape it. With constant fluctuations, sometimes great, sometimes small, it reveals to us an element of our identity from a constantly changing viewpoint. Our relationship with history, however, is an unconscious one, and it is only on rare occasions that we become aware of just how great a role it plays in both our individual and our national life.

The key moments of an excavation, when a monument that has been buried beneath the mist and earth of centuries resurfaces – these are the moments at which we find ourselves confronting our history. Most of these moments are personal and any dialogue is restricted to the monument and the archaeologist. When the finds are of major importance, however, they acquire an added dimension: they escape their confines and their fame spreads to broader interested circles. And when the finds happen to be of a monumental character or are connected with figures and events known from historical sources these moments are charged with emotion and excitement and satisfy our national pride.

The story of Greek archaeology, as it emerges from the introductory chapter by Vasileios Petrakos, is a continuous struggle to uncover, preserve and project the material remains of Greek civilisation. This struggle began immediately after the outbreak of the Greek War of Independence in 1821 and before the creation of the modern Greek state, and has continued without a break down to the present day. It is full of great moments of archaeological discovery which, when examined closely, also can reveal to us pieces of our modern history. Excavation and research themselves, that is, are not simply a series of isolated events, as one might believe as one examines the 'end product', but are the result of many factors and circumstances which, consciously or unconsciously, influence the archaeological reality of the day: national aspirations and ideological orientations, international political junctures and Great Power confrontations, personal motives and ambitions, or purely scientific objectives are some of these factors that have moulded, and still mould, the archaeological event.

From this perspective, and using these considerations as criteria, we have selected some of the great moments of Greek archaeology for this book. We have given priority to those that reflect their period, which impressed their contemporaries and which reveal, as strongly as possible, certain features of the modern Greek identity over the approximately 200 years of the existence of Greece as a free nation.

Our story begins with the sacred rock of the Acropolis, which was properly the first concern of the newly founded Greek kingdom. The first Greek and 'Bavarian' archaeologists 'cleansed' the monuments of the consequences and remains of Ottoman rule and transformed the Acropolis from a castle into a monument. At the same time, they endowed these monuments with the national, emblematic character required by Greeks as the foundation of their national identity, and also provided Europeans with the exemplar of the pure Classicism that they were seeking.

In the spring of 1861, the chance discovery of a stele 3.5 m. high, which still stood upright in its original position near Pireos Street, led to the gradual uncovering of the Kerameikos cemetery, which not only yielded tombs with their imposing funerary monuments, but also brought to light sections of the Themistoklean fortifications of the city, along with its two most important gates.

A new chapter in Greek archaeological exploration opened after 1870. It was signalled by the start of the major excavations funded and conducted by foreign archaeological missions, and by wealthy devotees of the ancient world, whose objective was to uncover ancient cities and sanctuaries. In 1873, the French School at Athens began the excavation of Delos, which unearthed the panhellenic sanctuary of Apollo – the religious centre of the Ionians – and also the large Hellenistic city with its wealth of house remains.

In 1875, after long years of negotiation, the Greek state granted the right to excavate at Olympia to the German Archaeological Institute. This led to the uncovering of the greatest of the panhellenic sanctuaries with its fine monuments and rich dedications, and also the facilities in which the ancient Olympic Games were held.

One year later, in 1876, Heinrich Schliemann, a wealthy merchant from Germany, achieved his second personal ambition, after the discovery of Troy, by excavating the pit graves in Grave Circle A at Mycenae and demonstrating to the scholars of his day that the Homeric epithet 'rich in gold' was not merely a linguistic device, and that the Homeric poems refer to many events of early Greek history.

The great excavation of Delphi by the French School at Athens began in 1892. The French claims to the privilege of conducting this excavation had for a long time experienced many, occasionally amusing vicissitudes. The sanctuaries of Apollo and Athena Pronaia came to light, as well as the structures used for the Pythian athletic contests: and along with them, thousands of other finds that document the great importance of the Delphic oracle in ancient times, already known from literary sources.

The great moments of Greek archaeology at the beginning of the 20th century are associated with three significant phases of Greek prehistory. In 1901, the British benefactor Arthur Evans began the excavation of the palace of Knossos, which exposed the splendid monuments of Minoan civilisation. In 1903, the first monumental installations of Neolithic culture – the citadels of Dimini and Sesklo – were revealed by Professor Chr. Tsountas. And later, in 1930, the Italian Archaeological School uncovered the oldest city in Europe – Poliochni on Lemnos, a characteristic example of Early Bronze Age culture in the northeast Aegean.

The year 1931 was a landmark in the archaeological investigation of Athens: the American School of Classical Studies began the excavation of the Ancient Agora. Since that date dozens of buildings and thousands of finds have come to light, associated with the economic and cultural centre of ancient Athens, the city that devised and practised the first democracy in the history of civilisation.

There have been two exciting moments in the recent history of Greek archaeology. In 1967, Professor Sp. Marinatos sought to confirm his theory that the Minoan civilisation was destroyed by an eruption of the Thera volcano by excavating on the island and discovered an astonishingly well-preserved Middle Cycladic settlement at Akrotiri. And in 1977, Professor Man. Andronikos excavated the Great Tumulus at Vergina and found, among other things, a large, unlooted royal tomb, which he attributed with considerable probability to Philip II, the king of the Macedonians and father of Alexander the Great.

Finally, Yorgos Chourmouziadis began the systematic excavation of the prehistoric lake settlement at Dispilio, Kastoria, the finds from which gave a new dimension to our knowledge of the lives and activities of the Neolithic inhabitants of north Greece.

Since the influence of Greek civilisation in ancient times went far beyond the borders of the present Greek state, great moments of Cypriot archaeology could not be omitted from the present volume. Important amongst these were the discovery of the royal tombs at Salamis by Vasos Karageorghis, which contained rich grave offerings and revealed 'Homeric' burial practices, and also Michael Katzev's underwater excavation of a trading ship of the 4th century BC in the sea off Kyrenia. Its excellent state of preservation not only enriched our knowledge of ancient shipbuilding, but also made it possible to construct a copy of it, which travelled the Aegean – the first example of nautical experimental archaeology.

Another, more recent, underwater exploration (1984), led initially by George F. Bass and later by Cemal Puluk, revealed the wreck of a trading vessel of the 14th c. BC off Cape Uluburun in Asia Minor, near ancient Antiphellos. The unimaginable wealth of its cargo is changing our views about the commercial activities and international contacts of the Mycenaeans in the area of the eastern Mediterranean.

The book closes with two chapters on the exciting circumstances surrounding the discovery of a number of individual Greek sculptures. The first is devoted to statues found on dry land, such as the Aphrodite of Melos and the Nike of Samothrace, the bronze statues of Piraeus, Phrasikleia and the kouros of Merenda, and the enormous kouros of Samos. The second chapter deals with bronze statues found at the bottom of the sea: from the earlier investigations of the Antikythera and Artemision shipwrecks, which yielded the superb statues in the National Archaeological Museum of Athens, to the more recent discovery of statues at Riace in southern Italy, the Apoxyomenos of Lysippos off the coast of Croatia, and the statues from the bottom of the sea off Kalymnos.

Great Moments in Greek Archaeology aspires to be much more than a mere collection of memories. Behind the superficially fragmentary, fortuitous nature of the story of the great archaeological discoveries can clearly be traced an internal – genetic, even – logic that binds together the individual moments, giving the book the character of a synopsis of the epic of excavation in modern Greece.

PANOS VALAVANIS
Professor of Classical Archaeology at the University of Athens

15

1. Admission card of B. Leonardos, who attended the First International Archaeology Conference (1905). Archive of the Archaeological Society at Athens.

2. Lottery ticket of 1882 in the Lottery in Support of Antiquities run by the Archaeological Society (AAE, Lottery Archive p. 57, fig. 23).

3. Crown Prince Constantine at the Parthenon, declaring the First International Archaeology Conference open (1905). Archive of the Archaeological Society at Athens.

4-6. Articles in Figaro and the New York Times on the discovery of the bronze statues of Piraeus. Archive of the Archaeological Society at Athens.

7. Ioannis K. Papadimitriou in the Piraeus Museum, describing the bronze kouros to the Prime Minister, Konstantinos Karamanlis. Archive of the newspaper 'Kathimerini'.

8. Visitors to Georgios Ikonomos's excavation of Klazomenai (12 August 1922). Archive of the Archaeological Society at Athens.

9. The excavation of the stoa at Brauron, with Ioannis K. Papadimitriou at the right. Archive of the Archaeological Society at Athens.

10. The cover of the first issue of Ephemeris Archaeologiki. Archive of the Archaeological Society at Athens.

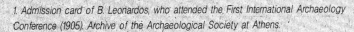

1

3

2

QUATORZE — LE FIGARO — 22 OCTOBRE 1959

MUSE OU DÉESSE ?

- LES ARTS - LES

SCULPTURES

Emmanuel Bondeville reçu à l'Académie des Beaux-Arts

NEW YORK : Léo SAUVAGE

Ascension périlleuse du temple
(en forme de tiare renversée)
de la peinture "non-objective"

4

Bust found in Piraeus

Experts Hail Sculpture Discovery in Greece

Two Bronze Statues and Marble Work Are Highly Rated

By A. C. SEDGWICK
Special to The New York Times.

ATHENS, July 20—Laborers pulling up pavement to repair sewers in a busy section of the Athens seaport, Piraeus, have discovered three outstanding ancient works of sculpture.

Archaeologists describe the two life-size bronze statues and a marble column surmounted by a man's head as some of the most beautiful art treasures

Statue of the young man may be an Apollo

Bronze figure, slightly larger than life

The New York Times.

NEW YORK, SUNDAY, JULY 26, 1959.

6

The stages of Greek archaeology

Ὁ Πρόεδρος τῆς Κυβερνήσεως κ. Κ. ΚΑΡΑΜΑΝΛΗΣ, ὁ Διευθυντὴς Ἀρχαιοτήτων τοῦ Ὑπουργείου Παιδείας κ. ΙΩ. ΠΑΠΑΔΗΜΗΤΡΙΟΥ (εἰς τὸ μέσον) καὶ ὁ Δήμαρχος Πειραιῶς κ. Π. ΝΤΕΝΤΙΔΑΚΗΣ, ἐξετάζοντες τὸ ἄγαλμα τοῦ Κούρου ποὺ ἀνεκαλύφθη τὸ Σάββατον εἰς τὸν Πειραιᾶ.

7

9

8

ΕΦΗΜΕΡΙΣ
ΑΡΧΑΙΟΛΟΓΙΚΗ,

ΑΦΟΡΩΣΑ ΤΑΣ ΕΝΤΟΣ ΤΗΣ ΕΛΛΑΔΟΣ ΑΝΕΥΡΙΣΚΟΜΕΝΑΣ

ΑΡΧΑΙΟΤΗΤΑΣ.

ΕΚΔΙΔΟΜΕΝΗ ΔΕ

ΚΑΤΑ ΒΑΣΙΛΙΚΗΝ ΔΙΑΤΑΓΗΝ

ΥΠΟ ΤΗΣ

ΑΡΧΑΙΟΛΟΓΙΚΗΣ ΕΠΙΤΡΟΠΗΣ.

ΑΘΗΝΗΣΙ.
ΕΚ ΤΗΣ ΒΑΣΙΛΙΚΗΣ ΤΥΠΟΓΡΑΦΙΑΣ.
1837.

10

Vasileios Petrakos

The stages of Greek archaeology

The archaeology of Greece may be divided into clear chronological and political periods. Their sequence exhibits unbroken progress: in the material sphere through the constant discovery of new monuments and in the academic through the consolidation of this progress by publications of the excavations and monuments. During the long period of its birth and growth, beginning in 1829 and continuing to the present day, 2006, there are phases that belong to the activities of the foreign archaeological schools. The oldest of these is the French School, which was founded in 1846, followed by the German in 1874, the American in 1881 and the British in 1886. New foreign schools continue to be founded, with some intensity, indeed, in recent decades.

The progress of archaeological investigation by Greek and foreign archaeologists is marked by interruptions, periods of inactivity and, on occasion, exaggerated advances, due mainly to military and political events. After Greece won its liberation from the Turks, a large number of military and political events made an impact on archaeology. The Crimean War in 1853-1856 brought foreign forces to Piraeus, where they conducted excavations. Later events that led to productive, systematic scientific excavations included the creation of the modern Greek state, the unification of the Ionian islands with Greece, the acquisition of Thessaly, the unification with Crete, the Balkan Wars, the First World War, the Asia Minor campaign, the Second World War, the annexation of the Dodecanese, the economic development of the country and the construction of new buildings attendant on it, and the execution of major public works projects, such as dams, roads, and the Athens underground railway. Finally, the 2004 Olympic Games also led to the discovery of many antiquities, though they also caused great destruction.

Another factor on which the progress of archaeological investigation depends is the attitude taken towards antiquities by governments, particularly the view of individuals that influence this attitude. For individuals have often influenced the fortunes of archaeology. Examples of this that spring readily to mind are the antiquities thefts of the 1870s, the building of hotels and industries on archaeological and historical sites and their consequent damage and destruction. The academic competence of the staff of the Archaeological Service and the members of its councils is another decisive factor influencing the fortune of antiquities: the councils, which are dependent on the political authorities, have been subjected to pressure from the government, in earlier periods but above all in recent years, to adapt their scientific views to party political perceptions, which are created in accordance with the interests of financial bodies or the self-interested friends of political figures.

These phenomena are part of an important chapter in the political history of Greek archaeology, relating principally to the academic personnel of the Archaeological Service and to a lesser extent of the universities. The Service began to function in 1829 with a single individual forming its academic personnel, and continues to operate at present with a staff of about 500. This is connected with its administrative structure. In 1829, the whole of Greece constituted a single administrative unit for archaeological purposes. Today, according to Decree 191 (Govt. Gazette 146 I/ 13.6.2003), the one-man Archaeological Service of 1829 has expanded into a Central Service with 2 General Directorates, 15 Directorates, 1 Centre, and 2 Secretariats. The Provincial Services comprise 39 Ephorates of Prehistoric and Classical Antiquities, 28 Ephorates of Byzantine Antiquities, 4 Special Ephorates, 6 Archaeological Institutes and 8 Museums that function independently of the Ephorates. This enormous increase in size has obviously led to differences, mainly in the ideas about antiquities held by the members of the Service. The views of the old guard are not always identified with those of the archaeologists of today.

Great moments in Greek archaeology

Fani Mallouchou-Tufano

The vicissitudes of the Athenian Acropolis in the 19th century
From castle to monument

1833: THE BLUE AND WHITE FLAG FLUTTERS ON THE ACROPOLIS

*O**n 29/30 April 1833, we were given orders to capture the Acropolis of Athens. At nine o'clock in the morning, we ascended, or rather climbed with difficulty, up the steep, narrow path, full of stones and ruins. When we arrived before the entrance, we were met by the Turkish garrison, a force of about two hundred and fifty men, which looked more like a band of robbers than a regular army battalion. Their clothes were wretched and worn, many of them in tatters, and their shoes were worn down to the heel. Silent and sullen, they passed before us, showing no interest in what was happening, or in greeting us, though I ordered my detail to present arms.* With these words, the surrender of the Acropolis is described in the memoirs of a leading actor in the events, Christopher Neezer, the lieutenant of the army corps that received the surrender of the fortress (fig. 1). The ceremony of the surrender was very simple and brief. The garrison commander Osman Efendi *handed over a document issued by his government to the representative of the Greek government, the Bavarian major Palligan, and accepted a similar document from him. In this way, the Acropolis was surrendered and acquired by Greece [...] and I had the honour, as lieutenant of the Bavarian royal reserve army, of being the first regular Christian garrison commander of the town of Cecrops.* That evening, Neezer, highly excited *finding himself on Classical soil,* spread a straw mat *beneath the gigantic columns of the Parthenon,* used *a fragment of a column* for a pillow, and dreamed *with open eyes [...] of the archon Perikles, of Sokrates and his pupils, of Euripides, Demosthenes and so many other great men of glorious Greece, walking beneath these columns and entering the immortal temple of Pallas.*

The following morning a Chiot sailor and his son went up to the Acropolis. The sailor *was called Captain Dimitris, and he had left his boat in Piraeus. This Chiot carried a pole and blue flag with white stripes, and with a cross in the middle,* and he received Neezer's permission to raise it on the Parthenon. *With the aid of some soldiers, the pole was set up on the Parthenon, and I called on my few soldiers to parade, presenting arms, and I saluted the old seafarer, who raised the Greek flag, shouting, with his son: Long live Greece! Long live the king! And I and my soldiers repeated his words [...] Tears of joy fell from the eyes of the old Chiot, and a short time later, I went about observing the marbles, piled up higgledy-piggledy on the Acropolis. Amidst the jumble, amongst column capitals, broken columns, small and large pieces of marble, were cannon balls, parts of shells, human skulls and bones, many of which were gathered together, mainly near the slender Caryatids of the Erechtheion [...]*

Neezer's text reveals two elements that were to characterise and define the approach to and treatment of the Acropolis monuments throughout the 19th century: the admiration for the Greek Classical spirit, nurtured by romanticism, with which educated Europeans of the day were imbued, and the profound, spontaneous feelings of love and pride experienced by ordinary, uneducated Greeks for the creations of

their forefathers and in particular for the Acropolis and the Parthenon which, from the very day of their liberation, they felt to be their own, their national monuments and the symbols of the regeneration of their native country. At the same time, Neezer gives an epigrammatic, yet clear account of the image presented by the castle of the Acropolis after the two successive sieges (1821-22, 1826-27) it had suffered during the recent War of Independence.

The neighbourhood of houses known from earlier depictions, with its picturesque streets and gardens (fig. 4), which seems to have covered the plateau of the Acropolis after its conversion into a fortress as early as Byzantine times, had been transformed into piles of ruins. Amongst these, and amongst a few wretched huts that had survived, rose the Classical monuments, themselves in ruins and deformed, ghosts of their glorious past. The Parthenon (fig. 5) with the small 18th-century mosque inside it, had been split in two in 1687 by the bombardment during the Veneto-Turkish war, a large part of its walls had been destroyed during the Greek National Uprising, and its surface was scarred by bullet-marks from recent battles. The monument had suffered equally deep wounds when it was stripped by the

1. The Acropolis as a strong castle, seen from the Hill of the Muses, from about the site of the church of Ayios Dimitrios Loumbardiaris. The Pinakotheke in the Propylaia can be seen on the Sacred Rock at the left, in the form it assumed after conversion into a residence for the Frankish dukes of Athens and the Acciaiuoli. The so-called Frankish Tower (centre) was demolished in 1875. In the foreground can be seen the strong fortifications of the west approach to the hill. Detail from an oil-painting by Louis Dupré, 1825. Athens, National Historical Museum.

1

3

agents of Lord Elgin during the years 1801-1803. The Erechtheion (fig. 6) was in an even worse condition: the long walls of the cella were almost completely razed to the ground and the two porches were deformed, with only three of the Caryatids in position. As for the other monuments on the Sacred Rock, the temple of Nike had disappeared from the landscape as early as the 17th century, when the Ottoman Turks, in anticipation of an attack by Morosini, dismantled it in order to construct the second large bastion at the western approach to the castle (fig. 1), while the Propylaia, though preserved, was unrecognisable beneath the imposing later fortifications and additions that had begun to conceal it already in the Frankish period (fig. 3).

LEO VON KLENZE AND THE DEMILITARISATION OF ACROPOLIS

The situation had not changed by the summer of 1834, when Leo von Klenze (fig. 2), the powerful architect at the Court in Munich and confidant of Ludwig of Bavaria, father of the Greek monarch Otto, visited the Acropolis. Despite the small-scale excavations that had taken place at various points of the Rock during the previous months, and the first attempts by the archaeologist Kyriakos Pittakis to create a rudimentary museum in the Propylaia to house the scattered antiquities, the Acropolis was still a fortress. The Bavarian soldiers were installed in the mosque inside the Parthenon and in a few habitable shacks around the Propylaia, and their careless, unheeding behaviour was causing additional damage to the monuments. And the predominant view in government circles was that it was necessary to maintain its function as a fortress. Klenze's brief visit was a landmark in the fortunes of the Acropolis monuments. Making use of his great influence with the Regency, he managed to have the Acropolis declared an archaeological site, through a royal decree issued on 18 August 1834. By so doing, he put a final end to more than one

5

5. The Parthenon. Watercolour by J.J. Wolfensberger, 1834. Moscow, Pushkin Museum.

6. The Erechtheion from the southeast. Watercolour by J.J. Wolfensberger, 1834. Moscow, Pushkin Museum.

thousand years of constant association of its use with the city of Athens and gave the monuments a supra-local, national and emblematic character in the eyes of Greeks. At the same time, Klenze formulated proposals for the enhancement of the monuments that were to form the guidelines for interventions on the Acropolis throughout the 19th century.

On 10 September 1834, the eve of his departure from Greece, Klenze ceremoniously inaugurated the restoration of the Parthenon at a public ceremony. In the presence of Otto, seated inside the building on a throne adorned with olive, myrtle and laurel branches, and of the entire Athenian people, wearing their picturesque costumes, the irregular Independence fighters with their dress scorched by gunpowder, and the political and military leaders of the land, he delivered a speech steeped in his love of the ancient world and charged with overt references to the expected political benefits to be anticipated from the restoration of the Acropolis: *Your Majesty's foot has today trod for the first time, after many centuries of barbarity, on this sacred rock on the road of civilisation and glory, the road of Themistokles, Aristeides, Kimon and Perikles. In the eyes of the world, this will, and should, be the symbol of the blessed period of*

6

7. Work on removing the fortifications at the west approach to the Acropolis, in front of the Propylaia. Watercolour by M. Rørbye, 1835. Copenhagen, Statens Museum for Kunst.

8. Ludwig Ross (1806-1859).

Your Majesty's rule over this land, and Your decision with regard to the sacred rock. The traces of a barbarian period, ruins and formless rubble, will be effaced here, as everywhere in Greece, and the remains of the glorious past will be restored with new brilliance, as the most stable foundations of a glorious past and future. The ceremony closed with Otto symbolically placing a drum in position in a column of the north colonnade of the building.

LUDWIG ROSS AND THE FIRST YEARS OF THE ACROPOLIS AS A MONUMENT OPEN TO THE PUBLIC

In September 1834, on Klenze's recommendation, the German archaeologist Ludwig Ross (fig. 8) was appointed Ephor of all antiquities in Greece, and undertook to implement the programme for the Acropolis. Ross had come to Greece in 1832 as a very young man, and already in August 1833 had been appointed Ephor of the Antiquities of the Peloponnese. A man of the world, he was acquainted with people and affairs and with all the highly placed foreigners who visited or lived in Greece during these years. He was also connected with the circle of the Regency, the royal family and Otto's father, Ludwig, and indeed became their indispensable companion and guide on their archaeological excursions. On the Acropolis, Ross was assisted in technical matters by the architects Eduard Schaubert, Christian Hansen and Eduard Laurent. He also took care to employ sculptors and mould-makers. The work commenced in January 1835, but was hindered by the presence of the garrison, which was still quartered on the Acropolis, despite the decree passed the previous August. [...] *The then Minister of Defence, General von Lezouir, could not get rid of the idea that the security of Athens demanded the military occupation of the Acropolis [...]*, writes Ross in his memoirs. *Every day at 12 o'clock, in the absence of a clock, a cannon was fired from the fortress, proclaiming that it was midday [...] But the presence of the soldiers was a great hindrance to my work. Moreover, I needed all the buildings* (in which the soldiers were billeted) *for sheds and storerooms for means of transportation, crowbars, pulleys, and other technical equipment. I therefore pressed constantly for the fortress to be evacuated. Mr. von Kombel* (a member of the Regency), *gave me considerable verbal support, bringing great 'pressure' to bear on the Regency, and finally, in February, the order to evacuate was issued. [...] The general received the order to leave the mosque and hand over all the buildings to me [...] I had won a great victory [...] If I had not been so determined, the Propylaia might still have been a barracks and garrison look-out post.*

Work was carried out at two points on the Acropolis: at the west approach, where the large second bastion (fig. 7) between the tower of Athena Nike and the pedestal of Agrippa was demolished, and around the Parthenon. As Ross wrote to Klenze, the demolition work began with the bastion, partly in order to prevent once and for all the return of the soldiers to the Acropolis. For this same reason, Ross began to demolish the mosque inside the Parthenon. There, however, he was unable to proceed with any substantial restoration work, since he lacked suitable lifting tackle. He merely began to demolish the Christian apse of the church, and conducted excavations around it that yielded a wealth of finds and scientific observations.

One of the greatest moments in the history of the Acropolis at this period was the recovery of a monument that had disappeared from the sacred rock for about 150 years. This was the temple of Athena Nike, the architectural members of which were uncovered in the earth deposits of a bastion in the process of being dismantled at the western approach to the Acropolis, in front of the Propylaia. This, in combination with the discovery *in situ* of the crepis and some of the column bases led to the partial restoration, from December 1835 until May 1836, of the elegant Ionic building (fig. 9). During this work, the north and east side of the temple were almost completely restored, and the south and west to about half their height. The members of the temple were placed in random positions, and the existing

gaps were filled with stone blocks lying scattered on the ground, many of which came from the neighbouring Propylaia. Despite this, the restoration of the temple of Athena Nike (fig. 10) – the first restoration of a Classical temple in Europe, in the literal sense of the word Classical – was well received by all and greeted with enthusiasm in Greece and the rest of Europe as a tangible example of the regeneration of the Greek people and of the Classical ideal of beauty.

Amongst the first steps taken to facilitate the transformation of the Acropolis into an archaeological monument open to the public were the appointment in September 1834 of six custodians, from the company of the Monemvasia veterans and the issuing of the first tickets in May 1835. The duties of the

9. The temple of Athena Nike from the southeast during the restoration work of 1836. F.W. Newton, February 1836 (detail).

10. General view of the Acropolis from the west. At the right can be seen the restored temple of Athena Nike. Watercolour by J. Skene, 1838. Athens, National Historical Museum.

11. One of the first entrance tickets to the Acropolis, dating from 1835. Athens, National Historical Museum.

12. Kyriakos Pittakis (1798-1863). Athens, Archaeological Society at Athens.

custodians were defined in detail by a regulation issued by the Secretariat of State for Religious Affairs and Public Education, and Ross and Schaubert saw to it that a little house was built above the Odeion of Herodes Atticus to house them. Ross writes that it was constructed for the most part of useless ancient ruins, pieces of columns, capitals, reliefs and inscriptions.

The first tickets to the Acropolis (fig. 11) were governed by a management policy of surprisingly modern spirit, and were divided into categories, individual or group/family tickets, valid for various periods of time (three days, fortnightly, three-monthly, etc.), with the price varying accordingly. The revenue raised was intended to pay the wages of the custodians and meet the expenses of excavation and restoration work.

A more appreciable source of income was the sale of the formless stone blocks – 'cornerstones' according to Ross – that came to light in large quantities during the demolition of the later buildings on the Acropolis. At the beginning of February 1835, a royal decree fixed the terms of the sale of these blocks to the work-sites of the new buildings being constructed in Athens (the National Press Building, Cathedral, Amalieion Orphanage, Arsakeion Girls' School, and many other imposing buildings in the Athens of the Othonian period were constructed with marble from the Acropolis. The practice continued throughout almost the entire 19th century, and indeed was later extended to the provinces).

KYRIAKOS PITTAKIS, THE 'SACRED CUSTODIAN' OF THE ACROPOLIS

From July 1836 until the end of the Othonian period, the work on the Acropolis was dominated by the figure of Ross's successor in the Archaeological Service, Kyriakos Pittakis (fig. 12) and his incessant, indefatigable efforts to preserve and embellish its monuments. Much has been said – most of it negative – about Pittakis, an Athenian reared literally in the shadow of the Sacred Rock and the self-taught "first Greek archaeologist," as he is known to history, particularly by his contemporaries. He has been heartily condemned for his considerable academic shortcomings and for much else, but no-one has ever doubted his great passion and missionary dedication to the preservation of antiquities, particularly those of the Acropolis. *I worked invariably, and I swear this in fear of God, with the most fervent zeal and attention, imagining the shades of our ancestors visiting and judging my work*, wrote Pittakis himself. The portrait sketched by the French historian Jean Alexandre Buchon, when he met him on the Acropolis in 1840/1, is revealing for his idiosyncratic personality: *Mr. Pittakis, it seems, was actually discovered by our old consul Fauvel beneath a forgotten cornice of the Acropolis, which protectively sheltered his cradle. There he grew up, there he lived, there he will die: for the Acropolis is his country, his family, his God – and after his death he will surely be found transformed into an extra Caryatid, intended to replace those that have been lost – so lively, constant, and all-consuming is his passion for the Acropolis. I often went with him amongst the piles of ruins in his Acropolis-country, and on each occasion I was impressed by the very dignified sorrow of his gait, his gestures, his gaze, his discourse. He is the finest possible collector and Ephor of antiquities of the city of Athens.*

Pittakis excavated continuously down to 1860, with brief interruptions, and engaged in general cleaning, removal of earth deposits and demolition of later buildings on the Acropolis Rock. The remains of the medieval palace of the Propylaia, the ruined mosque in the Parthenon, a large part of its Christian apse, the gunpowder magazine in the north porch of the Erechtheion – nothing escaped his spade. His cleaning work was not confined to the major monuments, but extended also to the areas around them: the ascent to the Propylaia, the area to the east of the Erechtheion, that to the west, south and southeast of the Parthenon, and the area of the Sacred Rock between the three great monuments. He returned often to this, and by end of the period, he had uncovered virtually all the bedrock (fig. 17), which led him to believe that the excavations on the Acropolis had been completed. During all this work, the earth that was removed was dumped outside the circuit walls, on the south and east slopes, creating the mountains of earth that can be seen in photographs of the period (fig. 23). The formless stone blocks that were to be sold were piled up along the circuit walls of the Sacred Rock, awaiting transportation.

At the same time, in the belief that *the repair and restoration of the monuments of the ancient Greeks is a sacred task*, Pittakis restored the monuments, repositioning the older members that had collapsed, and also the new ones that came to light constantly. In the case of the Erechtheion (fig. 13), he restored a large part of the side walls of the cella, and supplemented and consolidated the columns at the west of the north porch and the half-columns on the west façade. During the course of the work, the Caryatid that collapsed during the second siege of Athens (4th from the west) was found and placed in position on the monument. The restoration of the porch was completed in 1844-45 by the French archaeologist A. Paccard (fig. 15), who placed the remaining two Caryatids in position, the 3rd in a copy sent by the British Museum, the 6th repaired and restored (fig. 14).

In 1841, after Klenze had sent a powerful hoisting machine, it was possible to begin work on the restoration of the Parthenon. There, Pittakis collaborated with Alexandros Rizos Rangavis, the Secretary of the newly created Archaeological Society, and by 1844 they had re-erected a large part of the side walls of the cella and some of the columns and drums in the north and south colonnades. They went on to restore the temple of Athena Nike (fig. 16), completing the rest of the unfinished walls, the architraves, the coffered ceilings of

13. The Erechtheion from the southwest after the first restoration work. Watercolour by Chr. Hansen, 1845. Copenhagen, Kunstakademiets Bibliotek.

13

the two porches, and the southwest column. They also placed on the temple casts of the frieze slabs that had been carried off by Elgin, which they ordered from the British Museum.

Pittakis's final interventions on the Acropolis involved the partial reconstruction of the staircase leading up to the Propylaia, in 1850 (fig. 16), and, some four years later, the radical repair of the outer, west side of the podium of the Pinakotheke, which was on the point of collapse. Another notable project of these years was the excavation by the French archaeologist E. Beulé, of the Late Roman gate that bears his name.

gate that bears his name.

Pittakis carried out these extensive interventions in a fever of enthusiasm and zeal – in keeping with the unrealistic national expectations and visions of the Othonian period – that helped him overcome the great technical deficiencies and economic difficulties. During these projects, trial and error, improvisation, and the lack of scientific method reached their height. Pittakis was proud, when he announced to the Archaeological Society the removal from the Propylaia of the large, *imposing bastions of the Middle Ages, at little cost, within a few months.* This very fact called forth the scepticism of Ross, however, who censured Pittakis's haste, mainly for not making a rudimentary record of the finds. During the restoration work, the architectural members were placed in position at random, without regard for their original position on the building (members from one part of a monument were commonly placed in another), or even for their provenance (occasionally members of one monument were used in the restoration of another). To erect and consolidate the walls and columns, Pittakis used any material to hand, ancient fragments, unworked stone blocks, bricks, tiles, and even tree trunks (!). This became clear during the modern restoration work on the Acropolis, when the orthostates of the south wall of the Erechtheion, which had been restored by Pittakis, were dismantled. The manner in which the horizontal bedding surface was restored for the drums of the southernmost column in the east porch of the Propylaia is legendary, and gives a good idea of the enthusiasm, and also the innocence, naivety and ignorance of complex technical problems and interventions. It is described by Rangavis in his memoirs: *When [...] it was observed that one of the internal columns of the Propylaia was leaning strongly from the vertical, and there was a fear that it might fall [...] the thought occurred that perhaps we should take down all the upper parts of the building and put them back in their proper place, vertically and solidly. This, however was a very expensive [...] and also highly dangerous task. I then talked to Mr. Pittakis and he ordered a large, wide saw, longer than the diameter of the column, from a blacksmith. And one day, at a time when the Acropolis was empty of people, we placed two ladders, one each side of the column, and he and I climbed up on each side and, grasping the two ends of the saw, we began with great piety and care to saw at the foreign materials in the space between the drums, removing them with a dust-brush, until we heard a strong cracking noise, and the column and all this part of the huge structure swayed, as though from a great earthquake, and for a moment it seemed that it would collapse on our heads. This did not happen, however, fortunately for us and for the Propylaia; when the impedimenta were removed, the column settled vertically into place, and all the stone blocks, beams and architraves of the enormous ceiling also returned to their positions, to stay there forever. This huge task of repairing and securing Mnesikles' masterpiece did not require the expenditure of thousands or hundreds of thousands of drachmas, which would have been needed to take it down and put it back up, but only five or six drachmas for the price of the saw; this was squashed and trapped beneath the drum, as it now occupied its original position, and the projecting ends of it can be seen, as an eternal monument to the improvised repair, which was successful beyond our hopes.*

14. View from the east of the 6th Caryatid, restored by G. Andreoli. Photograph by W. Hege, 1930s. Athens, German Archaeological Institute.

15. View of the Erechtheion from the southeast after the restoration of the porch by A. Paccard. On the east side of the porch (right) can be seen the 6th Caryatid, restored by G. Andreoli. Photograph by Fr. Frith, 1861. Boston, N. Catsimpoolas Collection.

16. The west approach to the Acropolis from the southwest. The staircase restored by Pittakis can be seen. Photograph by W. J. Stillman, 1869. Athens, National Historical Museum.

17. View of the interior of the Acropolis from the east. Photograph by P. Moraitis, 1870. Athens, National Historical Museum.

17

Later history largely vindicated Rangavis's prediction: 'Pittakis's saw' began to be mentioned in guide books and became a tourist sight. Nikolaos Balanos, who restored the Propylaia at the beginning of the 20th century, kept it in its place, and even placed it in a special recess in the bedding surface of the drum. At some point in the 1960s or 70s, some Ephor of the Acropolis cut off the rusty ends, which still projected, and after that the great saw fell into obscurity, until it was rediscovered on 8 April 2003, during the modern restoration of the Propylaia (figs 18, 19). It was then finally removed from the monument, the victim of strict (and rigid) academic ethics.

Equally legendary is Pittakis's ingenuity in devising ways to protect the scattered ancient members, varied, heteroclite material drawn not only from the Acropolis, but also from monuments in the lower town. (He took such antiquities up to the Acropolis to protect them better, particularly in the early years.) Pittakis made agonised efforts to protect the ancient pieces from the rapacity of various visitors. He created 'archaeological collections' in the four major monuments, or in later buildings on the Acropolis, such as the large medieval cistern in front of the Parthenon, in a second cistern known as the 'tholos', and in a Turkish house to the east of the Erechtheion (fig. 20). He also stacked them up like walls on the surface of the Sacred Rock or along the south circuit wall (fig. 22). He even – in a display of personal ingenuity – used plaster to fix them in wooden frames and hung them up like paintings inside the Pinakotheke in the Propylaia (fig. 21).

During these years, the crews of the foreign fleets that frequently anchored in Piraeus were a true scourge. A kind of collector's rivalry seemed to prevail amongst them – not for scattered fragments, but for pieces chipped off reliefs and statues. Favourite targets were the Caryatids and the blocks of the Parthenon frieze, which had been discovered during the recent excavations and lay leaning against the walls inside the monument.

Pittakis's work on the Acropolis in the reign of King Otto was legendary, improvised, makeshift, empirical and anti-scientific. It was commented on, criticised, sometimes praised beyond reason, but usually censured by his contemporaries, both foreigners and Greeks, whether scholars or not. Whatever it was, it gave shape and volume to the monuments and an archaeological character to the group as a whole (fig. 23). And it prepared the ground for the great interventions that were to follow.

18, 19. Uncovering the 'large saw' in the Propylaia on 8 April 2003. Athens, Committee for the Conservation of the Acropolis Monuments (ESMA).

20. The Turkish house to the east of the Erechtheion, in which the finds from Pittakis's excavations were kept. Watercolour by H.C. Stilling, 1853. Copenhagen, Det kongelige Bibliotek.

21

22

21. Wooden frames with the scattered antiquities found by Pittakis, placed like 'paintings' inside the Pinakotheke in the Propylaia. Photograph by F. Margaritis, ca. 1855. Athens, Th. Theodorou Collection.

22. Archaeological finds stored along the south circuit wall of the Acropolis. Photograph by F. Bonfils, ca. 1871, Munich, Dietmar Siegert Collection.

24

23. General view of the Acropolis from the southwest. The mountains of earth from the first excavations on the Acropolis are visible on the south slope. The so-called Frankish Tower dominates the Propylaia. Photograph by D. Konstantinou, ca. 1860. Boston, N. Catsimpoolas Collection.

24. View of the Acropolis from the church of Ayios Dimitrios Loumbardiaris after the demolition of the so-called Frankish Tower at the Propylaia (1890).

25. Stephanos A. Koumanoudis (1818-1899). Athens, Archaeological Society at Athens.

THE MUSEUM, THE FRANKISH TOWER, THE DAILY ROUTINE OF THE ACROPOLIS

During the first two decades of the reign of King George I (1863-1913), a somewhat more pragmatic spirit prevailed and is reflected in the work on the Acropolis.

The great dreams of re-erecting all the monuments on it gave way to a policy of regular conservation and infrastructure works. The men responsible for the Acropolis, and for the other monuments of Greece, were Panayiotis Efstratiadis, the General Ephor of Antiquities, and Stephanos Koumanoudis (fig. 25), Secretary of the Archaeological Society, a brilliant figure, thinker and scholar, and a true Classicist, the last of the Enlighteners in a time of change.

During these years, two major projects had a direct impact on the image of the Acropolis: the construction of a museum, in the years 1865-1874, and the demolition of the so-called Frankish Tower, which had dominated the entrance to the Sacred Rock since the 15th century. The construction of the Museum – an old dream of Klenze, Ross and Pittakis – was to become the occasion of extensive earth removal and excavation at the north and northeast of the Acropolis, which yielded some outstanding finds (fig. 26), such as the Kritios Boy, the Calf-Bearer, the head of Athena from the Gigantomachy group, and so on. The Museum, built to a design by the architect Panagis Kalkos, who worked with the General Ephorate of Antiquities, was an austere, discreet building of a clearly functional character, lacking in architectural pretensions that would have competed with the monuments. The various 'collections' from different parts of the Rock began gradually to be transferred to it from 1874 onwards, as well as casts of the Acropolis sculptures in the Elgin Collection, which had been sent to Athens by the British Museum many years earlier.

The Frankish Tower at the Propylaia was demolished between 21 June and 20 September 1875 (fig. 24), raising a storm of protest. In contrast with the earlier cleaning of the medieval remains on the Acropolis, which had by and large met with general agreement, the removal of the Tower was carried out at a time of a general re-evaluation and acceptance of the medieval past of Europe and the enhancement of the period's status. The demolition of the tower provoked strong protests from historians, at the effacing of features representative of the rule of the West in the East during the Middle Ages (French historians in particular protested at the destruction of a 'French national' monument), and also by artists, who explicitly condemned the radical alteration of the romantic setting of the Acropolis through the obliteration of one of its venerable picturesque features (fig. 23). The demolition of the Tower was advocated by the Archaeological Society, an intransigent ideological exponent of pure Classicism throughout the 19th century, against the background of national crisis and controversy (with the rekindling of the Eastern

26. Sculptures from the Acropolis that came to light during the digging of the foundations for the Museum: the torso of the Kritios' Boy, the Moschophoros (Calf-Bearer), the head of Athena from the Gigantomachy group, and the torso of Athena no. 140 (ex-voto by Aggelitos). Anonymous photographer, ca. 1864. Athens, Th. Theodorou Collection.

Question), which encouraged modern Greeks to have recourse to their ancient heritage as a source of belief in and affirmation of their national identity. Ignoring the critics, the representatives of the Society, Stephanos Koumanoudis and Lysandros Kaftantzoglou, voiced their support for *the embellishment of one of the two wings of the architectural monument of Mnesikles, in accordance with its original design, and the restoration of the Greek character of the shining face of the Acropolis, pure and unsullied by anything foreign.* Kaftantzoglou, indeed, used the stone blocks from the demolished tower to reconstruct the retaining walls to the north of the base of

Agrippas and to the west of the Pinakotheke in the Propylaia, keeping, as he notes with pride, *the ancient line and masonry style of the structure, without the slightest deviation from the original line, or the use of different material.*

The 'Archaeological Service Daybook' carefully kept by Efstratiadis brings to light the daily routine of the Acropolis, and particularly the problems that arose and had to be solved by the archaeologist responsible for the protection of the site: problems during the sale of the formless stone blocks (arising out of profiteering by the buyers), problems with the residents of the surrounding area (protests that earth and formless blocks were dumped outside the circuit walls, threatening to crush their houses), above all the great problem of the illicit trade in antiquities (theft of ancient objects from the site and later also from the Museum, was common, as was the subsequent appearance of the stolen antiquities at auctions), and problems relating to the wear of the surface of the monuments as a result of their exposure to the atmospheric conditions (already!).

Two entries in the Daybook are worth citing, since they transmit with great immediacy the working conditions and specific dangers threatening men and monuments at that period:

- 11 April 1869. Last night, about 10 o'clock, the king went up to the Acropolis with the heir to the British throne. On it had gathered politicians, men and women, admitted by tickets, which the police distributed on the day, with the knowledge of the minister. The ancient monuments were lit up by fireworks (fig. 27), *which had been sent to the Acropolis by the garrison commander three days ago, after verbal communication between the minister and the minister of Military Affairs. The Acropolis was vacated about 11 o'clock. About 2 after midnight, it was reported to me that the corporal in charge of the fireworks returned about half past midnight. He entered the room in front of the inner gate of the Acropolis where the fireworks had been placed, with the first*

27. Photograph of the Acropolis during a visit by the Prince of Wales in 1875. Engraving from an issue of The Illustrated London News *(1842-1885).*

28. Panayiotis Kavvadias (1850-1928). Athens, Archaeological Society at Athens.

of the veterans, carrying in his hand a torch, the flame of which ignited the remaining fireworks. It was reported that the room was on fire and those who entered it had been burnt. At about half past 3 I was told that the room had been completely destroyed by fire and that it was with great difficulty that one next to it, in which the custodians lived, had been saved, but that there had been no damage to the antiquities next to the room.
- 21 April. On this night – last night – the veteran Spyros, who had been burnt in the fire in the room, died. He had been charged with supervising the other custodians of the Acropolis. This duty has now been assigned to Panagis.

29

GREAT EXCAVATIONS AND DISCOVERIES

On 11 November 1885, Panayiotis Kavvadias (fig. 28), a dominant personality who reorganised the archaeological affairs of Greece at the turn of the 19th to the 20th century, and who held the posts of General Ephor of Antiquities and Secretary of the Archaeological Society simultaneously, began to excavate the entire surface of the interior of the Acropolis systematically down to bedrock (fig. 30). After the end of the work, the intention was to restore the surface of the Acropolis to its presumed level and condition in the Classical period, leaving the important remains visible and suitably arranging the scattered ancient members. This programme was carried out constantly and without deviation by Kavvadias, in collaboration with the German architect Georg Kawerau, down to 1890.

As Kavvadias himself reports, *the excavations commenced in the northwest part of the Acropolis, near the Propylaia, and proceeded to the east along the north wall, as far as the Belvedere; here they turned to the south and proceeded along the whole of the south part as far as the Propylaia and the temple of Athena Nike, after which they were extended to the area to the west of the Propylaia as far as the Beulé gate and beyond.* The excavation was also to be extended to the central part of the Acropolis between the Erechtheion and the Parthenon, to the interior of the Museum, the interior of the Parthenon – the exposed parts of the floor were to be excavated – and the interior of the Pinakotheke in the Propylaia. The excavation was completed by February 1890. On the entire Acropolis, writes Kavvadias, *there remained not the slightest quantity of soil which had not been removed down to bedrock, and which was not investigated.* During the course of the work, any medieval or early modern buildings that remained on the rock were removed. The appearance of the Acropolis was completely changed (fig. 29).

By modern standards, the excavation was conducted in an unscientific manner: there was no daily record

30

29. General view of the interior of the Acropolis from the northwest, after the excavation of the years 1885-1890. Athens, National Historical Museum.

30. Excavation of the Acropolis down to bedrock in the years 1885-1890. The full height of the stereobate of the Parthenon was uncovered. Athens, German Archaeological Institute.

of the work and, above all, no study of the stratigraphy. The photographic record was inadequate and confined to general views, and the drawing was uneven, carried out by Kawerau and occasionally by Wilhelm Dörpfeld, then Director of the German Archaeological Institute. The results, however, *were truly very important, unexpected, and astonishing* as Kavvadias trumpeted. *On 24 January* (5 February 1886), *late in the day, in an area to the northwest of the Erechtheion that had been previously investigated, and in the presence of the king, a daily visitor to the excavations, - the spade struck a veritable nest of statues, which emerged from the ground one after the other over the following day* (fig. 31). *There were fourteen of these statues, all of female type, and of different size. Eight of*

31. Dignitaries visiting the site of the discovery of the korai to the northwest of the Erechtheion in 1886. Engraving from an issue of The Illustrated London News *(1842-1885).*

32. The Korai room in the first Acropolis Museum. Athens, 1st Ephorate of Prehistoric and Classical Antiquities (A' EPCA).

them still had the head preserved, and retained their bright paint in different degrees. The spade worked wonders here [...] The success with which these excavations, inaugurated with such brilliance, continued every day and were brought to an end is well known. The fourteen korai [...] were shortly followed by others, discovered here and there inside the precinct of Athena. This sacred band continued to increase until the end of the work. The discovery of the Archaic *korai* (figs 32-34), which caused a great stir in Greece and abroad, was the prelude to what was to come. The whole of the long history of the Sacred Rock, from Mycenaean to Roman times, was uncovered, the literary sources were confirmed, the Persian Wars were relived, and completely unknown monuments came to light under the archaeologist's spade: the Cyclopean walls, the northeast entrance, the traces of the Mycenaean megaron, the Archaic temple-shaped structures with their colourful poros architecture, the Old Temple of Athena, the 'Hekatompedon' (the hundred-feet temple), the

Arrephoroi staircase, Building B beneath the Pinakotheke, the Brauroneion, the Chalkotheke, and the temple of Roma and Augustus. Along with them emerged a vast number of unique sculptures, architectural members, vases, bronzes, figurines and inscriptions, that lent lustre to the Acropolis Museum. This was now radically reorganised and became *unique throughout the world*, in Kavvadias's expression. The great excavations and discoveries provided a huge impetus, both internationally and in Greece, to the scientific investigation of the history of the Rock, its topography and architecture, and in general to epigraphy, pottery, and the history of ancient art. Kavvadias's objectives had been achieved when, in February 1890, he announced in the *Archaeologikon Deltion* with great pride: *Greece presents the Acropolis to the civilised world, a monument of Greek genius, dignified, purified of all barbarity, a model, unique repository of outstanding works of ancient art, which challenges all civilised peoples, without distinction, to study, collaboration and noble rivalry in order to advance the science of archaeology.*

From the "random pile of marbles" of 1830 to the "purified monument of the Greek genius" of 1890, the vicissitudes of the Acropolis in the 19th century, with the small and great, light-hearted and tragic moments, had come to an end. The transformation of the Rock from castle to monument was fostered by the love of the antiquity and the general atmosphere predominant at the beginning of the century, and was required by the changed external circumstances and by new needs that arose, particularly by the na-

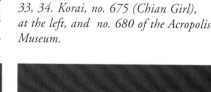

33, 34. Korai, no. 675 (Chian Girl), at the left, and no. 680 of the Acropolis Museum.

tional aspirations of the new Greek state. It was embraced by all Greeks: by scholars and educated men in their efforts to solidify the national identity, then still being formed, and by ordinary people out of a need for a steady source of pride, hope, and affirmation. The modern history of the Acropolis was continued by the interventions of N. Balanos (fig. 35), which began with the Parthenon from 1898 onwards and lasted until the Second World War, amidst repeated national crises and wars. These interventions extended to all the monuments on the Rock and formed its well-known image, the 'trade mark' of modern Greece in the post-war world.

The vicissitudes of the Acropolis have continued down to the present day. New restoration work that began in 1975 (fig. 36) to resolve a number of crucial problems is producing a new image of the monuments on the Sacred Rock – one that conforms to the perceptions and technological and social demands of the early 21st century (figs 37, 38).

33

34

35. *The beginning of N. Balanos'
restoration work on the Erechtheion, 1903.
In the foreground can be seen, at the left,
the draughtsman N. Ioannitis and, at the
right, the Ephor of the Acropolis,
D. Philios. The figure at the centre is
probably N. Kambanis, the foreman.
Athens, P. Venieris Collection.*

36. *The new restoration of the Acropolis
that began in 1975 and is still continuing
under the direction and supervision of the
Committee for the Conservation of the
Acropolis Monuments (ESMA) constitutes
the modern great moment in the history of
the Sacred Rock. The architect Manolis
Korres, one of the most important contributors
to the restoration of the Parthenon, can be
seen stooping above the pediment. Athens,
Committee for the Conservation of the
Acropolis Monuments (ESMA).*

37. *View of the Parthenon from the west.
A part of the frieze with the original
sculptures is visible.*

38. *Panoramic view of the Acropolis from
the Lycabettus Hill. Athens, Committee
for the Conservation of the Acropolis
Monuments (ESMA).*

35

36

Jutta Stroszeck

Kerameikos I
The discovery of the ancient cemetery

BEGINNING OF THE EXCAVATION

In the spring of 1863, a workman was busy near the church of the Holy Trinity, digging sand for the construction of Pireos Street, which was just being laid out. During this work in a thick layer of mud and sand from the river Eridanos, he struck the palmette *akroterion* of a marble *stele* (fig. 2), which he recognised to be an ancient one. In order to uncover it, he dug along the stele to a depth of 3.50 m. When he realised, however, that it was still standing upright in its ancient position, with its full height vertical in the earth, just as it had been erected, he informed the body responsible for archaeological matters at that time, that is the Archaeological Society of Athens. After an on-the-spot inspection by the Secretary of the Archaeological Society, it was decided to finance and carry out an excavation. Responsibility for the conduct of the excavation fell to K.S. Pittakis and A. Rousopoulos. Over the months that followed, it proved possible to uncover an entire row of preserved funerary monuments, with their marble decoration, on the southwest side of the Street of the Tombs (opposite the church of the Holy Trinity). Over the millennia, these tombs had been covered by deposits with a depth of many metres. The excavation site rapidly became a pole of attraction, even for tourists (figs 1, 8). Initially, the new area was called the 'cemetery near the Holy Trinity', after the church, and it was still referred to in this way on postcards at the beginning of the 20th century. Today, this section is the finest part of the archaeological park of the Kerameikos. Without the attention and curiosity of the workman, or if he had not contacted the responsible services, this unified archaeological park that we still enjoy today would certainly not exist.

IDENTIFICATION OF THE SITE

The Kerameikos in Athens was already known to archaeologists in the 19th century. They had devoted intensive study to the ancient literary sources, from which it emerges that at the Kerameikos (ἐν Κεραμεικῷ) was to be found the well-known public cemetery of the Athenians – that is, the place in which Perikles delivered his famous Funeral Oration for those who died in 431/430 BC (Thucydides II, 34). Parts of grave stelai erected for the fallen by the city of Athens had also been found before. After the discovery of the grave stele of Dexileos (figs 7, 11) along the Street of the Tombs in 1863, Rousopoulos believed that he had found the Kerameikos, since this stele was obviously the funerary monument of a warrior. This hypothesis appeared to receive confirmation when, as the excavation of the Archaeological Society of Athens proceeded, under the direction of St. A. Koumanoudis, the fortification walls and gates were also discovered and finally, in the year 1870, the inscription *ΟΡΟΣ ΚΕΡΑΜΕΙΚΟΥ* ('boundary of the Kerameikos') came to light close by the fortification wall (fig. 3). The word 'Kerameikos' was used in Classical times for the majestic way leading through the demos of the Kerameis, that is, the quarter occupied by the potters, and linking the Academy with the Agora. Only now it applies to the archaeological park of 38,500 m². The Archaeological Society excavations in the Kerameikos were later resumed by K.D. Mylonas (1890), V. Stais (1896) and G. Oikonomos (1897), and uncovered large parts of the cemetery, the fortification walls and the gates.

1. The imposing funerary monuments in the Street of the Tombs as depicted a few years after they were excavated. Watercolour by Angelos Yiallinas, (1857-1939). George David Collection.

1

THE EXCAVATION OF THE GERMAN ARCHAEOLOGICAL INSTITUTE

The archaeologist Alfred Brueckner knew Attic tombs and funerary inscriptions better than most people of his time. As a young man, he worked for many years in Athens on the Corpus of Attic Grave Reliefs under the direction of Alexander Conze. He also carried out a series of excavations in Athens at the end of the 19th century and from 1907 to 1909, with the permission of the Archaeological Society of Athens, in which he explored the cemetery near the church of the Holy Trinity (figs 6-9). The outcome of this investigation was the publication in 1909 of a seminal monograph entitled *Der Friedhof am Eridanos* (The Cemetery on the Eridanos). Four years later, at the age of 52, he was charged with directing the Kerameikos excavation, after the Greek state and the Archaeological Society of Athens had come to an agreement with the German Archaeological Institute to transfer the excavation rights to the institute (DAI). There is a brief reference to this event on page 4 of the *Deutscher Reichsanzeiger und Königlich Preussischer Staatsanzeiger*, no. 178, Wednesday 30 July 1913, under the title "Art and Science":

3

2

4

The imperial German Archaeological Institute of Athens has been given by the royal Greek Ministry of Education – after a decision taken by the Archaeological Council on the 16 of this month – the authority to complete the uncovering of the Kerameikos of Athens, using German financial means. This is an important region of the ancient city near its main gate, the Dipylon. Here, from 1863 onwards, the Archaeological Society has already uncovered the perimeter of the fortification walls and parts of the excellently preserved Street of the Tombs. From 1906 onwards, thanks to the readiness and support for the preliminary studies offered by the Greek authorities and the Greek Archaeological Society, German scholars such as the university Professor F. Noack at Tübingen and Professor A. Brueckner, headmaster of the royal Prinz-Heinrich Gymnasium at Schöneberg, have succeeded after many years of work in penetrating ever deeper into the problems raised by this site. The former has established the history of the Themistoklean Walls, and the latter the building plan of the cemetery, and the water-supply system at the entrance to the city, after digging a number of trial trenches. The German Archaeological Institute has thus undertaken the obligation, insofar as it is associated with these preliminary works, to uncover completely an area of about 45,000 m², which has already been expropriated by the Greek government. This has made it possible for the researchers of the institute, too, to acquire a large body of new material for study. At the same time, the Institute has undertaken the obligation to attend to the preservation and restoration of the finds, to lay out the area of the ruins in a fit manner, and also to express thanks, in a prominent place at the centre of the city, for the hospitality enjoyed by all Germans in Greece. The Institute may hope, when the excavations begin next spring, as planned, for donations by German friends eager to support this project, as they have done with great success during Professor Brueckner's work on the restoration of the monuments on the funerary way, and in his preliminary study. Of equal importance is a letter written by K. Kourouniotis, Director of Antiquities, on 2 July 1913 to Alfred Brueckner:

4. The grave relief of the two sisters Demetria and Pamphile. A copy of it has now been placed on the pedestal. The original was taken to the Kerameikos Museum in 2004.

5. View of the first burial monuments uncovered in the Kerameikos by the Greek Archaeological Society during the second half of the 19th century. Athens, German Archaeological Institute.

Athens, 2 July 1913

My Dear Friend, Professor
Yesterday I spoke with Mr. Svoronos and Mr. Tsountas about the excavation in the Kerameikos. They both agreed with your request that the excavation should be carried out by the Institute. Mr. Tsountas will be away from Athens today, so there is no need for you to take the trouble to ask for him.

Ever yours
K. Kourouniotis

6. Reconstruction drawing of the north side of the Street of the Tombs with the succession of grave enclosures adorned with superb funerary monuments. From the left: precinct of a family from Thorikos (Dexileos), the tomb of a family from Herakleia on the Black Sea, the monument for Dionysios of Kollytos (bull), and part of the monument of Lysimachides (with the dog). Drawing by A. Brueckner and A. Struck (1904).

7. Street of the Tombs. Burial plot of a family from Thorikos with the monument for the horseman Dexileos, one of the first finds from the excavation of the cemetery. Athens, German Archaeological Institute.

8. The Street of the Tombs and the Tritopatreion during excavation in 1907. In the background lies the former vegetable market of Athens on Pireos Street, to the right the old church of Ayia Triada. Athens, German Archaeological Institute.

9. The marble bull that stands above the funerary naiskos in the grave enclosure of Dionysios of Kollytos. The sculpture has been replaced by an exact copy and was taken to the central yard of the Archaeological Museum of Kerameikos for its protection in 1997.

6

7

8

10. The funerary monument of Hegeso, from the enclosure of Koroibos, that stood on the northwest side of the Street of the Tombs. A copy has been placed on the site, while the original is now kept in the National Archaeological Museum.

11. The grave stele of Dexileos, a monument erected by the family of a young warrior who fell in battle in 394 BC. Athens, Archaeological Museum of Kerameikos.

Since then, the German Archaeological Institute has excavated in the Kerameikos every year, apart from two breaks during and after the two World Wars. The work is funded by the German state, which also shoulders the expenses for the employment of permanent and temporary staff (archaeologists, workmen and conservators), as well as the maintenance of storerooms and the publication of the finds and results of the excavation. Some members of the excavation staff are the second generation to work in the Kerameikos. Great expense was incurred in the extension of the site by the purchase of a number of buildings on the periphery of the excavation. The old buildings were demolished and the additional area was excavated. After the excavation, these extensions were added to the archaeological park between Melidoni, Ermou, Pireos and Salaminos Streets. Other projects – such as the erection of the museum and its extension, and also the various conservation programmes – have been supported for many years by German sponsors

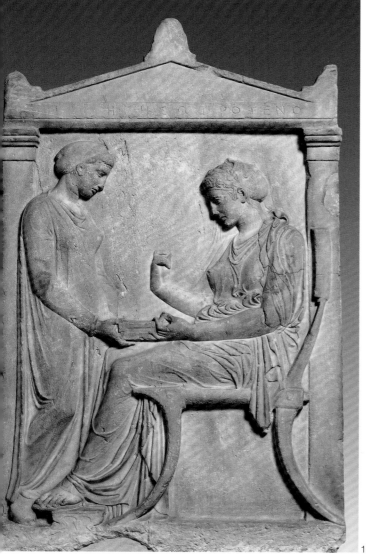

12. *Marble sphinx from the crowning of a grave stele dating from 550-540 BC. Found in the Themistoklean wall at the Sacred Gate. The sculpture preserves vivid traces of colour. Athens, Archaeological Museum of Kerameikos.*

13. *Reconstruction drawing showing the bright colours with which the sphinx in fig. 12 was painted.*

14. *Reconstruction drawing of a grave relief with a maiden and her parents found in the Kerameikos in 1870. Engraving from an issue of* The Graphic *(1869-1885).*

15. *Excavating the Pompeion in 1930. At the bottom left can be seen the columns of the internal colonnade. Athens, German Archaeological Institute.*

16. *The monument of the Lakedaimonians (403 BC) under excavation in 1914. Athens, German Archaeological Institute.*

THE MONUMENT OF THE LAKEDAIMONIANS

The programme of new excavations included the investigation of the street, along which the Athenians erected common tombs (known as Polyandria) for those who died in war. The names of those buried here are mentioned in many ancient literary sources, and Pausanias, in particular (I 29ff.), lists a series of battles, the casualties of which were buried on this site at the expense of the Athenian state. Brueckner's first excavations along the southwest side of this street yielded important results, since he was able to establish that the funerary buildings, erected here above a series of warrior's tombs, were part of the public burial ground (fig. 16). He was nevertheless obliged to suspend his work by the outbreak of the First World War. It was not until 1926 that work resumed, again under his direction. Alfred Brueckner's last excavation season took place in the Kerameikos in 1930 (fig. 17). Brueckner intensified his investigations in order to complete his study of the funerary monuments on this street, and at this point, he made a final find of exceptional importance: during the demolition of a later wall near the Polyandrion, he discovered part of an inscription that solved the problem of the interpretation of the monument (fig. 19): in the inscription were recorded the names of the Lakedaimonian *polemarchs* Chairon and Thibrakos, who are mentioned by

17. The excavators of the Kerameikos in 1930: Alfred Brueckner in the centre, to his left Hubert Knackfuss, Karl Kübler and A. H. Hess, to his right F. Wirth and Willy Zschietschmann. Athens, German Archaeological Institute.

18. Skeletons of Lakedaimonian fighters who fell in 403 BC. From the monument of Lakedaimonians in the Kerameikos. Athens, German Archaeological Institute.

19. Part of the inscription from the monument of the Lakedaimonians in the Kerameikos. Athens, German Archaeological Institute.

Xenophon (Hellenika 2, 4, 33) in connection with a conflict that took place in the year 403 BC between the supporters of the democrat Thrasyboulos and the allies of the Thirty Tyrants. Xenophon adds that the two polemarchs, as well as an Olympic champion named Lakrates and other warriors were buried before the gates of the Kerameikos (πρὸ τῶν πυλῶν ἐν Κεραμεικῷ).

Thus, after many years of investigation, it had proved finally possible to identify archaeologically a public tomb known from the literary sources. Down to the present, this funerary monument remains the only surviving example of a tomb of Spartan warriors (figs 16, 18).

17

18

19

THE DISCOVERY OF THE DIPYLON HEAD

Greece's entry into the First World War signalled the temporary suspension of the German Archaeological Institute's excavations directed by Alfred Brueckner in the Kerameikos. In the spring of 1916, excavation on the Kerameikos street was still going on. During the course of the work, it was judged necessary to make a thorough investigation of the north tower of the Themistoklean Dipylon Gate, the walls of which were not so clearly defined, in contrast with the other towers of the monument. One of the most important finds from the Kerameikos came to light during this work: amongst the broken stones in the foundations of the Themistoklean fortification tower lay the larger than life-size head of an early Archaic statue of a young man, which became famous as the Dipylon Head (fig. 20). It is made of Naxian marble and, in stylistic terms, may be assigned to the early period of Attic large-scale sculpture – that is, the early 6th century BC. In 1929, after the resumption of the excavations at the Dipylon, the hand of the youth was also found in the same foundations. Today, the two pieces are on display in the National Archaeological Museum of Athens. This find is splendid confirmation for Thucydides' statement that the fortification walls were erected hastily by the Athenians just after the expulsion of the Persians in 478 BC. Stones from surrounding tombs and anything else suitable such as statues (fig. 21) and funerary reliefs, for the purpose were used in the construction of these walls (Thucydides I. 89,93).

20

KÜBLER AND THE SUB-MYCENAEAN CEMETERY

Not all archaeological discoveries are necessarily connected with great, unique moments. Many findings of the utmost importance are the product of long years of painstaking excavation, arrangement and classification of the material, and publication of the excavation data. New conclusions that advance research are often reached only after the study of the excavation record in combination with the finds kept in the storerooms, and comparison with published finds of similar material from other parts of Greece. A characteristic example of this kind of investigation is provided by the work of Karl Kübler, who, in 1930, succeeded Alfred Brueckner as director of the Kerameikos excavations. Kübler devoted himself to two main topographical areas of the site: the excavation of the Pompeion (fig. 15) between the Eridanos River and the Dipylon Gate, and the uncovering of the great funerary tumulus found beneath the church of the Holy Trinity. When the church was demolished in 1931, it was replaced by the large new building on Pireos Street that still dominates the site today. Both at the Pompeion and beneath the former church of the Holy Trinity, Kübler encountered important cemeteries: to the north of the Eridanos and beneath the Pompeion he was able to uncover a significant

20. The Dipylon Head. Athens, National Archaeological Museum.

21. Fragment of an Archaic marble statue, as found built into the Themistoklean wall. Athens, German Archaeological Institute.

21

number of tombs of the Sub-Mycenaean and Protogeometric period (fig. 24) – that is, the Early Iron Age (1050-950 BC). Beneath the hill on which the church stood, he found a large cemetery of the Geometric period covered by tombs ranging from the Archaic (7th-6th century BC) to the Hellenistic periods (figs 22, 23, 25). These excavations enabled him to undertake a thorough study of the burial practices and grave offerings of Attic tombs over a period of more than 1,000 years.

Over the years, more than 6,000 tombs have been uncovered in the Kerameikos. From 1939 to 1976, six volumes of the series *Kerameikos – Results of the Excavations* were published, written by Kübler and devoted to the cemeteries from the Sub-Mycenaean down to the Classical period. Since then, they have constituted a seminal work for anyone studying the funerary culture and customs of this period. Kübler also made sure that the finds were put on display in the museum built at this time in the Kerameikos to designs by the excavation architect, Heinz Johannes. The museum was donated to the Greek state in 1938. For the first time, grave groups were placed there on display in an unbroken sequence from the Sub-Mycenaean to the Classical period, thus giving non-specialists, too, a picture of ancient burial customs and an appreciation of the evolution of Attic pottery. These grave groups still form an important part of the exhibition in the Museum, which has now been renovated and was reopened in 2004.

22, 23. Late Geometric female burial accompanied by many offerings, as found during the excavation (right) and as displayed today in the Archaeological Museum of Kerameikos (left). Athens, German Archaeological Institute.

24. Protogeometric burial during excavation. Athens, German Archaeological Institute.

25. Detail of a red-figured hydria by the Meidias painter, ca. 410 BC. Athens, Archaeological Museum of Kerameikos.

OSTRACISM

In 1966, the direction of the excavations was assigned to Franz Willemsen. He set as his aim to clarify the building activity in front of the middle fortification outwork – that is, the area between Kerameikos Street and the bed of the Eridanos River. The high level of the water, however, was a serious obstacle, and work could only be carried out after the water had been pumped away. The ground in front of the outwork is furrowed by water conduits and drainage channels more than the rest of the Kerameikos, and these destroy the ancient layers. The natural bed of the Eridanos crossed this area before the river was channelled in 478 BC. To the south, following the direction of the river, the ground falls away. Amongst a row of conglomerate blocks, a huge *pithos* and a well, Willemsen discovered a uniform level that had filled the earliest bed of the Eridanos. In this level thousands of inscribed *ballots-ostraka* (potsherds) for ostracism were found (fig. 26). They were presumably thrown here after the vote and used as supplementary filling material. Significant evidence was thus found, quite unexpectedly, for the study of ostracism, well-known from the ancient literary sources. The sherds are probably the refuse from one, or at most two ostracisms. The ostraka contain unique information for conditions in Athens in the 5th century BC, and for one of the most famous mechanisms of Athenian democracy.

The excavations of the German Archaeological Institute in the Kerameikos are continuing at the present moment (fig. 32). It is worth noting at this point that over a quarter of its total area has not yet been

26. *Potsherds used for ostracism in Athens. They were found as fill in the old river-bed of the Eridanos.*

27. *Burial stele for the comic actor Aristion from Troizen, found in front of the Dipylon Gate. Athens, Archaeological Museum of Kerameikos.*

28. *The painted mask on the stele of Aristion, with the colour digitally enhanced.*

29. *Showcase with finds from the 6th c. BC as displayed since 2004 in the splendidly renovated Archaeological Museum of Kerameikos.*

fully investigated. The impressive new finds of the year 2002 (see the chapter by W.-D. Niemeier) give a precise idea of the surprises that the Kerameikos still holds in store.

Quite apart from these finds, however, the archaeological investigation continuously raises very different questions, and uses new methods of documentation, in the hope that there will be new, interesting conclusions in the future.

An example of the new methods which yielded new results is the use of digital photographs. A stele found in front of the Dipylon Gate in 2002 bears the inscription for the comic actor Aristion from Troizen, who died around 265 BC and was a well-known, prize-winning artist of his time (fig. 27). Faint traces of a red painted comic mask survive just below his name. They were made visible by intensifying the colour digitally without otherwise changing the photograph (fig. 28).

To this work should be added concern for the conservation and safekeeping of the monuments, as well as the publication of the finds and their display in the Museum (figs 29-31). In this way, not only will the interest of the public in Greek civilisation be aroused and kept alive, but also the knowledge acquired will be handed on to future generations.

30

30. Fine Attic sculptures of the 6th c. BC on display in the Archaeological Museum of Kerameikos.

31. The inner courtyard of the renovated Kerameikos Museum, with a display of inscribed bases and funerary monuments, one of which is the marble Bull from the Street of the Tombs.

32. Panoramic view of the Kerameikos from the north.

31

Wolf-Dietrich Niemeier

Kerameikos II
The Archaic sculptures of the Sacred Gate, Spring 2002

A great moment in the archaeological investigation of the Kerameikos occurred in the recent past, on 29 March 2002. The spring excavation season of 2002 at the Sacred Gate, which on the date in question was drawing to its planned close, did not have any spectacular objectives: a few small trenches were to contribute to the resolution of a number of questions that remained unanswered, in order to prepare for the publication of the monument, the Sacred Gate in the city fortifications, through which the Sacred Way passed, after 19 kilometres, en route to the sanctuary of Demeter and Kore at Eleusis. Amongst other things, a conduit was excavated in the Sacred Way (fig. 1), in the hope that pottery to which a date could be assigned would be found inside. No such pottery was discovered, but quite unexpectedly, the experienced excavation workman Tasos Boundroukas was astonished to find, beneath the bottom of the pipe, the left shoulder and hair of a marble *kouros* that had fallen on its face (fig. 2). No-one expected a spectacular find of a kouros in the middle of Athens. We couldn't believe our luck... The hair, with the beaded tresses tied in a so-called 'Herakles knot' immediately reminded us of the famous Dipylon Head, found in the Kerameikos in 1916 and now on display in the National Archaeological Museum. At our feet lay a piece of sculpture from the dawn of Attic marble-working, about 600 BC. And it was not alone. Next to it could be seen a fragment of a marble Sphinx (fig. 3, left), the head of which was covered by a stone block of the conduit.

The excavation was extended for six weeks in order to uncover the kouros and the Sphinx. Clarification was also sought for the questions of how and why they came to be this position, and whether there were other sculptures in the area. The heavy stone blocks of the conduit had to be removed by crane. We all turned in anticipation to the task of uncovering the Sphinx's face. Had the face been preserved, concealed for almost 2500 years beneath the conduit, or not? It was indeed preserved, and rewarded us with an Archaic smile as it gradually emerged from the earth. The head of the Sphinx was next to the head of the kouros. They looked just like an Archaic couple, and we found it very hard to separate them after so many centuries.

Every so often, as the excavation continued, one of the workmen would shout: "Another marble here!" In the end, we found ourselves – entranced and speechless – before a group of sculptures lying side by side: from west to east (fig. 4, from front to back), a reclining lion, a fragment of a Doric capital, the kouros, the Sphinx, the front part of the seated lion, a fragment of an Ionic column with its capital, and the back part

1. The conduit crossing the Sacred Way. Its excavation led to the discovery of the group of Archaic sculptures.

2-4. The Archaic sculptures of the Sacred Gate, as found during various phases of the excavation.

of the seated lion, which is unfortunately in a poor state of preservation. Apart from the Doric capital, which was of brown limestone, they were all made of marble. The two capitals did not belong to an architectural ensemble, but had been used as statue bases.

The statues originally stood on the funerary monument of an aristocratic family, and had fallen victim to the plundering of Athens and its cemeteries by the Persians in the year 480 BC. In the 6th century BC, marble lions and Sphinxes guarded the tombs of aristocrats, with the lions symbolising both the strength and the spirit of the dead. Kouroi probably commemorated the glory and posthumous fame of the deceased and their families. With their 'ideal nudity' they reflected the athletic skill of the men they depicted; they were not realistic portraits of the dead aristocrats, but symbols of them at the height of their virtue and nobility, which the kouroi perpetuated for eternity.

But how did these sculptures come to be where they were found, beneath the Sacred Way? When the Athenians were able to return to their city after the Greeks defeated the Persians in the naval encounter at Salamis and the battle of Plataia in the autumn of 479 BC, Themistokles' first concern was to erect new fortification walls. The programme was implemented between autumn 479 and spring 478 BC, with all the citizens helping, using all available building material. It was then decided to increase the space enclosed by the wall, which, with its two gates, the Dipylon and the Sacred Gate, cut through the ancient cemetery in the Kerameikos. Funerary sculptures that had fallen here and been damaged during

5. The first cleaning of the Archaic kouros, on the site of the excavation, just after it had been raised from the position in which it was found.

6. Modern means were used to transport the Archaic sculptures from the Sacred Gate. Here, the kouros is raised with the aid of a crane.

7, 8. Two views of the kouros from the Sacred Gate, an outstanding work of sculpture from a great artist. Athens, Archaeological Museum of Kerameikos.

the Persian attack were incorporated as building material in the foundations of the wall: one of these was the Dipylon Head, which was found in one of the towers of the Dipylon Gate. The group of sculptures found in spring 2002 had been placed beneath the earth road that ran from the newly created Sacred Gate. They were put here to strengthen the road at a point where it was increasingly flooded by the Eridanos River. Evidence for this second use of the sculptures is provided by the traces of wear on them from the wheels of carriages. In a later phase, the banks of the Eridanos were protected by a wall, and some of the water was channelled off through the overflow pipe, beneath which we found the kouros.

Comparison of the head of the kouros from the Sacred Gate with the Dipylon Head (figs 9-12) leaves virtually no doubt that they were created by the same sculptor about 600 BC. He was the first Athenian marble-carver of consequence and the founder of a tradition that was to culminate 150 years later in the marble sculptures of the Parthenon. His name remains unknown, and archaeologists have therefore baptised him the Dipylon Artist. The kouros of the Sacred Gate gives us an idea of the way in which this leading Athenian sculptor rendered the male body in ideal nudity.

The reclining lion, which is dated about 570 BC (fig. 13), is an unusual work of art, for which no parallels are yet known. The stylised muzzle is the so-called Assyrian palmette muzzle, a motif that comes from the Near East and goes back to the Orientalising Period of the 7th century BC. This lion, however, has completely shed the menacing, daemonic features of lions of the late 7th century.

The latest work in the group is the Sphinx, which is dated to about 560 BC. All that we found was the

9

11

9-12. Comparison of the Dipylon Head (Athens, National Archaeological Museum; figs 9, 10) with the head of the Sacred Gate (Athens, Archaeological Museum of Kerameikos; figs 11, 12) leaves virtually no doubt that they were created by the same sculptor about 600 BC.

13. Despite the influence of Assyrian art, the predominant features of the reclining lion from the Sacred Gate are those of Greek Archaic sculpture. Athens, Archaeological Museum of Kerameikos.

14. The Sphinx as reassembled from fragments found in 1907 and 1983 and placed on an Ionic capital found during the excavation. Athens, Archaeological Museum of Kerameikos.

10

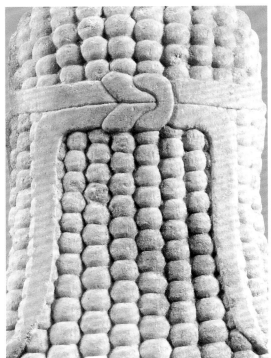

12

upper part of the body, partly preserved wings, and the head. We remembered, however, that in 1907 and 1983, two fragments of the back of the body of a Sphinx had been found in the area of the Sacred Gate, and these indeed proved to be the back of the newly found Sphinx. All the finds in the Kerameikos down to 1938, when the Kerameikos Museum opened, had been taken to the National Archaeological Museum, and this was where the 1907 fragment was kept. Thanks to the attention of the Director of the Museum, N. Kaltsas, it was handed over to the Kerameikos Museum, to make it possible to restore the Sphinx (fig. 14). Sockets for wooden tenons of equal sizes are to be found in the top surface of the abacus of the Ionic capital, and also in the lower surface of the plinth of the Sphinx. This indicates that the Ionic capital was used as a base for the Sphinx, as now shown in the restored monument on display in the Kerameikos Museum.

The sculptures were conserved in exemplary fashion by colleagues of the Third Ephorate of Prehistoric and Classical Antiquities of the Hellenic Archaeological Service. They have been placed on exhibition in the Kerameikos Museum, which was completely redesigned for the 2004 Olympic Games, and is now a jewel amongst Athenian museums and houses a highly successful permanent display, from both a teaching and an aesthetic point of view. In this context, the new sculptures from the Sacred Gate form a new attraction for visitors to Athens. At the same time they enrich our picture of Archaic Athenian marble sculpture.

13

14

Dominique Mulliez

Delos
The excavation of the sacred island of Apollo

Delphi and Delos, the two sites excavated by the French Archaeological School of Athens, which were linked by the figure of Apollo, are often compared and contrasted: Delphi is located in a mountain setting, while Delos is an island; the excavations at Delphi were confined to the sanctuary of Apollo, while those at Delos extended to the city and the harbour; Delphi was protected by the village built in the area of the sanctuary which sealed the site; Delos, on the other hand, is an island, exposed and therefore an easy target for plunder.

THE MAPPING OF DELOS

In contrast with Delphi, Delos did not have to be discovered, since its existence was always present in people's memory. Abandoned at the beginning of the 7th century, it owes its appearance in a relatively large number of maps to its location on a much-frequented sea route.

The earliest such map, of the entire Archipelago, is attributed to the geographer Claudius Ptolemaeus and was reproduced by G. Mercator in 1584. The world atlas designed in the 17th century by Abou Abdallah Mouhammed Al Idrisi is undoubtedly incomplete, but it is the first representation, after Ptolemaeus, that may be described as geographical. Delos is referred to as follows: "From it (Mykola = Mykonos), east to the island of Antzilo (Zdilo = Delos), twelve miles. Antzilo is circular, an abandoned, uninhabited island, however it does have a harbour." In later times Italian seafarers laid down the lines for the character of the mapping of the Archipelago, in a tradition lasting from the 14th to the 17th century.

It was not until the beginning of the 15th century that the first map devoted exclusively to Delos made its appearance. The work of Christopher Buondelmonti, it was published in the *Liber*

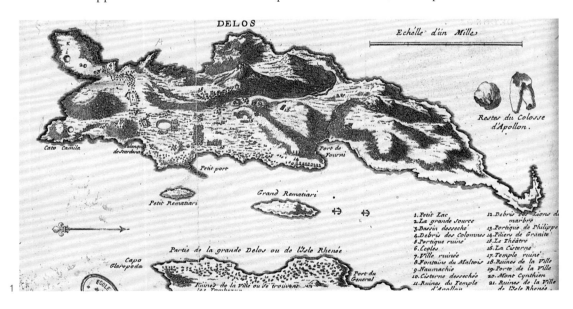

1. Old map of Delos showing the position of several of the monuments visible at the time, such as the Sacred Lake, the Theatre, etc. Drawn in 1717 by the botanist J. Pitton de Tournefort.

2. Aerial photograph of the archaeological site of Delos from the northeast. In the foreground can be seen the Theatre, with the extensive remains of the Theatre Quarter next to it.

Delos. The excavation of the sacred island of Apollo | 79

insularum Archipelagi in 1420. After this, alongside the maps drawn by seafarers, astronomers or hydrographers to locate a route, or refer to the natural resources of a place, maps produced by those who would soon be called "foreign travellers" gradually appeared (fig. 1). The travellers were the first to locate the ancient ruins on Delos and mark them on the map, offering descriptions of whatever had escaped the looting of ancient times.

The first map that may reasonably be called scientific dates from the beginning of the 19th century. Almost a century later, in 1909, the French Archaeological School of Athens published a map of the Island of Delos at the scale 1:10000. This map was the outcome of a programme that began in 1906, and was drawn "as an indispensable aid to archaeological work by É. Ardaillon and H. Convert." Applying the methods used by the military geographical service, it aimed at "the most faithful depiction of the region." Ardaillon and Convert also attempted to identify as many ancient ruins as possible, whether excavated or not, that were visible on Delos and the east coast of Rheneia (A. Bellot.)

3

THE FOREIGN TRAVELLERS AND THE FIRST EXCAVATIONS

The list of foreign travellers who visited Delos and left a record contains about 100 names and begins with Cyriacus of Ancona, who came to the island in 1445. The narratives of these visitors reveal an island that was abandoned, inhospitable, exposed to the elements, where there was no water and where nature was far from liberal; the only animals found in great numbers were rabbits. They also stress the striking contrast between the former grandeur and the random disorder of the ruins currently encountered by the eye, which discouraged any reference to them. In his *Les ruines des plus beaux monuments de la Grèce* (2nd edition, 1770), the traveller Le Roy comments: "even the most splendid buildings have bowed to the laws of time, or to assault by barbarity. The famous temple of

3. View of Delos as depicted in 1829 by the French Mission to Morea. This visit signalled the beginning of French academic interest in Delos.

4. Ruins on Delos. Drawing by Seger de Vries before 1673. At the left are parts of the columns of the Temple of Apollo and at the right the two fragments that then survived of the Naxian statue of Apollo, which was about 9 m. high.

4

Apollo […] now appears as a random heap of column fragments, so mixed up that I found it impossible to form a picture." More than a century later, in his account of an excursion made in 1847, but published long afterwards, Charles Benoît wonders, for his part, how Théophile Homolle could extract a plan of the site from the total confusion he found before him. Summarising the picture of abandonment in a single phrase, J. Spon spoke of "the miserable 'shoal' of Delos…"

In *Antiquities of Athens measured and delineated …etc.* (vol. 3, p. 57, London 1794), by J. Stuart and N. Revett, painters and architects, we read the following description: "This island, once so celebrated […] is now an uninhabited desert, every where strewed with ruins, so various, and so well wrought, as to evince its once populous and flourishing condition. The only animals we saw here, beside rabbets and snakes, were a few sheep brought occasionally from Mycone, a neighbouring island, to crop the scanty herbage which the ruins will permit to grow. Travellers, who have visited this place, have been distressed for water […]. The number of curious marbles here

5. Reconstruction drawing of the Apollo of the Naxians, one of the largest ancient Greek statues. It was erected next to the House of the Naxians in the sanctuary on Delos at the beginning of the 6th c. BC.

6, 7. The two fragments of the Naxian statue of Apollo and the enormous base, weighing 32 tonnes, as preserved in 1910.

is continually diminishing, on account of a custom, the Turks have, of placing, at the heads of the graves of their deceased friends, a marble column; and the miserable sculptors of that nation come here every year, and work up the fragments for that purpose, carving the figure of a turban on the top of the monumental stone. Other pieces they carry off for lintels and window cells; so that, in a few years it may be as naked […]." In a note, the publisher of the volume pointed out: "In the year 1785, there were no remains but one single altar of marble, broken into pieces, with heaps of ruins of buildings, but not even a stone of any regular form, or any ornamental fragments. The antiquities, described in this chapter, are said to have been taken away by a Russian fleet, in the last war against the Turks."

The travellers also describe an island exposed to plunder, either in order to procure building material for new construction work or to create collections of antiquities. In his book describing his impressions of his journey, J. Spon gives the following account of the Colossus of the Naxians (figs 5-7): "We found ourselves on the site of the temple of Apollo. We would probably not have noticed it if we hadn't seen the statue, fallen to the ground, so badly worn that it resembles a formless torso; this was the consequence of its age, or of the poor treatment it received at the hands of those who visited Delos. Some took away a leg, others an arm, without respecting the great esteem in which this statue had been held in the past. It is not very long ago that a governor of Tinos sawed off the face since he reckoned that the head was very bulky and he would not be able to load it on his boat." At another point in the book, Spon speaks of the Stoa of Philip (figs 8, 9): "The majority of the columns that we see are fluted at the top and polyhedral at the bottom. In the prevailing confusion, we saw only two or three capitals of the Corinthian order, the rest having been taken off by the Turkish or Christian ships that have put in here since the island was abandoned." In a letter to His Highness the Count of Pontchartrain, Tournefort describes Delos as he saw it in the winter of 1700/1701. He remarks that "The people of Mykonos [...] go to Delos every day to cut wood, to fish, or to hunt," but that "the best parts of the island are covered with ruins and marble fragments, and the land is barren and completely unsuitable for sowing. All the builders from the neighbouring islands come here as though to a quarry and choose the pieces that serve them best. They break a beautiful column to make staircases, window supports, and frames for doors: they smash a statue base to make a mortar or a salt-cellar. Turks, Greeks, and Latins break, overturn and remove whatever they like. What is strangest is that the inhabitants of Mykonos pay only ten silver coins to the sultan for rights to an island on which is kept the public treasury of the League of the Greeks, of the country that was the richest in Europe at that time." The first excavations that ever took place on Delos were not followed up. Reference should be made to the excavation conducted in 1772 by H.L. Pasch van Krienen, an officer in the Russian army, and those by L.S. Fauvel. In an undated letter that does not bear the name of the place at which it was written, and which is now in the Bibliothèque Nationale in Paris, the latter boasts of the excavations conducted by him during his stay on the island in 1791: "I also drew a plan of Delos; and I conducted excavations. Much had escaped the earlier travellers."

Reference should be made to the work of the eminent British architect C.R. Cockerell in October 1810: Cockerell employed a number of workmen and uncovered a sizeable part of the temple of Apollo, enough to enable him to make a drawing of the temple. He drew and measured all the architectural features, and was able to copy the inscriptions. His endeavours ceased at this point, however, because the site was in a state of confusion: "you would think that it had been used as a sculptor's workshop," he commented. The sequel to these ventures however, according to A.J. Reinach, was brought about by the architect W. Kinnard. He relied on Cockerell's references when he went to Delos in 1818, in order to bring back ancient sculptures for the British Museum, amongst which was the leg of the Colossus of the Naxians. And if Cockerell had seen Delos as a "sculptor's workshop," Kinnard, for his part, looked on it as "an insignificant marble quarry."

Two years after Cockerell, in 1812, Thomas Leigh employed twenty workmen, but without great success: "Although our researches were carried on for three days, our labour was not discovery of consequence, nor were able to carry off one of the numerous altars which are lying upon the adjoining island, called the Greater Delos" (*Narrative of a Journey in Egypt*, 1817).

The Kapodistrias Government very soon showed itself determined to put an end to this uncontrolled, irregular exploitation. In 1825, Colonel Rothiers, who wished to implement "a programme of excavations which he had been thinking about for some time," was refused permission by the

Greek authorities. This does not mean that after this time there were no illegal excavations: in his *Souvenirs*, Viscount Marcellus notes in 1826 that he saw "on the shore traces of recent excavations just as unsuccessful as those carried out by a company of architects based in Athens." In the same year, according to Reinach, inhabitants of Mykonos complained of the tactics of the consuls of France and England. The plundering of the island and neighbouring Rheneia continued until the end of the 1820s. This accounts for the dispersal of the *stelai* and gravestones from Rheneia to numerous European museums, in Austria, Great Britain, France, Italy, Norway and even Russia. The decisive intervention of the Kapodistrias Government was needed to bring this to an end. In 1829, the sculptor E. Wolf noted that the authorities on Syros confiscated twenty funerary monuments that had been removed by a Frenchman. Some forty pieces are also said to have been confiscated from the inhabitants of Mykonos, who were selling them for commercial profit, and which are now in the Mykonos museum. About one hundred items confiscated in 1828 were sent to Aigina in 1872.

8, 9. The Stoa of Philip V at the time of the excavations (bottom), and a reconstruction drawing of it (top). The stoa, which stood on the Sacred Way very near the harbour, was often the object of plundering by ships that put in at the island. Archive of French School of Athens.

8

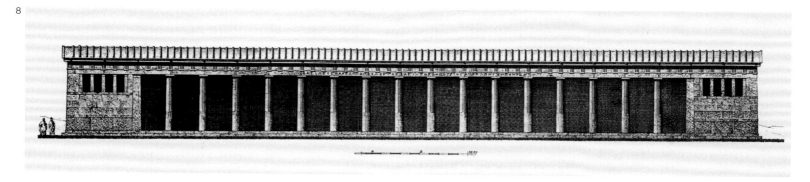

9

THE FIRST FRENCH EXCAVATIONS (1873-1894)

In addition to individual initiatives, the Mission to Morea (Expédition Scientifique de Morée, 1828-1831) marked the beginning of French interest in Delos: widening its investigations to include the Cyclades, this mission bequeathed a fairly unimportant text on Delos. The engravings accompanying it (fig. 3), however, are still valuable, since, as L. Terrier notes in his *Memoirs* in 1864, "some of the monuments depicted in them have now been destroyed or suffered considerable damage since the time of the mission."

Following what was "an entirely philological mission" by Ch. Benoît in 1847, and a preliminary reconnaissance by L. Terrier, the fruit of which is the *Mémoire sur l'île de Délos* of 1864, Delos was the first major excavation entrusted by the Greek state to the French School of Athens. It was a concession, not a monopoly: it was so arranged that the investigations made by the French archaeologists would be supplemented, enriched and carried out under the supervision of the members of the Greek Archaeological Service, particularly the Ephors of the Cyclades and successive Curators of the island. Set against the background of French-German rivalry, the archaeological investigation of Delos coincided with a major change of direction in the missions of the French School, which decided its archaeological priorities. Georges Radet wrote, "Delos was more than a brilliant chance event. The enterprise carried out in 1877 in the precinct of Apollo demonstrated that the renewal of the School would only be complete and constant on condition that it explored the bowels of the earth continuously, not occasionally."

In fact, the archaeological investigation of the island commenced in 1873 with A. Lebègue. It was directed to the "Cave of the Dragon" (figs 10, 11), situated on the slopes and summit of Mount Kynthos. The sanctuary, which was dedicated to Zeus Kynthios and Athena Kynthia, was easily reconstructed, but the cave itself left the field open to the imagination. In his book *L'histoire et l'oeuvre de l'École française d'Athènes* (Paris 1901), Georges Radet vividly recounts the various imaginative interpretations given to the Cave on Mount Kynthos due to the lack of any significant finds at that time:

10, 11. The cave on Mount Kynthos: as drawn (right) and as it was at the beginning of the 20th century (left). It was dedicated to Herakles, though the local tradition knew it by a variety of names, such as Cave of the Dragon. Archive of French School of Athens.

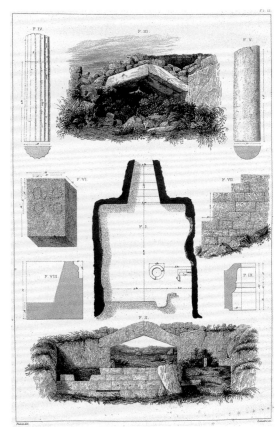

"Ross saw in it an entrance from above to the peribolos of the temple, Leake a treasury, Tourne-fort a guardhouse, Spon a kind of castle. For Burnouf, the orientation of the passageway betrayed astronomical concerns. From the time of Homer the Ionians used the cave as an observation post. It is none other than the 'cave of the sun' mentioned by Eustathios and Didymos. For Lebègue, it was primarily a prophetic adyton, the earliest temple of Apollo on Delos, the seat of the oracle consulted by Aeneas, Odysseus and Agamemnon."

In 1876, Albert Dumont sent Théophile Homolle, then a member of the French School, to Delos. He decided to leave the mountain aside and concentrate on the sanctuary of Apollo, which was placed at a site called Marmara on a map dating from the time of the Mission to Morea. He began fresh excavations on Delos in 1877 and continued until 1880, starting at the heart of the sanctuary and steadily widening the investigation until he found the *peribolos*. These excavations yielded a wealth of architectural, topographical and epigraphic finds, as well as large items of Cycladic sculpture. The Nike of Archermos (fig. 12) and the statue of Artemis of Nikandre (fig. 13) were first brought to light at this time. These early years of systematic archaeological excavation made it possible to determine the general lines of the topography of the sanctuary.

Th. Homolle believed, however, that the excavation of the temple should be accompanied by an investigation of the city. The programme for this investigation, drawn up with 'perfect logic', was summarised by G. Radet as follows: "on Delos, since religious life gave rise to commercial life, the sanctuary and the agora were next to each other. Visitors were led inescapably from the buildings devoted to the cult to those intended for commerce. Beyond the commercial quarter spread the city proper, with its public and private buildings, gymnasia and palaestras, stadium, theatre (figs 18-20), entertainment centres, clubs, and religious areas in which foreigners worshipped their own national gods, the harbours and the quays. For a project of this size, the work of a single individual was not enough." The work was accordingly shared in 1881 between A. Hauvette, S. Reinach, P. Paris, F. Dürrbach, G. Fougères, G. Doublet, L. Couve and Th. Homolle himself, for the years 1885 and 1888. The project was completed in 1894 by the compilation of an archaeological map of Delos to the scale 1:2000 by É. Ardaillon and H. Convert, which was published in 1902.

How should we assess this first period? F. Dürrbach, who was to resume the work eight years later, made the following comment: "fifteen successful missions failed to exhaust the archaeological interest of Delos. In the sanctuary itself there are still areas of virgin, unexplored ground [...]. Around the enclosure, a series of excavations [...] defined the important points of the Delian topography, placed the Agora , the School of the Italians and the area of the Sacred Lake to the north, the harbours and quays to the west, and the Stoas and a second Agora to the south. However, even these excavations need to be repeated, to be taken to greater depths, in order to unify the site. Finally, a little further off, the efforts of members of the School were directed to various buildings that dominate our attention: such as the temple of

12. The Nike of Archermos, one of the first attempts in Greek sculpture to render a winged figure. Athens, National Archaeological Museum.

13. The statue of Artemis of Nikandre, the first large marble statue. Athens, National Archaeological Museum.

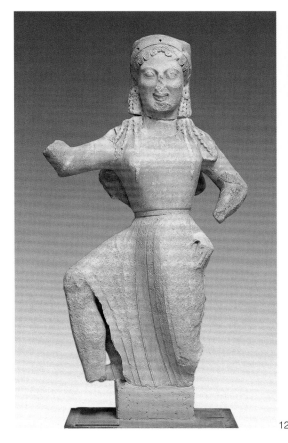

12

13

Zeus Kynthios and the temple-cave, the sanctuaries of the foreign gods and the Kabeiroi, the theatre, and the gymnasium uncovered by M. Fougères. Without taking into consideration the many other buildings mentioned in inscriptions, the traces of which have disappeared, it may be said that the entire Greco-Roman city, with its streets and squares, remains unknown. The few houses uncovered here and there by MM. Paris and Couve give only a foretaste of the city" (*BCH* 26/1902, p. 481-482). Despite this, there was another major excavation that tied up all the available energy and finance: Delphi, the exploration of which began in 1892. Théophile Homolle, who had in the meantime become the director of the French School of Athens, was convinced that the archaeological work on Delos should be continued. In his report on the excavations on the island in 1894, after L. Couve's discovery of the Diadoumenos (fig. 14), and while the excavations at Delphi were still in progress, Homolle wrote: "nothing could be more encouraging than this beginning for a general excavation on Delos [...]." He expresses his desire that "the earth should be removed and the whole of Delos excavated, because no other city can provide so complete, varied and lively a picture of the life of the ancient Greeks." It is his hope that "as soon as the excavations are completed at Delphi, the equipment can be transferred to Delos and the funds gathered for a patient, methodical and general excavation" (*BCH* 19/1895, p. 538-539). Despite the evident sense of incompletion, this first phase of the archaeological excavation of Delos, which is often overshadowed by the "great excavation" of 1903 at Delphi, did have an impact. The Paris Exposition of 1889, for which the Eiffel Tower was built, included a pavilion devoted to Delos, and on 30 June 1889, Théophile Homolle addressed a *Conference sur les travaux de l'Ecole française d'Athènes à Délos* from the platform of the Trocadero.

14. Some important marble statues came to light in 1894. The Diadoumenos, immediately after its discovery, supported by two workers from Mykonos (today, Athens, National Archaeological Museum). Archive of French School of Athens.

15. Also in 1894 the pseudo-athlete, a portrait of an important Roman citizen of Delos, came to light. Archive of French School of Athens.

14

15

THE GREAT EXCAVATION OF DELOS

The excavation of Delos was resumed in summer 1902, after a break of eight years. In his very first report, F. Dürrbach considered that: "the interest of this new mission should be measured only by its direct results. In fact, the mission inaugurates an overall programme that will continue the excavation of the entire island with new resources and methods." The first of the preconditions laid down by Th. Homolle in 1894 had been fulfilled: the excavations at Delphi had finished and freed a substantial quantity of equipment, which was taken to Delos as early as 1902 and enabled F. Dürrbach to continue successfully, to reveal the Agora of the Delians.

In 1903, as Dürrbach reports, "from the second mission, we had unexpected good fortune that allowed us to give the work a dynamic impulse" (*BCH* 28/1904, p. 265). He refers to the fact that the second precondition stated by Th. Homolle – " that the funds be gathered for a patient, methodical and general excavation" – had been met, thanks to the generous annual sum of 50,000 francs donated by the wealthy Joseph Florimond, Duke of Loubat (fig. 16), a liberal patron of the arts.

An American citizen and a member of the Historical Society of New York, the Duke of Loubat (1831-1927) repeatedly showed his generosity to the Académie des Inscriptions et Belles-Lettres of France, of which he subsequently became a corresponding member (1901) and foreign associate (1907). In 1908 he established the Loubat Prize, to be awarded every three years for "a published work relating to North America (History and Historical Geography, Archaeology, Ethnography, Linguistics and Numismatics)." In 1903, a grant of 50,000 francs, which was renewed in the following years, "made it possible," according to the relevant entry in the Government Gazette of 5 January 1911, "to give a very dynamic impetus to the excavation of Delos." His generosity towards Delos did not stop here, but proved of decisive importance in the publication of the *Corpus des Inscriptions de Délos*, the first two volumes of which were included in the collection *Inscriptiones Graecae* (1912-1914). The First World War, however, put an end to the earlier agreement between the Berlin Academy and the Académie des Inscriptions et Belles-Lettres, and the latter proceeded with the venture alone. The generosity of the Duke of Loubat enabled F. Dürrbach to publish the first volume of the series, *Choix d'inscriptions de Délos* (1921 and 1923), while the income from a foundation created in 1920 was later used for the publication of the five volumes of the *Corpus français des inscriptions de Délos* between 1926 and 1937. The Duke of Loubat never visited Delos. He at least had the pleasure, however, of receiving the thanks of His Highness the King of Greece, who sent him the following telegram after visiting the island in August 1910: "From Delos, 8 August, 6 in the afternoon - via Malta. After visit to Delos, I send you my congratulations."

The grant enabled the excavation of Delos to be given the greater scope desired by Th. Homolle. Thanks to the financial support and advanced technical means, as well as an enlarged scientific group, it finally became possible to make a start on a systematic excavation. This required a re-examination both of the available equipment and of the workforce undertaking the enterprise. Th. Homolle asked the Ministry

16. *The American millionaire Joseph Florimond, Duke of Loubat. His generosity enabled both the excavations and the related publications to proceed at the beginning of the 20th century.*

17. *The group of French scholars who brought the great excavation to a successful end, photographed on Delos at the beginning of the 20th century. Seated, Ch. Dugas, A. Gabriel, J. Paris, J. Chamonard (?), J. Hatzfeld. Standing: P. Roussel, R. Vallois, H. Convert, G. Poulsen, F. Courby, J. Replat. Archive of French School of Athens.*

18

19

to seek the temporary assignment of F. Dürrbach, then a professor in the Philosophical School at Toulouse University, as director of the project. The direction of all technical matters was entrusted to Henri Convert (fig. 17) director of the Engineering School, "whose experience had proved so invaluable during the excavation of Delphi" (*BCH* 28/1904, p. 266). In the archives of the French School of Athens is a valuable report compiled by H. Convert at the end of 1903 on "the technical side of the project." The following extract enables us to assess the extent of the equipment used, which was distributed to the six teams working simultaneously.

"The equipment for the excavations is that used at Delphi. At 19 June [1903], it included 35 wagons, one platform and 1700 metres of tracks 0.90 m. wide, which were brought to Delos last year for the excavation of the square stoa. This material is not enough for the work we are undertaking. Moreover, when we began to organise the work towards the end of June, Sotiris Ayious was sent to Delphi and returned with 1300 planks, 22 wagons, 2 platforms, all the equipment of the conservation laboratory, various other materials, timber, bricks, etc. We then called for more workmen, the work multiplied and the project went ahead at a rapid rate. The impulse given to it was so great that the equipment is now inadequate. On 10 October, a caïque came from Piraeus carrying equipment that had been used in the excavation at Tegea, which included: 11 wagons, one platform, 478 metres of tracks 0.90 m. wide, 2 junctions (crossed tracks to enable the wagons to change direction) and a number of tools. The same caïque also brought us a supply of double-headed nails, bolts, wedges, iron and steel rods, seatings, etc., which will enable us to repair any material that has been damaged after 10 years of use.

"Consequently, the equipment now on Delos consists in total of: 68 wagons with a capacity of half a cubic metre, 4 platforms, 3,478 metres of tracks 0.90 m. wide, with eight junctions, a windlass capable of lifting 5,000 kilos, and a boat with a sail. The rest of the light equipment consists of shovels, spades, pickaxes, crowbars, lifting tackle, wheelbarrows, panniers and barrels. The blacksmith's shop contains a kiln, anvils, a drill, and clamps, all from Delphi. Finally, the situation is such that we are able to undertake any repairs on site. All this equipment can be kept in 3 storehouses, one of which is adjacent to the workshop, while the other two are contiguous with its east and west sides. There is also a stable that can hold two horses next to the workshop on the west."

A project of this nature required sound organisation, since in the twenty-one weeks the excavations lasted in the year 1903, there were from 42 to 192 workmen, depending on the period: "apart from a number of former workmen from Delphi," notes Henri Convert, "all the rest are from Mykonos. Every Monday morning a caïque transports them from the harbour of Mykonos with a week's supplies, because there is nothing on Delos, and the following Saturday, the same caïque returns them to Mykonos, in order to restock and spend Sunday with their families." Convert kept detailed notes each week of the number of workmen employed, the number of wagons in action, and the number of animals used (up to 10 horses and mules). Nor did he fail to note the holidays "on account of the large number of festivals in their calendar," or days lost due to the bad weather that prevented the caïque from leaving Mykonos or, at the beginning of October, because "many of the workmen have gone to sow their fields." We find the same numbers for the year 1904. In a letter to the General

18-20. Characteristic pictures of the French excavation in the Theatre Quarter at the beginning of the 20th century. They show the great depth of the earth deposits, the impressive state of preservation of the ruins, and a large number of workmen. Archive of French School of Athens.

20

Ephor, dated 16 April 1904, M. Holleaux, who had recently been appointed director of the French School, writes: "we intend to employ 150 to 200 workmen, and we shall start with four or five teams simultaneously." This presupposed the taking of the appropriate measures, which were M. Holleaux' concern when he presented the following requests to the president of the Greek Council:

"1. The presence of police in sufficient numbers –five or six men– to keep order, and if and when quarrels arise, to discipline the shepherds or the villagers from Mykonos residing temporarily on the island, or the sailors sitting in the harbour with nothing to do. To arrest any workmen who cause serious trouble.

"2. The installation of communications either by telephone or by telegraph between Mykonos and Delos, making it possible to request medical help from Mykonos in case of an accident, or other assistance, if any emergency arises" (letter dated 2/15 April 1904).

Accidents did arise, because the work was not without its risks. The archives contain a request from Konstantinos Nikolaos Zouganellis (generally known as Vavoulis), after an accident that happened to him in July 1904: "a wagon severed his left leg above the knee." He therefore sought from the French School of Athens "considerable assistance to maintain him." It is possibly as a result of this demand that in documents dated 1918, Zouganellis is referred to as "custodian of archives of the School of Athens."

Charged with the "technical side of the project," Henri Convert compiled a report on the work at the end of 1903: "to sum up, during these excavations we deposited 60,990 wagons of soil in-to the sea, representing 31,000 cubic metres, since the wagons were invariably overloaded. The soil was deposited from the following three points: in the north, from the ancient quay, in the west from Ardaillon's agora (the Agora of the Hermaistai), where a huge mole, formed from earth

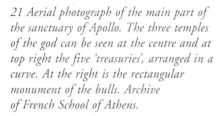

21 Aerial photograph of the main part of the sanctuary of Apollo. The three temples of the god can be seen at the centre and at top right the five 'treasuries', arranged in a curve. At the right is the rectangular monument of the bulls. Archive of French School of Athens.

22. The sculpture group of Aphrodite, Pan and the young Eros, which dates from 150-125 BC. It was found in the Institution of the Poseidoniastai and, according to the inscription on the base, was dedicated by Dionysios son of Zeno from Beirut to the ancestral gods. Athens, National Archaeological Museum.

21

that had been removed on the site, juts into the sea, at the west from the shop with the columns and at the south, from itself." These figures are not surprising; in some parts of the Theatre Quarter, the layer of earth covering the site frequently reached a depth of five metres (figs 18, 19).

However important the technical side of things, the tone was set by the scientific aspect of the project. In contrast with our observations on Delphi, the great excavations on Delos had a truly original form, due to the wider scope and the conception itself. Whereas the order issued in the case of Delphi concerned only the Sanctuary of Pythian Apollo, the great excavation of Delos went beyond the narrow confines of the Sanctuary of Apollo and extended to the entire city and surrounding countryside. Above all, it proved to be a truly interdisciplinary enterprise in the great tradition of the Mission to Egypt or the Mission to Morea. This is very evident from the papers of the Parliament, published in the Government Gazette of the French Republic on 5 January 1911: "we considered that the interest was mainly, though not exclusively, archaeological. It was important to show the links connecting archaeology with other sciences. The assistant scientists selected and sent to the island enabled us to integrate geography, meteorology, geology, hydrography, and so on, into the project we are planning."

Work was directed initially to the Sanctuary of Apollo, which had first to be cleared of the earth deposits left by previous excavations, and to which F. Dürrbach referred as "the toilet of the sanctuary." The earth was dumped in the sea, creating the mole, now used by ships as an anchorage. At the same time, it was planned to excavate the city bordering with the sanctuary on the north, east and west: "we wanted, through this city, the best-preserved of all ancient cities in Greece proper, to gain accurate knowledge, through methodical transitions from quarter to quarter, and to learn how it was connected with the Sanctuary of Apollo" (BCH 30/1906, p. 483). In this way, through the series of reports published in the Compte rendu de l'Académie des Inscriptions et Belles-Lettres and the Bulletin de Correspondance Hellénique, we see the topography and the name of the city being made very clear as this enormous project progressed.

In addition to the precinct of Apollo, the excavation turned its attention in 1903 to the quarter of the Agora of the Delians, in which is the house known as the House of Kerdôn, which at once became a reference point in the topography. As soon as the earth deposits had been cleared, an excavation was carried out along the line of the ancient street, revealing the houses on the left side and the peribolos of the House of the Kerdôn. At the same time, the methodical excavation of the market place along the commercial harbour continued. In addition to the ongoing excavation in the Sanctuary of Apollo, the 1904 season was marked by the excavations by L. Bizard at the north, in the Agora of the Italians, and that of the Institution of the Poseidoniastai, which was excavated by M. Bullard and yielded the group of Aphrodite, Pan and Eros (fig. 22).

At the south, the excavations of the Theatre Quarter were resumed under the direction of J. Chamonard: the House of the Trident had been excavated in 1894, and now came the turn of the House of Dionysos and the street of the Theatre, which had been partly cleared of its earth deposits in 1893 and had not been entirely revealed. The buildings lining the street, the majority of which were given over to commercial use, were also excavated at this time. A. Jardé resumed the excavation of the shops near the sea, to the south of the Agora of the Hermaistai. During this same year, 1904, and through supplementary excavations in 1906 and 1907, the main part of the façade of the Sanctuary of Apollo was revealed, "with the objective of determining the exact boundaries of the sanctuary, isolating it from the neighbouring districts of the town, and at the same time, identifying each of these

22

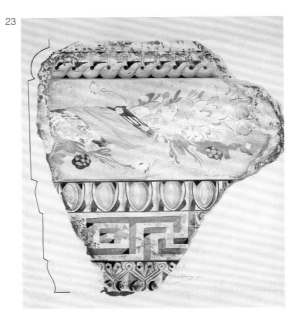

23

24

25

26

23. Reconstruction drawing of a wall-painting from the House of the Trident. Archive of French School of Athens.

24-26. The wall-paintings of the houses on Delos were rich and varied. Here are depicted Ariadne sleeping on Naxos – where she was abandoned by Theseus –, the preparations for a pig sacrifice and a young slave setting the table. Archive of French School of Athens.

districts" (*BCH* 31/1907, p. 470). At the end of 1904, M. Holleaux was able to give the following account, in an address to the Académie des Inscriptions et Belles-Lettres: "we measured the heights, drew the topographical plan and took photographs as the work proceeded. We compiled a complete inventory of the objects discovered, which numbers no less than 4,000 artefacts. All the inscriptions were deciphered and transcribed, and copies were made. The works of sculpture that were found broken have been temporarily repaired. We buttressed all the sides that were collapsing in all the buildings we uncovered. In particular, we attempted to save the wall-paintings and mosaics from destruction, found in many of the buildings" (*CRAI* 1904, p. 727).

Year after year, the excavations continued and were extended. In 1905, the projects of the previous year continued. Specifically, the Agora of the Italians was completely revealed in this year. In 1906, J. Chamonard finished excavating a small insula of residences in the Theatre Quarter, and M. Mayence and F. Courby discovered two more insulae: one of these contained 12 houses, including the House of Cleopatra (fig. 27), a workshop and 20 shops. In the north part of the site, the *Letoön* and the granite monument were found; after this, the excavation continued up to the Lion Terrace (figs 35, 36).

Although 1907 was dedicated mainly to the Sanctuary of Apollo, in the following year, 1908, after an explicit request from the Duke of Loubat, excavations were conducted at the harbour and on the cistern of Inopos, and the fountain of Minos was discovered. Collaboration between the architects A. Gabriel, G. Poulsen and J. Replat made it possible to produce a topographical plan of the precinct of Apollo. The year 1909 was marked mainly by the excavation of the sanctuary of the foreign gods by P. Roussel, of the

27. *The facade of the House of Cleopatra, with the statues of Cleopatra herself and her husband Dioskourides in the background. According to the inscription on the base, the couple were Athenians from the deme of Myrrhinous.*

28. *Two large building blocks near the theatre. At the top, the Delian House and, at the bottom, the House of the Masks, so called after the masks depicted in the mosaic floors.*

29

30

31

29. *The House of Hermes. Uncovered in 1908 in the Quarter of Inopos, near the sanctuary of the foreign gods.*

30. *Three hundred and fifty mosaic floors have been uncovered in the houses on Delos, a truly astonishing number. Most of them were found in the Theatre Quarter. Here, a common motif found in many of the houses on Delos.*

31. *The mosaic from a house of the Theatre Quarter.*

32. *The mosaic with the dolphins from the house of the same name.*

33. *Dionysos with the panther was a favourite subject of the inhabitants of Delos. Here, the head of the panther from the House of Dionysos.*

34. *Mosaic with Dionysos and the panther, from the House of the Masks.*

32

33

sanctuary of the Kabeiroi by J. Hatzfeld, of the residential quarters by J. Hatzfeld and Ch. Dugas, while the House of the Naxians was examined and measured. In this way the work developed year after year, marked by important finds such as the "bronze head of a Roman," the discovery of which was announced by Th. Homolle to his colleagues at the Academy on 11 October 1912.

During the course of all these projects, great use was made of external collaborations. In 1905, G. Simoes da Fonseca, who had also played a part at Delphi, was invited to Delos to copy "in very delicate water colours, most of the wall-paintings that adorned the houses on the island" (*CRAI* 1905, p. 762). This completed the work done the previous year on the mosaics by M. Bulard. In 1906 and 1907, L. Cayeux, professor of geology in the School of Metallurgy, compiled a geological and geographical study of the island. In 1907, Captain Bellot of the military geographical service drew a topographical map of the island (fig. 38), while the ensign Bringuier drew a hydrographic map of the south coast and the main anchorages of the island. In

34

35. Archaic lions dedicated by the Naxians. They were found in 1906 and placed on pedestals by the then Ephor D. Stavropoullos. In October 1999, the lions were taken to the Museum and replaced by copies.

36. A unique photograph showing one of the lions just after it had been uncovered. Archive of French School of Athens.

37. The public cistern of Inopos, found in 1908. Twenty-two marble steps led to the surface of the water.

1910, the work of Henri-Paul Nénot, who worked under the supervision of Th. Homolle on the original excavation of Delos, was resumed by Camille Lefèvre (Winner of the Prize of Rome), who stayed on the island for five months, engaged mainly in the drawing of the houses.

For these discoveries to receive the publicity they deserved, a publication was needed. This corpus was called *Exploration archéologique de Délos*, the first two volumes of which appeared in 1909. For the results of the project to be displayed to the public, a museum was required: in 1904, M. Holleaux again turned to the General Ephor, D. Stavropoullos, to whom he sent two letters (17 April and 3 May 1904), enclosing the "designs and budget for the Delos Museum," prepared by H. Convert. In his letter of 17/30 June, however, he spoke of confidential information to the effect that the plan "would meet with the opposition of the mayor of Mykonos. He will probably raise the issue that the structure will encroach on a piece of the territory of Delos that belongs to his municipality. I would like to assure you that this demand of the mayor's is totally unjustified." In July 1904, work had already begun, "despite the nature of the ground on which the Museum was

to be built, (which) requires that the foundations go to a great depth," despite the opposition of the mayor of Mykonos, and despite the lack of adequate support from the Ministry, which, though having no objection to the plan, nevertheless delayed it. In the end, the project was completed, though as early as 1909 it proved necessary to plan for its extension – that is, before the work had even started.

The second phase of the archaeological investigation of Delos, came to an end with the outbreak of the First World War. One of the most tangible influences of the excavations of this period, especially those in the residential areas, can still be seen at Beaulieu-sur-mer, where the Hellenist Théodore Reinach commissioned the architect Emmanuel Pontremoli (Grand Prix for architecture in the Rome competition, 1890) to build a house that was an exact copy one on Delos, equipped with reproductions of ancient furniture. The architect devoted six years, from 1902 to 1908, to the creation of what became known as the Villa Kerylos.

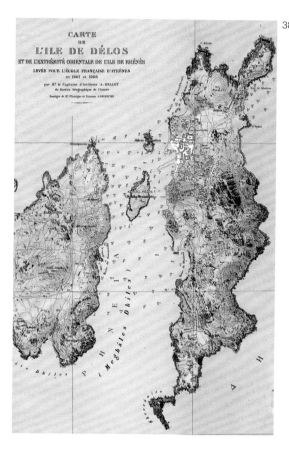

38

38. Map of the islands of Delos and Rheneia drawn by Captain Bellot of the French military geographical service. The French Mission to Delos had broader scientific interests, in addition to archaeology.

39. Reconstruction of the sanctuary of Apollo and part of the city. Drawing by Ph. Fraisse, owned by the French School. In the 1st c. BC, when Delos was at the height of its prosperity, it is reckoned that it had about 30,000 inhabitants. It was the most important commercial centre in the Aegean, and the more important harbour.

39

The First World War brought an end to these activities. On 17 April 1914, the second volume of *Inscriptiones Graecae*, containing the inscriptions of Delos, was published, after agreement with the Berlin Academy, and was presented and honoured at the Académie des Inscriptions et Belles-Lettres: this was the only report of this year on the work of the French School on Delos. In 1915 and 1916, the question of excavation was not raised, other than in a general report on the work of the School, whose activities had come to a standstill. J. Replat devoted himself to drawing the archaeological map of Delos, while A. Plassart carried out an excavation on Mount Kynthios in 1916. In a world thrown into utter confusion, in a year in which the French School was obliged to close its doors in Athens for the first time, "there was still the sacred island, which for forty-three years now has never betrayed the trust of the French, the island that has protected us from pirates, the deserted island on which we had nothing to fear from political or military disturbances: Delos" (*CRAI* 1916, p. 606). The echoes of war reached even Delos, however, and Plassart's correspondence reveals his anxiety and uncertainty: "we are impatient to receive news of the war," he writes. "The last newspaper we saw seemed to foreshadow a serious British counterattack." More immediately, he was anxious about the return of his curator D. Pipas, of whom his superior in the hierarchy, D. Stavropoullos, "does not believe that he will be able to avoid conscription, because he is in the officer cadet corps (at Chalkida) and will probably serve as the instructor for the new recruits. On the other hand, he regards his return as essential, because he alone has the keys to all the storerooms, chests and drawers in the museum." In the year 1918, there were no reports on the work of the French School.

DELOS AFTER THE GREAT EXCAVATION

When archaeological activity was resumed after the First World War, other sites attracted attention – Thasos, Philippi, Malia, Dikili Tash. This does not mean that Delos and Delphi were completely neglected, but the initial impetus had gone, and the pace was scaled down. The end of the funding by the Duke of Loubat exacerbated this. The excavations were not broken off, but whereas the objectives of the great excavation were to reveal entire complexes, areas and districts, the scale now changed and the focus was on the study of individual monuments, the publication of the catalogue of the finds by category, and the publication of the inscriptions. The day of the great excavation had gone, and a new generation of archaeologists took over the baton.

Much later, between 1950 and 1970, true excavations were resumed, on the House of Hermes (fig. 31), the House at Fourni and the district of Skardana. The cemetery on Rheneia was also revealed. Later still, in the 1980s, the landscape of Delos and its agricultural areas were studied, and precise measurements made it possible to clarify a number of chronological and topographical points.

TOWARDS AN ASSESSMENT

The rapid development followed by the premature abandonment of one of the liveliest centres in the heart of the Mediterranean explains the good fortune of Delos. Théophile Homolle was correct in his view that "no other city in Greece can provide us with so complete, so varied and so lively a picture of the life of the ancient Greeks." No other city in Greece can offer us such a great wealth and variety of finds: architecture, sculpture, painting, pottery, mosaics, and the furniture used in everyday life. All of these are reflected and finally depicted on Delos. Religious and political, public and private, urban and rural life, all have their place and expression. Literary sources and inscriptions, finally, complete the knowledge provided by the island.

The collection *Exploration archéologique de Délos* now numbers forty-one volumes, supplemented by nine volumes of inscriptions, about twenty monographs, and many hundreds of articles. The work is still incomplete, however: because the excavations covered only half the island; because the study of the parts already excavated need to be brought to a conclusion, or to start anew; because new questions arise as to the methods used for development. Testimony to this is provided by three recent programmes dealing with the water of Delos, the use of colour in the sculptures, and the clarification of the atlas of the island, which aspires to use modern techniques in order to bring to a conclusion the original plan entrusted by Th. Homolle to A. Ardaillon and H. Convert.

40. Aerial photograph of the archaeological site of Delos from the north. The characteristic feature of the archaeology of Delos is that the great sanctuary of Apollo, the panhellenic Ionian religious centre, existed alongside a large settlement with imposing houses, which were created by the development of the harbour of Delos into the largest commercial centre in the Aegean.

40

Helmut Kyrieleis

Olympia
Excavations and discoveries at the great sanctuary

Unlike today, the Greece of the ancient world was not a unified state, but was fragmented into small, competing city-states that were often hostile to each other. The ancient Greeks were united, despite their political opposition, by their common religion, mythology and language. The idea of a culture common to all Greeks emerged not so much within the city-states as at the great panhellenic sanctuaries. Amongst these, the sanctuary of Zeus at Olympia played a leading role as a gathering place for all Greeks, thanks to the prestige of its cult and the athletic contests held there every four years under the protection of a sacred truce. The significance of Olympia as a reference point for ancient Greek religion and culture was also reflected in the exterior appearance of the sanctuary, in the buildings and the wealth of artworks that arrived here as dedications from all parts of the ancient Greek world.

The glory of Olympia survived the decline and destruction of the ancient sanctuary and its athletic facilities. And the idea that cult games were held every four years under the aegis of the supreme god of the Greeks, uniting athletes and leading figures from the whole of the ancient Greek world, and also that a panhellenic sacred truce interrupted the constant hostilities between the Greek cities, made an impression on modern scholars from as early as the age of Humanism.

The exceptional importance of Olympia and the Olympic Games was brought to life in the victory odes composed by the great Greek poet Pindar, and also in Pausanias's detailed description of Olympia in the

1. The valley of Olympia at the beginning of the 19th century. Coloured lithograph from Ed. Dodwell, Views and Descriptions of Remains in Greece *(1821), Athens, National Historical Museum.*

2. View of the ruins of the temple of Zeus immediately after the 1875 excavation. The temple was the main cult building in the sanctuary and the focus of the excavations and studies. Athens, National Historical Museum.

1

2nd century AD, in the 5th and 6th books of his famous *Description of Greece*, which is of even greater importance to academic research. It was precisely this description of the sanctuary, with its dedications and buildings, that gave rise very early to the view that excavations at Olympia would be worthwhile and would yield rich finds. In 1767, the founder of the science of archaeology, J.J. Winckelmann, had already expressed a desire to carry out excavations at Olympia. The site of the sanctuary, buried beneath thick layers of mud, had already been located shortly before by the British traveller Richard Chandler (fig. 1). The first archaeological excavations were conducted by the French Expédition Scientifique du Morée in 1829. At this time parts of the temple of Zeus were uncovered on the surface, as well as parts of early Classical marble metopes from the temple, now in the Louvre.

Nevertheless, almost half a century was to pass before a thorough investigation of Olympia began, after long diplomatic and political negotiations. For many reasons, these excavations, from 1875 onwards, served as a guide in the course followed by Classical archaeology in Greece. This was already true of the contract entered into in 1874 by the Greek and German Governments regarding the excavations at Olympia. For the first in time the history of modern archaeology, this contract laid down that all the finds from the excavation should remain the property of Greece, while the German side acquired the right to undertake the academic publication of the finds and results of the excavation. It was left to the

3. *The Heraion after its discovery during the excavations in 1877. The large earth deposits 3-4 metres thick, that had been deposited by the flooding of the rivers Alpheios and Kladeos and covered the ruins, can clearly be seen. Athens, German Archaeological Institute.*

judgement of the Greek side whether certain reduplicated finds should be given to the excavator. These principles, which are formulated for the first time in the Olympia contract, still form the basis for the work of the foreign institutes in Greece and other Mediterranean countries. From the point of view of the history of scholarship, the fact has not been properly appreciated that, both through the contract and through the investigation itself, the main objective of archaeological excavation was defined as scientific knowledge and not the acquisition and ownership of museum objects. The new role played by archaeological and historical research in the political rivalry between the nations of Europe is attested by the fact that the German Parliament approved significant sums of money for conducting the excavations at Olympia, despite the fact that the finds were to remain in Greece. It is worth noting that the German Chancellor, Bismarck, was originally opposed to this contract. He believed that the German state was making a bad agreement and had to be persuaded personally by Kaiser Wilhelm I to add his signature to approval for the funding for the excavations and publication. It was only in 1887, after the release of a number of authentic finds that now belong to the valuable collection of the Berlin Museum, that the chancellor became more reconciled to the idea.

In a way, the importance of the discovery of Olympia for the history of Greek art matches the supreme importance of the site in ancient times. It is no exaggeration to claim that the excavations at Olympia from 1875 onwards marked the beginning of the first great chapter of modern archaeology in Greece. When one reflects that before the commencement of the great excavations, the entire area of the ruins was covered with a layer of sediment 3-4 metres thick, it becomes apparent that brief archaeological campaigns like that by the French in 1829 were not enough to carry through the enormous task of uncovering Olympia (fig. 3). One can also comprehend, albeit partially, the huge problems facing the archaeologists at Olympia, and the spirit of the excavators who ventured upon this gigantic enterprise. The famous sanctuary of Zeus and the place where the ancient Olympic Games were held emerged again before the eyes of the modern world in October 1875, in the lower slopes of Kronios Hill, which had been covered by flat, cultivated land since the early Middle Ages (fig. 2). In the course of six excavation seasons down to 1881, thanks to the work of eminent archaeologists and architects such as Gustav Hirschfeld, Adolf Bötticher, Georg Treu, Wilhelm Dörpfeld and Adolf Furtwängler, under the general direction of Ernst Curtius and Friedrich Adler, the larger part of the ruins of Olympia came to light, along with a large collection of inscriptions, sculptures and dedications of all kinds that permitted a completely new view of the history and importance of Olympia, and shed new light on hitherto unknown

4. The temple of Zeus after it was uncovered, in 1876. Athens, German Archaeological Institute.

5. Group of German excavators – archaeologists and architects – at Olympia, photographed on the ruins of the temple of Zeus. Athens, German Archaeological Institute.

4

spheres of Greek art. In the 19th century, the excavation at Olympia was the first major excavation achievement in Classical archaeology with specific scientific objectives.

The great influence on the development of archaeology exercised by the excavations and finds at Olympia in their time is due mainly to the fact that the results of the work were published in a very short space of time, and with great accuracy. A mere sixteen years after the end of the excavations, the entire academic publication appeared in five volumes, which are still regarded as a seminal work in the archaeological bibliography, for the quality of their texts and illustrations. The

5

6

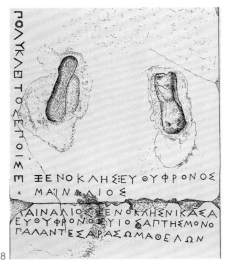

7

8

9

Olympia Museum, donated by the Athenian banker A. Syngros, was inaugurated only six years after the end of the excavation, in 1887 (fig. 6). This Museum is of special importance in the history of European museums, since it was the first in Greece founded to house the finds from an excavation in the provinces. The modern settlement of Olympia was created later, as a result of the ever-increasing tourism attracted by the Museum and the archaeological site.

The text of Pausanias, which gives a detailed description of the monuments of Olympia, served as a valuable guide for the excavators and at the same time an invaluable source of information by which to identify the various buildings and monuments. Without the detailed descriptions of the travel-writer, it would still be impossible today to assign a name the majority of the buildings at Olympia. The excavators of Olympia conducted their investigations following Pausanias's text to the letter. For he was the first, with his description of the artworks assembled at Olympia, to provide a powerful motive for commencing archaeological investigation. During his tour, he enumerates hundreds of statues, either honorific dedications by Olympic victors or dedications by Greek cities or private individuals, which were all crowded together in the sanctuary, including works by the most famous sculptors of the ancient world, such as Myron, Onatas, Pythagoras, Kalamis, Polykleitos, Pheidias, Silanion, Praxiteles, Leochares and Lysippos. It was the hope of finally uncovering once more unique pieces of ancient sculpture that gave wings to the first plans to excavate at Olympia. However, this hope was in practice to prove false. The more the work of excavation proceeded, the clearer it became that virtually nothing remained of the large number of bronze statues that had once adorned the sanctuary. Only their bases had been preserved, several of which could be identified with the monuments described by Pausanias, thanks to the inscriptions on them; even these, however, were quite badly damaged as a result of being moved from their original position and used later as building material (figs 8, 9). The statues themselves had fallen victim to Roman plundering, or to recycling in Late Antiquity. Only a few fragments had escaped the comprehensive destruction to enable us to reconstruct to some extent the form and style of the bronze dedications at Olympia. The most important of these fragments is the life-size head of a boxer, which came to light in 1880, a unique work of mature Classical sculpture. In the view of some archaeologists, it is the head of the boxer Satyros of Elis, who was victorious at Olympia on two occasions, probably at the games of the years 332 and 328 BC. According to Pausanias, his statue was the work of the Athenian sculptor Silanion (fig. 7).

When account is taken of the thoroughness with which the votive statues at Olympia were destroyed in modern times, it is almost a miracle that it has nonetheless been possible to recover, through the excavation, and restore to their original form at least two of the Classical statues mentioned by Pausanias: the Nike of Paionios and the Hermes of Praxiteles, the most famous antiquities of Olympia.

The larger than life-size statue of Nike, broken into two pieces, came to light just a few weeks after the beginning of the excavation, on 21 December 1875 (fig. 11). It was found not far from its original position, about 30 m. southeast of the temple of Zeus. The flying messenger of victory once stood on a marble pedestal of triangular cross-section, the original height of which has been calculated to have been about 8.80 m. What Pausanias knew and recounts of this Nike was obviously derived from the inscriptions on the pedestal, which are still fully preserved. According to these, the Messenians and Naupaktians dedicated the monument, the work of the sculptor Paionios of Mende, to Zeus, as a tithe from the spoils of war (fig. 10). The political event that lies behind this statement is probably the victory won over the Spartans by the Athenian allies during the Peloponnesian War, in 425 BC, on the island of Sphakteria. The statue fell from its tall pedestal and broke into countless pieces, only some of which were found during the excavations and reassembled. Although, for this reason, significant parts of

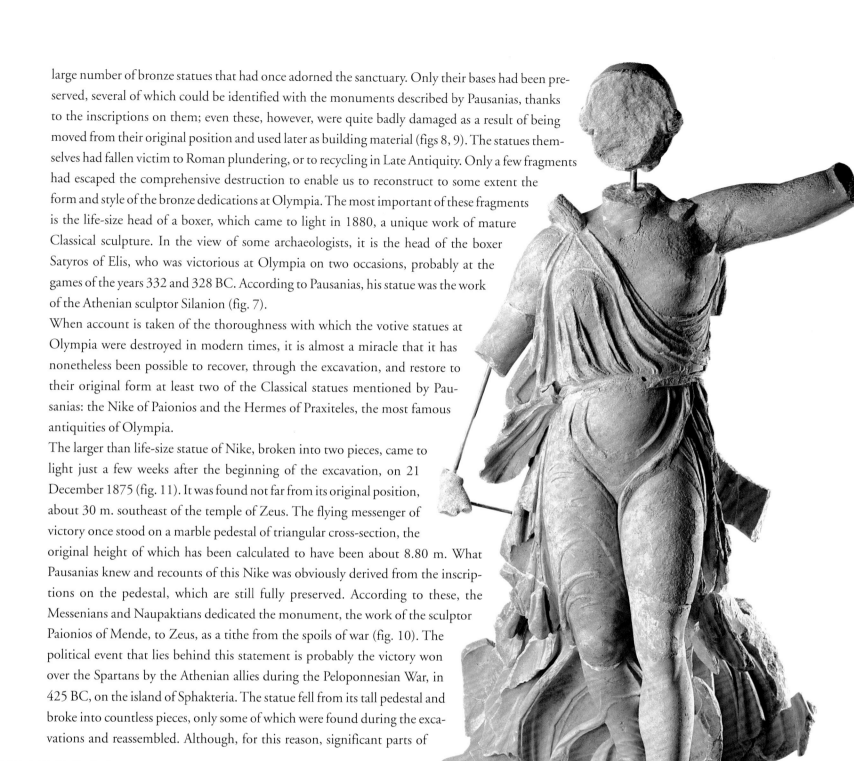

ΜΕΣΣΑΝΙΟΙΚΑΙΝΑΥΠΑΚΤΙΟΙΑΝΕΘΕΝΔΙΙ
ΟΛΥΜΠΙΔΙΔΕΚΑΤΑΝΑΠΟΤΩΜΠΟΛΕΜΙΩΝ
ΠΑΙΩΝΙΟΣΕΠΟΙΗΣΕΜΕΝΔΑΙΟΣ
ΚΑΙΤΑΚΡΩΤΗΡΙΑΠΟΙΩΝΕΠΙΤΟΝΝΑΟΝΕΝΙΚΑ

10

11

the original composition are lost – the wings are almost completely missing, as are large parts of the clothing and arms, as well as the face – the preserved statue is very striking and enables us to recognise in it the unprecedented boldness of its artistic design.

The temple of Hera must have already served as a kind of museum for earlier dedications by the time of Pausanias. During his enumeration of these pieces, the travel-writer also refers to a "marble Hermes holding the infant Dionysos, the work of Praxiteles." The excavators must have known their Pausanias by heart, because when, on 8 May 1877, the larger than life-size statue of a god was found with the figure of a young child preserved on its left arm, it was immediately identified – as we read in the day-book of the excavation – as the Hermes mentioned by Pausanias. The astonishing state of preservation, the delicate, masterful workmanship, and the serenity in subject and expression led properly to this unique sculpture, the Hermes of Olympia, being described only a few years after its discovery as the ideal of Classical beauty (fig. 12). Whether it really is an authentic work by the great Late Classical sculptor Praxiteles, or whether it is an ancient copy, is a question that is still debated in the academic world. The popularity of this unique figure, however, remains untouched by the scholarly dispute.

The second major excavation period, under the direction of Emil Kunze, began in 1937 and lasted until 1967, with a break of ten years at the time of the Second World War. During this period, the stadium was excavated and restored to its original form, sectors in the southeast and south of the excavation site were explored further, and areas that had hitherto only been uncovered at the surface were dug to deeper levels. The number of finds, mainly of bronze, multiplied incredibly during these decades. The excavation from 1967 onwards, under the direction of Alfred Mallwitz, helped to fill out the topography of the sanctuary to the south and west of the excavation site.

The latest investigations at Olympia, from 1985 onwards under the direction of the present author, are concentrated on two different points. They involve, in simple terms, the investigation of the earliest, and also of the latest, period of the history of Olympia. On the one hand, we are investigating the beginnings and earliest history of the sanctuary. Thus, it has proved possible through supplementary excavations in the Pelopion to clarify the prehistoric stratigraphy of Olympia and document the beginning of the cult of Zeus at the end of the 11th century BC. On the other hand, there is a programme of investigation under the direction of Ulrich Sinn on the Roman imperial period and Late Antiquity at Olympia, with excavations in the Roman ruins to the northwest and southwest of the sanctuary that have produced a wealth of results.

The archaeological investigation of Olympia is a complex process, which, in addition to the continual enrichment of our knowledge and the inevitable daily routine of excavation, has been characterised from the very beginning down to the present day by very important finds and discoveries. In this brief article, only a few characteristic examples can be mentioned.

The 19th-century excavations at Olympia opened up a new chapter in the investigation of the beginnings of Greek art. Thousands of votive figurines made of bronze or clay, which differ in their abstract form from all those previously known in Greek art, were found in the lower levels of the excavation. Most of these figurines were depictions of horses and bovines, though there were also numerous human figures. Some of the figurines were used to adorn large bronze tripod cauldrons, several fragments of which were also found. The style of all these figurines is marked by the reduction of their natural shapes into simplified basic forms, and by the emphasis placed on their few characteristic features. This style, which the

12

astonished archaeologists at Olympia encountered in thousands of examples, is now known to us – after long scholarly debate and as a result of finds made in cemeteries and sanctuaries all over Greece – as the Geometric style of Greek art of the 9th and 8th century BC. At first greatly differing views were expressed about the date and interpretation of these finds. Wilhelm Dörpfeld, for example, was convinced that these were prehistoric figurines, while Adolf Furtwängler – who had undertaken the responsibility for the publication of the bronzes from the 19th-century excavations at Olympia – has properly recognised the significance of these figurines as testimony to early Greek sculpture. In this way, he laid the foundation for the study of early Greek art from the period of Homer.

The discovery of the sculptures of the temple of Zeus in 1876/77 was completely groundbreaking in the history of Classical sculpture. The pedimental sculptures and the reliefs on the metopes of the temple are assigned on historical grounds to the period 470-456 BC. The powerful, larger than life-size pedimental compositions depict the mythical chariot-race between Pelops and Oinomaos and the battle of the Greeks against the Centaurs at the wedding of Peirithoos. The twelve metopes from the front and back of the cella are carved with representations of the twelve labours of Herakles (fig. 13). The discov-

12. The Hermes of Praxiteles. Marble masterpiece of the Late Classical period (340 BC), found inside the temple of Hera. Olympia, Archaeological Museum.

13. The best-preserved metope of the temple of Zeus depicts Herakles, with Atlas bringing him the apples of the Hesperides. Olympia, Archaeological Museum.

14. Zeus abducting Ganymedes. Typical example of the terracotta statues found at Olympia, which were probably akroteria of the treasuries that stood in the lower slopes of the Kronios Hill (480-470 BC). Olympia, Archaeological Museum.

13

ery of fragments of sculptures dispersed over a wider radius beneath the ruins of the temple, and the restoration of the pedimental groups and the metopes from thousands of broken pieces – on which Georg Treu, in particular, worked – are amongst the pioneering achievements of Classical archaeology. This highly important ensemble of early Classical sculpture, and its rediscovery and publication, completely changed modern perceptions of Classical sculpture, which had hitherto been dominated by the Parthenon sculptures or Roman copies of Greek masterpieces. Their dramatic expressive power and sculptural weight places them amongst the finest works of Greek sculpture. The heavy, strong forms and the serious, almost melancholic, style of these figures gave birth to the name Severe Style for this phase of Greek art history (figs 15-18).

14

The admiration of the ancient world, however, was focused not on the sculptures of the pediments and metopes of the temple of Zeus, nor on the size and harmony of its architecture (fig. 21), but on the superb gold and ivory sculpture inside the temple, the colossal cult statue of Zeus from the hand of Pheidias, the greatest artist of his time. No other ancient artwork was cited as often or with as much admiration in ancient poetry and prose as Pheidias's Zeus, which was one of the seven wonders of the ancient world. Its astonishing size and the grandeur of its appearance, and also the divine aura of the masterpiece must have made a profound impression on ancient spectators, as is evident from contemporary sources. It was said, indeed, that anyone who had seen Pheidias's Zeus even once in his life would not suffer unhappiness thereafter.

The famous work was destroyed during the upheavals of Late Antiquity. Pheidias's Zeus can now only be imagined from Pausanias's description and from a much simplified representation on bronze coins dating from the time of the Roman emperor Hadrian (figs 19, 20). Apart from the foundations for the huge base, not the smallest fragment of the cult statue was found in the temple itself. Its traces, howev-

15

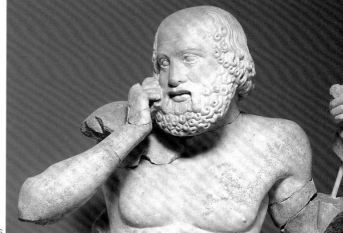

16

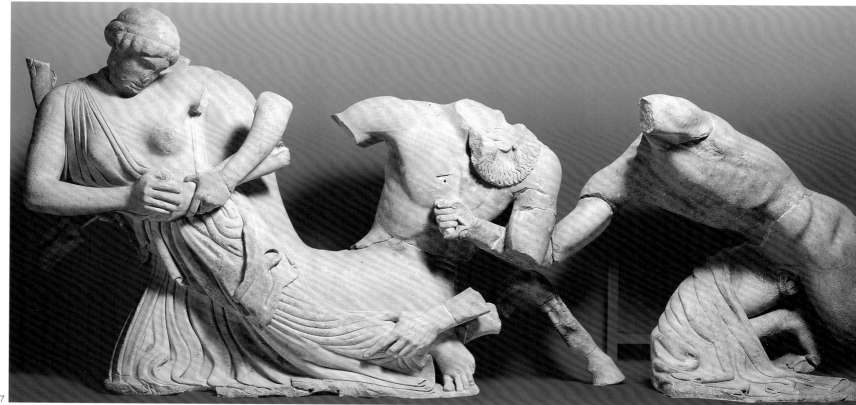

17

19, 20. The chryselephantine statue of Zeus, one of the seven wonders of the ancient world. Proposed reconstruction of the front and side of the statue inside the temple. Athens, German Archaeological Institute.

21. The temple of Zeus. Detail of an imaginary reconstruction drawing of the sanctuary of Olympia by V. Laloux (1883). Paris, École Nationale Supérieure des Beaux Arts.

er, were not completely effaced at Olympia. This is due to an archaeological discovery that caused much ado at the time. Architectural investigations and excavations from 1954 to 1958 in the Early Christian basilica to the west of the temple of Zeus revealed that the Classical building on whose foundations the 5th century AD church was erected (fig. 22), was none other than the workshop mentioned on this site by Pausanias, in which Pheidias created the chryselephantine statue (fig. 23). The discovery of Pheidias's workshop permits a small, but authentic look at the place in which this famous work of art was created. The statue, which must have been over 12 m. high, according to ancient sources, presumably consisted of a wooden core with a shell of gold and ivory. The various parts of the cult statue were carved and assembled in the workshop, the size of which corresponded roughly with the space inside the cella of the temple of Zeus. The enormous statue, which could not pass either between the columns or through the

22. *Some of the first tourists to visit Olympia in the second half of the 19th century. They were given a guided tour by the German archaeologists, who showed them the ruins of the Early Christian basilica, into which the workshop built by Pheidias to create his chryselephantine statue was converted. Athens, German Archaeological Institute.*

23, 24. *The 1954-1958 excavations to the south of the Early Christian basilica (fig. 23) revealed the remains of Pheidias's workshop and the waste from the work on the chryselephantine statue of Zeus (fig. 24). Athens, German Archaeological Institute.*

25. *Detail of the small black-glaze cup bearing the words ΦΕΙΔΙΟ ΕΙΜΙ ('I belong to Pheidias'), inscribed at the bottom (ca. 430 BC). Olympia, Archaeological Museum.*

door when complete, was disassembled into its separate parts, taken to the temple, and then reassembled once more. Interesting remains of the artistic and technical work on the statue have been found in the pit outside the workshop building (fig. 24): ivory and obsidian waste, bone spatulas, a goldsmith's hammer, lead moulds for jewellery, remains of floral decoration made of glass and the clay moulds in which they were made, and also clay moulds for the construction of drapery. These remains enable us to imagine the meticulous handwork and skill that went into every detail of the colossal Zeus, and the majesty of the decoration radiated by the statue of the god and his throne. However, the finest find amongst these workshop remains was an insignificant black-glaze cup, on the bottom of which was scratched the inscription: ΦΕΙΔΙΟ ΕΙΜΙ ('I belong to Pheidias'). A moving personal document of the great artist, possibly even the autograph of Pheidias himself (fig. 25).

26. View of the site of the ancient stadium before the excavations. The discovery of the stadium was a major excavation feat, since thousands of tonnes of earth had to be removed. Athens, German Archaeological Institute.

27. Excavation activity in the stadium in 1958. Athens, German Archaeological Institute.

The larger part of the ruins of Olympia had been uncovered already by the German excavations in the 19th century. The Olympic stadium, however, the most famous athletic venue in the ancient world, still remained buried beneath deep layers of mud deposited in later times. Plans to excavate the stadium did not mature until half a century later. The initial motivation was furnished less by the needs of scientific research and more by the modern Olympic movement and the increasing public interest in the birthplace of the Olympic Games. Amongst the archaeologists, in contrast, the view prevailed for a time that all that could be expected from an enterprise of this nature were a few finds and very little additional scientific knowledge – not enough to justify the effort and expense of removing the enormous volume of earth (fig. 26).

The immediate impulse for the excavation of the stadium was provided by the Olympic Games of 1936, held in Berlin. The excavation lasted from 1937 to 1942 and was resumed after the Second World War from 1953 to 1960 (fig. 27). Immediately after this, the stadium was reconstructed as it had been in ancient times, with earth embankments and without stone benches, with grass growing in the spectators' seating areas. By the end of this work, in 1963, a venerable historic sporting monument, impressive in its simplicity and size, had been recovered. Today, the stadium is an essential part of the overall picture of Olympia, and it is difficult to believe that one of the most extensive excavation projects of the 20th century was required to reconstruct it. Despite the initial reservations, the scientific conclusions to emerge from these excavations were of great importance. From the stratigraphy of the spectators' seating areas and of the competition arena, it proved possible to establish the various phases in the evolution of the stadium, which was converted and extended many times during its history of almost a thousand years. The wealth of finds was truly astonishing, especially the bronzes that had been buried beneath the soil when the earth was deposited for the embankments. These finds enrich our knowledge of the variety and artistic quality of the dedications made at Olympia in the 7th-5th century BC by people from every part of the world. Additionally, however, the finds from the stadium illuminated yet another important aspect of ancient Olympia.

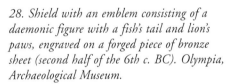

28

In general, the excavations at Olympia yielded a great wealth of weaponry and armour: helmets, greaves, shields, cuirasses, spear- and arrow-heads, and so on (figs 28-32).

This great 'Greek arsenal' in the Olympia Museum today offers a unique insight into the highly developed manufacturing technique and artistic flowering of Greek metalwork and weapon-making in the Archaic and Classical periods. An explanation of the large number of weapons found at Olympia is afforded by the inscriptions engraved on many of them: they are booty, dedicated to Olympian Zeus after victorious wars. Victors and vanquished are often named in the votive inscriptions, and the dedications of weapons may therefore be associated with specific historical events. One famous example is the oriental helmet which, according to the inscription engraved on it, was seized by the Athenians as spoils from the Persians, and which must therefore come from the battle of Marathon in 490 BC. This event, of decisive importance to Greek history, is also recalled by a Corinthian helmet inscribed with the name of Miltiades, the victorious Athenian general at Marathon (fig. 29). It is not only victories won by the Greeks over foreign peoples that are hymned in these inscriptions on the weapons at Olympia: much more frequently, they celebrate victories of the Greek city-states over other Greeks, a very common phenomenon in the political history of ancient Greece. These conflicts between Greeks were the reason for the sacred truce, under the protection of which the Olympic Games were held every four years. It was therefore very surprising that a large proportion of the weapons was found in the stadium, in and above

28. Shield with an emblem consisting of a daemonic figure with a fish's tail and lion's paws, engraved on a forged piece of bronze sheet (second half of the 6th c. BC). Olympia, Archaeological Museum.

29. During the excavation of the stadium hundreds of weapons and pieces of armour were found in the earth covering the embankments. They came from trophies erected here by the Greek city-states for propaganda purposes. Amongst them are a number of monuments of historical significance, such as the bronze helmet of Miltiades, the victor of the battle of Marathon (490 BC). Olympia, Archaeological Museum.

30. Bronze Corinthian-style helmet with inlaid silver decoration at the edges (7th-6th c. BC). Olympia, Archaeological Museum.

the earth embankments of the Archaic and Classical building phases. From the position in which individual objects were found, and from the identification in the surface of the embankments of holes in which posts were set, it may clearly be deduced that the booty was basically treated as trophies. The objects, that is, were spoils of war that were suspended from wooden poles and displayed on the terraces of the stadium. It is no doubt a shock to the modern view of the peaceful character of the Olympic Games that in the very place where the athletic events took place, such bellicose monuments, reminders of

29

30

military confrontations between Greeks, were on display before the eyes of tens of thousands of visitors. From these archaeological finds, however, it is evident that ancient Olympia cannot be understood from the perspective of the modern Olympic ideal. The guiding idea at ancient Olympia was not peace, but victory, in both athletic contest and in war. This emerges from many inscriptions and monuments at Olympia and it is no coincidence that the cult statue of Zeus in the main temple on the sacred site depicts the god holding Victory in his right hand.

Our picture of Archaic and Classical art would be much poorer without the numerous bronze figures, reliefs, vases and vessels that can now be admired in the Olympia Museum (figs 33, 34). A large and signif-

31. A forged bronze cuirass, one of the hundreds finds, found during the excavation of the ancient wells in the stadium area, which were used every four years to serve the needs of the spectators (first half of the 6th c. BC). Olympia, Archaeological Museum.

32. The discovery of the bronze cuirass during the excavation of a well shaft. Athens, German Archaeological Institute.

33. No other archaeological site in Greece has yielded as many bronzes as Olympia. Here is seen a bronze statuette of Zeus dedicated by a believer (first half of the 5th c. BC). Athens, National Archaeological Museum.

icant part of these finds comes from the resumed excavations from 1936 onwards and is due to a discovery that produced rich finds, made during the excavation of the stadium. It was established that before the construction of the Classical stadium, there were many wells in the area that could be distinguished during the excavation only by the different colour of the soil. They were circular pits, presumably dug during the games to supply the visitors with drinking water. Since they were used only for a few days, they were not walled on the inside, and were closed again after the end of the festivities and filled with earth. When they were sealed with earth, many dedications were also thrown into them which, though broken or old, still had to remain in the god's possession within the sacred precinct. During the excavation of these earth wells characteristic of Archaic and Classical Olympia (about 240 of which have been found in different parts of the sanctuary), many works of ancient art were uncovered, some of them in an exceptionally fine state of preservation (figs 31, 32). Mention may be made only of the impressive discovery of the life-size forged bronze bust of a winged goddess dating from the early 6th century BC, which emerged from one of these wells in 1965.

New finds can sometimes lead to great changes in our picture of ancient history and shed new light on hitherto unknown data and views. One such case involves the discovery of part of an inscribed bronze plaque, measuring 75 x 40 cm., that may originally have been part of a larger plaque, during Ulrich Sinn's excavation of the so-called southwest building, a Roman bath of the Imperial period. The inscriptions engraved on this plaque at different periods

33

and in different scripts form a catalogue of Olympic victors. Each record includes the name of the victorious athlete, the nature of the event, and the number of the Olympiad at which he won the victory. Since, as we know, historical dates in ancient Greece were based on the Olympiads, the data in this catalogue provide the exact date, in the form of letters, for the Olympic victories inscribed in it. With one exception, all the records come from the 4th century AD. Earlier victories were probably entered on the now lost parts of the plaque. It was apparently a kind of honorific panel dedicated by a union of professional athletes, one of the many that are so characteristic of the history and development of sport in the Late Hellenistic and Roman period.

The unexpected information provided by this find relates to the late history of the Olympic Games. From the inscriptions on the bronze plaque, we learn of 18 hitherto unknown names of Olympic victors from Greece and Asia Minor in the 4th century AD, a period from which only a single victor was formerly known – the winner of the boxing competition at the 287th Olympiad, of AD 369. He had been regarded for some time as the last known Olympic victor, and it seemed a matter of doubt whether the Olympic Games were regularly held during the 4th century AD. These doubts are now dispelled thanks to the new source, which also contains another important piece of information: that the Classical Olympic events continued to be held until the end of Late Antiquity. And although AD 369 had hitherto been regarded as the final secure date in the annals of the Olympic Games, the list has now been extended significantly thanks to the new find. For mention is made here of two athletes, Marcus Aurelius Eukarpides and Marcus Aurelius Zopyros of Athens, who were victorious in the pankration and boxing respectively, in the class of ephebes at the 290th and 291st Olympiads, that is in AD 381 and 385, a mere 8 years before the Olympic Games were banned by a decree issued by the emperor Theodosius (fig. 35).

34. A bronze stele dating from the 3rd c. BC inscribed with the text of a decree of the Eleians honouring Demokrates of Tenedos. Athens, National Archaeological Museum.

35. Bronze plaque engraved with the names of Olympic champions in the 4th c. AD – one of the latest finds from the excavations, which sheds light on the late history of the Olympic Games. Olympia, Museum of the History of the Ancient Olympic Games.

34

35

SPONSORS OF THE RESTORATION PROGRAMMES

Apart from excavating, the archaeologists and architects working at Olympia have attached great importance to the conservation of the monuments and their visual revaluation through partial reconstruction of the original architecture. The completely restored Classical stadium, for instance, the re-erected columns of the palaestra and the Heraion and parts of the terrace of treasuries are impressive testimonies of these activities. The latest restoration works, undertaken on the occasion of the modern Olympic Games of 2004 at Athens and Olympia, were the anastylosis of one of the huge columns of the temple of Zeus and the partial reconstruction of the Philippeion (figs 36-39). These challenging and highly expensive restoration projects would not have been realised without the generous financial support given by sponsors who, in the tradition of ancient donors and euergetai to the sanctuary, supplied the necessary means: The Anastasios G. Leventis Foundation has financed the whole Philippeion project and has borne the lion's share of the costs for the column of the great temple, while one third of the costs for the latter were contributed by the Society of Friends of the German Archaeological Institute - Theodor Wiegand Gesellschaft.

36. View of the temple of Zeus from the southeast in recent years, with the scaffolding for the restoration of a column.

36

37. The crepis of the Philippeion, the circular building erected by the kings of Macedonia, ready for the restoration of three of its columns and part of the epistyle. Two blocks of the crepis were returned from the Museums in Berlin to which they had been taken during the early years of the excavation.

38. The column of the temple of Zeus after the restoration was completed.

39. The Philippeion after a partial restoration which was completed in 2004 and gave the monument the three-dimensional aspect it lacked.

Olympia. Excavations and discoveries at the great sanctuary | 117

Spyros Iakovidis

Schliemann and Homer's "Mycenae Rich in Gold"

To His Majesty King George of the Hellenes:

It is with great pleasure that I announce to Your Majesty that I have discovered the graves which tradition, echoed by Pausanias, recognises as the tombs of Agamemnon, Cassandra, Eurymedon and their companions, who were all killed during the course of a dinner by Clytemnestra and Aigisthos. They are enclosed by a double circle of parallel slabs that can only have been built in honour of these figures. Inside the tombs I found enormous treasures of archaic gold objects [...] As I am working purely out of love of science, I naturally have no claim to these treasures, which, with lively enthusiasm, I present intact to Greece. With God's will, may these treasures become the corner-stone of a boundless national wealth.

Mycenae, 16 (28) November 1876

Heinrich Schliemann

The signatory of the above text was a very wealthy German merchant and businessman (figs 1, 6). The son of a poor pastor, he was born in 1822 at Neu Buckow in Mecklenburg-Schwerin near the Baltic coast, and grew up at Ankershagen, where his father had been assigned. When the boy was seven years old, the pastor, who occasionally told him stories that he remembered of ancient Greece and Homer, gave him a copy of the *Illustrated World History* by Jerrer, in which Aeneas was shown carrying his father Anchises away from the walls of the burning city of Troy. "Is that what Troy was like?," asked the boy. "And everything of that has been lost, does no one know where it was?" "That's right," replied his father. "I don't believe it," said the seven-year-old boy. "When I grow up, I'm going to find Troy and the treasure of its king."

At the age of fourteen, he was obliged to break off his schooling and work in a grocer's shop in nearby Fürstenberg. In 1841, when he was nineteen, he embarked as a cabin boy on a ship bound for Venezuela, which was wrecked off the island of Texel on the Dutch coast. A family friend then secured

1. Portrait of Heinrich Schliemann about the time of the excavations at Mycenae. His signature can be seen at the bottom. From Heinrich Schliemann's Autobiography *(Leipzig 1892).*

2. View of the citadel of Homer's "Mycenae rich in gold" from the south. The earth from the excavations can be seen at the left and in the centre.

3. Aerial photograph of the citadel of Mycenae, showing the fortification walls, the remains of the palace on the summit of the hill, the Lion Gate and Grave Circle A.

3

him a position as an errand-boy and assistant accountant in Amsterdam, in a company that traded with Russia. He had meanwhile taught himself six languages, thanks to his very good memory and to a method of his own devising, which was based on comparing known texts with corresponding ones in the language to be learned. He now added Russian to these and in 1846 his company sent him to St Petersburg as its representative. In two years, he founded his own business and made a fortune by supplying the Russian army during the Crimean War. In 1850 he was in California at the time of the gold rush and the incorporation of this state into the United States of America. He took out American citizenship and founded a bank that dealt in gold. Now a millionaire, he travelled to Egypt, Tunisia, India, China and Japan. Meanwhile, he had learned four more languages, making it a total of eleven, and in 1856 he began in St Petersburg to learn modern Greek and acquire a more profound knowledge of the ancient Greek language. "God," he wrote, "blessed my commercial enterprises in a most wonderful way, so that by the end of 1863 I owned an estate that surpassed my ambitions. I withdrew from trade," he added, "in order to devote myself solely to the studies that attracted me more." The studies that attracted him more were those that led him to confirm the truth of the Homeric poems, and, secondarily, of other ancient Greek authors (mainly Pausanias and the tragic poets), which he believed literally. The only way to make this confirmation was through the material remains of the culture described by the sources on the sites mentioned by them. These remains, buried with the passage of time by natural forces and human activity, had to be revealed by excavation. Only in this way could he refute the view, generally held at the time, that the Homeric poems were nothing more than myth, the creations of a poet whose very existence was disputed.

In order to achieve this, he had first to acquaint himself with the Homeric sites, and the first task of this new period of his life was therefore to make a reconnaissance visit in 1868 to the areas to which he was to devote the rest of his life: Ithaca, the east Peloponnese (Mycenae and Tiryns) and Troy. In 1869, he published his conclusions. Impromptu excavations at Aetos and two or three other places on Ithaca did not yield encouraging results. At Mycenae and Tiryns, he confined himself to confirming the identifications of the surviving ruins made by the travellers who had visited them before him. In the Troad, he ruled out the village of Bunarbashi, which almost everyone was agreed was the site of ancient Troy, on the grounds that its distance from the sea, the form of the terrain, and the large number of springs around it precluded its identification with Troy as described or implied in the *Iliad*. Instead, he focused

4. *The Iliou Melathron, designed by E. Ziller and built in 1878-1881 as the residence of Heinrich and Sophia Schliemann. Watercolour by E. Ziller. Athens, Municipal Art Gallery.*

5. *Sophia Schliemann with their son Agamemnon, who was born on 10 March 1878. Photograph taken by Jacques Pilartz at Bad Kissingen in July 1879.*

6. *Portrait of Heinrich Schliemann by Sydney Hodges in London in 1877, when Schliemann was 55 years old. Berlin, Museum für Vor- und Frühgeschichte.*

his attention on the hill of Hissarlik close to the coast, where the owner of the site, the British vice-consul of America, Frank Calvert, had carried out a number of limited excavations, and on which the few known finds placed the Ilium of historical times, which had been visited at various times by Xerxes, the Spartan general Mindaros, and Alexander the Great. Here, Schliemann believed, was the city of Priam. After his divorce from his Russian wife, Ekaterina Lyschina, Schliemann decided to find a new companion from the land to which he had turned his interest. On his return to Athens he married Sophia Engastromenou in 1869 (fig. 5), a beauty who recited Homer with the same passion as he did himself, the daughter of a good Athenian family and niece of his old friend from St Petersburg, a theologian and his teacher of modern Greek, Theoklitos Vimbos, who had in the meantime been appointed archbishop of Mantineia. With his new wife, who would henceforth follow him everywhere he went and share in all his endeavours, his set-backs and his adventures, he returned to Hissarlik in 1870 and began to excavate the site, though he was obliged to suspend the excavation due to misunderstandings with the responsible Turkish authorities. The difficulties were smoothed over and he resumed the following year, and particularly in 1873 and 1874, indifferent to the sarcastic comments of various scholars and men of learning from over almost the entire world, for whom he was nothing more than an opinionated dreamer.

And he was right: beneath the Hellenistic and Classical ruins of the later Ilium, he found not the one Homeric city he expected, but seven prehistoric cities in distinct, successive levels: that is, a total of nine Troys of various periods, the deepest of which had only a few, primitive finds, from which metals were almost completely absent. Which was the city of Priam, the city which, according to Homer, was destroyed by the Achaians, who burnt it? The third level (which later proved to be the last phase of the second city) had traces of a strong fire, stout walls, and a fortified gate and, most importantly, contained a total of sixteen hoards, groups of objects that were not necessarily valuable but certainly useful, on account of their shape and/or material, and had been concealed in some hiding place at various times. The richest of these, consisting mainly of jewellery, vases and other gold items, was found in 1875, and had been buried in such a way that it clearly formed the contents of a wooden box that had disintegrated. Fortification walls, a gate, a fire and treasure. Schliemann had no doubt that he had found the city captured and torched by the Achaians. And the hoard was presumably the treasure of Priam! Given the state of knowledge at the time, he could not yet know that this city was much older than the Trojan War, with which later scholarship tends to identify the seventh city, 1000 years later in date (figs 7, 8).

7. *Sophia Schliemann wearing the jewellery found by her husband in Troy and attributed by him to the 'treasury of Priam'. However, this jewellery was about 1000 years later than the time of the king whose city was besieged by the Achaians.*

8. *Drawings of the jewellery and other objects found by Schliemann at Troy. From C. Bacon,* The Great Archaeologists *(1976).*

The sarcastic comments were silenced, and, although certain doubts continued to be expressed, it was generally agreed that, with regard to Troy, Schliemann had been vindicated, and Homer with him. Lacking confidence in how the Turkish authorities would deal with his finds, Schliemann arranged to have them taken to Greece, and when this country, under Turkish pressure, refused to accept them, he sent them to Germany "for eternal possession and to be kept together in the capital of the state," after being obliged to pay great compensation to the Museum of Constantinople. The excavation was suspended and would not resume until 1879. Meanwhile, he turned his attention to his second Homeric objective: "Mycenae rich in gold" (figs 2, 3).

9. A depiction of the drawing of the Lion Gate at the citadel of Mycenae, to illustrate the article "Antiquarian Discoveries in Greece." Engraving from an issue of the Illustrated London News *(1842-1885).*

10. Heinrich Schliemann giving an account of his discoveries at Mycenae to the members of the Society of Antiquaries in London (1877). Engraving from an issue of The Illustrated London News *(1842-1885).*

Here, the site was known, but not the spot of the grave monuments of Agamemnon and his companions, who had been buried in five separate tombs. Foreign travellers believed that these were the *tholos* tombs located outside the citadel, but Pausanias placed them inside it. Here, too, therefore, an excavation was necessary. And if he were right, the burials would not have been in the fairly steep sides of the hill, but near its lower slopes. Schliemann came to Mycenae and began the investigation, following one of his trial trenches inside the Lion Gate, which he had dug in 1874 (figs 9, 11, 12). "I began the great work," he writes, "on the 7th August 1876, with sixty-three workmen, whom I divided into three groups: twelve at the Lion's Gate, to free up the entrance to the citadel; I set forty-three to dig a trench 113 feet wide by 113 feet (about 37 m.) long at a distance of 40 feet (13 m.) from the Gate; and I left the other eight to make a trench to the south of the treasury found near the Gate, to find its entrance."

These trenches brought to light an abundance of pottery and assorted finds which proved that Mycenae, despite the comments of ancient geographers and travellers, had also been inhabited in historical times. At a deeper level, 'archaic' vases began to appear, similar to those he had observed at Tiryns, where he had carried out a provisional excavation. Along with them were found clay figurines of women and cows, which he supposed depicted Hera, and a variety of small finds made of stone, ivory and bronze. At a depth of 3-3.50 m. stone house-walls appeared, something which he thought was an aqueduct, and two relief stelai of soft stone, that were presumably gravestones.

12

13

On 19 August, he was already employing 125 workmen who, he says, "work much better and more conscientiously than those of the Troad." He had already uncovered part of the circular sloping retaining wall that supported the double slabs of the enclosure, had noted that this circular enclosure was full of earth deposits, and had observed that at a depth of about 1 m. beneath the surface of these deposits, the fill contained ash and many animal bones, but none of humans. He also noticed, and notes, that the space between the two rows of upright slabs of the circle was full of earth and pieces of 'archaic' vases and figurines, but contained no bones at all. He continued to find, at various depths, which he notes carefully, fragments of eleven relief and five plain grave stelai, which he illustrates and describes in detail, adding that they undoubtedly belonged to graves dug at greater depths. He also found a variety of architectural reliefs, vases and building walls constructed of rubble. The double row of upright slabs, which had a row of horizontal covering slabs on them, were interpreted by him, following the opinion of various learned friends, as a circular bench on the perimeter of the agora, the gathering place of the Mycenaeans. On this the Mycenaeans sat to listen to the orators, as described in the Iliad (XVIII 497-505), and at the centre of them were the tomb or tombs of local heroes, as at Megara, according to Pausanias, or like the tomb of Bottos at Cyrene, according to Pindar (Pyth. 5, 124-125).

This interpretation is invalid for many reasons, but mainly because the enclosure wall is 1.10 m. high, at least 0.60 m. higher than the standard height of any seat at any period. It did reinforce Schliemann's conviction, however, that the circle must enclose tombs: specifically, again according to Pausanias, the five tombs of Agamemnon, Cassandra, Agamemnon's charioteer Eurymedon, Cassandra's twins, Teledamos and Pelops, and their companions (fig. 13). He therefore continued with the excavation, cleaned a building to the north of the circle that was later called the Granary and another to the south; in the latter he found a krater with a depiction of warriors on both sides. At a depth below the surface ranging from 3.50 to about 6 m., he uncovered three large and two smaller graves, at which stage he stopped, convinced that he had found the ones he was looking for (fig. 15). He could not know at that time that these graves were about 400 years earlier than the period at which the ancient literary sources placed Agamemnon and the Trojan War; or that there was another grave, that would be discovered later by Panayiotis Stamatakis, the Ephor of the Archaeological Society, state representative and overseer of the excavation – a man whom Schliemann so disliked that he refers to him only once , without even mentioning his name.

The earth above the graves had already yielded not only the stelai (whose position did not invariably correspond with the burial trenches), but also abundant pottery in fragments, hundreds of clay figurines, glass-paste beads, a mould for making jewellery, sealstones, a bronze axe, and an inscribed sherd

14. Aerial photograph of the west slope and part of the citadel of Mycenae. At the centre can be seen the 'Tomb of Aigisthos', and at the left the 'Tomb of Clytemnestra', very close to Grave Circle B.

14

dating from the 6th century BC – all mixed up in earth deposits that were undoubtedly disturbed. The graves, however, were intact. They were all dug in the west, strongly sloping part of the circle, and take the form of four-sided pits, with dimensions ranging from 2.90 x 2 (II) to 6.60 x 4.10 m. (IV). Along all four sides, or, in some cases only the two long sides, they had low dry-stone walls, on which rested the ends of the wooden transverse beams supporting the layer of matting, reeds or stone slabs that roofed the grave and kept its interior free beneath the earth that filled it after every burial. The floor was strewn with pebbles, on which the bodies were placed. Schliemann insisted, on the basis of the burial customs reflected in the Iliad, that the bodies had been cremated (imperfectly, he says, on account of the haste of the murderers to get rid of them), though at the same time he carefully describes in detail the individual parts of the skeletons and skulls and the position occupied by them in the grave. The cremation and the smoke from the pyre, he says, were responsible for the dark colour of the bones and the dry-stone walls. This is an error still made by those not familiar with the sight of burnt bones. The fire shatters them and splits them along their dynamic lines, and, depending on the degree of burning, gives them the white or grey colour of the calcium they contain. Burnt bones do not form skeletons, but lie scattered in small, whitish heaps. Unburnt bones and stones owe their colour to the dampness of the soil.

15. Grave Circle A just after Schliemann's excavation. Engraving from an issue of The Illustrated London News *(1842-1885).*

16. Grave Circle A, at Mycenae, today.

17. Some of the 701 gold roundels with repoussé decoration of spirals, octopuses, leaves and rosettes. They were found in Grave III of Grave Circle A at Mycenae, and may have been sewn to the luxury clothing of the dead women (16th c. BC). Athens, National Archaeological Museum.

18. Bronze dagger with an embossed representation of a lion-hunt in gold and silver on niello. From Grave IV of Grave Circle A (16th c. BC). Athens, National Archaeological Museum.

19, 20. Gold cutouts depicting a tripartite shrine with horns of consecration and birds (left), and a nude deity with birds (right). From Grave III of Grave Circle A (second half of the 16th c. BC). Athens, National Archaeological Museum.

21, 22. Two gold rectangular seals cast in a mould, depicting a wounded lion (left) and a man wrestling with a lion (right). From Grave III of Grave Circle A (second half of the 16th c. BC). Athens, National Archaeological Museum.

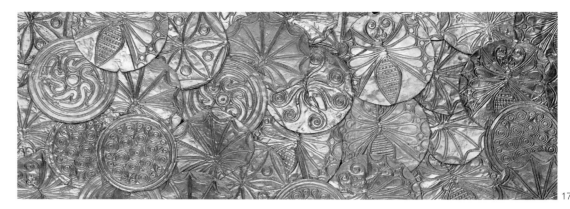
17

All the graves contained burials, and all the bodies were accompanied by grave offerings in varying numbers. Schliemann numbered the graves in the order in which he excavated them. Later, however, particularly after the addition of the sixth grave discovered and excavated by Stamatakis, the numbering was partly changed, and the graves have been referred to ever since by Roman numerals (fig. 16).

Grave I (Schl. 2) contained three bodies, each adorned with five gold diadems. Two of them had in addition five four-lobed gold rosettes, and a third had four. There were also cylinders of glass paste, obsidian blades, pieces of a silver gilt vase, a silver bowl, a knife, various beads and clay vases, figurines, and a tripod vessel.

In Grave II (Schl. 5) there was a burial with a gold diadem on the skull and a spear, two daggers and two bronze knives to the right of it. Next to these lay a gold one-handled cup with repoussé decoration, a vase made of green Egyptian porcelain, and a clay nippled jug.

Grave III (Schl. 3) contained three burials, probably female, accompanied by rich offerings, amongst which gold jewellery was prominent: 701 gold roundels with repoussé decoration, rectangular engraved

18

23. Silver pin ending in a gold cutout with a depiction of a female figure. From Grave III of Grave Circle A (second half of the 16th c. BC). Athens, National Archaeological Museum.

24. Gold pin with a double head of rock crystal and a bronze shaft. From Grave III of Grave Circle A (second half of the 16th c. BC). Athens, National Archaeological Museum.

25. Striking group of gold vases from Grave IV in Grave Circle A (16th c. BC). Athens, National Archaeological Museum.

19

20

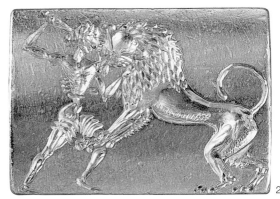

21

22

seal beads, attachments for sewing to clothing, in the shape of insects, griffins, animals, sphinxes, rosettes and octopuses, two crowns on the forehead of two of the bodies, a diadem on the skull of a third, earrings, bracelets, necklaces, a fibula with a silver pin and a representation of a woman holding plant symbols and branches arranged in a semicircle, a gold balance, a small pyxis, and a gold cup. There was also jewellery made of agate and rock crystal, vases of silver, bronze and clay, and four bronze cubic objects pierced by bronze rivets, which had probably been attached to the ends of the beams that supported the roof of the grave (figs 17, 19-24).

In Grave IV (Schl. 4) were found five interments with a large number of rich offerings. The faces of the three men were covered with gold masks, two additionally had gold breast-plates, and another had a gold crown. The bodies were accompanied by 36 bronze swords, either complete or in pieces, some of them wrapped in material. Fragments of scabbards with gold ornaments were also preserved. There were also two daggers, the bronze blades of which were decorated with embossed gold representations on a

23

24

25

Idole und Gefässe aus Mykenae.

26. Reconstruction drawing of elaborate vases and other of Schliemann's finds from Mycenae. From the publication of his work at Mycenae: Mykenae, *Leipzig 1878.*

27, 28. These two gold signet rings with thick oval bezels are examples of wealth and the advanced level of the goldsmith's art. On the bezel at the left is depicted a scene of hunting from chariots, while the bezel at the right has a battle scene set in a rocky landscape. From Grave IV of Grave Circle A at Mycenae (second half of the 16th c. BC). Athens, National Archaeological Museum.

29. Three handled vase of outstanding art made of white marble with its surface polished to make it look like alabaster (16th c. BC). Athens, National Archaeological Museum.

30. Silver rhyton in the shape of a bull's head with a double gold rosette on the forehead. The horns, the inside of the ears, and the nostrils are gilded. From Grave IV of Grave Circle A (second half of the 16th c. BC). Athens, National Archaeological Museum.

niello ground. On one is a depiction of a lion-hunt by armed men, and on the other a row of galloping lions (fig. 18). With them were found 10 single-edged swords, the handles of which ended in rings. The handles of some of the swords were sheathed in gold leaf with repoussé decoration, and one was embellished with coloured enamel. The weapons also included knives, two double axes, obsidian ar-row-heads, and a gold baldric, which was found wrapped around part of a sword blade.

The bodies were also accompanied by four rhy-tons made of noble metals: one of gold sheet in the shape of a lion's head, which had been completely crushed, a silver bull's head with a gold rosette on the forehead (fig. 30), a third so deformed from the weight of the earth that it originally went un-noticed, and which has a repoussé representation of an attack from the sea on a coastal town (the so-called Siege Rhyton), and finally, another one of silver depicting a hind, whose models are to be sought in Hittite art. There were also nine gold vases, one with two handles adorned with birds, which has been identified (erroneously) with the

Homeric *depas amphikypellon* of Nestor, one of gold and silver alloy decorated with gold plants against a niello ground below the rim, a silver jug and an alabaster three-handled vase (figs 25, 29). The bronzes include five cauldrons, one of which was full of about 100 wooden conical attachments sheathed with gold, and also a jug, a tripod vase, and a pair of fire-tongs. Mention should also be made of a greave of gold sheet, found sticking to a shin-bone, an ostrich egg and a large quantity of gold jewellery: a crown with repoussé rosettes, four diadems of regular size and two smaller ones (for children?), two finger-rings with bezels engraved with a representation of a deer hunt with a chariot and a battle between men set in an open landscape (figs 27, 28), a bracelet decorated with a large rosette, gold pins and assorted lozenge-shaped and round clothing attachments. There are also human figures cut out of gold sheet, some with birds on their heads, two bull's heads with double axes between the horns, and cutouts of tripartite shrines (fig. 19). Finally, an Egyptian decorative porcelain sacred knot was found, and a large number of sherds.

The last Grave V (Schl. 1) is possibly the most interesting. It contained three burials, one along the north side, one in the middle, and one on the south side, the middle one of which had been plundered already in ancient times. "Here," writes Schliemann, "the ash had been disturbed, and the clay with which the other two bodies and their jewellery were covered, and the gravel on the layer of clay, had disappeared. In addition to this, it was evident that the grave had been robbed since the skeleton was found virtually without gold offerings. This view is supported by the twelve small gold cones, small pieces of gold sheet and many bone objects found along with small quantities of black ash at various levels beneath the carved stelai that adorned the grave. It is further confirmed by the fragments of later clay vases that were in this grave, mixed up with sherds of much earlier handmade vases. Someone probably dug a pit here in order to search the grave, came upon the middle body, robbed it without hesitation and, fearing discovery, left with his booty, taking care to preserve only the large gold objects […] leaving behind many of the smaller ones […] which were thus found at various levels." This observation, which reveals the care with which Schliemann excavated, is undoubtedly accurate.

The other two burials still had their offerings. The body to the south had on its face the well-known mask with strong, distinctive facial features. It differs from all the others and shows a mature man with an oval face, straight, thin nose, moustache and short beard (fig. 33). On the breast was a breast-plate decorated with spirals and with the nipples indicated. At the right of it were two swords with gold-sheathed handles and scabbards. A little further away, on its right side, were found 11 bronze swords, nine of which were corroded by the damp. The handles of these, too, were sheathed with gold sheet, decorated with spirals. Near them had been placed cylinders of gold sheet wrapped around wood, 124 plain or engraved roundels, knives, a

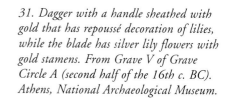

33

31. Dagger with a handle sheathed with gold that has repoussé decoration of lilies, while the blade has silver lily flowers with gold stamens. From Grave V of Grave Circle A (second half of the 16th c. BC). Athens, National Archaeological Museum.

32. Wooden hexagonal pyxis sheathed with twelve rectangular pieces of gold sheet, which have three decorative motifs repeated four times each. From Grave V of Grave Circle A (second half of the 16th c. BC). Athens, National Archaeological Museum.

33. The best-preserved gold death mask, in which the facial features of the dead man are rendered with great emphasis on the details. From Grave IV of Grave Circle A (second half of the 16th c. BC). Athens, National Archaeological Museum.

31

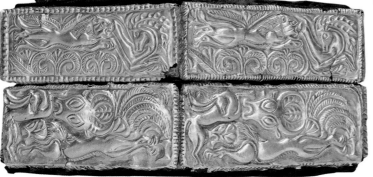

32

spear, and a battle axe. There was also a heap of beads made of electrum, 36 sheets of gold, two silver vessels, a silver tweezers, and another vase made of alabaster.

The burial at the north was also covered by a gold, round-faced mask and a plain breast-plate, like those in Grave IV. When these covers were removed, however, it was clear that the body was much better preserved than the others, offering support for the hypothesis that it had been subjected to a process of mummification. Schliemann at once summoned a painter who made an oil-painting of the mummy, and a pharmacist, who consolidated it with a solution of sandarac in alcohol. The deceased, a man of about 35 years according to the doctors who examined him, had a round piece of gold sheet on his forehead, another on his right eye, two gold roundels on his breast, and another on his right hip. On him, lay a gold baldric, though not in its proper position, wrapped around a sword blade. Next to him there were two more swords with gold-sheathed handles and a wooden scabbard adorned with gold roundels. At his right side were found 11 more bronze swords and 242 decorative roundels. He was also accompanied by a *pyxis* sheathed with gold cutouts decorated with repoussé lions hunting deer (fig. 32), a gold cup with repoussé decoration, a *kylix* with a representation of running lions, and two silver jugs. The grave contained three more daggers, on the blades of which were inlaid lilies (fig. 31), a network of spirals, and a riverine landscape with papyrus plants, fish and felines hunting birds on a niello background. There were also 340

34. The tholos tomb called the 'Treasury of Atreus' was known in the 19th century and was used as a shelter by the local shepherds in Schliemann's time. During his excavations at Mycenae, the emperor of Brazil, Don Pedro II, visited the site and Schliemann gave a dinner in his honour inside the tholos tomb. Lithograph of the drawing by Ed. Dodwell from his Views and Descriptions of Remains in Greece *(1834). Athens, National Historical Museum.*

35. Façade of the tholos tomb of 'Clytemnestra', with Sophia Schliemann at the entrance. Engraving from the publication of H. Schliemann's work at Mycenae: Mykenae, *Leipzig 1878.*

36. The 'Treasury of Atreus' or 'Tomb of Agamemnon'. A handwritten note gives the date Mycenae, 25 March 1839. Watercolour on paper by J. Skene. Athens, National Historical Museum.

roundels, two gold greaves, a wooden box decorated with an ivory dog and lion, a Middle Helladic vase, a heap of seashells, and many boar's tusks, probably from the sheathing of a helmet.

In addition to the Grave Circle, Schliemann – Sophia Schliemann, to be precise – also partly excavated the tholos tomb known as 'the tomb of Clytemnestra' (figs 14, 35). Work in the Grave Circle was completed in 1878 by Stamatakis, who discovered and excavated the sixth grave in the enclosure and cleaned a point near the northwest corner of the Ramp House (as it was later called), which, according to Schliemann, had been shown him by the surveyor and engineer V. Drosinos. There he found a hoard in which had been concealed five gold vases, nine hair rings and finger rings of gold wire, and one of silver, two gold finger-rings with engraved representations on the bezels, a statuette of a seated lion, and an assortment of gold beads. These objects, which became known as Drosinos's Treasure, seem to have come from a plundered grave, possibly Grave V.

Schliemann thought he had succeeded in doing what he wanted: locating and bringing to light the graves of Homer's Mycenaean heroes. He could not know – no-one knew at that time – that these graves were centuries earlier, that they belonged to the early years of Mycenaean civilisation, that they revealed contacts at this early date with Egypt, the Cyclades and Minoan Crete – which Evans was to discover 25 years later – and that the enclosure was much later than the graves, which belong to an extended cemetery. At the other, west, end there was another group of graves of the same kind and with similar offerings, which were only discovered 75 years later. Schliemann, convinced that he had done his duty to Homer and the heroes of the Trojan War, published his excavation in 1878 (figs 10, 26, 38), returned this same year to Troy, and in 1886 excavated Tiryns in collaboration with W. Dörpfeld. He died in 1890 at Naples while on his way back to Greece and was buried in Athens. His work was continued by W. Dörpfeld at Troy and Chr. Tsountas at Mycenae, who was succeeded by A.J.B.Wace, I. Papadimitriou and G.E. Mylonas. The investigation is still in progress, under the direction of the present author.

The numerous finds from the graves (12,000 ceramic and 3,200 other finds, according to Stamatakis, who recorded them), are kept in the National Archaeological Museum (fig. 37). Some of them are on display in the Mycenaean gallery and attract hundreds of thousands of visitors every year, as Schliemann predicted and hoped (fig. 39). The new Museum at Mycenae unfortunately has only some copies.

In his own lifetime, and still today, Schliemann has been condemned for many things. He was egocentric, authoritarian, stubborn and unscrupulous, and particularly vain. Moreover, the manner in which he exca-

37. The National Archaeological Museum in Athens, in which Schliemann's finds were ultimately housed, in the late 19th - early 20th century. The Mycenaean gallery is one of the most important sources for our knowledge of Mycenaean civilisation.

37

38

38. The first exhibition of Schliemann's finds in the National Bank of Greece, immediately after the excavation at Mycenae. Engraving from an issue of The Graphic *(1869-1885).*

39. View of the Mycenaean gallery in the National Archaeological Museum, as arranged at the beginning of the 20th century for the exhibition of Schliemann's finds from Grave Circle A at Mycenae. The upper part of the walls and the ceiling were covered by compositions of various motifs drawn from Mycenaean decorative art. Photograph of 1910 from material supporting the official participation by Greece in the International Fair in Rome, 1911.

40. Honorary diploma awarded to Heinrich Schliemann by the German Anthropological Society in 1877.

vated, the large number of workmen he employed, his haste and his mania for treasure-hunting caused much serious damage to the antiquities he was investigating. None of this is of significance any longer, nor are the imperfections in his methods. Now, after over 100 years of excavations, our experience and knowledge have multiplied, and the material that has accumulated permits secure identifications, comparisons and parallels, and fairly accurate dating. When Schliemann excavated, however, guided only by his faith in Homer, none of this was known and he himself proceeded in the dark, which was lit only by his own investigations. Minoan Crete and Mycenaean Greece were completely unknown. The literary tradition of historical times – that is, what the ancient Greeks believed they knew – was the only recognised guide, and the technique of excavation, combined with an admittedly partial knowledge of what he was looking for, was inadequate. Schliemann was the pioneer, and the only one to conceive of searching for the past through the remains themselves (fig. 40). Today we know much more than he suspected, and our knowledge is based on much securer data. Without him, however, it is debatable whether these data would exist. To condemn him and belittle him for errors of technique and identifications is unfair, ungrateful, and injudicious.

39

Henricum Schliemannum,

virum et ingenii sollertia et animi fervore prae-
cellentem, qui sedibus

Priami et Agamemnonis

post longam multorum saeculorum obli-vi-
onem in claram lucem protractis de antiquita-
tibus **gentis Graecae et carminibus**
Homeri rectius cognoscendis optime meruit,
societas anthropologica Germanorum
Constantii die VIII. cal. Oct. a. MDCCCLXXVII

socium honoris causa

nuncupavit, cujus rei in testi-
monium hoc diploma nominibus
praesidum subscribi jussit.

Bonnae, Berolini,
Stuttgarti, Monachii,
Idibus Nov. a. MDCCCLXXVII.

Hermann Schaaffhausen

And. Pirson

Oscar Fraas.

Kollmann

Dominique Mulliez

Delphi
The excavation of the great oracular centre

Delphi was abandoned in the period AD 610-620 and the sanctuary, central to the ancient world, was forgotten. It was not until the 15th century that Delphi, even for a short time, re-acquired something of an identity.

The merchant Cyriaco of Ancona visited Delphi in March 1436. He stayed for six days, copied inscriptions, observed the theatre that was subsequently concealed by houses, noted the site of the Stadium, and identified the Monument of the Kings of Argos as the temple of Apollo. For the first time since the early 7th century AD, Delphi was to re-emerge, after eight centuries in limbo. Several more centuries were to pass before the village located on the site, Kastri (fig. 3), would once more become Delphi. In 1858, the name of Delphi was finally restored on the lintel of the local school.

In 1676, almost a century and a half after the visit by Cyriaco of Ancona, travellers Jacob Spon and George Wheeler were the first of a number of foreigners to identify the village of Kastri with ancient Delphi. They located the site of the ancient gymnasium beneath the Monastery of the Panayia. They noted with some disappointment, however, that "we had to stop there and be satisfied with what we could learn from books of the former wealth and grandeur of this place: for now we encountered only wretchedness, and all its splendour had passed like a dream." Those following in the footsteps of Jacob Spon and George Wheeler included scholars, clerics, artists, diplomats, merchants, professors and military men. They reiterated the destitution of the place, in which they managed to identify only a few rudimentary remains. There were many who, following their pilgrimage, departed from Delphi disappointed.

1. Steps cut into the rock at the east end of the Stadium at Delphi. One of the few remains that was visible before the excavations. Engraving by A.M. Chenavard (1843).

2. Reconstruction of the sanctuary of Apollo giving a general picture of the sanctuary buildings and dedications. It is quite faithful from an architectural point of view but contains several imaginary features, particularly with regard to the dedications. Drawing by the French architect A. Tournaire, 1894. Paris, École Nationale Supérieure des Beaux-Arts.

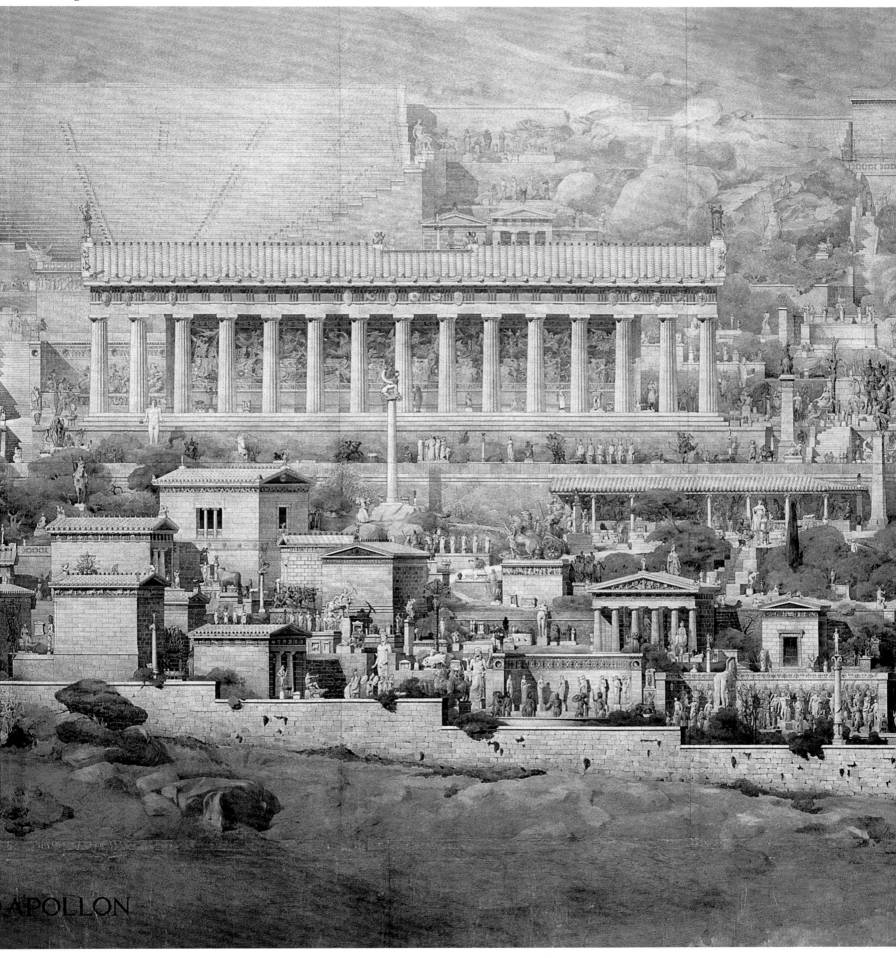

APOLLON

Prince Hermann von Pückler Muskau gives a profoundly disenchanted account following his visit in September 1836: "Full of reverence, I hesitated to enter this sanctuary, even though all that I saw on the site of the temple was a lamentable village of wretched ruined houses, while the mysterious cavern where intoxicating fumes were inhaled by the prophetess, Pythia, no longer exists, and the actual site of the temple is uncertain. Careful inspection revealed many ruins of ancient walls built at various periods, fragments of columns, and detached blocks of stone with the remains of inscriptions. Apart from the Stadium, however, which lies in the upper part of Kastri, and of which a few rows of benches can still be seen (fig. 1), no building from the ancient city of Delphi can be identified with certainty." The Englishman Th. Chase offers an equally graphic description at the beginning of the 1860s: "Kastri, as the modern town is called, is a dirty, straggling village, with narrow break-neck streets (fig. 4), and in every respect – except its delightful situation – as unpoetic in its aspect as possible." Pavlos Kalligas, a lawyer of the National Bank of Greece and member of the Antiquity-lovers Society formed in 1862, also writes: "What sight does the village present? A miserable, wretched one. A pile of poor houses no larger than dovecotes, built chaotically one above the other up to the summit, on such a steep incline that they seem as if they are tumbling down, pushing each other to the edge of the cliff. What terrible sacrilege! All these stables are built directly on ancient monuments (fig. 7)."

3. The village of Kastri, built above the ruins of the ancient sanctuary of Apollo, from the southwest. In the background can be seen the Kastalia ravine between the Phaidriades rocks. Athens, National Historical Museum.

4. Street in the village of Kastri, with the public fountain. Archive of French School of Athens.

5. Photograph of Delphi showing the east end of the polygonal wall of the sanctuary and the Stoa of the Athenians, amidst houses of the village that were still standing. Archive of French School of Athens.

THE EXPLORATION BEFORE THE GREAT EXCAVATION

There was no talk as yet of a systematic excavation. Nevertheless, the curiosity motivated the foreign travellers to conduct a few excavations of limited success from 1828 onwards. Between 1828 and 1831, after a request from Ioannis Kapodistrias, Edmund Laurent began an excavation in the east cemetery, during which he uncovered the sarcophagus of Meleager. In 1838 he revealed the foundations of the temples at Marmaria (fig. 47), and drew the first ground plan of the site. Ernst Curtius and Carl Otfried Müller commenced work on the first real excavations in 1840, and revealed the polygonal wall for a length of about 10 metres and the sub-foundations of the temple, which they interpreted as being "underground rooms." During this same year, two scientific descriptions of the site were published: one by Friedrich Wilhelm Thiersh, who visited Delphi in 1831, and another by Heinrich Nikolaus Ulrichs, which was to become a reference point. The articles written by Alexandros Rizos Rangavis, professor of archaeology at Athens University, and Kyriakos Pittakis, director of Greek Antiquities, were of an equally high standard.

Carl Otfried Müller died on 1 August 1840, from sunstroke suffered while reading the inscriptions on the polygonal wall (fig. 6). On 26 July, he wrote to his wife: "we worked with great zeal to decipher and copy the inscriptions, 68 in number, and the majority of them very long. These

were engraved on the south-facing wall, which is exposed to the sun all day: exhausting work. I gambled on my ability to endure the heat and began to copy the inscriptions on an upturned stone, hanging upside down with the sun beating on my face. I paid dearly for this, however: I felt a burning on my skull, together with pain and irritation. I have reached the point where, I am able to do no more at Delphi since every new attempt on my part re-awakens the pain, and I cannot even escape this incessant heat."

From this period onwards, the French evinced a more scientific interest in the site. During his visit *(Voyage archéologique en Grèce et en Asie Mineure)* in 1843-1844, Philippe Le Bas called at Delphi, where he conscientiously copied inscriptions, many of them unpublished. The French School was founded a few years later, in 1846, and many of its members took an interest in the site. Eugène Gandar visited Delphi in March 1849, though his journey was not followed up. In 1850 the Academy included a full study of the site in its programme, but Joseph Guigniaut died on 19 December 1851 before completing the report he was preparing, and Henri Raynald composed a piece that was described as "mediocre." The Academy included the same subject in its programme in 1859. Paul Foucart began excavations in earnest in the autumn of 1860, at his own expense: he uncovered the polygonal wall for a length of about 40 metres, revealed the remains of the column with

6. Throughout almost the whole of antiquity, the stones of the polygonal wall were used as an open-air archive on which hundreds of inscriptions were inscribed. The reading of these was a very difficult task.

7. Artist's reconstruction of the archaeological site of Delphi during the Great Excavation. In the middle can be seen the polygonal wall, with the foundations of the temple of Apollo above it, and the houses of the village in the background. Drawing of 1893. Archive of French School of Athens.

the Sphinx of the Naxians (fig. 32), and excavated the sub-foundations of the temple. He initially believed he had discovered underground rooms, in which were stored the treasures sought by the Phokians when they captured the sanctuary between 356 and 346 BC (Diodorus Siculus 16.56.7 and Strabo 9.3.8). He resumed his investigations in 1861, together with Carl Wescher, who brought them to completion in 1862, revealing part of the east corner of the polygonal wall. In 1868, P. Foucart attempted, unsuccessfully, to commence excavations in a different sector of the site. In 1879, he became director of the French School at Athens and, in 1880, assigned to a member of the French School, Bernard Haussoullier, the task of initiating a series of excavations in a plot of land purchased by the Archaeological Society of Athens. There he uncovered another part of the polygonal wall, as well as the Stoa of the Athenians, though he failed to reveal the east end of the stoa – which was occupied by a house – and part of the paving of the Sacred Way.

All these, however, were incomplete excavations and were subsequently back-filled or repossessed by homeowners: the foundations of the temples at Marmaria revealed by Edmund Laurent in 1838

8. *The columns of the poros temple of Athena Pronaia as found during the excavation of 1903. They were destroyed by a huge falling rock in 1905. Archive of French School of Athens.*

8

were no longer visible in 1860: Captain Dimos Frangos, a colourful figure in Kastri, appropriated the east section of the polygonal wall excavated by C.O. Müller in 1840 and built the ancillary rooms of his house on it. While the trenches dug by P. Foucart and C. Wescher between 1860 and 1862 were also back-filled. As much as possible, the various parts of the polygonal wall were recorded as they were successively discovered. As the work proceeded, the need became ever clearer for a large-scale excavation on the site. There were precedents for such an undertaking: the excavation of Olympia (1875-1881), of Mycenae (1874-1876) and the archaeological investigation of Delos undertaken by the French School in 1873.

THE EXPROPRIATION OF THE SITE

One prerequisite for a large-scale excavation on the site, however, was the demolition of the village and its restoration elsewhere. W.M. Leake, in 1802 and 1806, followed by P.O. Brønsted in 1812, were the first to reach this conclusion after their visits. The finances available were insufficient, however, to satisfy the demands of the inhabitants. These increased as they realised the true value of the archaeological heritage upon which they dwelt. As a result, the opportunity to carry out the relocation was lost. At a disturbed political juncture, in an exhausted country in which national unity and military expenditure were the priorities, it was rather too early to undertake an enterprise of this nature in 1823, and rebuild the village which had been destroyed during the Greek War of Independence. In the absence of the necessary funding, the Greek government passed measures merely to protect the site. In 1838 they decided to include Delphi in a list of zones in which "it is prohibited to give as a dowry any plot of land on which there are antiquities." It was also planned to remove houses built on ancient ruins and pay compensation: King Otto visited Delphi in 1837 and 1845 and decided that "the dwellings shall not be rebuilt as they collapse one by one, and that it is forbidden to make significant repairs." The political will, however high-minded, foundered on the resistance of the inhabitants: despite the fact that the decision to confiscate the house of Captain Frangos was taken at this time, it was not enforced until 1878.

The mutual efforts of the authorities began with the first expropriation order for the village issued in 1860, and litigation began in 1864 against the inhabitants "who refused to make their plots of land available at the lawful price." Various bodies intervened to solve the problem, such as the Archaeological Society, which was founded in 1837, and the Antiquity-lovers Society, created in 1862 but dissolved two years later. The Committee for the Excavation of Delphi was set up in 1867, and was equally unsuccessful. The villagers were not even persuaded by the prospect of a "daily crowd of travellers," accurately predicted by A. Rangavis.

Natural disasters helped to settle the matter. The torrential rains of 1864 and 1866 revealed ancient ruins that could not be excavated because of the existence of the village. A devastating earthquake in 1870 caused the death of thirty people, thus providing an unexpected opportunity to relocate the village. This was increasingly regarded as essential. Even the inhabitants became aware of just how dangerous their location beneath the Phaidriades rocks was. However, a site and the necessary financial recompense had to be found in order to carry out the proposal. Another committee was formed for this purpose, though it, like its predecessor, was unsuccessful. Other efforts also proved to be in vain, despite the proposal by the Archaeological Society in 1872 to procure a loan: "so as to free the area of the archaeological site of Delphi, as soon as possible, of the inhabitants who currently occupy it, before the latter, under the pressure of the approaching winter, proceed to make fresh repairs to their houses damaged by the earthquake, and change their minds or increase their demands." Meanwhile, the inhabitants were faced with the consequences of the earthquake: they were not allowed to rebuild, but neither were they given alternative accommodation.

This issue was to play a decisive role in the negotiations, which would last for ten years.

9. P. Foucart, director of the French School at Athens, did all he could to ensure that the excavation of Delphi was assigned to the French.

THE PERIOD OF NEGOTIATIONS

Paul Foucart (fig. 9) was appointed director of the French School at Athens in 1879. He subsequently received a permit from the Archaeological Society to excavate the plot of land that the Society had purchased from Captain Frangos. This permit was issued for both political and financial reasons. France had lent decisive support to Greece at the Congress of Berlin in 1878, and as early as 1880, Paul Foucart had announced his plans for Delphi to the responsible ministry. These included his intention to expropriate about thirty houses. The first phase of Foucart's plans involved only the excavation of the temple and the immediate, surrounding area. An extraordinary budget was required to carry this out, as well as to implement the compulsory purchases. He entered into negotiations with Prime Minister Alexandros Koumoundouros and, after four months, reached an agreement that envisaged the signing of a contract on the model of the one drawn up for the excavation of Olympia. The speed of the entire procedure is accounted by the political juncture: Alexandros Koumoundouros was relying upon support from France for the signing of the Treaty of Constantinople to ratify the annexation of Thessaly and Epiros to Greece.

This was only the start of negotiations, culminating in 1892. Obstacles such as changes of political leadership and diplomatic games played by both sides, delayed the negotiations. Each waited for the other to take the first step that would lead to agreement. Even on the very day that the protocol of the agreement was signed, the French minister was informed by Alexandros Koumoundouros in a letter dated 14 June 1881 that the inhabitants of Delphi, "who have for some time been aware of the archaeological value of their land, are making unacceptable demands and seeking compensation at least twenty times greater than the real value of their properties." This situation required the passing of a law about expropriations in the public interest, and delayed the implementation of Foucart's proposal. Before the question of expropriation had been settled, a contract was signed on 2 February 1882 on the model of Olympia. It remained secret, however, to avoid the inhabitants' increasing their demands even further.

The issue of expropriations was not the only obstacle in the way of reaching agreement. On 12 March, Alexandros Koumoundouros resigned. He was replaced by Charilaos Trikoupis, who linked the granting of the right to excavate with the negotiation of a commercial treaty, in particular with the reduction of tariffs on the export of Greek currants. Soon, however, a third obstacle emerged: the convention stated that where two similar objects were found, one was to be given to France, which gave rise to lively debate in Parliament. This was obviously a way of gaining time and influencing the commercial negotiations. Finally, to these disagreements was added the appointment of Alexandros Kondostavlos to the office of Foreign Minister in 1882. Kondostavlos was hostile to France, which had brought pressure to bear on Alexandros Koumoundouros to desist from his initial claims relating to the annexation of Thessaly and Epiros. He was, moreover, president of the Archaeological Society, which had agreed, in 1880, to the French excavating the plot of land that they had purchased. The Society was not, however, at all well disposed to the more general granting of excavation rights. Everyone clung intransigently to his position and could not come to any agreement, and it seemed, for about three years as though things would remain this way.

10. Photograph of the first excavations, immediately after the houses were demolished. Archive of French School of Athens.

Following complex negotiations, progress was gradually made, with regard both to the commercial agreement and to the granting of excavation rights, after the rescinding of the article speaking of giving one copy of duplicated finds to France, and the obligation of Greece to pay 60,000 francs for the expropriations. After intensive consultations with a view to amending or improving a number of articles, a second agreement was signed on 4 February 1887, defining the boundaries of the excavation "on the site enclosed by the ancient walls." The parliamentary procedure began, though at a very slow rate. The agreement was delayed a further eight months due to the insistence of Charilaos Trikoupis upon linking the archaeological convention with the commercial agreement, and the fact that the French government was not competent to ratify such an agreement. It was achieved on 21 December 1887, but the French Parliament refused to ratify the commercial agreement, thereby torpedoing the plan.

During all these years, France remained in a somewhat privileged position in negotiating with the Greek authorities. It had been leaked, however, that other powers were aspiring to excavate the sanctuary of Pythian Apollo. The old rivalry between France and Germany lay behind the negotiations, kindled by the intervention of Hans Pomtow, who began an excavation in 1884, which continued until April-May of 1887. In 1886 the Americans began to show an interest in excavating Delphi, and made contact with the Greek authorities with this end in mind. The interminable negotiations between Greece and France encouraged this plan. In 1888-1889, W.R. Thayer addressed an appeal to American millionaires with the aim of collecting the necessary capital for the excavation, while Harvard professor Charles Norton gave a lecture and attempted to collect contributions to meet the expenses of the expropriations. In Athens itself, the director of the American School, Charles Waldstein, and the US ambassador continued their negotiations, even after the French ambassador, the count of Montholon, "received assurances [...] that America would not lay claim to this privilege until it became clear that France no longer has the slightest interest in the plan in question."

When obliged by Charilaos Trikoupis to respond, France, free of the demand that a commercial treaty should first be signed, gave a reply in the affirmative on 4 November 1890. In the same month, Deliyiannis succeeded Trikoupis, and in the following month, Th. Homolle (fig. 15) replaced P. Foucart. The discussions started once more, but the contract on the excavations at Delphi was finally signed in France on 10 March 1891, and in Greece during May 1891.

THE GREAT EXCAVATION

The expropriations could now begin, and were on a very large scale: "they included the entire village," says Th. Homolle in *BCH* 1923. "About a thousand building plots belonging to over 300 owners. A new village had to be created on the site that was to be compulsorily purchased, divided into sections and distributed. Houses had to be built and a water-supply secured." A few village houses remain, and can be distinguished by their brick walls reinforced with timber frames. The procedure was time-consuming, often stalled by the inhabitants and the cumbersome bureaucracy. The evaluations came to an end in December 1891, but the Committee of Experts did not submit its findings until March 1892. The inhabitants still had to relinquish their titles of ownership. Delays in payment of compensation enraged the inhabitants, who prevented the work from commencing, until they received it. The first cheque was issued on 7 October 1892; the excavations began on 10 October.

The announcement published in the Greek press, reporting the commencement of the work, is very conciliatory: "The Greek and French flags flew on the wagon taking the first load of earth to the ravine. The inhabitants showed feelings of sympathy. [...] The Greek Government, having always adopted a positive attitude to the enterprise, took the necessary measures to speed up the final formalities and smooth out the difficulties." In fact, they had to resort to the army on two occasions. The first – as Th. Homolle notes in a letter written by him on 29 September 1892, to the French Minister of Education – when H. Convert (fig. 15), a craftsman and foreman, was sent to Delphi to install the Decauville railway tracks (figs 12, 16).

"The threats made against us and your warn-

11. View of the excavation of part of the sanctuary, showing the ruins revealed. Most of the finds (e.g., statues) were found in similar circumstances. Archive of French School of Athens.

12. A rail network 1,800 metres long was installed to remove the earth deposits. Archive of French School of Athens.

11

12

ings were to no avail: as soon as the site office opened, the entire village assembled and the most militant of the inhabitants rushed at the workers and seized the tools from their hands, declaring that there would be no work as long as the compensation was not paid. Convert very prudently offered no resistance. […] At my request, the prime minister and minister of Foreign Affairs agreed to give instructions to the mayor and prefect to assist us, putting at our disposal an officer and eleven armed soldiers: thanks to them, we were able to lay the tracks, which will be finished this week. At the same time, we are building a house for the site, and the excavation will commence next week."

But the beginning of the work was beset with conflicts: Th. Homolle in *BCH* of 1893 notes (p. 185): "Having postponed the excavations from the spring to the summer 1892, we now had to postpone them again until the autumn, waiting for the financial allocations to become available and for

13. Removing earth from the higher areas to the lower with the aid of huge planks. Characteristic picture of the first excavations in the sanctuary. Archive of French School of Athens.

14. The area of the Roman agora and the stepped entrance to the sanctuary of Delphi, with the beginning of the Sacred Way, as discovered during the Great Excavation. Archive of French School of Athens.

15. The men in charge of the Great Excavation of Delphi in 1893. In the centre is the Director, Th. Homolle, with the engineer H. Convert at bottom right. Archive of French School of Athens.

the payment of the first cheques. These were signed on 7th October and on this same day, Mm. Homolle and Couve arrived in Delphi: the site office opened on the 10th of the month.

Despite zealous efforts to resolve the situation with the inhabitants, the conflicts continued, as they put obstacles in the way of every task until the compensation was paid. They occupied the site office and routed the workers, having first removed their tools from them, just as when they attempted to lay the tracks for the wagons. So the excavations only began after a great struggle, and under the protection of the armed forces."

This excavation required the distribution of sizeable financial allocations. A rail network 1,800 metres long, the traces of which are still visible today, was installed to remove the earth deposits and empty them, courtesy of a wooden ramp spanning the road (figs 13, 16), into the

16. *The rail system with wagons that gradually spread over the entire site of the excavations and made it possible to remove the tonnes of soil that covered the sanctuary. Archive of French School of Athens.*

17. *The terrace in front of the temple after the removal of the earth deposits. The finds, most of them large-scale sculptures, are placed provisionally on improvised bases or rest against the ancient walls. Archive of French School of Athens.*

17

Delphi. The excavation of the great oracular centre | 143

18, 19. The Treasury of the Athenians (left) and the Treasury of the Siphnians (right) are two of the most interesting buildings in the sanctuary. Drawings by the French architect A. Tournaire. Paris, École Nationale Supérieure des Beaux-Arts.

20. Drawing of the frieze of the Treasury of the Siphnians made immediately after its discovery. Archive of French School of Athens.

21. Fragment of the Delphic Hymn to Apollo, found carved on two stones of the Treasury of the Athenians. The symbols between the lines and text are musical notes. The decipherment of these made it possible to give a musical performance of the hymn. Archive of French School of Athens.

22. Plan of the sanctuary of Apollo immediately after the end of the Great Excavation. Paris, École Nationale Supérieure des Beaux-Arts.

FAÇADE PRINCIPALE

18

19

20

21

ravine of the Pleistos. In 1895, more than 160,000 wagons of earth were emptied in this way. In 1893, the excavation of the sanctuary, on occasion, employed as many as 220 workmen, though there were fewer in mid-summer or during the harvest season.

During the brief excavation season of 1892, the work begun by Bernard Haussoullier in 1880 was resumed. The years 1893-1894 matched up to expectations and the telegraph conveyed information about the discoveries: the Treasury of the Athenians (figs 18, 44, 45) with its sculptural decoration and, amongst the inscriptions, the Hymn to Apollo (fig. 21), the Great Altar, the Halos, and the Rock of the Sibyll, the Treasury of the Siphnians (figs 19, 20) and the Treasury of the Sikyonians have since found their place in the Delphi landscape. The year 1894 was marked by the discovery of the archaic twins Kleobis and Biton of Argos (figs 23-25), statues from the dedication of Daochos, hieromnemon of the Thessalians. One of the most impressive finds of 1894 was the statue of Antinoös (figs 26, 27).

The finds in 1894, caused a great sensation, especially that of the Delphic Hymn to Apollo (fig. 21). At the meeting of the Institut de Correspondance Hellénique on 15 March 1894, an 'official performance' took place in the presence of the king and queen of the Hellenes, the crown prince and princess, "with the diplomatic corps, the admiral and officers of the French naval

DELPHES
PLAN DV TEMENOS D'APOLLON

DIAZOMA

THEATRE

LESCHÉ DE CNIDE

BARRAGE DE PROTECTION

Fontaine Kassotis

Scène

Offrande des Thessaliens

La Chasse d'Alexandre

Citerne romaine

PORTIQVE   Thermes

Offrande de Gélon

GRAND TEMPLE D'APOLLON

Grand Autel de Chio

Char des Rhodiens

Paul Emile

Trépied de Platée

Thermes romains

TERRASSE DE SOVBASSEMENT

Portique des Athéniens

Colonne des Naxiens

VOIE SACRÉE

Bouleutérion

Trésor des Athéniens

MAISON DE L'ÉCOLE
FRANÇAISE

Trésor des Béotiens

Mur

Trésor des Thébains

Trésor des Corinthiens

Trésor des Siphniens

Trésor des Cnidiens

Mur

VOIE

Trésor des Sicyoniens

SACRÉE

Rois d'Argos

Ex-voto d'Ægos-Potamos

PORTIQVE

Épigones

Enceinte

Entrée principale du Sanctuaire

ROVTE   ACTVELLE

Thermes

D'ITÉA

ETAT ACTVEL DES FOVILLES   A

ECHELLE

ARACHO

22

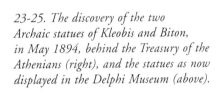

23-25. The discovery of the two Archaic statues of Kleobis and Biton, in May 1894, behind the Treasury of the Athenians (right), and the statues as now displayed in the Delphi Museum (above).

squadron of the Eastern Mediterranean, the entire cultural world and the cream of Athenian society" (*BCH* 18/1894, p. 172).

After Th. Homolle's address to the king, in which he stated that "these exceptional monuments will bring decisive progress for science, and it is certain that they will occupy scholars for ever, "the hymn was interpreted by Mm. Roc, Rodios, Laskaris and Papageorgiou, Athenian amateurs, with precision and ease, and, one might say, with true religious and patriotic sentiments. His Majesty the King, starting off the applause, asked for the hymn to be performed a second time." The hymn then became the subject of lectures and academic meetings: in May, performances of it took place in St Petersburg and Johannesburg. It was performed in Paris at the international athletics conference organised by Pierre de Coubertin in 1894, during which it was decided to revive the Olympic Games and hold them in Athens.

However, as one moved away from the main areas of the sanctuary, the excavation became rather disappointing, and in 1895, the only addition to the landscape was the Knidian Club in the northeast corner. In 1896, interest was rekindled: the Stadium, the polygonal wall, including its southeast end, the base of the Messenians, and the base of the Roman general Aemilius Paulus, were completely revealed.

The greatest moment of 1896, however, came on 28 April, with the discovery of the lower part

26, 27. The discovery of the statue of Antinoös next to a brick wall behind the temple of Apollo on 12 July 1894 (right), and the statue as now displayed in the Delphi Museum (left).

26

27

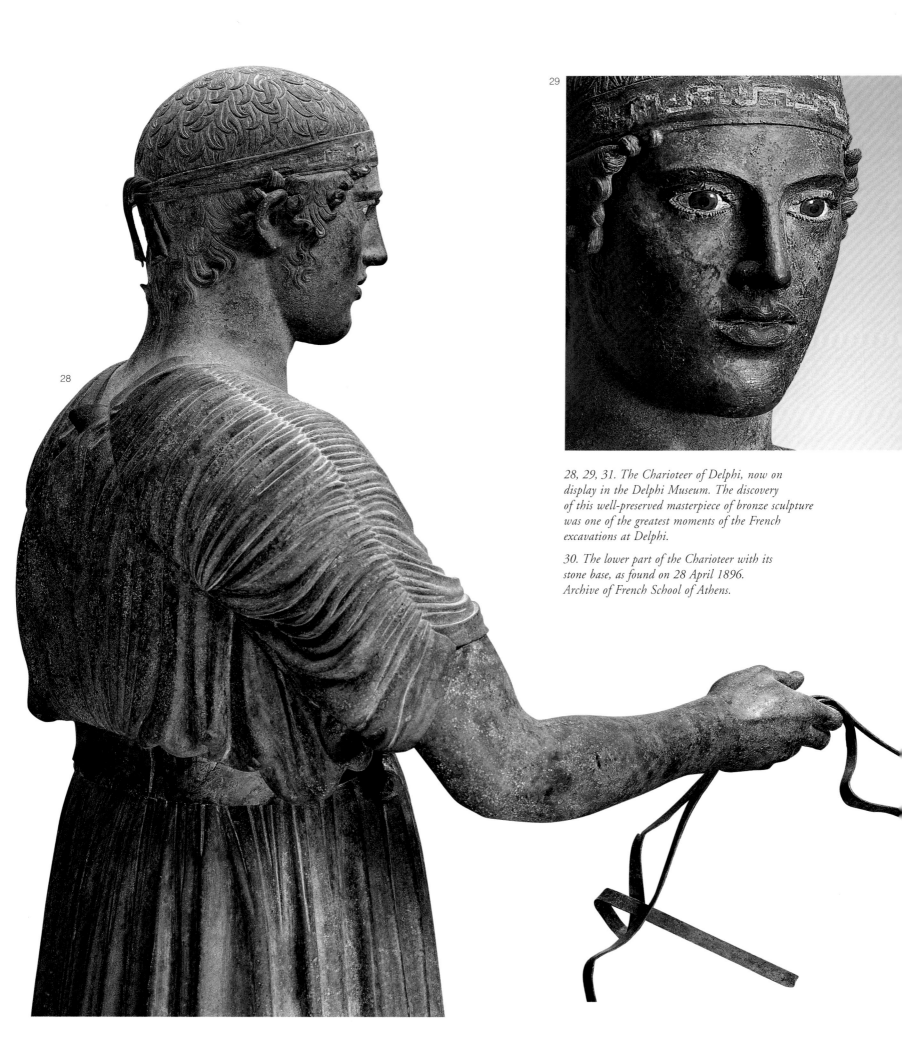

28, 29, 31. *The Charioteer of Delphi, now on display in the Delphi Museum. The discovery of this well-preserved masterpiece of bronze sculpture was one of the greatest moments of the French excavations at Delphi.*

30. *The lower part of the Charioteer with its stone base, as found on 28 April 1896. Archive of French School of Athens.*

of the Charioteer (figs 28-31), along with the stone base with the votive inscription and a few bronze fragments. On 1 May, the upper part of the statue was found, with more bronze fragments belonging to the dedication. The discoveries continued until 9 May. That day Théophile Homolle sent a telegram to the Académie des Inscriptions et Belles-Lettres: "Life-size bronze found: young victor - chariot-races - Pythian games - masterpiece of bronze-working - patina intact - Report follows." On 11 May, a second telegram offered clarification: "Inscription shows bronze is Hiero I of Syracuse, victor at the Pythian Games. Historical importance equal to artistic value." On 12 May, he wrote a preliminary report, in which he considered it to be "possibly the most valuable and exceptional find," accompanied by two photographs. Finally, as early as 5 June 1896, he presented a communication before the Academy on this major discovery, hoping that "the pleasure, at this superb find has not clouded the perspicacity of my judgement, nor influenced the strictness of my method."

The daybook of the Great Excavation (figs 35, 36), which is kept in the archives of the French School and has entries by many contributors

with dates recorded according to the Julian and Gregorian calendars, preserves the memory of this outstanding archaeological adventure, revealing the focus of interest of each participant, and enables us to follow the progress of the identifications. There was some doubt about the identification of the Treasuries of the Siphnians and Knidians. The Argos Twins (Kleobis and Biton) were initially thought to be statues of Apollo, the floral decoration of the column surmounted by the Dancing Women (fig. 34) was at first thought to be a stalk of the plant sylphium, and the dedication was therefore thought to come from the Cyrenaica. Along with the record of the finds, one can find details of life on the work site, the rainy days that often interrupted the work, or the holidays, which took advantage of the double calendar. As Anne Jacquemin wrote, this diary records "the birth of a kind of scientific work, the rules of which had not yet been defined."

Paul Perdrizet was the first to show interest in the site's archaeological sequence and its stratigraphy, a term unknown at the time. The following is an extract from his notes of 30 April 1895: "Between the Great Altar and the east wall of the precinct, beneath the foundations of the wall, a 50cm layer of greenish earth mixed with a large quantity of bone fragments, burnt wood and ashes was discovered.

32

32. The Sphinx of the Naxians, displayed as it appeared originally, set on a column about 9 metres high. Delphi, Archaeological Museum.

33. The marble omphalos. According to the latest research, it was set on a tripod cauldron carried on the heads of the three Dancing Women. Archive of French School of Athens.

33

A zimbile [container] of this earth was taken to the Museum. The so far known surface of this layer is in excess of 100 square metres, and is a continuation of the layer found last year beneath the Treasuries to the east of the base of Gelon, a layer in which Mycenaean and Geometric vases were found (Tuesday 10 October). The layer discovered yesterday and today no longer contained Mycenaean vases, but only Geometric finds (of Delphi)".

In 1897, marked by the Greek-Turkish war, work was devoted to keeping the site in order. Finally, the years 1898, 1899 and 1900 were dedicated to the excavation of the Gymnasium, the church of Prophitis Ilias, and Marmaria, respectively (fig. 47).

In addition to the exceptional technical means used at that time, the Great Excavation of Delphi resorted to two methods for studying the finds and disseminating information: the copy and the photograph. Two experts worked on the manufacture of moulds; one, Giovanni Buda, an Italian, was mentioned on the stone slab erected on the occasion of the inauguration of the Museum. The French School itself had a workshop for copies in its garden in Athens. The copies enabled the archaeologists to make the finds known and ensure that they were widely disseminated. At the first performance of the Delphic Hymn to Apollo, for example, Théophile Homolle "gave a brief description of the Treasury of the Athenians demonstrating its rare architectural perfection with the aid of photographs and also copies on display in the hall" (*BCH* 18/1894, p. 173).

Wide use was also made of photography, an art that was growing and spreading at the time of the Great Excavation, though the excavation diary provides evidence of only 18 exposures. The collections of the French School contain a total of almost 2,000 glass plates, which provide valuable testimony to the state of the site before the village was moved, and also of the progress of the excavation and the objects uncovered there. They are still used as evidence by archaeologists today.

34. The upper part of the column with the three Dancing Women, as discovered in front of the temple of Apollo. Archive of French School of Athens.

35-36. Two representative pages from the daybook of the excavations at Delphi by the French School. The text, written by major personalities in modern archaeology, is still important as historical evidence. Archive of French School of Athens.

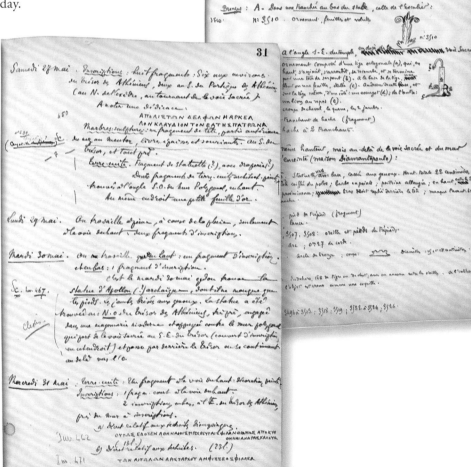

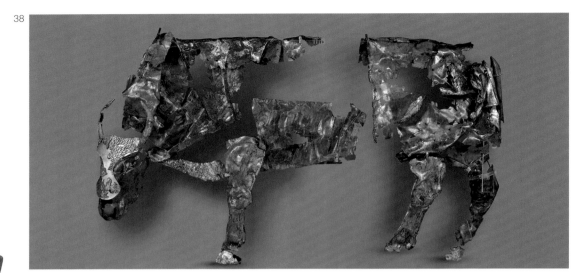

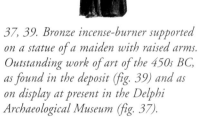

*37, 39. Bronze incense-burner supported
on a statue of a maiden with raised arms.
Outstanding work of art of the 450s BC,
as found in the deposit (fig. 39) and as
on display at present in the Delphi
Archaeological Museum (fig. 37).*

*38, 40. Dedication of an Archaic bull
rendered at almost life size, as found, with
its metal sheeting crushed (fig. 40), and as
superbly reconstructed from hundreds of
fragments of silver sheet that had been forged
on a wooden mould and riveted to an inner
copper frame (fig. 38). The horns, ears,
forehead and hooves were gilded.
Middle of the 6th c. BC. Delphi,
Archaeological Museum.*

*41. In 1939, the excavation of the Sacred
Way led to the discovery of a deposit
containing works of art dedicated in
the sanctuary at Delphi that had been
destroyed in ancient times and then buried.
Archive of French School of Athens.*

THE MUSEUM AND SUBSEQUENT EXCAVATIONS

The handing over of the site and the inauguration of the Museum on 20 April/2 May 1903, signalled the end of the Great Excavation. Before the excavations began, the archaeologists imagined that five years would be enough for what was considered the 'definitive' publication of the finds. This was delayed, first by the excavation of Delos, which began in 1903 and absorbed both energy and financial allocations, and secondly by the First World War. Above all, however, the amount of time required for the study of the monuments discovered over the course of ten years, had been miscalculated.

If we do not take into account the request for the construction of a museum, addressed by the inhabitants of Kastri to the king in 1834, the first reference to a museum is to be found in the daybook of the Great Excavation on 28 May 1894. Until this time, the finds had been placed in the village school. The first museum was extended before it was even inaugurated, and two wings were added to the original main building, thanks to the generosity of A. Syngros (fig. 42).

A new museum was built between 1935 and 1938, but the layout had not been completed by the outbreak of the Second World War. The Charioteer and the gold and ivory objects that had not yet been conserved were sent to Athens, while the stone statues were concealed in the basement of a Roman *heroön*, that was covered by a cement slad, and in pits dug in front of the museum. They remained there until July 1952. After the war, a new building included an adaptation and extension to the old museum. The only significant modification made thereafter was the creation in 1974 of a gallery exclusively for the finds from the pits at the Sacred Way, the conservation of which had been completed. The Delphi Museum experienced a final development with the inauguration of a new building and a radically revised display, on 9 August 2004 (fig. 43).

The site of Delphi would never again experience such intensive activity over such a long period. Later excavations did take place, but they were on a smaller scale and different methods were used. Apart from a few trenches dug with

42. The first Museum at Delphi under construction. The two additional wings were built with a donation from A. Syngros. Archive of French School of Athens.

43. The new building of the Museum inaugurated on August 2004.

the aim of confirming data, Robert Demangel completed the archaeological investigation of Marmaria in 1920 and Pierre de La Coste Messelière that of the West Stoa in 1923 and 1924. Later, in four excavation seasons between 1934 and 1937, Lucien Lerat uncovered levels associated with Mycenaean and Geometric settlements in the northeast part of the sanctuary. Between 1936 and 1949, Jean Bousquet and Pierre Amandry investigated the phases of the sanctuary preceding the monumental phases, when the systematic dismantling of the paved Sacred Way, with a view to retrieving architectural members or inscribed stone blocks led, in 1939, to the discovery of two pits (fig. 41) containing valuable dedications, mainly of gold and ivory, buried there after a fire. Reference should also be made to a number of trenches sunk in 1970 and 1971 to the east of the

sanctuary, and in 1970s in the Stadium. From 1985 on, the Ephorate and the French School at Athens joined forces to complete the uncovering of the Gymnasium, only the ends of which had been brought to light by the Great Excavation. The systematic study of the Early Christian town, which commenced in 1983, was resumed from 1990 to 1997 with the excavation of a large villa to the south of the sanctuary. In 1990, archaeologists finally took advantage of the dismantling of the base of the Chariot of the Rhodians to excavate the archaeological strata beneath it, revealing part of the first precinct and remains of a settlement destroyed when the sanctuary was extended. These were the most recent outstanding excavations to be conducted at Delphi.

In addition as the excavations continued, the French School at Athens began at an early stage to

44, 45. One of the first concerns of the French archaeologists was to restore some of the monuments that were preserved in good condition. Here, The Treasury of the Athenians during the restoration of 1903-1906 (left) and as it is today (right).

46. The excavation of Delphi yielded many new finds important to the study of epigraphy and sculpture. Apollo seated on a tripod, restored as the central figure of the east pediment of the 4th c. BC temple (drawing by K. Iliakis). Archive of French School of Athens.

47. Aerial photograph of the Gymnasium at Delphi and the sanctuary of Athena Pronaia below it. These buildings were discovered in the years 1898, 1899 and 1900.

undertake restoration work that has given the site its present appearance. Several monuments were restored in the galleries of the first museum, including the base of Aemilius Paulus and the base of the Messenians (1902). The most important example of these early restoration projects, however, is the Treasury of the Athenians. As early as September 1902, Th. Homolle proposed to the municipality of Athens that it should shoulder the expense of rebuilding it (figs 44, 45). The work lasted from 1903 to 1906. The French School also partly restored the Altar of Apollo (1902, 1920 and 1959), the Tholos (1930), part of the colonnade of the temple (1941) and the base of Prusias (1947). Several monuments were also restored on the first section of the Sacred Way, and more recently the base of the Krotoniates and the base of the Chariot of the Rhodians.

46

Preliminary studies were undertaken for several other monuments, particularly the bases of the Attalids. Between the works of restoration and organisation of the area, it is worth mentioning the case of the theatre, for which, the French School undertook an in depth study in 2001 and 2002, which has been delivered to the appropriate Greek service.

TOWARDS AN ASSESSMENT

The story of the Great Excavation of Delphi is, from one point of view, a story of disappointment. The excavation of the temple, in particular, did not live up to expectations: "It is remarkable," wrote Théophile Homolle in 1894, "that a study on such a wide scale uncovered so few characteristic architectural members, and the complete absence of sculpted decoration may be considered highly discouraging for the future. Not a single metope has been found, nor a fragment of a frieze, and not even a little toe of a figure from a pediment." The preserved fragments were only identified in 1971. The very site itself at which the oracles were issued proved to be unexpectedly empty, and the Pythia kept her secret.

On the other hand, the excavations at Delphi proved to be definitive in some spheres: this was true of epigraphy and sculpture, for which the site provided basic reference points, particularly in archaic sculpture. For architecture, too, Delphi is a veritable workshop in which creations from all the great periods of history are to be found side by side in a relatively small space.

Several pieces of the puzzle are missing, preventing the resumption of large-scale excavations. Almost 60 volumes have been published to date, in which the progress of the investigation is delineated, and others still wait to appear. "The names have strength, the 'shadows' have authority," wrote Georges Daux, to account for the attraction exercised by the sanctuary, even after it had lost its meaning. This strength, this authority is still exercised by Delphi today on scholars and visitors.

48. Panoramic view of Delphi with the sanctuary of Apollo, seen from the top of the Phaidriades rocks.

Colin F. Macdonald

Knossos
The discovery of the Minoan palace

Knossos was not *discovered* by its main excavator, Sir Arthur Evans, nor by his native Cretan predecessor, Minos Kalokairinos. Knossos had long been known from fantastic myths that ultimately had been woven in the first millennium BC from distant memories of the second. These myths revolved around Minos, king of Knossos, the main city of one-hundred in Crete; husband to Pasiphae whose unnatural passion for a bull led to the birth of the *Minotaur*; father of Ariadne who helped the Athenian Theseus kill the Minotaur (fig. 1) and escape from the *labyrinth* built by the architect Daedalos; son of Zeus and brother of Rhadamanthys, a judge of the Underworld; Minos himself a law-giver and master of a thalassocracy that maintained peace over the Aegean sea. That the name Knossos had been correctly given to the area where ultimately the Palace was found was confirmed largely by the frequent discovery of Hellenistic and Roman coins with "ΚΝΩΣ" on the obverse and the image of a maze on the reverse (fig. 3).

The site of a Roman theatre had been located and a large Roman basilica outlined by Onorio Belli in AD 1586. The labyrinth itself had long been known and was described in some de-

1. 6th c. Attic black-figure amphora with a scene depicting Theseus killing the Minotaur. Paris, Louvre Museum.

2. Aerial view of the Palace at Knossos from the south-east. The Central Court is surrounded by ceremonial areas on the west (top left) with the storage magazines beyond bordering the West Court. On the east side (lower right), the Residential Quarter rises two storeys to the level of the Central Court. To the north is the North Entrance Passage and its bastions with the relief wall-painting of a raging bull restored under the eaves.

tail by Pliny (*Nat.* 36. 19. 85) where he may even allude to the great West Magazines as Sara Paton has pointed out (pers. comm.): "doors are let into walls at frequent intervals to suggest deceptively the way ahead and to force the visitor to go back…." Thus, Knossos may have been a tourist attraction even in the 1st century AD and Pliny's description still resonates today. However, it was the investigation of the site at *Tou Tselevi Kephala* by Minos Kalokairinos in 1878-1889 that first excited the modern antiquarian world. By no means all those who became interested in Knossos were *bona fide* scholars belonging to respected institutions, even though some tried to enlist academic support. Kalokairinos had dug in certain parts of what was to become known as the West Wing of the Palace as well as on the southern terraces. He recovered *pithoi*, large storage jars (figs 4, 5), as well as decorated pottery of a kind linked with that being called *Mycenaean* from the Argolid, from Mycenae itself, and from the tombs of Ialysos on Rhodes. One of Kalokairinos's trenches touched part of what was later the greatest discovery of Sir Arthur Evans's

3

3. Hellenistic coin from Knossos depicting the Labyrinth on the reverse. Athens, Numismatic Museum.

4. West Magazine V with deep cists (or kaselles) and some of the storage pithoi. The storage jars were in use when the palace was finally destroyed by fire, traces of which can be seen on the gypsum piers at the bottom of the picture. At the top is the paved West Court.

5. The Long Corridor from the north. The corridor gave access to the eighteen, long storage magazines that were filled with pithoi (e.g., in the foreground). There were sunken cists in the corridor as well as several of the magazines to increase storage capacity. From C. Bacon, The Great Archaeologists *(1976).*

4

5

first season, the Room of the Throne (figs 10, 12). As Crete was still under Turkish rule, it seems to have been thought unwise for Kalokairinos to uncover what might be a site rich in treasure that could disappear to Constantinople. Yet, the finds that had come to light caused great excitement, prompting unsuccessful attempts to secure the site by French (Bertrand Hassoulier and later André Joubin of the French School at Athens), Italian (Federico Halbherr), American (W.J. Stillman, former consul), British (Thomas Sandwith, consul) and German (Heinrich Schliemann) individuals.

EVANS AT KNOSSOS

Sir Arthur Evans (figs 6, 7), Curator of the Ashmolean Museum, Oxford, had been interested in Crete as a possible source of inscribed sealstones that might bear witness to early, pre-Hellenic scripts in the Aegean area. He was introduced to Crete by Federico Halbherr, most famous for the discovery of the Law Code of Gortyn, whose knowledge of the island's landscape and antiquities was probably unrivalled among foreign scholars. During an impromptu and strictly illegal forage in the Diktaion Cave at Psychro in 1896, Evans recovered part of a stone *offering table* with seven inscribed signs, apparently a development of the *hieroglyphic* or *pictographic* script found on sealstones. This demonstrated the existence of a linear, indeed syllabic script in Crete during a pre-Hellenic era. At the same time, it had been noted that signs were inscribed on some of the great cut blocks uncovered by Kalokairinos at Knossos, signs that appeared close to the pictographic script of sealstones, including evocative double axes, stars and tridents. Evans had already tentatively sug-

gested that *Minoan* as opposed to *Mycenaean* should be used to describe the material culture that was latent in the earth of Crete and of Knossos in particular. He had also begun to formulate ideas on Bronze Age worship in Crete based on the iconography of sealstones, gold rings and even a conical, stone rhyton with relief decoration found at Knossos.

Evans was able to triumph in his bid to buy the Kephala Hill of Knossos due to independent wealth, personal persistence, the helpful interventions of Joseph Hatzidakis, a Melian doctor turned philologist and head of the Cretan Philological Committee, and the independence of Crete in 1898. His finds were to stay in Crete although 'duplicates' might be transported abroad, notably to his home museum, the Ashmolean, where today a healthy collection of Minoan originals and copies occupies a room given over to Crete.

The first ground was broken on the 23rd of March 1900. During the first season, the west half of the 'Mycenaean' palace was uncovered (fig. 8), already putting the Mainland palaces of the 14th-13th centuries in the shade due to its size, monumentality and prolific use of glittering white gypsum for facades and architectural embellishments such as doorjambs and paving. It was important for Evans that he had enlisted the help of Duncan Mackenzie, a Scot who had experience at excavating *stratigraphically* (by layers, the lower layers being earlier than the upper layers). Yet, despite this,

6. *Sir Arthur Evans portrait painted in 1907 by Sir W.B. Richmond. Evans is surrounded by clay vessels, relief and figural frescoes and a stone lamp from the excavations at Knossos. Oxford, Ashmolean Museum.*

7. *Sir Arthur Evans next to a cast of the throne from the Room of the Throne (now in the Ashmolean Museum, Oxford). In front is a pithoid jar of the 15th c. BC, decorated with an octopus. Oxford, Ashmolean Museum.*

much information was lost in the early seasons due to the fact that some less distinct occupation levels were almost certainly missed in a drive to reach the first paved floors. Nonetheless, most of these floors were in use at the time the Palace was destroyed, none more clearly than those in the Room of the Throne that was fully uncovered in the first season (fig. 10).

The West Wing was not deeply buried under later accumulations of earth nor was later occupation (Early Hellenic) much in evidence. Indeed, the original earth that lay on top of the walls of the great series of storage magazines was still in place and formed no impediment to excavation. It seems likely that in various parts of the site, ancient walls were protruding from the earth so that Evans was by no means excavating a blank knoll. On April the 13th, excavation of a room, the ante-chamber of which had already been investigated by Kalokairinos, revealed an elaborately carved gypsum seat with a tall straight back of curvaceous outline, set against a wall covered in wall-paintings (fig. 12). It was only four weeks into the excavation and Evans had come across what was to become the most famous room of the Palace, rapidly dubbed 'Room of the Throne' (figs 10, 12), although *whose* throne was clearly the question on the mind of all who saw it. Evans was taken with the idea of a female occupant, the mytho-

8. The Central Palace Sanctuary and Room of the Throne (right) with its first protective roofing in 1901. All these rooms lead directly onto the Central Court. Oxford, Ashmolean Museum.

9. The West Court with the original gypsum orthostat base blocks, which were put in place by 1900 BC. The paved, raised walkways were first laid down in the 20th c. BC. This western border of the palace remained in place until the building was destroyed some time in the 14th c. BC.

8

9

logical Ariadne, influenced somewhat by the fact that opposite the throne lay what was later termed a *Lustral Basin* (fig. 13), although then known as a sunken bath chamber. We now know that lustral basins were never actually filled with water since they were lined with soluble gypsum slabs and had no drainage facilities, although cleansing with unguents may have taken place as part of rituals connected with a chthonic deity. Descent into the basin by a number of steps may have been symbolic.

The seat was flanked heraldically by griffins, and Evans ultimately proposed not only that this was the oldest European throne but also that it was the seat of Minos (or 'the Minos', equivalent to 'Pharaoh'), or at least a male king or priest. Evans imagined a final scene in the palace where, as flames engulfed its magnificence, Minos, as the *papa ré*, sat in sombre state surrounded by elders seated on the carved gypsum benches lining the walls. On the floor were a number of gypsum *alabastra* (fig. 14), a Mycenaean shape adopted in Minoan Crete around 1400 BC, with

11

10. The Room of the Throne immediately after excavation with the broken pithos near the gypsum throne. The room was surrounded by gypsum benches that had probably been added in the 15th c. BC. Oxford, Ashmolean Museum.

11. Steatite rhyton fragment from the area of the Lustral Basin. The exquisite relief carving, known as the "ambushed octopus," depicts part of an octopus and seaweed. It either dates to the 16th c. BC or the early 15th c. when Marine Style pottery was in vogue. Herakleion, Crete, Archaeological Museum.

12. The Room of the Throne as finally restored by Evans (and re-restored by the Knossos Conservation Office). The great stone basin was not found here but rather in a corridor to the north. The wall-paintings depict griffins placed antithetically on either side of the throne.

compass-guided spirals decorating the rim. These magnificent vessels lay where they were at the time of the destruction of the Palace, and next to them was a pithos, perhaps holding a liquid for the *alabastra*. No finely decorated clay vessels were found that might help to date the destruction to a specific ceramic phase, yet the *alabastra* were decorated in a manner that could only belong in the 14th century BC. Although Evans dated the destruction of the Palace to around 1400 BC, scholars now lean towards a later 14th century BC date, somewhat closer in time to the use of the Mycenaean Linear B script at Chania and on the Greek mainland.

Among the most exciting finds of the first season were the numerous clay tablets (fig. 17) inscribed with a script new to Evans – he had previously seen pictographic/hieroglyphic scripts, and an earlier Linear script. This new script was termed Linear B to show that it was a development of the script (Linear A) that had been in use from the 17th to early 15th centuries BC. The tablets were temporary documents, fortuitously baked during a fiery destruction, of an administration that regulated many aspects of the palace economy. Livestock, grain, chariots and weapons are all recorded in painstaking detail on the rectangular clay tablets, sometimes accompanied by clay sealings made by metal rings and stone seals of the 16th-14th cen-

13

13. *The Lustral Basin of the Room of the Throne. This was part of the original design of the complex and was lined with gypsum slabs. The bench to the right was probably inserted later (15th c. BC) when the focus of activities was transferred to the Room of the Throne.*

turies BC (figs 15, 16). One set of tablets dealing with chariots may have been preserved in an early conflagration that engulfed part of the palace around 1375 BC, after which many changes took place, to the detriment of the palatial grandeur of the building. The numerous deposits of clay tablets that date from the time palace's final destruction evoke a sense of intense bureaucratic activity hitherto unknown. Many of these deposits of tablets were found in the first two seasons of excavating. Their very existence alongside small impressed sealings caused Evans and Mackenzie to exercise greater care during the excavation than might otherwise have been the case. When similar clay tablets were found at the Palace of Nestor at Pylos in destruction layers post-dating Knossos by up to a century (not two centuries as Evans would have it), Evans considered this as proof of the civilizing of mainland culture through Minoan influence and invasion. It was only after Evans's death that the Linear B script was found to represent a very early form of Greek, in contrast to 'Minoan' Linear A, thereby indicating

that important influence, if not invasion, had rather stemmed *from* the mainland, creating a superficial Mycenaean veneer on Cretan Bronze Age culture.

However, the excitement generated by the discovery of written documents in the Palace of Minos was understandable since they allowed Minoan palatial society to join the Near Eastern club of civilized societies. Indeed, after the second season, with the discovery of monumental and well-planned architecture, written records, fine art of a public character and complex religious paraphernalia, Knossos exhibited many of the attributes of Near Eastern and Egyptian civilizations. Knossos, however, lacked and still lacks the obvious or prominent portrayal of a ruler. The empty 'throne' found in the first year had been assigned first to a female priestess and then a male ruler or perhaps 'Priest King'. It could well have been the seat of one or the

15   16

17

14. Gypsum 'alabastron' found in the Room of the Throne. The shape and the engraved spirals allow it to be dated to the 14th c. BC, when the Throne Room complex was last used. Oxford, Ashmolean Museum.

15. Clay seal impression made by a bronze ring. The scene may represent a goddess and a votary holding an elaborate cup with another woman facing left. Part of the destruction debris of the palace and made by the same ring that created the sealing from which the 'matrix' in fig. 16 was made. Herakleion, Crete, Archaeological Museum.

16. Famous clay 'signet' or 'matrix', actually an intaglio impression of a relief seal impression made by the same bronze ring that impressed fig. 15. Although associated with 14th c. destruction in a south room of the palace, the ring itself was made no later than the earlier part of the 15th c. BC. It could have been used by officials to confirm that seal impressions were genuine and not forgeries from a similar ring. Herakleion, Crete, Archaeological Museum.

17. Linear B clay tablet (14th c. BC) from West Magazine XV mentioning cloth and people. Herakleion, Crete, Archaeological Museum.

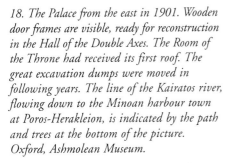

18. The Palace from the east in 1901. Wooden door frames are visible, ready for reconstruction in the Hall of the Double Axes. The Room of the Throne had received its first roof. The great excavation dumps were moved in following years. The line of the Kairatos river, flowing down to the Minoan harbour town at Poros-Herakleion, is indicated by the path and trees at the bottom of the picture. Oxford, Ashmolean Museum.

19. The Temple Repositories were two large stone-built cists on the north side of the central palace Sanctuary area. They were filled with mostly antique clay vessels (17th c. BC) for storing and pouring liquids as well as exquisite objects made from faience, rock crystal and other materials. The 'Snake Goddess' and her 'votaries' are the most famous statues found in repositories, their clothes beautifully decorated in different colours. These objects probably date to the later 16th c. BC, as do most of the clay sealings found with them. The sealings must have been burnt in a fire destruction before deposition in the cists. Oxford, Ashmolean Museum.

19

20

21

20. The faience 'Snake Goddess' from the Temple Repositories. Later 16th ce. BC. Herakleion, Crete, Archaeological Museum.

21. The best known faience 'votary' of the 'Snake Goddess' – head restored. Later 16th c. BC. Herakleion, Crete, Archaeological Museum.

22. The Prince of the Lily Crown, a relief wall-painting from south of the Central Court – probably 15th c. BC. It is incorrectly restored since the 'crown' probably belonged to a sphinx; only the torso and one thigh of the youth remain. Herakleion, Crete, Archaeological Museum.

other depending on the period of use. Yet, the very fact that Evans was ambivalent as to the sex of its occupant emphasises how little we know of the institutions of the Knossian palace during both its long Minoan phase (20th-15th centuries BC) and the period of mainland Mycenaean influence (mid-15th-end of 14th century BC).

During the second year of excavating (1901), Evans began to uncover the east slope, exposing another wing (fig. 18) that showed the court on the east side in reality to be a Central Court at the heart of the most massive prehistoric complex uncovered in the Aegean. On this slope, where archaeological deposits were deep, a quarter was uncovered that was a suitable candidate for *Royal* apartments. It was called the *Domestic* or *Residential Quarter* and rose two to three storeys from ground level (fig. 2). Ground level here was some 9 metres below the Central Court since the Minoans had cut into the old Neolithic mound on which the Palace lay and terraced the resulting drop with massive masonry. In fact, the digging began in the middle as excavation proceeded from a corridor on the north side (Corridor of the Bays), so that the excavators alighted on the first landing of the *Grand Staircase* (fig. 23) that gave access to the floors below and above. Although the stairs were in a collapsed state, Evans was able to replace many of the broad gypsum steps in their original position and faithfully to recreate the magisterial descent from the Central Court (figs 24, 26 and 35).

As excavation progressed, a series of rooms were revealed with some walls of the first floor in place if somewhat sunken (fig. 24). In one instance, part of a wall-painting depicting a bull

22

23. *The middle landing of the Grand Staircase of the Residential Quarter during excavation in 1901. The view is from the Corridor of the Bays, which provided access for Evans and his excavators. Oxford, Ashmolean Museum.*

24. *The middle landing of the Hall of the Colonnades before full reconstruction. Note the circular holes where wooden columns once stood. Oxford, Ashmolean Museum.*

23

24

25. The Hall of the Double Axes from the east, after excavation in 1901 with scaffolding in place to reconstruct pier-and-door partitions. Oxford, Ashmolean Museum.

26. The lowest flight of the Grand Staircase with wooden columns reconstructed in concrete.

27. The Queen's Megaron after excavation but before reconstruction. Oxford, Ashmolean Museum.

was found still adhering to the wall of the first floor above the *Hall of the Double Axes* (fig. 25), aptly named after the double-axe sign that appears so abundantly carved on the walls of the west lightwell. This title is more appropriate than *King's Megaron* since we shall continue debating the character of these rooms for many years to come.

The plan of the quarter appears complex, yet is deceptively simple. We know most about the ground floor. The *Grand Staircase* gave access to an airy interior court called the *Hall of the Colonnades* (fig. 24), bordered as it was originally by wooden-columned verandahs or loggias, one of which was decorated with wall-paintings depicting life-size figure-of-eight shields (fig. 28) that were taken down before the palace was finally destroyed. From here, two corridors exited east and south that ultimately emerged facing one another on the north and south sides of the west lightwell of the *Hall of the Double Axes* (figs 25, 32), the focus of the entire complex. The east exit from the *Hall of the Colonnades* led directly to the *Hall of the Double Axes*, while

28. The Hall of the Colonnades, first floor with wall-paintings depicting 'figure-of-eight' shields reconstructed. The wall-painting fragments were actually found dumped down a stairwell to the south-west and were not on the walls of the palace when it was finally destroyed. Oxford, Ashmolean Museum.

29. The hall of the House of the Chancel Screen from the south-east. Evans's use of reinforced concrete for restoration purposes is well illustrated.

30. The clay bath in the bathroom of the Queen's Megaron. Some original spiral wall-paintings can be seen as well as reconstructed fresco to the right.

31. Well-preserved female upper torso and head from the Queen's Megaron. Herakleion, Crete, Archaeological Museum.

32. The much restored – impressively so – Hall of the Double Axes from the southeast. The main structural and load-bearing elements were of wood, giving an impression of lightness. The crucial role of wood in multi-storeyed structures emphasizes how different were Minoan architectural techniques from those employed elsewhere in the Mediterranean in the middle of the 2nd millennium BC.

29

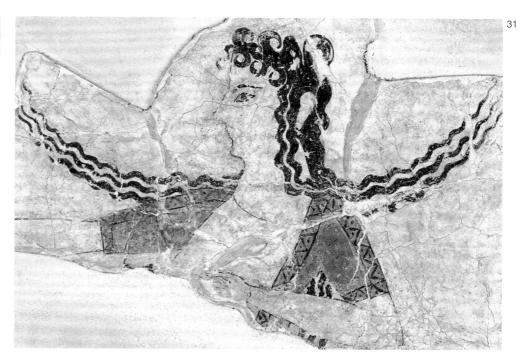

the south exit meandered through smaller apartments, including a bathroom, where an outlet led to the great stone drainage system, and a hall embellished with benches and frescoes, together with a small room that was later (14th century BC) used as a bathroom when the original no longer functioned (fig. 30). This complex has been inappropriately named the *Queen's Megaron* (figs 27, 34), whereas *Hall of the Benches*, though less evocative, could more suitably point to a notable physical attribute. Another corridor (The Dog's Leg Corridor) led from this hall into the *Hall of the Double Axes*.

When Evans found the *Queen's Megaron*, an upper balustrade or room had collapsed, which had been filled with storage vessels of a kind known as a false-necked jar with a

side-spout. These were associated with more Linear B clay tablets, yet scholars still argue over their date, storage vessels being very difficult to date stylistically. In the *Hall of the Double Axes* (figs 25, 32) finds were very few, perhaps not surprising for a grand suite that was the main public reception area. A simple spiral band had been painted on the wall around the room. However, the sense of luxury was imbued by tall gypsum slabs or dadoes acting as veneer on the rubble walls. This was a feature of many of the finer public rooms of the Palace during the 16th-15th centuries BC. Floors too tended to be of polished gypsum, giving a light alabaster sheen to otherwise shady ground-floor rooms.

EVANS AND THE RESTORATION

Evans conducted his most successful restorations in the Residential Quarter, allowing visitors their only chance to experience Minoan design and architecture at its best (figs 26, 28, 32-33). After WW I, Evans and his architects began to use re-enforced concrete, a technological innovation that was particularly useful for flat ceilings; this method can be seen side-by-side with the old barrel-vaulted brick ceilings in the Residential Quarter. A good example that can be examined by visitors today is the partial restoration of the so-called House of the Chancel Screen, to the south of the Residential Quarter (fig. 29). Although re-enforced concrete was innovatory, it is possible to argue that the post-WW I restorations, or 'reconstitutions', as Evans liked to call them, went beyond what was necessary. The restored floors above the Room of the Throne complex (fig. 37) are a case in

33

34

33. *Door in the north side of the Queen's Megaron with stairs leading to the upper storey. The blue rosettes that surround the frame are part of the restoration.*

34. *Watercolour reconstruction of the Queen's Megaron by Piet de Jong. Note that the 'Dolphin Fresco' was found outside to the east and is more likely to have been a floor painting from an upper storey.*

35. *Reconstitution in progress. Evans standing on the Grand Staircase inspecting reconstruction work in the Residential Quarter. Oxford, Ashmolean Museum.*

36. *The façade of the Room of the Throne complex as finally restored in concrete in 1923. The Stepped Portico to the upper floor, or 'piano nobile', is on the left. Oxford, Ashmolean Museum.*

37. The restored light well above the Lustral Basin of the Room of the Throne.

38. The back of the North Entrance Bastion (left) and the restored Northwest Lustral Basin (right). Both these elements dwarf the real archaeological remains of which they formed an integral part.

39. A reconstruction of the raging bull relief that may have adorned the Bastions of the North Entrance Passage, although almost certainly not in this precise form. From C. Bacon, The Great Archaeologists (1976).

40. The Bastion of the North Entrance Passage, restored by Evans and recently re-restored by the Knossos Conservation Office.

37

38

point since the whole represents Evans's 1930 vision of what a façade overlooking the Central Court would have looked like, based on the discovered architecture and representations of architecture in frescoes and the famous faience plaques known as the 'Town Mosaic', probably of the later 16th century BC (fig. 44). Earlier roofing attempts had taken place in 1900 and 1904, neither having in mind the blending of new reconstruction with ancient walling. The recurring question is "did Evans go too far?" There is no absolute answer to this. Unquestionably, the modern ethics of archaeological conservation would never have allowed this relatively irreversible form of reconstruction, an act which obscures important architectural information. On the other hand, Evans rarely attempted full reconstruction, preferring to use what might the called the 'etcetera' principle, which can best be seen in the great North Entrance Passage Bastions (fig. 40). Here Evans restored the west set of bastions, but not those on the east; he restored three full columns in order to preserve the reconstruction of the magnificent relief fresco of a bull (fig. 39) which may or may not have surmounted the bastions. Two other columns were restored as a half and a stub respectively to give the impression of a continuing loggia.

The North Entrance Passage and the Residential Quarter were the most successful attempts to reconstruct, conserve and catch the eye. A disastrous re-enforced concrete structure above the North-West Lustral Basin, the finest of all sunken chambers with chthonic overtones, has the effect of isolating this architectural element from the Minoan Hall system of which it was an integral part, suggesting a public convenience rather than an ancient remain (fig. 38). The restored interior, however, is aesthetically attractive and informative.

The wall-paintings from both the Palace and town of Knossos were the first vivid images presented to the world of the 'new' Minoan civilization. The public could quickly relate to these two dimensional depictions of the people, architecture, flora and fauna of prehistoric Crete. The human figures, in particular, were far more animated than their Egyptian and Near Eastern counterparts. While 'La Parisienne' (c. 1400 BC) (fig. 42), titillated the Edwardians, the more formal Procession Fresco, which originally depicted between 300 and 500 figures taking part in a ceremony,

41. The Cup-bearer, the best preserved male figure in Minoan frescoes. It was one of hundreds of figures depicted in the Procession Fresco from the southwest area of the Palace. 15th c. BC. Herakleion, Crete, Archaeological Museum.

42. 'La Parisienne' is known as an individual painting yet she formed part of the much larger 'Camp-stool Fresco' with many other seated ladies facing each other. It was found in fragments on either side of the west wall of the Palace and dates to its final phases in the 14th c. BC. Herakleion, Crete, Archaeological Museum.

43. The Toreador Fresco from the Court of the Stone Spout. The fragments have been restored to make this single panel when, in fact, they formed a series of panels showing different stages of bull-leaping. Herakleion, Crete, Archaeological Museum.

provoked Egyptian comparisons with the tribute-bearing Keftiu in tomb paintings of the XVIIIth Dynasty. Crete was seen to have played a notable role in the history of the East Mediterranean in the 15th century BC. However, hand-in-hand with history, mythological references to Knossos were brought to life with the discovery of the Bull-leaping frescoes (fig. 43), which evoked memories of the Athenians sacrificed to the Minotaur.

The wall-paintings also provided a more solid basis for Evans's reconstructions at Knossos.

41

42

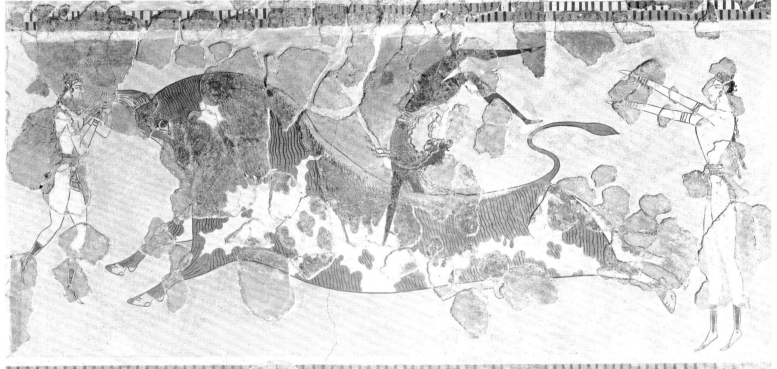

43

The Temple Fresco (fig. 45) may depict the west side of the Central Court with a tripartite Shrine in the middle. It shows architectural details such as 'inverted' wooden columns painted in red ochre, providing firm evidence for the reconstructed columns that are such a feature of the restorations in the Palace. The faience plaques that compose the so-called 'Town Mosaic' (fig. 44) were found in levels dating to the late 18th or early 17th century BC (Middle Minoan IIIA). These early polychrome plaques include illustrations of building façades that reveal structural details in the period immediately before the acme of Minoan palatial architecture, as represented by the Temple Fresco. The plaques show the use of timber for doorways and window frames as well as horizontal beams within walls. These features, combined with the wooden columns, illustrate the lightness of even three-storey structures. These construction methods were suitable in an earthquake prone area such as Crete. No other culture in the East Mediterranean appears to have understood the science of statics and dynamics in architecture so well as the Minoans.

44. Polychrome faience plaques from the so-called 'Town Mosaic'. Evans dated these to around 1700 BC, which may be right since, despite being executed in a polychrome technique, the plaques look artistically earlier than the elaborate faience objects of the Temple Repositories dated to the end of 16th c. BC. The plaques depict architecture, altars, flora and fauna. The architectural plaques and fresco depicting structures (like fig. 45) were useful to Evans and his architects when restoring parts of the palace. Herakleion, Crete, Archaeological Museum.

45. The Temple Fresco was found in fragments in the area of the Early Keep on the northwest side of the Central Court. It depicts, in miniature, a great gathering of men and women in a columned structure, the central element of which is a tripartite structure that may have existed on the west side of the Central Court in the late 16th c. BC and later. Herakleion, Crete, Archaeological Museum.

46. Overleaf, the palace of Minos from the air.

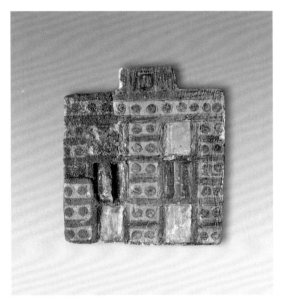

44

45

46

47. Marble statue of Emperor Hadrian now in the garden of the Villa Ariadne. Its discovery in a field to the north led to the excavation of the Roman Villa Dionysos.

48. The Villa Ariadne, designed by Christian Doll and the headquarters of Evans's work at Knossos from 1906. The garden was formally planned in the manner of English gardens although populated by Mediterranean flora.

49. The Roman Villa Dionysos from the northeast just before new wooden protective roofing was erected. The column on the right, with a Corinthian capital, was raised back to its original position in the late 1990's during a season of first aid for the mosaic floors. These have now been covered with protective materials, including pumice, with a view to their future conservation, consolidation and display.

Interestingly, the best illustration of Evans's early techniques in restoration is the Villa Ariadne, the house designed by one of his architects, Christian Doll. Built in 1906, the Villa Ariadne nestles in a planned Edwardian garden and overlooks the Knossos valley with views towards the Palace (fig. 48).

There is a verandah for every hour of the day and bedrooms are in a semi-basement to maintain a cool temperature in summer. This was the 'dig-house' and residence for British archaeologists working at Knossos. The workmen would walk up to the Villa and, amid palms and pine trees, be paid for their week's work.

Evans donated the Villa to the British School of Archaeology at Athens in 1926 and it was used as the German headquarters during WW II. The German surrender in Crete, the last act of the war in Europe, was signed here on 9 May 1945. Later, financial pressures encouraged the School to hand it over to the Ephoreia of Antiquities in the 1950's along with the rest of the land purchased by Sir Arthur. It is fortunate that Evans was a wealthy man who had the foresight to buy so much land in what is now an Alpha Archaeological Zone. The Villa was recently restored by the Greek authorities after years of neglect by both the British and the Greeks, yet the increasingly unstable bedrock of the Knossos valley, due to unchecked drilling for water, continues to be a cause for concern.

50. Central medallion of one of the 2nd c. AD polychrome mosaics depicting Dionysos. The photograph was taken during recent, preliminary conservation works. Major funding is needed to restore all the mosaics so that they can be on display for the public in their original context, the Villa Dionysos.

During Evans's last visit to Knossos in 1935, when his bronze bust was unveiled in the West Court of the Palace (fig. 55), some workmen planting vines on the northern edge of the estate came upon a Roman statue of Emperor Hadrian (fig. 47). Searching for its missing head they uncovered a panel of a polychrome mosaic floor with an image of a peacock. This led to the unexpected discovery of the so-called Villa Dionysos, part of a fine Roman *villa urbana* of the 2nd century AD (fig. 49). Five large reception rooms with magnificent mosaic floors (fig. 50), several of them depicting Dionysos and his followers, were arranged around a peristyle courtyard enclosing a garden with a fountain. The house was destroyed by an earthquake in about AD 200.

North of the palace, on either side of the Kairatos river, were Minoan cemeteries, although none was used before the end of the 15th century BC, when Knossos became involved in an intense, reciprocal relationship with the Argolid that might even have included some form of Mycenaean

49

50

domination. Some of the tombs, whether from the great Zapher Papoura cemetery or that at Sellopoulo or even the more distant Isopata cemetery with its so-called 'Royal Tomb', were very rich in funerary gifts, sometimes displaying a military character that had previously not been seen in Crete. The metal-working skills of the Knossians are elegantly demonstrated by the gold, silver and bronze vessels as well as by the magnificent swords, where gold hilt plates are complemented by the most delicate spiraliform engravings on the hilt and blade.

GOLD RINGS AND STONE-BUILT TOMBS

The Isopata 'Royal Tomb' yielded a fine example of miniaturist art in the form of a gold ring (fig. 52) on which four women in flounced dresses are seen enacting a ritual amidst flowers and fronds as a miniature deity hovers in the air. The gold ring that has recently rekindled interest and controversy is the so-called 'Ring of Minos' (fig. 53), which depicts the most extraordinary array of Minoan religious elements, including the hovering deity seen on the Isopata ring, a goddess seated on a shrine with 'horns of consecration', two tree worshippers, male and female, and a boat ferrying a shrine and altar across water. Apparently found by chance in a vineyard south of the Palace in 1926, this great ring was seen and copied by Evans, rejected as a forgery by Spyridon Marinatos, accepted as genuine by Nikolas Platon, and then lost until it was found and placed on display as genuine in the Herakleion Museum in 2002. Much as the discovery of the statue of Hadrian had led to the discovery of the Villa Dionysos, so the Ring of Minos led to the excavation of the Temple Tomb (fig. 51) just east of the vineyard where the ring had been found. This tomb is so far the only candidate for a royal funerary monument at Knossos. However, when excavated in 1930, no primary burial was discovered as it had been used over a long period (17th-14th centuries BC). Architecturally, it is of the highest quality, with fine ashlar masonry lining the walls of different chambers leading to the original rock-cut and pillared burial chamber. The latest offerings accompanied a disturbed burial made at about the time the Palace of Minos and its Linear B administration were engulfed in final flames.

Evans died in 1941 over a decade before it was discovered that the Linear B script was used to write a very ancient form of Greek on the administrative clay tablets. Discoveries continue although Evans

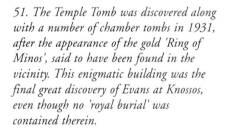

51. The Temple Tomb was discovered along with a number of chamber tombs in 1931, after the appearance of the gold 'Ring of Minos', said to have been found in the vicinity. This enigmatic building was the final great discovery of Evans at Knossos, even though no 'royal burial' was contained therein.

51

uncovered the jewel in the crown. Excavation by the British School has been sporadic yet focussed, each new investigation having specific aims in mind. The town of Minoan Knossos was large with a maximum of 18,000 inhabitants – far less than supposed by Evans, yet large in prehistoric terms. Highlights of the discoveries since Evans include the "exploration" of the "Unexplored Mansion" next to Evans's Little Palace, deep soundings by the Royal Road to clarify Minoan stratigraphy from 3000 BC onwards, excavation of a sector of the town where modest houses yielded evidence for ritual and human sacrifice, as well as the author's own excavations where the earliest written clay tablet (ca. 1800 BC) was found in a house on the terraced slopes of the palace hill.

52

It is this prehistoric Knossos that holds our imagination and it is due to Sir Arthur Evans and other early pioneers, both Greek and foreign, that the Bronze Age of Crete has shaken off the chains of later mythology to become a true prelude to the history of Greece. Knossos is less labyrinthine than it was but still holds many secrets for archaeologists of the coming centuries to discover.

53

I am very grateful to SARA PATON for comments on the first draft of this contribution.

52. The Isopata gold ring came from a fine built tomb to the north of the Palace. It depicts women attending a priestess or goddess with a male deity descending. (16th/15th c. BC). Herakleion, Crete, Archaeological Museum.

53. The integrity of the gold 'Ring of Minos', considered by many to have been a fake, has been restored and it is now on display in the Archaeological Museum of Herakleion, Crete, having been missing for many years. (14th c. BC). Herakleion, Crete, Archaeological Museum.

54. Evans during his last visit to Knossos in 1935. Oxford, Ashmolean Museum.

55. Bronze bust of Sir Arthur J. Evans in the West Court at Knossos. It was unveiled in 1935 during his last visit to the site. The ceremony was attended by the young Stylianos Alexiou, who remains a doyen of Cretan studies, including prehistoric Crete.

54   55

George Ch. Chourmouziadis

Sesklo and Dimini
The prehistoric citadels

J *ust as Denmark formed a notable museum of the Stone Age, Greece, too, may create one like it.* *Any expense on such a project would be not only justified, but even essential, a sacred obligation to our self-respect. Greece, a weak state, cannot rest its future hopes anywhere else but on the intellectual development of the entire nation. Through this it will one day succeed in winning the affection of the great scientific family of mankind, which is the dominant family and imposes its views on policy. If modern Greece, which used to be regarded only as a treasury of the fine arts and the golden ages of human civilisation, succeeds through the achievements and study of its children in providing information of similar certainty about the prehistoric period, we may believe that it has, in the eyes of the wise world, acquired new rights to its affection and respect* ('A Prehistoric Pompeii', newsp. *Eon,* no. 2496, 20.10.1869: 1-2*).*

THE CHRONICLE AND THE QUESTIONS

'Greece, a weak state' had to seek for its European identity, its 'conflicting' potentialities, as we would say today, 'in the intellectual development of the entire nation,' according to the leader of the newspaper *Eon* in October 1869. And it would achieve this, in the view of the anonymous columnist 137 years ago, by 'providing information, of similar certainty, about the prehistoric period.' This view of the importance of 'information about the prehistoric period' to 'the intellectual development of the entire nation' does not seem to have persuaded the then immature modern Greek state to devise and implement a concrete policy that would include the investigation of prehistoric sites, which had not at that time begun to be destroyed by the farming and building activities of modern Greek farmers and stock-raisers. It was undoubtedly this lack of specific investigation in the sphere of prehistory, combined with the negative views that circulated in relation to such research, that led one of the greatest Greek prehistorians, D.R. Theocharis, just before his death in 1977, to formulate a view that was very bold for the time: 'Today, there is a general conviction,' he wrote, 'that Prehistory is an essential part of the History of Mankind, and even that there is no real difference between them, nor even a clear dividing line. Both have human activity as the object of investigation.' This view, referring to the need to develop prehistoric research in Greece, just as in other small, 'weak' European states, was expressed roughly a hundred years after the publication of the *Eon* article. It has still not been accepted by 'official' Greek archaeology, which accordingly, as it carries out its investigations and transfers the conclusions of these investigations to the area of Greek education, whether organised or not, inclines to the theoretical position that prehistory is 'one thing' and history 'another.' According to this approach, the former forms the object of a different theory and a different method, based on the description of 'things,' and not on the search for and interpretation of causes of these 'things' and the people who invented them, made them and used them. As for the latter, it is the research object of an activity that does not need a specific theory, and perhaps not even a method, but only a specialised 'vision' that facilitates the description and dating of art objects. This approach has led to the strict separation of prehistoric archaeology from the archaeology of historical times, as fields with a different scientific interest. It has also prevented the proper evaluation of the findings of the first prehistoric excavations carried out in Greece, which yielded the first 'information' so valued by the *Eon* columnist, and which, without exaggeration, laid the foundations of prehistoric investigation in Greece.

The point of reference here was, of course, the excavations conducted by Chr. Tsountas (fig. 1) at

1. Christos Tsountas, the first excavator of the Neolithic settlements at Sesklo and Dimini.

2. The low hill ('Toumba') on which the settlement of Dimini was discovered, photographed at the beginning of the 20th century. In the middle can be seen the opening of the Mycenaean tholos tomb, the location of which led V. Stais to discover the remains of the Neolithic settlement. From Chr. Tsountas, Αι προϊστορικαί ακροπόλεις Διμηνίου και Σέσκλου (Athens 1908).

3. The archaeological site of Sesklo, photographed at the beginning of the 20th century. The Neolithic settlement of Sesklo was discovered on the Kastraki Hill and is not a 'typical' Thessalian Neolithic site, consisting of a tumulus in a flat plain. From Chr. Tsountas, Αι προϊστορικαί ακροπόλεις Διμηνίου και Σέσκλου (Athens 1908).

3

Dimini and Sesklo (figs 2-6) at the beginning of the 20th century – though the first news of the location of the tholos tomb that led to the excavations at Dimini was published in the newspaper *Neai Ideai* in May 1882. 'At Dimini,' said *Neai Ideai*, 'a tomb has been discovered that is said closely to resemble those at Mycenae.' Schliemann's excavations and the well-known structures and portable finds thus brought to light had made Mycenaean civilisation famous. The discovery, therefore, of a similar tomb at Dimini near Volos attracted the attention of the Archaeological Society, which decided to carry out a systematic excavation in the area with the aim, and of course the secret hope, of uncovering the Mycenae of the north. Of locating, in other words, a second important centre of Mycenaean civilisation, which was thought by scholars of the time to be the earliest mainland Greek civilisation. In 1882, of course, Volos and the surrounding area had only just been liberated from the Turks, and it would have been difficult to organise an excavation of this kind along the scientific principles followed at the time. The programme of the Archaeological Society was therefore confined initially, in 1887, to excavating the tholos tomb, and systematic excavations did not take place at Dimini until 1901. This is clear from a statement made by Ch. Tsountas: 'The Ephor of Antiquities, Valerios Stais,' writes Tsountas, 'discovered a second tholos tomb, which he excavated in 1901.' 'After the excavation of this,' he goes on, 'he continued his investigations on the hill, hoping to find one or more similar tombs, instead of which, there appeared the remains of a prehistoric citadel. […] Stais at once saw the importance of these remains, and worked zealously to uncover them. […] But since he was occupied elsewhere for the next two years and was unable to visit Thessaly in person to resume the excavation, I undertook to complete it in the summer of 1903.'

The information provided by Tsountas, of course, is not confined to the excavations at Dimini. It relates also to those that were carried out at the same period in the equally important prehistoric settlement of Sesklo, which had already been visited about 1880 by Leake and Lolling. Leake, indeed, identified the stone ruins of the prehistoric settlement as the remains of the historical city of Aisonia. In connection with this, Tsountas writes in the second chapter of his book on his excavations at Sesklo and Dimini: 'After Leake and Lolling, Stais visited Kastraki (Sesklo) while excavating at Dimini in 1901 and ascertained that its citadel belonged to the same Stone Age. On his recommendation, I also visited the place in this year. […] The uncovering of the ruins began immediately, that is, in 1901, but was completed the following summer.'

It is my view that this information supplied by Tsountas is not merely historical comment on the pioneering excavations at the two important prehistoric settlements of Dimini and Sesklo. It also raises problems and questions. One of these problems, for example, is related to the role played in these particular excavations by Stais, who, while 'seeing' the importance of the archaeological remains at both these sites, did not show any interest in 'resuming' their investigation, and assigned this task to

4. To construct settlements, Neolithic men used materials that could be found in abundance in the surrounding area. In this photograph, taken at the beginning of the 20th century, can be seen part of the stone foundations of the defence wall of Dimini, with the modern settlement, also stone-built, in the background. From Chr. Tsountas, Αι προϊστορικαί ακροπόλεις Διμηνίου και Σέσκλου (Athens 1908).

5

6

5, 6. Photographs taken at the beginning of the 20th century showing part of the stone foundations of the settlement of Dimini. The foundations of the buildings and the defence walls of the two Neolithic settlements were made of stone up to the height of about a metre, while the rest of the superstructure consisted of unbaked bricks.
From Chr. Tsountas, Αι προϊστορικαί ακροπόλεις Διμηνίου και Σέσκλου (Athens 1908).

Tsountas. These problems may be merely minor formalities in the course of an exciting history, but they nevertheless bring to the surface issues directly connected with the conditions under which archaeological investigation is conducted – investigation that is formed as the result of questions that are just as interesting as the problems. One such question: How could two prehistoric settlements of such importance be excavated almost completely in the space of three years and under the pressure of the fearful Thessalian summer? And another: How did the society of the area react to so pioneering an excavation, the results of which would shed light on the first European civilisation? Naturally, neither problems nor questions diminish deeds accomplished under adverse conditions. On the contrary, they enhance the heroism of those who carry them through to completion, without the moral or practical support of any precedent for such investigation. And it is a fact that the excavations at Dimini and Sesklo were without precedent and may therefore be regarded as great moments in Greek archaeology. It is in this light that we should view the excavations of D.R. Theocharis at Sesklo (1956-1972) and of the undersigned at Neolithic Dimini (1975-1977). These excavations had as a precedent the findings of Stais and Tsountas and, in the case of the former, sought to set the Sesklo finds, as archaeological material of historical significance, in the context of the debate that had developed in the meantime. This debate was devoted not only to prehistoric research in Greece, but also to the answers to a number of basic questions, concerning: (a) the circumstances of the transition from the hunter-gatherer stage of the Palaeolithic-Mesolithic to the farming stage of the Neolithic; (b) the origins of the relevant changes in Greece, in particular, permanent residences, domestication of crops and animals, consequent development of farming and stock-raising, and manufacture of clay vessels,

that is, did these things originate in Greece, or, did they imitate much earlier similar developments in the Middle East, as has been asserted by the supporters of the theory of Diffusionism, particularly G. Childe as early as the 1930s; (c) the study of the character of the preceramic period (which had already been identified stratigraphically by Miloijic at Argissa), with reference to its autonomy as a cultural horizon; and (d) the study of intra-community organisation in connection with the birth and evolution of the architectural features of the settlement.

In the excavations at Dimini (1975-1977), the undersigned essayed a new interpretation, based on archaeological and theoretical observations, of the intra-community functioning of the settlement, and particularly the 'enclosures' of Dimini, seen as design elements of the settlement, rather than as defensive features, as they were described by Tsountas.

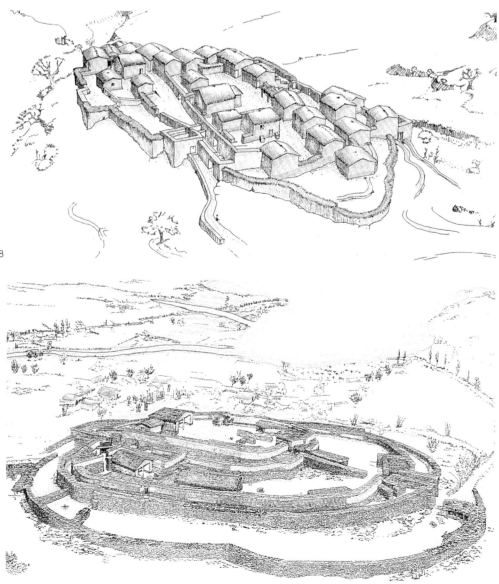

10. Dimini from above. The main courtyard and part of the enclosure walls that bounded the activities of Neolithic households.

THE FINDS

According to the view that was once widely held (and can still be found today), not only amongst the general public, but also within the archaeological community, the evaluation of an excavation-archaeological find is based not on the importance of the information it provides, nor the social and historical significance of which it is the conduit, but on details of its physical dimensions, such as its size, the intrinsic value of the materials of which it is made, and its aesthetic perfection, judged by the aesthetic standards of the person studying or evaluating it. For this very reason, finds from pre-historic excavations are still today not regarded as notable in the current view of archaeologists and others. They are treated simply as the products of humble need, not as creations of 'high' inspiration. I could argue, then, that this view is the reason why prehistoric collections in Greek archaeological museums are not the object of any special museological attention. They are usually kept in store-rooms inside wretched boxes. There is, of course, a tendency to rectify this situation. The enrich-ment of archaeological theory and the grounding of its interpretative schemata on the findings and methods of anthropology have led to acceptance of the view that archaeological finds are primarily important sources of information, irrespective of their size and the material of which they are made. It would be no exaggeration to assert that a carbonised vegetable (fig. 11) is a find. A significant number of carbonised figs found at Dimini with a hole in their centre furnish important information about to the efforts of the people of the period to meet their dietary needs using methods that are still current.

Nevertheless, quite apart from the theories and particular formal evaluations, the finds made during the excavations at Dimini and Sesklo are interesting for the information they provide about the economy, the technological expertise of the people of the time, and the social organisation of the Neolithic period. Tsountas himself, while believing that the findings of his excavations "still leave many problems and doubts regarding the details, which, of course, will be resolved by fresh excavations and observations," did not hesitate to reach the conclusion, regarding the excavations carried out at Dimini and Sesklo, that "the results of their work were unexpectedly rich. For they uncovered a wealth of remains of stone structures and defensive enclosures, and a large number of stone and bone tools, clay vases, clay and stone figurines and other things, from which emerges a thriving and occasionally paradoxically advanced civilisation." It is this conclusion that makes me believe that the excavations at Dimini and Sesklo should be described as 'great moments in Greek archaeology' not on account of their extent or the place they occupy in the history of the investigation of European prehistory, but because, on the basis of the importance of the finds, Tsountas spoke of a 'thriving' and 'advanced' civilisation, describing, albeit indirectly, a cultural region to which archaeological research ought to turn its attention, and thus founding a special branch of it. A branch that, it should not be forgotten, has as the object of its investigation the roots and foundations of Greek civilisation. A branch, too, that has been systematically developed in the other Balkan countries and has yielded notable finds and important information regarding the birth and dissemination of Neolithic civilisation in Europe.

This conclusion not only gives expression to a generalised view of the culture revealed by Tsountas's excavations. It also contains elements that help us to compile the table of contents that describes the

11

kind of finds made in the two great excavations in Magnesia. Naturally, I cannot discuss these finds in detail within the confines of this article. Nor do I believe that such detailed descriptions of artefacts are still of interest to the general public: indeed, they tend to alienate it.

It is the established practice, not only in the bibliography of the field, but also amongst the general public interested in archaeology, to assign Sesklo to the Early (6500-5800 BC) and Middle (5800-4800 BC) Neolithic and Dimini to the Late Neolithic (4800-4300 BC), in keeping with the initial assessment of the excavator, who writes: "Kastraki (Sesklo) was occupied a long time – probably centuries – before Dimini"; the finds from the site are, of course, also included in this chronological system, with the basic objective of finding, identifying and interpreting the differences in the material. An objective which, in the case of serious scholars, is not confined to a description of the finds and an account of their morphology, but extends to a search for the causes behind the differences, which are connected with the transition from one cultural period to the next. I shall not follow this approach. I shall not refer to these differences. Nor shall I seek for an interpretation for them, because I do not believe that differences in shape, size, material of construction, or, finally, the simple decorative motifs, are related, in any case, to transitions from one cultural period to another. I prefer to attribute these changes to deliberate, or occasionally accidental, inspirations on the part of the 'manufacturers', in their efforts to serve basic human needs, such as housing, exploitation of the environment, nutrition, personal protection against natural phenomena, social organisation, and the management of fear in general. To those endeavours, that is to say, which are expressed in different ways on different occasions, by every human being and in every place, at one point in time or another, and that form the content of the unified global civilisation. Cultural periods, their chronological termini, and the desperate attempt to identify and describe characteristics and models, types and categories, are 'inspirations' of scholars, deliberate devices that ultimately form a closed language and therefore alienate from their otherwise interesting accounts all those who speak a different language – the language of everyday life.

On the basis of an approach of roughly this kind, it is my view that the finds brought to light by the excavations at Dimini and Sesklo should not be assigned to categories, groups, types or chronological systems, but should be regarded as functional elements of human activity, as D.R. Theocharis wrote. The activity of the people who lived in these two important settlements 8000 years ago, and who succeeded, through their own thought and their own acts, in producing a 'thriving,' 'advanced' culture – in Tsountas's assessment – a culture that is also part of the global culture of mankind. However, in order to make this article easier to read, I shall simply classify the finds in question in four large groups. It is in these that, if one had the interest, one might locate the differences and all those features that reveal the ingenuity of Man and his creative relationship with the objective world, which may be stone, fire, clay, bone, hunger, birth and death!

11. Finds from Dimini. Carbonised corn, scythe for reaping, grinding tool, etc. Volos, Archaeological Museum.

12. Neolithic 'grill supports.' Athens, National Archaeological Museum.

12

The houses uncovered at Sesklo and Dimini were built of stone slabs (fig. 14), with a limited use of mortar and timber. They had pitched roofs (fig. 15); some of them consisted of a single room, and others of two or three. The latter are called *megara* (fig. 14) and various theories and some simple questions have been formulated regarding their function and the place of their origins. The major question is whether *megara*, as an architectural idea, came from the East, or whether it belongs to the 'western tradition.' And also: who lived in them? Was it the ruler of the settlement? The wealthiest man? The one who had the largest family? It is true that a house as impressive as this inevitably raises questions, but a more important truth concerns the existence of *megara* over the centuries, for they are not found only in the Neolithic period. *Megara* were also built in Mycenaean times, as residences of the kings of Mycenae, rich in gold, and in the Classical period, as imposing temples of the gods of Mount Olympos. *Megara*, however, are also the structural basis for Byzantine basilicas and many of the modern churches that imitate them. There is a view, of course, based on the excavation record, that men and animals lived in the same

13

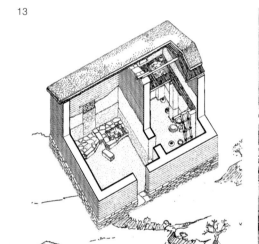

15

14

room in Neolithic houses, though at Dimini and Sesklo ancillary rooms have been discovered which may have been stables, workshops, storerooms or ovens.

If we add enclosures to the simple and complex houses, huts and *megara*, it may be claimed without exaggeration that, taken together, enclosures and residences, ancillary areas and *megara*, courtyards and narrow streets, and the impressive nature of the material used to build all these, compose an imposing picture that reflects a striking early approach to the organisation and use of an inhabited site, based on the needs of the people who live in it. This precise observation led me to the view that Dimini and Sesklo were not simply well-fortified settlements, but two sites excellently organised on the basis of a "thriving" and "advanced" approach to town-planning!

SECOND GROUP: THE VASES

Vases, as we know, are assigned to the more general category of pottery, which forms the largest category of excavation finds. Every excavation yields whole pots and also tens of thousands of sherds which may, with careful, painstaking work, also produce whole pots, the shape and structural details of which provide important evidence that would have escaped us amidst the multitude of thousands of sherds. At Dimini and at Sesklo, a large number of whole pots has come to light (figs 16, 17), along with many thousands of sherds. This material has, unfortunately, not yet been published and this is not the place for the "of necessity very long" discussion of them, to which Tsountas refers. "Amongst the finds," he writes, "the first place is occupied by the vases, both on account of their number and on account of their other significance. Consequently, the discussion of these will, of necessity, be very long."

First of all, it should be noted that the vases found at Sesklo and Dimini are characterised by an astonishing variety of shapes, which means that they served a large number of uses. For the purposes of study, all these shapes have their own names, still used by pottery experts: *lekanis, phiale, kypello,*

16

16. Closed painted vase from Dimini, Late Neolithic. Athens, National Archaeological Museum.

17. Incised vases of the Late Neolithic. Volos, Archaeological Museum.

17

skyphos... The second observation that obliged Tsountas to divide the vases brought to light by his excavations is that the Sesklo-Dimini vases are either monochrome or decorated. The monochrome pots have a red, dark or light brown, and in some cases white or black surface. This colour variety is due to a combination of the quality of the clay and the temperature at which it was fired. A combination that does not appear to have been, at least in the beginning, an aesthetic choice on the part of the potter. As for the decorated vases, their motifs are executed in light-coloured paint applied to a dark surface, or vice versa (painted vases) (fig. 16), or are incised (incised wares) (fig. 17). Finally, it should be noted that the quality, particularly of the vases from Sesklo, with their flammiform, geometric and freely drawn decorative motifs, led to the establishment of the term 'Sesklo culture', which undoubtedly reflects Tsountas's description of it as 'thriving' and 'advanced.'

THIRD GROUP: THE TOOLS

The tools found at Sesklo and Dimini, not only in Ch. Tsountas's excavations but also in those of other excavators, are made mainly of stone (fig. 19). Those of bone, however, are no fewer in number, followed by those made of clay (fig. 18). Naturally both Tsountas and other scholars sought to classify the Neolithic tools in categories based mainly on the way in which they were manufactured and the purpose for which they were intended. In my opinion, the information deriving from one of these categories, that of use, is the more important. This information reveals that the farmers/stock-raisers of Sesklo and Dimini invented and manufactured tools with which they could meet all the daily needs of their mixed economy. Tools, that is, with which they cut, dug, struck, ground, melted, smoothed, polished, made holes, sewed, killed. Depending on these uses, one can recognised in these tools, adzes, chisels, awls, axes, grinders and so on.

FOURTH GROUP: THE FIGURINES

Figurines are an archaeological material that is attended by endless debate, focused on establishing their function. What purpose did they serve, these mysterious statuettes, dozens of which were found complete at Sesklo and Dimini, depicting male (fig. 24) and female figures (fig. 22), houses, furniture (fig. 23), animals, and foodstuffs, and which are sometimes made in a meticulous, almost naturalistic manner (fig. 23) and sometimes hastily or with a deliberately extreme stylisation (fig. 24)? Many have claimed that the female figurines represent the Great Mother (Magna Mater), Mother

18

19

20

21

18. Neolithic clay bobbins and spindlewhorls. Volos, Archaeological Museum.

19. Silex tools. Volos, Archaeological Museum.

20. Obsidian blades and cores. Volos, Archaeological Museum.

21. Reconstructions of stone axes. Volos, Archaeological Museum.

Earth. The goddess of fertility, in other words. They were therefore elements of 'religious' belief, a functional part of cult worship. Others have asserted that they are toys, others that they were objects of initiation, and others still that they formed part of a primitive communication system. According to this last view, they were a kind of proto-script. Let us assume that the female figurines depict the Great Mother. What about the male figurines? The charming little animals, tables, houses, spoons? What did they represent? I therefore prefer to follow the last interpretation: Neolithic people used figurines to communicate, to send and receive messages –that is, to 'write'!

EPILOGUE

Sesklo and Dimini were not two major excavations that yielded large numbers of interesting finds. Nor were they simply a 'great moment' in Greek archaeology. They revealed to us an inexhaustible 'small, yet large world,' as the poet would have said. They truly revealed to us a 'thriving' and 'advanced' culture: the Neolithic culture, the roots and foundations of the Greek culture!

22. Female figurine ('kourotrophos') from Dimini. Athens, National Archaeological Museum.

23. Tiny clay furniture and vessels from Sesklo. Volos, Archaeological Museum.

24. Seated male figurines from Sesklo. Volos, Archaeological Museum.

22

23

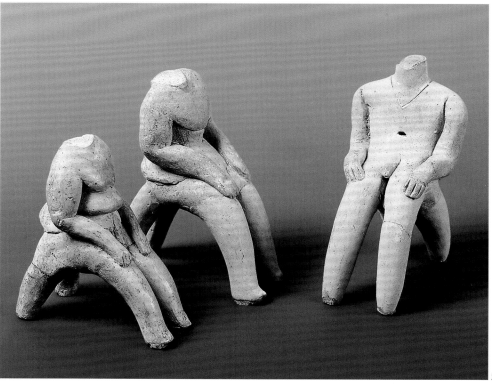

24

Alberto G. Benvenuti

Poliochni on Lemnos
The earliest city in Europe

Although the excavation of Poliochni on Lemnos is not widely known, the discovery of the first settlement of urban character in Europe is indeed one of the great moments of Greek archaeology. The Italian Archaeological School at Athens, which conducts excavations on Lemnos, was founded on 9 May 1909, as successor to the Italian Archaeological Mission on Crete, the most important activities of which were the excavations of Gortyn and the Minoan Palace at Phaistos.

The idea of excavating on Lemnos was born in 1923, based on Della Seta's wish to clarify the culture of the Tyrrhenians, a non-Hellenic people whose name and language were connected with those of the Etruscans in the Italian peninsula, and who seem to have dwelt on Lemnos and neighbouring Imbros before these islands were captured by the Athenians in about 500 BC. It was at this time, indeed, that the theory of the eastern origins of the Etruscans was widely discussed, based on the theory of their Lydian descent, guaranteed by the authority of Herodotus. The archaeologists at that time believed that the island might preserve traces of the passage of the Etruscans on their way from the East.

The excavation permit, the request for which was submitted immediately after the investigation of 1923, was long delayed. It was not to arrive until 10 August 1925: over ten years had elapsed since the unification of Lemnos with motherland Greece, and about five from the appointment of the new director. This was the fifth archaeological mission of the School: in 1930, a detailed surface survey began in the area around the village of Kaminia, where, in 1886, a stele dating from the 6th century BC had been found bearing the relief figure of a warrior, surrounding which were inscriptions that resembled the Etruscan inscriptions of Italy (fig. 1). The most important and encouraging result of this investigation was the location of a prehistoric city on the hill of Poliochni, a few kilometres to the east of Kaminia. The hill dominates the wide bay of Vroskopo on the east coast of the island, a distance of about 40 nautical miles from the coast of Asia Minor, opposite the entrance to the Hellespont.

1

There thus began an intense, very interesting period in which, during six excavation seasons, Della Seta, the scholar of Classical antiquity, who nevertheless had the precision of the prehistoric archaeologist with regard to stratigraphic investigation, uncovered one of the earliest proto-urban settlements in Europe. The settlement, or at least its main phases, dates from the Early Bronze Age in the north Aegean, and its complex architectural and cultural development covers the whole of the 3rd millennium BC (fig. 2).

The discoveries relating to the most important architectural structures occurred in 1934. In this year, a section came to light that was identified at once with the fortifications of the settlement, considered to be the most important defence work in the entire Aegean (fig. 3). The so-called *bouleuterion* was also excavated, an open-air structure with steps on the long sides, which is believed to have been a place for public gatherings (fig. 4). Excavation then began of the equally interesting large area next to the bouleuterion, which became known in the bibliography as the city 'granary'. After the

1. The stele found at Kaminia with inscriptions that resemble Etruscan lettering. Athens, National Archaeological Museum.

2. Aerial photograph of the ruins of the settlement at Poliochni.

2

1937 season, the excavations at Poliochni were suspended, having uncovered only three fifths of the total area of the settlement.

It was not until the beginning of the 1950s that Doro Levi, then director of the School, decided to resume the work, planning to publish everything that had been uncovered. The task was assigned to Luigi Bernabò Brea, who, as a student of the School, had taken part in the excavations at Poliochni in 1935-36 and had become an authority in the field of prehistoric archaeology. The first season took place in 1951, but it was the season of 1956 that began with an unexpected discovery: during the clearing of vegetation from the area of the excavation, a jewellery hoard came to light in one of the rooms of the megaron of the Yellow Period that had been discovered in 1953 (fig. 5); this hoard greatly resembled the so-called 'Treasure of Priam' discovered by Schliemann in the second city at Troy. After the end of the work of this year, the small hoard was taken to the National Archaeological Museum in Athens, where it is still on display.

When the Myrina Museum was inaugurated on 20 April 1964, Luigi Bernabò Brea's mission was complete. With the publication of the first volume on the excavation, devoted to the early and middle phases of Poliochni in 1964, and the sec-

3

3. Archaeologists and workmen on the excavation just after the discovery of the first section of the fortification walls of Poliochni in 1934. Italian Archaeological School at Athens.

4. The bouleuterion, a rectangular building with steps on the long sides, has been interpreted as a place for gatherings of the most important inhabitants of Poliochni.

5. Jewellery from the prehistoric hoard found at Poliochni in 1956. Athens, National Archaeological Museum.

4

ond, concerning the Poliochni of the Yellow Period, in 1976, the mission of the Italian Archaeological School in Athens was also complete. There followed a long period of silence until 1987. In this year, Santo Tiné, professor at Genoa University, embarked on a programme of interventions, initially aimed at the restoration of the great enclosure wall, which was on the point of collapse; in recent years, he has been preparing the final publication of the excavation.

THE IMPORTANCE OF POLIOCHNI

Poliochni, the geographical location of which on the sea route between the islands and the Asia Minor coast, made it a safe haven for sea communications between North and South, was occupied as early as the Late Neolithic, about 3700 BC. From the end of the 4th millennium, however, it experienced rapid development, and already at the beginning of the 3rd it had acquired the first features of a proto-urban centre. For the first time on European soil we encounter specialisation and division of labour, and communal works – majestic fortifications, paved roads and squares, a drainage network, a communal granary, and a building for gatherings. All these presuppose planning and social organisation, hinting at a primitive form of urban formation. Poliochni, then, may be placed at the interface between the civilised world of the East, where the urban revolution had already taken place, and Europe, where the phenomenon of this kind of proto-urban organisation had not yet made its appearance. In fact, Poliochni may be described as the earliest city in Europe.

What were the factors contributing to this? It appears to have been due to the importance of the island to the importing and processing of metals, at a period when these played the most important role in the evolution of civilisation. The geographical location of Poliochni, directly opposite the straits of the Hellespont, accounts for its relations with areas around the Black Sea and explains its rapid development with regard to the importing and distribution of metals. The archaeological evidence attests not only to the use of metals, but also to their being worked locally, despite the fact that the island produced no raw materials. Physical and chemical analyses and mining exploration have ruled out the areas of Asia Minor and the Balkans as the provenance of the raw materials used in the northeast Aegean, and the metals and related technical expertise seem to have been imported from

5

the distant shores of the Black Sea. It is no coincidence that the region of the Caucasus, where metal-working is known much earlier than in the Aegean, is frequently connected with Greek myths. It was in the Caucasus that Prometheus was chained to the rock because he had given human beings fire, the primary element used in metal-working. The myth of the Argonaut expedition also reflects the first endeavours of the inhabitants of the Aegean to acquire the technical expertise required for metal-working. It should not be forgotten that the objective of Jason's campaign to Colchis was an object made of metal – the golden fleece. Moreover, in ancient mythology, Lemnos played a leading part in metal-working, since it was on the island that the first metal-worker, one of the Olympian gods, Hephaistos, had his workshop, followed later by his children or grand-children, the Kabeiroi.

It is therefore reasonable to suppose that the economy, and therefore the importance of Poliochni, was based on this early involvement with metals and maritime commercial activity. Both were the fruit of the collective work of a population of about a thousand inhabitants, organised in a society, while the bouleuterion, which may be interpreted as an early form of ancient agora, points to a kind of collective exercise of authority. The digging of wells up to 9 m. deep and lined with masonry, the construction and maintenance of fortification walls, roads and a system of pipes to collect rainwater, the paving of squares and roads, were decisions that required unanimity on the part of the community and a space in which people debated and came to agreement. Obviously, the bouleuterion was not a meeting place for elected officials of the people, but probably simply for representatives of each family,

perhaps the older men, who were regarded as the most suitable to take decisions. It was a society of equals that practised the simplest, early form of democracy.

Poliochni, along with Troy and Therme on Lesbos, is one of the few sites that have been sufficiently excavated to permit some estimation of the degree of urban infrastructure attained by the populations of the northeast Aegean in the Early Bronze Age. The earliest settlement, which consists of 16 levels with oval huts, has been called the Black Period (about 3700-3200 BC). Above this phase extended a large settlement with houses of rectangular plan, the so-called Blue Period (about 3200-2700 BC). This is followed by another two called the Green (about 2700-2400 BC) and Red Periods (about

2400-2200 BC). The phase of the settlement which is best known from the point of view of its architecture, and visible over a large area, is that of the Yellow Period (about 2200-2100 BC). This undoubtedly represents a phase of contraction, which was to continue until the end of the Bronze Age; nevertheless, the technological progress made in pottery (fabric without inclusions) and the discovery of the small 'hoard' of jewellery point to significant development in the technological and economic spheres.

The period of time with the greatest area of settlement corresponds with the Green, and possibly also the Red, Period. These building phases are almost successive and reach the greatest limits of the settlement area: new zones were created by the construction of stout terraces that could be linked together by defence works, the superstructure of which was made of bricks and not stones. It is interesting that the only room in which axes and spear-heads have been found dates from the Red Period. The settlement of these two periods occupied an area of about 13,900 m², with a population reckoned to have been 1,300-1,400 inhabitants. All this must have happened at the same time that a section of the inhabitants of Kum Tepe moved to the hill of Hissarlik and built the first enclosure wall around Troy; probably at this same period, Poliochni was transformed from a peace-loving village enjoying commercial relations with mainland Greece, as is attested by the abundance of imported pottery found in the levels of the Blue Period, into a kind of 'acropolis' defended by fortification walls against the pirate raids that had begun in the north Aegean as a consequence of the intense commercial seafaring activities of the inhabitants of the Cyclades.

6. View of megaron 605 from the north. At the right are the storerooms with large vases.

7. This large vase with two high lug-handles and a tall conical body is a characteristic find from Poliochni. Athens, National Archaeological Museum.

8. The interior of the 'temple' with two skeletons on the floor. Italian Archaeological School at Athens.

8

In the following, Yellow, period, the settlement can be seen to have contracted, and was now confined to a strip along the road leading from the central to the north square. The most characteristic building of the period is the one known as megaron 605 (fig. 6), the owner of which was probably the last ruler of Poliochni. Poliochni was abandoned about 2100 BC, possibly as a result of a terrible earthquake that damaged it irreparably. Moving testimony to this is provided by the two human skeletons found buried beneath the ruins of a large building (fig. 8), which, since it stood isolated in the square, may be regarded as a temple. After this time the entire settlement fell into oblivion. A few traces, however, attest to the fairly sporadic use of the site during the 2nd millennium BC.

Panos Valavanis

The Athenian Agora
Encounter with the first democracy

If the Athenian democracy represents one of the most important moments in the history of civilisation, the Ancient Agora of Athens is, without doubt, one of the most important archaeological sites in the world. For it was the place that democracy was born and functioned on a daily basis, the centre of the political, religious, juridical, economic, educational and cultural life of the ancient city of Athens. (fig. 2).

One hundred and fifty years of investigation have been required to uncover the monuments associated with the birth and practice of the world's first democracy. Over the last seventy-five years, the most productive, the excavations in the Agora have been conducted by the American School of Classical Studies. For the investigations to begin, 365 houses to the northwest of the Acropolis, which formed the neighbourhoods of Ayioi Apostoloi, Vlassarou, and Ayios Philippos, were expropriated. American devotees of ancient Greece, numerous foundations, and hundreds of named and anonymous donors contributed to the collection of the funds required for the expropriations, excavation, restoration work, conservation of the finds, and, of course, publication.

The excavations and the scientific labour of researchers have led to the discovery so far of over of 100 buildings, hundreds of statues, 7,500 inscriptions, 80,000 coins and 100,000 finds of all kinds. The careful study of these, when combined with the statements of the ancient authors (of which we have a greater number than for any other site in the Classical world), has enriched our knowledge, not only of ancient Athens, but of the whole of the ancient Greek world.

1. Panoramic view of Athens from the Pnyx Hill about 1895. The site of the Athenian Agora, in the area between the Theseion and the Acropolis, is covered with houses.

2. Panoramic view of the Ancient Agora from the west. The political, economic and cultural centre of the ancient city was created on a level area between the hills of the Acropolis and the Areopagos, on the right, and the hill of Kolonos Agoraios (Theseion), on the bottom.

1

2

THE FIRST EXCAVATIONS

The excavation of the ancient city of Athens was one of the first concerns of newly formed Greek state. In the first town plan, drawn up by the architects Kleanthis and Schaubert in 1834, provision was made for the expropriation of the entire area north of the Acropolis, in order to make possible its excavation in the future. The scanty finances of the state, however, and the prevailing circumstances did not allow for the implementation of this plan (fig. 1, 3).

An idea of the difficulties encountered by the expropriations required to reveal the ancient monuments is given by the General Secretary of the Archaeological Society of Athens, St. A. Koumanoudis, who attempted to uncover the ruins of the Stoa of Attalos in 1861: "*If those who still dwelt on that site had been more open to reasonable negotiations to cede the plots of land required for the excavations, and if the Archaeological Society and the Government had more money at their disposal for their purchase, this excavation would have been completed as we wished and that part of the city would have been embellished, with the ancient building displayed to great effect for the whole of its magnificent length.*" A few years earlier, in 1858, Efth. Kastorchis, a professor at the University and member of the council of the Archaeological Society, excavated the so-called Stoa of the Giants, "*because this site was free of all contention, having already been purchased by the Government from its previous owners*" (figs 3, 6).

Later, in 1874, when D. Voulgaris was prime minister, and 1887, in Ch. Trikoupis's term of office, "*when there were enlightened men in the Government,*" it was decided to run a lottery in the name of the Archaeological Society of Athens, with the aim of collecting the money needed to "*purchase

3

the private houses to the north of the Acropolis, from the Theseion to the Tower of the Winds, in order to uncover ancient Athens in this way." Monuments in the Ancient Agora came to light during public works carried out in the area of the old town. In 1890-1891, the creation of the cutting for the electric railway from Athens to Piraeus brought to light the Sanctuary of the Demos, the Graces and Aphrodite and part of the Altar of the Twelve Gods, on the north side of the hill of Kolonos Agoraios (Theseion).

Great interest in the uncovering of the Ancient Agora was also shown by the German Archaeological Institute. In the years 1891-1898, members of the institute, led by the German archaeologist and architect W. Dörpfeld, excavated on the west and north side of the Agora, where the remains of several important buildings were discovered (figs 7-9). These investigations were resumed in 1907-08 by the Archaeological Society, which uncovered the two temples of Apollo Patroos and Zeus and Athena Phratria, the Metroon and the Old Bouleuterion, as well as the well-known statue of Apollo Patroos. However, these sporadic trenches did not yield the kind of finds that would have helped to identify these buildings with certainty and confirm that the area was in fact the Athenian Agora (fig. 10).

The question of the excavation of the Agora was again in the news during the first decades of the 20th century. But all plans were interrupted in 1912 by the Balkan Wars, and later by the Asia Minor disaster of 1922. A bill was introduced to Parliament by the Kafandaris government in summer 1924, providing for expropriations for excavation purposes, but it was rejected for financial reasons. This law envisaged the division of the site of the Agora into zones, which would be made available for excavation to various archaeological schools and foundations.

4

5

6

3-6. The statues of the Giants from the second phase of the Odeion of Agrippa (ca. AD 150), one of the few antiquities other than the temple of Hephaistos (Theseion) that was visible before the excavations in the Ancient Agora.

3. The area of the Ancient Agora from the east. At the left is a depiction of one of the statues of the Giants. Watercolour by J.J. Wolfensberger, 1834.

4. One of the statues on its pedestal in its present condition. The American School of Classical Studies at Athens, Archives of the Agora Excavations.

5. The area around the statues of the Giants, before the excavations in 1931. The American School of Classical Studies at Athens, Archives of the Agora Excavations.

6. View of the Stoa of the Giants in 1935, just after the excavations. In the near background can be seen the houses of the nearby residents. The American School of Classical Studies at Athens, Archives of the Agora Excavations.

THE EXCAVATIONS OF THE AMERICAN SCHOOL OF CLASSICAL STUDIES

Faced with the impasse that had arisen, the Greek government *"turned to the representatives of the archaeologists from foreign nations who work here."* The American School of Classical Studies responded immediately and positively to this request, out of a conviction that the United States, as the leading democracy of the modern world, ought to uncover the roots of the first ancient democracy. The Minister responsible granted the School an excavation permit for the Agora on condition that it secure sufficient financing to expropriate the houses that covered the area under investigation. The American School of Classical Studies, under the directorship of Ed. Capps, accepted the assignment with great satisfaction, and the necessary preparations were begun for an important project on this scale.

The lengthy procedure of expropriation had to be set in train, and this encountered countless difficulties. Moreover, the Ministry proposed to extend the area to be expropriated as far as the Roman Agora, and also towards Tripodon Street as far as the Odeion of Perikles. The result of this would have been to double the number of inhabitants affected from 5,000 to about 10,000. The newspapers wrote of "100,000 native Athenians who are being driven from their ancestral hearths by the Americans" (figs 11-13).

The problems were solved after painstaking negotiations and everything was ready for the first investigations to begin in 1931. The Americans had already begun to collect money for the excavations, but the sums raised were small. The problem was solved by John D. Rockefeller Jr., who donated one million

7-9. Views of the first excavations on the site of the Ancient Agora, conducted at the end of the 19th century by the German archaeologist and architect W. Dörpfeld. The difference in ground level between the ancient and the modern city is striking. Athens, German Archaeological Institute.

dollars, which was put to the best possible use. Within the space of about ten years, down to the eve of the Second World War, 365 houses had been expropriated and demolished, freeing an area of about 160,000 m². An outstanding academic and technical team led by T.L. Shear, the first director of the excavation (1931-1940), uncovered a large part of the Athenian Agora (figs 14, 16, 18).

The most important moments of the excavation were undoubtedly those involving the discovery of monuments attesting that this area was indeed the Ancient Agora. In 1934, the remains of a circular building were uncovered, which was at once identified with the Tholos. This made it possible to identify with certainty the other buildings on the west side, which the travel-writer Pausanias mentions in the order he encountered them as he proceeded. At the same time, an inscribed base of a dedication by Leagros, son of Glaukon, dating from the early 5th century BC, which was found erected in front of the Altar of the Twelve Gods, demonstrated that this monument was in fact the altar built in the Agora by Peisistratos the Younger, son of Hippias, as we are told by Thucydides. Finally, in 1938, a late 6th century BC inscription came to light in its original position, next to the Tholos, bearing the inscription *ΗΟΡΟΣ ΕΜΙ ΤΕΣ ΑΓΟΡΑΣ* ('I am the boundary of the Agora').

An important period in the uncovering of the Agora began after the end of the Second World War in 1946, under the direction of Homer A. Thompson (1946-1967) (figs 15, 18). Excavations were carried out over almost the entire area of the Agora, revealing all the major buildings of the Classical, Hellenistic and Roman periods. In this way, the area and buildings associated with the functioning of the Athenian democracy came to light once more after millennia of silence. The remains of the earliest public buildings, possibly dating from the time of Solon, were found, as well as other structures associated with Peisistratos and his sons. The course and successive levels of the famous Panathenaic Way, which led by way of the Agora to the Acropolis, had been detected; here, during the Panathenaic festival, theatrical, musical and athletic contests were held. We can now also stand before the ruins of the Bouleuterion, the meeting place of the Council of the Five Hundred, and also before the monument of the Ten Eponymous Heroes, who gave their names to the ten Attic tribes. The excavation of the Tholos, the headquarters of the executive of the Athenian democracy, in which the prytaneis met and dined, the Metroon, in which the public archives were kept, as well as other buildings that were the seats of other institutions, such as the Mint and South Stoa I, all revealed the political centre of the Athenian democracy. Religious activity in the Agora was

10. View of the Ancient Agora from the hill of Kolonos Agoraios. In the foreground can be seen the finds from the old excavations. Behind the wall, in front of the church of Panayia Vlassarou, are men working on the first excavations of the American School of Classical Studies (May 1931). The American School of Classical Studies at Athens, Archives of the Agora Excavations.

10

attested by the large number of temples and altars uncovered. Evidence for juridical activity is to be found in the indoor and outdoor meeting places of jurors, together with the *kleroterion* (a device for selecting jurors), the *klepsydra* (a water-clock for measuring the amount of time used by speakers), and the ballots used to condemn or acquit the accused. Finally, commercial activity was documented by the discovery of many shops, and also the workshops of potters, bronzesmiths, sculptors and shoemakers.

The monumental buildings of the Hellenistic period, such as the Stoa of Attalos, the Middle Stoa, and South Stoa II, all of them donated by rulers of the Hellenistic East to the cultural capital of the world, were preserved in very good condition. The ruins of the Roman period were also impressive, and included those of the Odeion of Agrippa and the Library of Pantainos. Traces were also found of the Nymphaeum, a building donated by the Roman emperor Hadrian in the 1st century BC, as well as traces of five Classical temples that had been transferred to the Agora from various parts of the Attic countryside, the best known being the temple of Ares, in order to serve the cult of the emperor imposed by Rome.

11

12

In many places, the excavation uncovered evidence connected with important historical events, such as remains of the three major destructions suffered by the city: the first by the Persians in 480 BC, the second by the Roman general Sulla in 86 BC, and the last by the Herulians in AD 267. Hermaic stelai were also found that had been damaged on that terrible night in 415 BC by the drunken friends of Alkibiades, an act that caused much suffering for Athens; also hundreds of inscribed ostraka, which threatened, sometimes successfully, to ostracise leading political figures, such as Aristeides, son of Lysimachos, Themistokles, son of Neokles, Kimon, son of Miltiades, Perikles, son of Xanthippos and Alkibiades, son of Kleinias.

Archaeological remains were also found in the Agora that confirm the continuous occupation of the area from the Late Neolithic period (4th millennium BC) to the early 20th century. These remains demonstrate that Athens is one of the few places in the world that has been inhabited without break for so long a period.

14. *The first director of the excavations T. Leslie Shear, in front of the altar of Zeus Agoraios. The American School of Classical Studies at Athens, Archives of the Agora Excavations.*

15. *The finds from the Agora excavation enthralled international public opinion. Here, Agatha Christie during her visit to the Ancient Agora at the beginning of the 1950s, accompanied by E. Vanderpool, H. Thompson and J. Caskey. The American School of Classical Studies at Athens, Archives of the Agora Excavations.*

14

15

16

16. *E. Vanderpool, an outstanding member of the scientific staff of the Ancient Agora and professor at the American School of Classical Studies, studies the stele with the decree against tyranny. The American School of Classical Studies at Athens, Archives of the Agora Excavations.*

17. *Another scene of the first American excavations. The soil from the excavation was carried in carts to an area south of the temple of Hephaistos (Theseion). The American School of Classical Studies at Athens, Archives of the Agora Excavations.*

17

18. The scientific personnel of the Agora excavations in 1934. The director, T. Leslie Shear is seated in the centre, with L. Talcott on his right. Standing, centre, is E. Vanderpool, with the next director of the excavations, Homer Thompson, at the extreme right. The American School of Classical Studies at Athens, Archives of the Agora Excavations.

19, 20. The excavation day-book for 4 June 1931 (fig. 20), describing the discovery of the hermaic stele depicted in fig. 19. According to the day-book the herm was used as a support for a large statue of a clothed woman (?) holding a child on her left arm, which rested on the top of the herm stele. In the end it was demonstrated that the herm belonged to a copy made in the 2nd c. AD of Praxiteles' statue of Hermes, and that the child, who is preserved, is the young Dionysos. The American School of Classical Studies at Athens, Archives of the Agora Excavations.

18

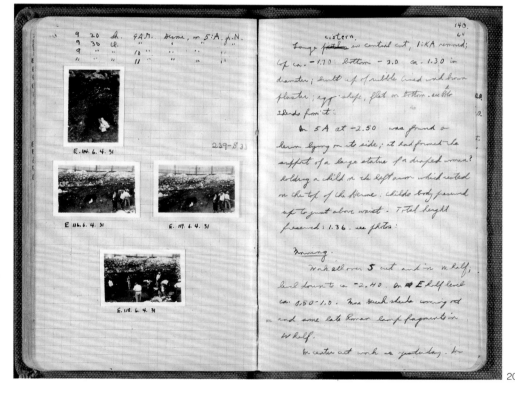

19

20

21

THE RECONSTRUCTION OF THE STOA OF ATTALOS

Alongside the excavations, work had to begin on another of the fundamental obligations of the archaeologist: the construction of a museum to house the thousands of finds. Many of these were important works of art, such as the large numbers of statues and black- and red-figure vases, while others were testimony to the use of the area at different periods, like the superb offerings found in the Mycenaean and Geometric tombs, and the vases and other artefacts from the Byzantine phase of the Agora. The most important items, of course, were associated with the political and social life of the Athenians in the Archaic and Classical periods, providing material witness to their public and private life.

The original idea was to build the museum outside the Agora, in the valley between the Pnyx and Areopagos Hills. Excavations conducted there, however, uncovered an important residential and workshop district, the remains of which could not be covered by a modern building. While the debate on all feasible sites for the new museum continued, a completely new idea was laid on the table: that the Stoa of Attalos should be reconstructed so that it not only formed a museum, storerooms, offices, workshops, archive, etc., but also restored a characteristic multifunctional ancient building.

Despite its innovatory character, the recommendation was accepted by the Greek archaeological authorities and in 1949 an agreement was signed between the Greek government and the American School to implement the bold venture.

The first concern of those responsible was to find the resources for both the excavation and the restoration of the Stoa, which came to the sum of 2 million dollars. It is worth noting that the first order for the Piraeus limestone with which the walls of the storerooms in the basement of the building were constructed was paid for with money from the final instalment of the Marshall Plan, designed to strengthen the Greek economy, which provided for funding even for the erection of museums. However, it proved to be a very difficult proposition to find the necessary funds. The solution to the problem again came from John D. Rockefeller Jr., who contributed a million dollars (fig. 21).

The study for the reconstruction of the Stoa was assigned by the American School to John Travlos, the architect of the Agora excavations (fig. 22). After long study of the ruins and the identification of members that belonged to the Stoa, he drew up the design for the reconstruction and detailed plans for carrying out the restoration. The statics study was done by the civil engineer Georgios Biris (fig. 22), while the

21. Bronze plaque installed in the Stoa of Attalos in memory of John D. Rockefeller, Jr., one of the major funders of the excavation. The American School of Classical Studies at Athens, Archives of the Agora Excavations.

22. The architect John Travlos (right) in conversation with the civil engineer Georgios Biris about the reconstruction of the Stoa of Attalos. Behind them can be seen the designs of the Stoa.

23

24

23, 24. Two views of the Stoa of Attalos, just before the start of the restoration works, at the beginning of 1950s, showing the parts of the ancient building preserved in situ. The American School of Classical Studies at Athens, Archives of the Agora Excavations.

25

26

27

building and the conversion of the Stoa into a museum was undertaken by the New York technical office of W. Stuart Thompson and Phelps Barnum. The general supervision of the project was by Anastasios Orlandos, then director of the Restoration Department of the Ministry of Education and Culture.

All that survived of the Stoa were parts of the walls, which had been incorporated in the Late Roman wall built after the destruction of the city by the Herulians in AD 267 (figs 23, 24). All the other parts of the building, which had two storeys and was 115 m. long, had to be built de novo. They included 124 marble columns and capitals (45 exterior Doric columns and 22 interior Ionic columns on the ground floor, 45 Ionic double-half columns and 22 interior Pergamene columns on the upper storey), as well as the marble entablatures of the two storeys. This work was carried out by about two hundred stone masons, in accordance with ancient methods, to designs by J. Travlos and under his direct supervision. This work provided an opportunity to study the technical methods used in ancient times, and other architectural issues connected with the construction of so large a building (figs 25-27).

25-27. Three views of the reconstruction of the Stoa of Attalos. Almost the entire building was made of new material, using the methods of the ancient marble-workers, which provided an opportunity for an experimental study of ancient building methods. The American School of Classical Studies at Athens, Archives of the Agora Excavations.

28, 29. Two views of the Stoa of Attalos in April 1956 (top) and September of the same year (bottom), before the inauguration. The building was erected with great speed. The American School of Classical Studies at Athens, Archives of the Agora Excavations.

28

29

Difficulties arose in the selection and procurement of suitable building materials. The wooden beams for the roof were in the end brought from America, while the tiles were made by the company owned by Kriton Deliveris. After three years of constant laborious work (1953-1956), the Stoa stood once more on the east side of the Agora, just as impressive as in ancient times (figs 28-30). The building was inaugurated on 3 September 1956, on the 75th anniversary of the founding of the American School of Classical Studies in Athens, exactly as planned. Immediately afterwards, all the finds were transferred to the new storerooms, the offices and workshops were installed, and an exhibition of artefacts was mounted in the new museum, which was handed over to the Greek Archaeological Service on 3 June 1957.

Alongside the Stoa of Attalos, another major restoration project was carried out in the Agora: the

30

restoration to its original form and consolidation of the church of the Holy Apostles, which had been a parish church for about 900 years. The study for the restoration was carried out by Alison Frantz and John Travlos, who also undertook to redesign the surrounding area and to assemble near the church all the Byzantine architectural members found in the area of the Agora. After the removal of the later in-elegant annexes, the church was restored to its original cross-in-square type (figs 31, 32). Wall-paintings from the church of St Spyridon near the Stoa of Attalos (demolished in 1939), and from the ancient temple of Hephaistos, dating from the time that it was used as a Christian church, were placed inside the original narthex.

Three monuments that call to mind important periods of Greek history now rise imposingly in the Agora. At the west, on the summit of the hill of Kolonos Agoraios, stands the temple of Hephaistos

31

32

30. Photograph of the interior of the Stoa of Attalos. The reconstruction of the ancient building not only provided a home for the Agora Museum, but also made it possible to experience one of the most characteristic buildings of ancient Greek architecture.

31, 32. Phases from the restoration of the Middle Byzantine church of the Holy Apostles. The monument was disencumbered of modern structures and regained its original form. The American School of Classical Studies at Athens, Archives of the Agora Excavations.

(known as the Theseion), an architectural jewel of the Classical period. At the east rises the Stoa of Attalos, donated by the kings of Pergamon of the Hellenistic period and at the south is the church of the Holy Apostles, a representative example of the Byzantine architecture of Athens (figs 2, 34).

THE ARCHAEOLOGICAL SITE

The American archaeologists were concerned to configure the archaeological site. The planning to restore the natural environment had begun as early as 1953, under the American architect E. Griswold, involving the planting of trees and shrubs that prospered here in Classical times. Expert agronomists searched Attica for suitable trees, and many individuals in both Greece and America contributed money for this purpose. Plants were donated by the royal estate at Tatoi, by A. Benakis and by many other prominent and ordinary Athenians. Amongst the most characteristic donations were those made by the Greek community of Toledo, Ohio, for the poplar that in ancient times provided shade for the statue of Demosthenes, and by the Ephorate of Antiquities of Epiros, which sent an oak, the sacred tree of Zeus, from Dodona, to be planted near the Stoa of this deity in the Agora.

The basic concern was that the site should regain its original form: rows of trees emphasised the road axes and others were planted at specific points, either mentioned by the ancient authors or where remains had been discovered during the excavations. An example is the restoration of the ancient garden identified to the south of the temple of Hephaistos. Two rows of pits were found there, which were dug in the 3rd century BC and contained clay flower-pots. These finds confirmed the statements in the ancient authors that the sanctuaries were sacred groves, full of trees, shrubs and flowers. Thirty-eight pomegranate trees were planted in the first, inner row, next to the temple, and twenty-two myrtles in the outer row.

The programme of tree-planting was inaugurated with great ceremony on 4 January 1954. The first trees, an oak and a laurel, were planted next to the altar of Zeus Agoraios by the then King and Queen of Greece, Paul and Frederica (fig. 33). Two years later, 654 trees (cypresses, pines, plane-trees, olives, oaks, poplars and figs) were planted, along with 2,800 shrubs (mainly laurel, myrtle and oleander), 400 vines, and thousands of wild flowers all over the site. Here, the voluntary help provided by both well-known and anonymous Athenians, with a leading role played by the Boy Scouts, was impressive. The final shrub, the one that produces hemlock, was planted in memory of Socrates. It was donated by Gorham Stevens, the architect known for his studies of the Acropolis and monuments in the Agora.

33. Festive inauguration of the planting of the Agora with trees on 4 January 1954. King Paul and Queen Frederica plant a laurel-tree next to the altar of Zeus Agoraios. The American School of Classical Studies at Athens, Archives of the Agora Excavations.

33

RECENT EXCAVATIONS

The excavation of the Athenian Agora was not yet finished, however, since a large part at the north of the archaeological site remained unexplored, still covered by modern buildings. In 1967, at the initiative of the then Director of Antiquities, Sp. Marinatos, a narrow strip between the railway line and Adrianou Street was expropriated. The excavation, which commenced in 1970 under the direction of T.L. Shear Jr. with the financial support of the Ford Foundation, brought to light, one of the most important monuments of the Agora, the Royal Stoa, the headquarters of the *archon basileus*. The threshold of this building was crossed by Socrates himself when, as the accused, he was to be interrogated by the archon, who would decide whether or not to send him to stand trial. This find increased the number of sites in the Agora, which the great philosopher is known to have visited: the workshop of the shoemaker Simon, which was one of his haunts; the Stoa of Zeus, where he liked to teach; the Bouleuterion, where he sat as a councillor; and the Tholos, where he served as a prytanis. A new round of expropriation, demolition and excavation took place at the end of the 1970s to the north of Adrianou Street. This led in 1981 to the discovery of the westernmost edge of yet another important building: the Stoa Poikile, which was decorated with fine paintings by Polygnotos, Panainos and Mikon. It was in this stoa that the philosopher Zenon from Kition on Cyprus taught,

34

and from it his school of Stoics took its name. The remainder of the building is expected to come to light when excavation, up to and behind the church of St Philip, is resumed in this area. These latest excavations are directed by J. McK Camp with the financial support of the Packard Foundation. This will bring to completion the long-term excavation project that has brought to light the centre of the ancient city of Athens (fig. 34). The finds, whether resplendent public buildings and sanctuaries, inscriptions and statues, or humble house remains and fragments of pottery, continue to increase our knowledge of Athenian history. Through the toil of many scholars from all over the world, and through the study and publications of the finds, the Athenian Agora continues to project before the entire world the ideals and values of ancient Greek civilisation.

34. Modern view of the archaeological site of the Ancient Agora from the Acropolis. The sign-posting of the monuments, the laying out of the archaeological park, and the housing of the Museum in the Stoa of Attalos form a triptych, making the site one of the most attractive in Athens.

Vassos Karageorghis

The "royal" tombs at Salamis in Cyprus

Salamis, the ancient city on the east coast of the island, was the most important city of Cyprus during the whole of the first millennium BC and is today the most imposing archaeological site on the island. In 1974 the area was occupied by the Turkish Army and continues to be so to the present day, inaccessible for legal archaeological activity by scholars of the Republic of Cyprus and elsewhere. The University of Ankara has been carrying out excavations at the site for the last five years, ignoring Unesco regulations which prohibit archaeological activity in areas occupied by a foreign army.

Although the site of Salamis has always been known, from the time of its foundation in the 11th century BC down to the present day (the city site was abandoned after its destruction by fire during the Arab invasions of the 7th century AD), it was during the 1960's that it became internationally known in the archaeological world, because of the astonishing discoveries in its Necropolis which are described below. In the 1890's, during the first years of British rule, an archaeological mission from the British Museum carried out extensive excavations at the city site, but these excavations have never been published in a scholarly fashion. The Necropolis of Salamis, situated west of the city site, was thoroughly looted by treasure hunters from the neighboring villages and also by foreign adventures (bankers and diplomats) who were collecting Cypriote antiquities during the second half of the 19th century.

In the autumn of 1952 I was sent by the Director of the Department of Antiquities of the colonial government to Salamis, together with another Cypriote colleague (a medievalist) to excavate. We excavated the Roman gymnasium and the Roman theatre, and we partially restored both buildings, providing unique monuments for the development of 'cultural tourism' (figs 1, 2). The theatre was frequently used for the performance of Greek plays with tremendous success.

1. The restored west colonnade of the Palaestra of the Gymnasium.

2. The theatre is ready to be used. One part of the cavea has been restored. The original cavea was very large, as one may see from the outer semi-circular wall. Our aim was to preserve harmony with the environment.

In November 1957 after a rainy weekend, an old man came from the nearby village of Enkomi to report that while he was ploughing his field west of the city site, in what we knew was the Necropolis of ancient Salamis, the surface soil collapsed; he dug a 'hole' and brought to the surface an imported Greek *crater* (a jar for mixing wine with water) of the 8th century BC. The then Director of Antiquities (two years after the independence of Cyprus), Dr. P. Dikaios, sent a technician from the Cyprus Museum, Symeon Klonaris, to excavate the 'hole' and report to him directly. In any case Dikaios considered that this tomb, if it was a tomb, must have been looted long ago.

Soon after Symeon started digging, the first large amphorae appeared about half a metre below the surface in the passage in front of the façade of a built chamber known in archaeological terminology as the 'dromos'. Symeon ascertained that the built chamber had been systematically looted and that the limestone plaques of its roof had been removed.

When Symeon reached the floor of the dromos, he found animal bones and, as far as he could

3. General view of the dromos and chamber of 'royal' Tomb 47, in the Necropolis of Salamis. In the background, to the right, the Monastery of Saint Barnabas. At the left is the tumulus of Tomb 3.

3

judge from previous experience, considered them to be modern, belonging to a donkey which had died only recently and had been buried by its owner away from the village, a very usual custom. So he got rid of them. But when more and more bones appeared, he became suspicious; he stopped throwing them away and informed Dikaios of this strange phenomenon. When Dikaios came to Salamis to supervise (fig. 5), he found that most of the bones of at least two skeletons had already been dumped. He ordered a careful cleaning of the remaining bones and it soon became clear that they did not belong to a donkey or donkeys buried recently, but that they dated to the original burial in the tomb (fig. 4). Next to two skeletons of horses – not donkeys – that were cleared more or less in situ, the impressions of two poles of a four-horse chariot were clearly visible. Thus 'royal' Tomb 1 was discovered. The incinerated remains of a young woman and a necklace of gold and crystal beads were found in a bronze cauldron. The importance of this 8th century BC tomb was obvious and it was not without embarrassment that Dikaios published what was left for him to record in an article in the German periodical *Archäologischer Anzeiger* in 1963. Later, in 1979, Swedish archaeologist Einar Gjerstad suggested that this was the tomb of a Greek princess who was married into the royal court of Salamis and that part of the 'dowry', which she brought from her fatherland (a set of Greek vases), was buried with her. This proposal was based on the fact that quite a lot of Late Geometric Greek vases (plates, bowls and a crater) were found among the tomb gifts, as well as the consideration that incineration of the dead was not the local custom, which favoured inhumation.

TOMB 2

One of the most notorious tomb looters from the village of Enkomi was Pachoumios, then about 70, but still strong enough to work with me as a specialist digger in the Gymnasium of Salamis. One winter afternoon in 1962, after heavy rain, we noticed that soil had subsided at a point in a field north of the Great Tumulus of the Salamis Necropolis, very close to the tomb excavated by Dikaios (Tomb 1). We suspected that this subsidence indicated the presence below of a funerary chamber, like the built chamber of Tomb 1. In the summer of 1962, I started excavating what is now known as the 'royal' Necropolis of Salamis. We began by excavating around the opening in the ground where the soil had subsided and came upon the large slabs of the roof of a built chamber (fig. 7). Through a hole that had been opened by the looters who had first entered the tomb, we gained access to the chamber. Pachoumios was with me when we entered and I was bitterly disappointed to see that it was completely empty, its floor 'swept' clean. Pachoumios smiled meaningfully and after a few seconds he said: "I excavated this tomb many, many years ago!" By the light of a torch, we cleaned the slabs of the floor and in one corner we noticed a cavity filled with soil. In it there was a corroded silver bowl. Pachoumios turned green and I

7. Camera in hand, I went up and down taking photographs and notes of all the details of the first tomb I excavated in the Necropolis of Salamis, Tomb 2.

7

heard him mutter to himself "Damn it, I missed that one." The silver bowl, which was later sent to the laboratory of the British Museum, London, for cleaning, proved to have rich, finely-engraved decoration on the interior which turned out, even more interestingly, to be a palimpsest, that is, it was decorated twice.

Conscious of the importance of the dromos of Tomb 1, we started carefully excavating the dromos of Tomb 2, having first defined its boundaries. It was long and broad, leading to the built façade of the chamber. Just below the surface, we found the bones of two human skeletons (fig. 9). One was very disturbed by deep ploughing, but the second, a male, was complete, in situ, with his hands bound together in front of him. Since the finds in Tomb 1 had already demonstrated the association of the burial customs in the 'royal' tombs of Salamis with the Homeric burial customs as described in the 23rd book of the *Iliad*, we quickly interpreted the male skeleton as that of a slave who had been killed to serve his

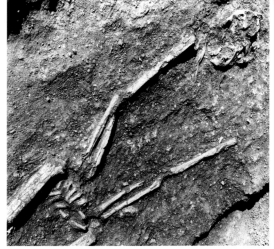

8. The skeleton of a horse and the impression of the wooden chariot-pole above it.

9. Two slaves were killed and placed in the fill of the dromos of Tomb 2, their hands tied in front. Here we see one of the skeletons in situ.

10. Detail of the head of one of the horses in the dromos of Tomb 2, with bronze blinkers, front band and iron bits in situ.

master in the after-life, sharing the same fate as the 'twelve young Trojans' who were killed by Achilles on the pyre of Patroklos. Book 23 of the *Iliad* was, from then on, our 'Bible'. We proceeded with the careful removal of the rest of the fill of the dromos. Close examination of the stratigraphy clearly showed how the soil was shovelled into the dromos from above, that the two 'slaves' were killed and placed in the dromos before it was completely filled and how more soil was then added to the dromos to fill it completely, flush with the surface. Near the sloping floor of the dromos, not far from the entrance to the tomb (the large slab which blocked the entrance being found in situ, since the looters entered the

chamber from above), we noticed the head of a horse resting horizontally, with the forelegs in a kneeling position. The animal was seated on its hind legs, while trying to escape (figs 6, 8, 10).

TOMB 79

The highlight of our investigations in the Necropolis of Salamis was the excavation of Tomb 79. In the plain of Salamis, not far from the Great Tumulus (see below), one could see a large flat stone on the surface, that covered the chamber of a built tomb which had been looted long ago (fig. 11).

With the experience of the excavation of Tombs 1 and 2 and the conviction that in front of each chamber there was a long dromos with horse and chariot burials as well as funerary offerings, we started the excavation of the dromos of the tomb in May 1966 and we completed it in August. This tomb proved to be the richest of all the tombs in the Necropolis, the one which established the fame of Salamis internationally; it is still referred to very frequently in the international bibliography and several doctoral dissertations have been written on its rich material and funerary customs.

In the second week of the excavation we came upon the material placed in the dromos, mainly large amphorae. But what excited us were the tops of some vertically standing ivory plaques (fig. 15) and what appeared to be the ears of some bronze 'monsters' arranged in a circle (fig. 12). Andreas, one of my technicians, undertook the excavation of the ivory and Kakoullis, the chief technician, that of the bronze. The excavation of both took several weeks. On the third week Kakoullis exposed the protomes of three sirens and six griffins which decorated a bronze cauldron of extraordinary beauty, the first of its kind to have been found in Cyprus (fig. 14). It was found standing on an iron tripod. With glue and fine cloth we were able to keep its pieces together for the necessary photographs, drawings and measurements, but after that the cauldron was taken to the Cyprus Museum, where it was carefully dismantled and its numerous pieces packed in boxes, grouped according to their relationship to each other. The pieces, including those of the iron tripod on which the cauldron stood, filled four large cartons. These were sent to the laboratory of the Landesmuseum in Mainz (Germany) in 1967, which kindly undertook to do the necessary conservation and mend the pieces. This process took four years. Andreas excavated the ivory plaques for one and a half months! It soon became clear that we were dealing with a chair of wood, dressed with ivory plaques, inset motifs and thin sheets of gold on the upper part of the backrest (figs 16-20). The wood, of course, had decayed and only the ivory plaques survived in situ. After all the soil around the chair had been removed, a delicate structure was created, consisting of the ivory plaques held together with cloth and wire.

11. General view of Tomb 79. It took three and a half months of hard work to prepare for this photograph, with all the objects in situ on the floor of the dromos of the Tomb.

11

12. One of the two bronze cauldrons was full of jugs, all of Phoenician type, of the 8th c. BC. Some of them were covered with a thin sheet of tin, to give the impression that they were made of silver.

13. Detail from the decoration of the second large cauldron found in the dromos of Tomb 79. The rim was decorated with two antithetic groups of bull protomes, looking into the interior of the cauldron. Below each handle there is a rectangular plaque decorated with a hathoric head in repoussé, flanked with papyri; above the head there is a winged solar disc. The cauldron belongs to a koine style, with oriental motifs, which prevailed in the Eastern Mediterranean at the beginning at the 8th c. BC. Nicosia, Cyprus Museum.

14. Two large bronze cauldrons were found in the dromos of Tomb 79, one standing on an iron tripod and decorated with protomes of griffins and sirens (left). The other, less well preserved, is decorated with bull protomes below the handles and a hathoric head (right).

One could easily remove the whole chair. It was taken to the laboratory of the Cyprus Museum in Nicosia, where Andreas took careful measurements of the position of each plaque and constructed a skeleton of wood on which he placed each ivory plaque in its correct position (figs 16, 17); a chair, or rather a throne, was born, a unique object embellished under the handles with two ivory plaques decorated in the cut-out technique, one representing a sphinx wearing the crowns of Upper and Lower Egypt and the other a stylized composite flower motif (figs 18, 20). It is a superb throne, which could easily recall 'the throne of Penelope' described by Homer in the *Odyssey*.

Bronze objects belonging to the gear of the horses and chariots (figs 23, 24) and ivory plaques belonging to a bed (fig. 21) constructed in the same way as the throne were piled up in a corner of the dromos. To separate and lift each piece demanded skill and patience and my technicians

15. Day after day more of the backrest of an ivory throne was uncovered in the northwest corner of the dromos of Tomb 79. Andreas undertook its excavation, drawing upon all his skill and patience.

16. Andreas uncovered the ivory throne, using glue, cloth and wire to strengthen it.

17, 19. One of the thrones which was found in the dromos of Tomb 79 and detail of its decoration. It was made of wood, covered with plaques of ivory. Its backrest was decorated with vertical frames filled with guilloche motifs and at its lower part were rows of inlaid anthemia. It is of Phoenician workmanship, like the ivory bed from the same tomb (8th c. BC). Nicosia, Cyprus Museum.

17

18

19

had both. It took Andreas and others more than two months to sort out the pieces and fix them
to a wooden skeleton.

Equally skillfully, Andreas and Kakoullis excavated the two chariots (one four-horse chariot
and one two-horse chariot) and their horses, rescuing every detail of the construction of the
chariots (fig. 25), and enabling us to recreate them later and to place their metal parts on the
wooden models.

A second throne with its footstool was also rescued from the fill of the dromos of Tomb 79. As we
found out later in the laboratory of the Cyprus Museum, this throne and its footstool were made of
wood covered with thin sheets of silver fixed with rivets, the heads of which were covered with thin
sheets of gold (fig. 22).

20

21

21. Detail of the hind part of the ivory bed, decorated with inset nonsensical hieroglyphics used for decorative purposes only and plant motifs of blue paste. The two corners are decorated with ivory heads of the Egyptian god Bes, protector of the household and of pregnant women (8th c. BC). Nicosia, Cyprus Museum.

22. Among the four thrones which were found in the dromos of Tomb 79, one (throne A), together with its footstool, was made of wood covered with a sheet of silver. The wood decayed, but the silver left its traces in the soil (8th c. BC). Nicosia, Cyprus Museum.

22

TOMB 3

Other important tombs were excavated in the Necropolis of Salamis including Tomb 3, which was covered by a tumulus. The chamber was built of ashlar blocks of stone (fig. 28). It had been reached by excavators from the British Museum in 1896, but the tomb had already been looted. The British excavators failed to excavate the dromos and we thus had the chance to discover chariot burials, weapons of iron and bronze and numerous amphorae (see below).

The results of the excavations of the 8th-7th century BC tombs in the 'royal' Necropolis of Salamis illustrate very effectively the cultural atmosphere in Cyprus during a period that is usually identified as 'Homeric', for reasons which we will explain below.

The kings or nobles who were buried in the 'royal' Necropolis of Salamis and in some tombs at Palaepaphos in the 8th-7th century BC cannot all be regarded as heroes, but they were accompanied by all those luxuries that a hero was due: a chariot, horses, slaves, firedogs and skewers for a proper meal of roasted meat, swords, helmets and luxury goods, such as ivory furniture of Levantine workmanship, silver drinking cups and bowls of Cypro-Phoenician workmanship.

Some of the funerary customs observed in the 'royal' tomb and some of the objects which were offered to the dead recall 'Homeric' conditions. In the fill of the dromos of Tomb 2 the skeletons of two humans were found. Examples of this custom of human sacrifice in honour of the dead have

23. Drawing of a bronze front band of a horse's headgear from Tomb 79.

24. Bronze blinder for a horse, from the dromos of Tomb 79. Decoration in repoussé with a winged sphinx striding over a fallen enemy, symbolizing the conquest of the Egyptian Pharaoh over his enemies. Nicosia, Cyprus Museum.

25. Skeleton of a chariot horse with bronze breastplate and iron bits in situ, on the floor of the dromos of Tomb 79.

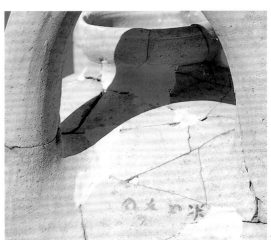

already been noted elsewhere in Cyprus from the 11th century BC onwards, and in the heroic burials of Eleftherna in Crete. This custom is also alluded to in the 23rd book of the *Iliad*, where Achilles sacrifices twelve young Trojans on the pyre of his dead friend Patroklos.

Particularly characteristic of the Salamis 'royal' burials are the sacrifices of horses and chariots in the spacious dromoi of the tombs. Sacrifices of horses are known from Anatolia, Palestine and the Aegean world, in Cyprus during the Late Bronze Age period and at Lefkandi c. 950 BC, but the reappearance of this funerary custom in the 8th-7th century BC in Cyprus is a novelty. Coldstream goes so far as to suggest that "the princely burials of Salamis were influenced in large measure by the circulation of Ionic epic poetry and especially of the *Iliad* in the royal court of Salamis." It is significant that this custom also occurred in Crete, a place where other characteristics of 'heroic' burials are encountered. But it should also be noted that in a Neo-Assyrian text there is a description of a royal funeral that involves the slaughter of horses and the offering of a bronze bed. Chariot sacrifices are also known from other places in the Eastern Mediterranean. The sacrifice of chariots and horses in Etruscan tombs formed part of the funerary customs of the Etruscan princes.

We have already referred to the tumulus above Tomb 3. Tumuli were also common above monumental built tombs in Phrygia and Etruria. In addition to impressions and remains of a chariot, a bronze spear, a *pharetra* (quiver) with iron arrow-heads, and a bronze shield, the same Tomb 3

26. The bronze shield and spear of the warrior who was buried in the chamber under the Great Tumulus. Next to them, the impressions of the chariot.

27. Detail of an amphora bearing a painted inscription in the Cypriot syllabary below its handle. The inscription reads "of olive oil" in Greek. It recalls the burial custom of offering olive oil on the pyre of the dead as described in the 23rd book of the Iliad.

28. The façade of the built chamber and the sides of the dromos of Tomb 3. The latter were built of mudbrick. A 'dome' of mudbricks formed the top of the tumulus.

yielded a silver-studded sword, of a type that was known to Homer, and of which several examples are known from Cyprus (figs 26, 29-32). Among the large storage jars found in the dromos of Tomb 3 there is one that bears a painted inscription in the Cypriot syllabary (fig. 27). It represents the Greek word for olive oil in the genitive, i.e. " [an amphora] of olive oil." It evokes the Homeric passage in book 23 of the *Iliad*, where Achilles places amphorae of olive oil or fat on the pyre of his friend Patroklos. Tomb 3 may date to ca 600 BC.

In Tomb 1, which may be dated to the early part of the Cypro-Archaic I period, the incinerated remains of the dead, probably a woman, were found in a bronze cauldron, together with her necklace of gold and rock crystal beads. The pottery found in this tomb included a 'dinner set' consisting of one footed crater, probably from Attica, twenty skyphoi from Attica, and two skyphoi and ten plates from Euboea. Such plates have been identified as Euboean imitations of a Cypriot shape made for

29. Andreas Gheorghiou and his two assistants prepare to lift the impressions of a chariot.

30. On the floor of the dromos of Tomb 3 bones of horses were found, as well as bronze parts of the yoke of a chariot. Large vases were found against the nearby mudbrick wall of the dromos.

the market in Cyprus and further east as far as the mainland. A similar 'dinner set' was found in a tomb at Amathus. They formed part of the lifestyle and ritual banquets that were widespread among the members of the elite society in the 9th-8th century BC. In Etruria the drinking cups and dinner sets are quite common, and they include cups and bowls of gold, silver, and bronze. They are found side by side with firedogs and oboeloi, craters for mixing wine and water, large jars for cooking etc. In Homer feasts with eating and drinking were the privilege of aristocratic society; they occurred during funerals, weddings and 'royal dinners'.

As mentioned above, the Salamis Necropolis has provided ample and important material for the study of social and cultural conditions in Cyprus in particular and in the Mediterranean in general. The question of interconnections in the Mediterranean during the 8th-7th century BC has been in the foreground of scholarly research in recent years. Cyprus, lying at a cultural crossroads of the

Mediterranean, helps us to achieve a better understanding of how the aristocratic ideology spread from East to West during the 8th-7th century BC and how the Homeric epic was affected by this pan-Mediterranean ideology. The Necropolis of Salamis is thus indispensable for such research and has rightfully gained an important place in international scholarship.

Salamis, however, did not yield only material from the early historical period. There was a second tumulus in the Necropolis of Salamis, which lies on the eastern outskirts of the village of Enkomi (fig. 33) and had long been a temptation for archaeologists and looters alike. The archaeologists of the British Mission, who excavated the first tumulus, attempted an excavation of this tumulus, but without any positive result. In their published excavation report they accorded to both tumuli the following statement: "[...] the two tumuli, so conspicuous in the district, were in themselves sufficient witnesses of an important settlement of the Mycenaean (sic!) age.

31. Foreman Athanasios Evangelou managed to make a cast of a whole wheel of the chariot by pouring plaster of Paris into the impressions left by the wood in the fill of the dromos.

32. The silver-studded sword of the warrior who was buried in Tomb 3. It recalls Homeric descriptions of swords (7th c. BC). Nicosia, Cyprus Museum.

33

33. Tumulus 77, belonging to the Necropolis of Salamis, near the village of Enkomi. Several attempts were made in the past to excavate it, but without success.

34. With patience and care we uncovered the steps of an exedra below the tumulus.

35. The complete exedra with a small mound of rubble in the middle of its floor was uncovered under the tumulus of earth.

It is true that these tumuli had been ransacked long ago as we ascertained by exploration and indeed knew beforehand as a matter of fact."

We started excavating this tumulus in mid-September. That it was a funerary monument was certain, but where were the dead? Underneath the pile of stones there was a large circular pyre with gifts (figs 35, 38, 39), including fragments of golden wreaths, which had melted in the fierce heat of the pyre to mere drops of gold; we found weapons of bronze and iron and the heads and limbs of clay statues, hardened in the fire (figs 36, 37). Uncovering the faces of two elderly males, two male youths and a young woman was like coming into direct contact with these individuals, whom we tried desperately to identify. Since we could find no traces of the dead on the floor of the exedra, we decided to dig underneath in the hope of finding, perhaps, a funerary urn with their incinerated remains. We reached the bedrock without finding anything. The style of the five heads, two of them portraits, could give us a date towards the very end of the 4th century BC. The impressionistic rendering of the hair of one of the male youths recalled the style of the Greek sculptor Lysippos. Who was the important person at Salamis, perhaps a king, who died at the

end of the 4th century BC? Reading the late historian Diodorus, we learned that the last king of Salamis, Nicocreon, his wife Axiothea and other members of the royal family of Salamis, not wishing to fall into the hands of Ptolemy, who besieged the city in 311 BC, committed suicide, having first set fire to the palace. Obviously their bodies would not have been retrieved. In 306 BC, when Demetrios Poliorketes decided to honour the dead, he may have built a cenotaph in honour of the members of the royal family who suffered a violent death. This was then a moving encounter with a specific moment in history, with the last king of Salamis!

38

36. Andreas cleaning one of the human heads of unbaked clay found on the pyre of Tumulus 77.

37. Having removed a few centimetres of earth from the top of the pyre, we uncovered a life-size female head of unbaked clay, which had been hardened in the flames of the pyre.

38, 39. Underneath the small mound, right on the floor of the exedra, there was a large circular pyre with many offerings.

Christos Doumas

Akrotiri on Thera
The excavation of a buried city

Spring 1967 saw the establishment of a military dictatorship in Greece and also marked an important event in Greek archaeology: the appointment of the academician Spyridon Marinatos to the position of General Inspector of Antiquities. Marinatos had earlier served as Ephor of Antiquities in Crete and had formulated the theory that the volcano on Thera had been responsible for the end of the Minoan civilisation. This suggestion was published in the 1939 volume of the British periodical *Antiquity* and was received with considerable reservation and a publisher's note to the effect that it could be proved only by excavation. The outbreak of the Second World War prevented Marinatos's proposal from becoming widely known: apart from a few copies of this volume of *Antiquity* that entered circulation, the rest were destroyed during the bombardment of London. Marinatos nonetheless felt himself obliged to prove his theory by excavating on Thera. However, the terrible experiences heaped on Greece by the vicissitudes of war, the foreign occupation, and the civil war that followed left no margin for 'luxuries' of this kind. Two decades had to pass before the country was able to stand on its feet and turn its attention to its archaeological heritage.

The dawn of the 1960s ushered in a phase for Greek archaeology which, with hindsight, may be described as its golden age. Thanks to the Public Investment Programme, it embarked upon a process of rapid development involving the designing of new displays for the finds in the museums, the configuration of archaeological sites, and the commencement of excavation programmes. It was about this time that Marinatos began his efforts to confirm his theory. Making frequent visits to Santorini and conducting surface surveys, he gathered information from the farmers of the island, in order to identify the best place to excavate.

Marinatos's appointment to the position of General Inspector of Antiquities was more than he could have hoped for: it gave him the opportunity to have the first and last word not only on the priorities of the excavation programmes of the Archaeological Service, but also on the allocation of the relevant finances. Marinatos took advantage of the Colonels' need for support from personalities of his standing to secure funding on a scale hitherto undreamed of for an archaeological programme.

From about a half dozen sites that he had identified on the island at which there were visible Minoan remains, he finally selected one on the south coast (fig. 2) near the village of Akrotiri. The criteria for this choice proved to be entirely correct. First, the south coast is protected from the prevailing north winds and was therefore an ideal anchorage for the boats of the time. Before the eruption of the volcano this area had been the largest plain on the island, in which the development of agriculture was possible. Finally, the site lay opposite Crete, which, though scores of miles away, can often be seen from Thera, especially in the limpid atmosphere of spring and autumn.

1. One of the Adorants (detail). Part of a wall-painting from the north wall of the Lustral Basin in the northeast wing on the ground floor of Xeste 3.

The area was crossed from north to south by the bed of a small winter torrent that served as a path linking the modern village with the coast. Archaeological remains often came to light along this torrent after heavy rainfall. Information to this effect brought the French volcanologist F. Fouqué to this site, and at his urging, a small French archaeological mission lead by H. Mamet and H. Gorceix carried out a small excavation in 1867, precisely one century earlier than Marinatos. Later, at the turn of the century, a more systematic excavation was conducted a few hundred metres to the east, at Potamos, by a group from the mission led by Hiller von Gaertringen, the excavator of ancient Thera (fig. 3). The preliminary publications of both these pioneering projects were contributing factors in Marinatos's decision to concentrate his interest in the area of Akrotiri. The first year, 1967, was devoted to trial trenches dug across the bed of the torrent with the objective of establishing the size of the settlement (fig. 4). From these trenches Marinatos ascertained that the settlement extended both to the north, towards the village, and to the south, in the direction of the sea, and also that buildings several storeys high lay beneath a thick layer of volcanic ash. He also realised that the walls of these buildings had now lost their cohesion, since the organic materials used in them – timber frames, straw, etc. – had completely vanished. The uncovering of these ruins and their exposure to the elements of nature would therefore lead inescapably and rapidly to their complete disappearance. These observations led him to conceive the ambitious design to protect the entire excavated area with a single shelter. Another bold idea, of uncovering the prehistoric city by opening tunnels along the routes of the ancient roads,

2. Aerial photograph of the area of Akrotiri.

3. The excavations carried out at Potamos in the area of Akrotiri by a group from the mission led by Hiller von Gaertringen. Photograph taken in the early 20th century. The modern village of Akrotiri can be seen in the background. Athens, German Archaeological Institute.

2

4. The excavations begun in 1967 by Spyridon Marinatos. Photograph taken in 1969 from the northeast, looking towards Sector Beta. The sunken paved floor belongs to the first floor of Room Beta 2.

proved completely unrealistic. Even if the entrance to the buildings had been found, they would have been impenetrable, since they were in ruins.

Working at an intense pace for seven successive years, Marinatos brought to light a small, but very important sector of the prehistoric city, which the volcano of the island had buried about three and a half thousand years ago. Removing the upper layers of volcanic ash, he had, by the time of his death on 1 October 1974, covered an area of about a hectare with a single shelter (fig. 5). Dozens of buildings had been located within this area, only four of which Marinatos had time to investigate to a satisfactory degree. Despite their small number, these buildings were enough to prepare us for the treasures and great civilisation concealed in the bowels of Santorini: quite apart from their imposing dimensions, they contained their household equipment virtually intact (figs 6, 7), along with a hitherto inconceivable wealth of wall-paintings of outstanding quality (figs 1, 10-14, 32-34, 38, 39).

The excavation has continued to the present day without a break. However, the rate at which

5. The discovery of the important
prehistoric city buried beneath the lava of
the volcano of Thera has attracted the
attention of thousands of visitors, who
converge on the island annually.

6. Storeroom with built-in pithoi, as found
in Room Beta 1.

7. Mill installation in Room Delta 15.
Workshops serving the needs of the
prehistoric Therans were located within
the settlement, usually on the ground
floor of the buildings.

8. Staircase bearing clear traces of
destruction in Sector Delta (area 5).

new buildings are uncovered has slowed significantly, not because such new buildings do not exist, but because the large number of finds brought to light by Marinatos are in immediate need of conservation and protection. Emphasis has accordingly been placed on this sphere, which involves time-consuming, costly procedures. Modern technology and science make it possible to adopt a more substantial approach to matters of conservation, which is no longer confined to the empirical reassembling and reconstitution of fragmented finds. It has extended its interest to the scientific investigation of methods and materials, so that greater information can be derived from the material evidence and a greater length of life can be secured for the ancient artefact that is

the object of the intervention. It has been remarked that conservation should not wait for the ancient object to be taken to a museum or laboratory, but should begin when it is still in the excavation trench.

The sudden interruption of the life of the prehistoric city of Akrotiri and its interment beneath thick layers of volcanic material – pumice and pozzuolana – sealed in its buildings and streets, along with the wealth of household equipment, a vast quantity of information that can only be extracted by special procedures and methods. This information has opened up new horizons for the study of the daily life not only of the Therans, but also of the inhabitants of the Aegean in general, during the Bronze Age. Conservators and archaeologists specialising in archaeozoology,

9. Plaster-of-Paris casts of three beds taken from impressions left by them in the pumice.

10. Part of the large Spring Fresco in the room in which it was discovered (Room Delta 2). Various household vessels can be seen on the floor along with the plaster-of-Paris cast of a bed, which is being cleaned by the conservator S. Perrakis.

11. The wall-painting of fig. 10 after its restoration. The naturalistic treatment of the subject (flowering lilies and swallows) is characteristic. Athens, National Archaeological Museum.

12. *The Fisherman. Wall-painting in the room in which it was found (West House, Room 5).*

13. *Boxing boys. Wall-painting from Room Beta 1 (south wall). The boy on the left is shown in profile and the one on the right in a three-quarters stance. They wear a boxing glove on their right hand and a sash around their waist. Athens, National Archaeological Museum.*

14. *Antelopes. Wall-painting from Room Beta 1 (west wall). Although the artist has rendered the animals solely through the use of outline, the entire scene exudes movement and vitality. Athens, National Archaeological Museum.*

archaeomalacology, archaeoicthyology, archaeoentomology and archaeobotany, working seasonally and occasionally, conserve and process finds connected with their own specialty and enrich our knowledge on spheres such as the ancient environment, flora and fauna, the temperature of the sea, the diet of the inhabitants of Akrotiri, the cultivation methods they used on their farms, the illnesses they may have suffered, and so on.

The salt from the sea and the oxides in the volcanic material form a very hostile environment, especially for metal structures. Over the years the metal in the shelter became dangerously corroded. In the meantime, it was demonstrated that the sheets of Hellenit (asbestos-cement) used to cover the site were a cause of cancer, and therefore a hazard to the health of those who visited or worked there. There was accordingly a pressing and urgent need to replace Marinatos's corroded shelter with a new one that was earthquake-proof and made of more durable materials (fig. 15). For the foundations of the pillars supporting this new shelter, shafts had to be dug through a sequence of archaeological levels, penetrating in many cases to a depth of over twenty metres beneath the modern surface. In order to avoid damaging the ancient remains, at least a hundred and fifty such shafts had to be dug, of which only ninety were used in the end. The digging of these shafts provided an opportunity to study the entire sequence of phases of the settlement, from its creation to its final burial beneath the thick volcanic layer. These phases represent a history of at least three and a half thousand years.

It is perhaps worth referring at this point to the role played by stratigraphy in the study of human history. Essentially a geological method, which relies in the fact that each geological layer is earlier than the one overlying it, stratigraphy was adopted by archaeology. Stratigraphy was applied as an excavation method for the first time in the Mediterranean by Heinrich Schliemann in his excavations at Troy. At the end of the 19th century the archaeologists who uncovered the prehistoric settlement of Phylakopi on Milos used this method to determine the sequence of the Bronze Age phases in the Cyclades: Early Cycladic period (3200-2000 BC), Middle Cycladic period (2000-1650 BC), Late Cycladic or Mycenaean period (1650-1100 BC). Throughout this long history

15. The new shelter covering the excavated area, designed to anti-earthquake specifications and of very durable materials. Archive of N. Fintikakis.

15

Phylakopi gradually developed into a notable urban centre. The strong walls that protected it, at least during the final period of its life, are impressive even in their present ruined condition (figs 16, 17). It is thus no coincidence that Phylakopi became established as the main point of reference for other sites, not only in the Cyclades, but in the general area of the Aegean. The stratigraphy of Phylakopi established the antiquity of Cycladic civilisation, which had been brought to light a few decades earlier by the founder of Greek archaeology, Christos Tsountas.

The relations and exchanges between Phylakopi and other Aegean societies, particularly Crete, helped Sir Arthur Evans to reconstruct the sequence of phases of the Cretan culture known as the Minoan civilisation.

This brief excursus into the history of the excavations at Phylakopi has been necessary in order to demonstrate the contribution made by the excavation of Akrotiri to the enrichment of our knowledge of Aegean civilisation in the Bronze Age. The new evidence brought to light by the deep excavation trenches sunk for the foundations of the new shelter has filled many gaps in the earlier investigations.

Today we are aware that at the tip of a low peninsula on the south coast of Santorini, near the village of Akrotiri, a small settlement was founded about 4500 BC, which is attested by the fragments of clay pots scattered over the region. From these sherds it emerges that the Neolithic inhabitants of Thera enjoyed the same material culture as the other islands of the Cyclades, such as Naxos and Mykonos, and above all the islet of Saliagos between Paros and Antiparos.

16

17

16, 17. Phylakopi on Milos. The strong fortification walls protecting the city are still impressive, despite their ruined condition.

The Neolithic fishing village on the coast at Akrotiri gradually grew and developed into a notable centre of Early Cycladic civilisation. The monolithic pithos made of andesite (fig. 18), with its impressive dimensions (height 1.30 m.), evidently the product of a local workshop, is an indication of the competence of the Theran stone-carvers of the 3rd millennium BC. Marble figurines in a great variety of types and variations (figs 19, 20), and marble and clay vessels reveal the active part played by Thera in the Cycladic civilisation throughout the 3rd millennium BC. The absence of marble from the geological composition of the island indicates that Thera imported finished products from other islands, with which it shared a common culture. And the presence at Akrotiri of a large number of clay transportation vessels of the 3rd millennium BC from various parts of the Aegean suggests that the settlement gradually evolved into a centre of commercial exchanges for the entire Aegean. From about the beginning of the 2nd millennium BC, relations with Crete became increasingly close.

The islands of the northeastern Aegean are known to have had a long tradition and advanced technological expertise in metal-working. The existence of evidence for the practice of metal-working at the same time as the appearance of northeastern pottery types cannot, therefore, be without significance. For at about the same period, some notable settlements on the islands of the northeast Aegean were abandoned by their inhabitants. The most important of these, Poliochni on Lemnos, had developed into the major Aegean centre of metal-working in the 3rd millennium BC. Lying at the entrance to the Hellespont, the island seems to have played a leading role in the importing and working of ores from the Black Sea and in the distribution of the products of metal-working. The reasons for the abandonment of Poliochni remain unknown. It is not impossible, however, that this abandonment led to the emigration of the metal-workers who inhabited the island and contributed to the rapid spread of metal-working in the south Aegean.

These junctures form a background against which the developments that occurred at Akrotiri towards the end of the millennium may be understood. Underground chambers hewn into the soft pyroclastic rock have come to light beneath the ruins of the city. They are probably chamber tombs dating from the Early Cycladic period, similar to those brought to light earlier on Milos, where the equally soft pyroclastic rock made it easy to dig them. According to the excavation record the underground chambers at Akrotiri were filled with rocks and earth about the end of the 3rd millennium. Apparently, as part of a broad, coordinated building pro-

18

19

18. The monolithic pithos made of andesite, which is exceptionally tall (1.30 m.), reveals the skill of the stone-carvers of the period (3rd millennium BC).

19. Early Cycladic marble figurines, as found in the cenotaph in the area of Shaft 17.

20. Figurines (from Fig. 19). Thera, Museum of Prehistoric Thera.

20

gramme, the Early Cycladic cemetery ceased to be used so that the settlement could expand into its area to meet the housing needs of the constantly growing society of Akrotiri. In this case, the deliberate filling of the chambers with rubble may be understood as an attempt to strengthen the subsoil on which large buildings were to be founded.

After the underground chambers were filled in, the development of Akrotiri was rapid. At no other time in its history does it seem to have experienced economic growth on such a scale. As pointed out above, this growth may conceivably be due to the impact of the abandonment of the settlements of the northeastern Aegean on the islands to the south. At the beginning of the 2nd millennium BC Cyprus emerged as an inexhaustible source of copper, while at the same time there was a constantly increasing demand for this metal in Crete, which was just entering on the development of the palace system. Thera, lying between these two large eastern Mediterranean islands, seems to have succeeded Lemnos as a centre for the working and distribution of metals. It is difficult to account otherwise for the wealth and prosperity characteristic of Akrotiri during its later history.

Our knowledge of the city of the Middle Cycladic period is still fragmentary, since the later city

21

22

21. Jug with bichrome decoration (black or brown paint on a light surface). The pomegranate was one of the most popular motifs used in this category of vase.

22. Jug with bichrome decoration, with a depiction of a swallow. Thera, Museum of Prehistoric Thera.

23. Jar with bichrome decoration. One side has a depiction of swimming dolphins and seabirds taking off from the surface of the sea.

23

was built above it. Certain aspects, however, can be traced from the finds associated with it. Metal-working, for which there is some evidence from about the end of the previous period, seems to have been a by no means negligible activity during the Middle Cycladic period, too. We do not expect, of course, to find pottery kilns in the city, much less metal-smelting kilns, which are even more damaging to the environment. Nonetheless, clay copper crucibles, moulds for making metal tools, and nozzles for metal bellows found in the rubbish of the city, are enough to confirm that metal-working was practised locally.

Of the large number of Middle Cycladic clay vases, both local and imported, that formed part of the household equipment of Middle Cycladic houses, some may be described as true works of art. These are either small or large vessels with figures of plants, animals (figs 21-23, 26) or human beings (fig. 24) painted in black or brown on their light-coloured surfaces.

The most popular motif in pottery with bichrome decoration, at least on the basis of the finds to date, was the pomegranate (fig. 21), which is shown hanging from its branch. The depiction of the pomegranate on vases of about the 18th century BC acquires great significance in the light of the fact that before this the earliest evidence for the presence of the pomegranate in Aegean art dated from the Mycenaean period. Even the pomegranates contained in the cargo of the ship that was wrecked at Uluburun (ancient Antiphellos), opposite the island of Kastellorizo, are dated no earlier than the 14th century BC.

The belief is commonly held amongst archaeobotanists that the pomegranate, an indigenous plant in the area to the south of the Caspian Sea, was disseminated from there to the eastern Mediterranean. However, a few pieces of charcoal, amongst which pomegranate wood has been identified, have been retrieved from a horizon in the late Early Cycladic period (late 3rd-early 2nd millennium BC) at Akrotiri. This find, apparently insignificant at first sight, is of great importance for the early history of the Aegean, since it places the importing of the pomegranate a few centuries earlier. It makes it easier to understand how the pomegranate became a fashionable decorative motif in the vase-painting of the following period: it was not simply an exotic fruit, but may also have been thought to have magical powers. For even when its skin dries up completely, the fruit does not deteriorate with the passage of time, but remains juicy. This quality, combined with the countless number of seeds, and the red colour of the juice, which recalls blood, has made the pomegranate a symbol of abundance, life and death, from ancient times to the present day.

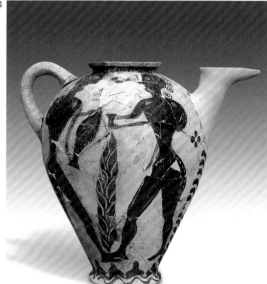

And it is not impossible that the specific vases on which the pomegranate was depicted were used in ritual acts during which this exotic, magic fruit played a leading role.

Vases with bichrome decoration were sometimes, though rarely, also adorned with narrative compositions, which presumably represent scenes either from everyday life, or from the now unknown mythical world of the inhabitants of the Cyclades. To this category belong two compositions that cover both sides of an ovoid pithos, between the handles. The subject of one of these compositions is rather static, depicting a bull flanked by two wild goats in a landscape with Aegean flora. The characteristic feature of the other composition is mobility, with a flock of seabirds flying up from the surface of the sea, presumably startled by the sudden appearance of dolphins (fig. 23). It is as though the vase-painter is attempting in these compositions to render the world of the land, sea and air, as he himself perceived it. There is greater detail in the scene on a bathtub depicting an Aegean landscape with animals and birds that seem to be startled by the appearance of the male figure at the left (fig. 26).

Quite apart from the symbolism and significance of compositions like these for the inhabitants of the Cyclades in the Middle Bronze Age, they may be regarded as works of art foreshadowing

24. Jug with bichrome decoration. One side has a scene involving two men.

25. The other side of the jug in fig. 24, with a depiction of an eagle lifting up its young, probably to train it how to fly.

26. Bathtub with bichrome decoration. Detail of a landscape with animals and birds that seem to be startled by the appearance of the male figure at the left, whose upper torso is missing.

large-scale painting. In fact, with the introduction of wall-painting, Akrotiri produced some unique monuments in the following and final phase of its life, which are an indication of the cultural level achieved by the society of Thera.

The thick layer of volcanic ash that blankets the soil of Thera has, for the past three and a half thousand years, preserved the final phase of Akrotiri. This phase was a period of great prosperity, judging by the imposing buildings, their furniture and general equipment, and their wall-painted decoration. According to the material evidence, the society of Thera had developed a cosmopolitan character, thanks to its contacts with the then known world, and an attitude that may be described as a consumer mentality.

The city of the final period – ca. 1700-1650 BC – was reconstructed from the ruins left by a major earthquake. The work of digging to great depths for the foundations of the supports for the new shelter coincided with a large earthquake in Athens. This circumstance was of great assistance in interpreting a number of archaeological finds that were probably connected with human behaviour in similar situations. Hitherto, for example, we had interpreted the absence of human skeletons beneath the earthquake ruins as evidence that the inhabitants of the city had managed to evacuate it and avoid being crushed by the ruins. This interpretation proved to be naive, at the least.

The reaction of the prehistoric Therans certainly seems to have been no different from that of any inhabitants of the planet after an earthquake: to drag the victims from the ruins, either in order to save their lives or to give them a dignified burial, or even for health reasons, since they were not intending to abandon their city. The archaeologist's spade has brought to life evidence demon-

27. Triangle Square with the West House at the left.

28. The excavation on the east side of Sector Delta.

29. General view of Sector Delta from the south. In the background are the Pylon and the West House.

30. The north facade of Xeste 2, with the timber anti-earthquake frames that have now been replaced with cement.

31. The south wing of Xeste 3, a large building that had at least three storeys. The staircase can be seen, in a fairly good state of preservation.

27

strating that after each great earthquake there followed a period of intense activity, involving clearing the ruins, rescuing the material equipment of the houses, and separating out the reusable building materials. The earthquake-stricken, living in temporary shelters, strove to save what was left of their material goods and at the same time began their preparations for rebuilding.

The manner and the speed with which the city of the final phase was rebuilt reflect not only its prosperity and wealth, but also the degree of organisation required to coordinate a programme of this scale. At some points of the city the urban tissue had to be modified to accommodate the new building programme. New construction techniques were used and imposing multi-storey buildings, both public and private, were erected at a rapid rate. The basic building materials used

28

29

30

31

were unworked stones and earth. Their experience of a thousand years of earthquakes led the inhabitants to devise ways and techniques to make their buildings earthquake-resistant. The imprint left by reinforcing timber frames can often be seen in the walls of ancient houses (fig. 30). Doors and windows were framed by carefully dressed stones (fig. 27), to prevent their corners from deteriorating. Dressed stones of larger dimensions were used at the outer corners of buildings, so as to protect them from rubbing by the loads carried by beasts of burden moving about the narrow streets of the city (figs 29, 30). More rarely the outer facades of some, normally public, buildings were faced with dressed stones. To these buildings, Marinatos gave the conventional name *Xeste* ('dressed-stone construction').

32. Saffron-gatherers. Part of a wall-painting from the east wall of Room 3a on the first floor of Xeste 3. Two female figures gather the flowers of the saffron plant. The one on the left holds a basket to put the flowers in.

33. Mistress of Animals. Detail of a wall-painting on the north wall of Room 3a on the first floor of Xeste 3. The majestic figure at the right wears impressive jewellery.

The floors on the upper storeys and the roofs of the buildings were very heavy structures. Beams consisting of tree trunks held layers of branches, on top of which was spread the floor of trodden earth, about 10-15 centimetres thick. The roofs of the buildings were made in a similar way. The floors of the upper storeys were in rare cases covered with large slabs of schist, while small pebbles from the sea were set here and there in the surface of the roof to prevent large cracks from emerging.

Only two structures have been identified as public buildings: Xeste 3 and Xeste 4, which dominated the southern edge of the city, not far from the sea. Of these, only Xeste 3 (fig. 31), which occupies the southwest edge of the excavated part of the city, has been fully investigated. It is a three-storey building with at least 15 rooms on the ground floor. Many of the rooms on both the ground floor and the upper storeys are connected with each other by *polythyra* (pier-and-door partitions), making it possible to unify them and create large assembly rooms. The north-eastern wing of the ground floor is occupied by an installation unique so far on Thera, though known in the palace architecture of Crete as a 'lustral basin'. The size and construction of the building, its design, the complete absence of household equipment to meet daily needs (e.g. stor-

32

33

age or cooking vessels), and its lavish wall-painted decoration (hundreds of square metres of paintings) form the criteria on the basis of which it has been assigned to the category of public buildings. The existence of the lustral basin, the general iconographic programme, and the individual subjects of the wall-paintings (figs 1, 32-33) have led all scholars, without exception, to the view that the building was devoted to rites of passage.

Xeste 4, which stands at the southeast edge of the city, is largely unexplored. It is of much larger dimensions than Xeste 3, and in the east wing reaches a height of at least four storeys. The entrance to the building is in the southwest corner, in front of an imposing staircase. The lavish wall-painted decoration of this staircase attracted Marinatos's attention, and he began his exploration of the building at this point. The excavation was in progress when fate cut the thread of his life. Although the excavation has not yet been completed and the conservation of these wall-paintings has not, therefore, begun, it is estimated that they cover a running length of over 50 metres. From the fragments that have so far been retrieved from the ruins it can be seen that the subject depicted is a procession of men rendered at life size, who are climbing the staircase holding various objects. It is naturally difficult to identify the building, given the paucity of evidence available at present. However, from its dimensions, the quality of its construction, and above all the iconographic programme of the staircase, it is reckoned to be a public building. If the procession of men on the staircase depicts foreign visitors bearing gifts, Xeste 4 may be supposed to have been a building connected with the administration, with authority.

Of the structures considered to be private buildings, the best studied and preserved is the West House, which owes its name to its location in the settlement at the time of its discovery. A building of at least two storeys, it dominates a square, the north side of which it bounds, which is known as Triangle Square after its shape (figs 27, 34, 35). A building erected in the previous period, it seems to have been repaired after the earthquake, at which time its entrance was redesigned to accommodate the raised level of the adjacent square. The rise in the level was due to the disposition of the rubble left by the earthquake, which converted the rooms that had hitherto been at ground level into semi-basement rooms, whence the low height of the windows. These rooms were now used solely for the storage of goods or the preparation of food. Two or three steps led to the new level of the rooms to the left of the vestibule before the entrance.

From the vestibule, a staircase led to the upper storeys. Of these, we may confidently describe the

34. Digital reconstruction of Triangle Square with the West House (left), Sector Delta (behind) and the House of the Anchor (front). Archive of Cl. Palyvou.

35. Digital reconstruction of the facade of the West House seen though the windows in the House of the Anchor. Archive of Cl. Palyvou.

36. Digital reconstruction of the L-shaped Room 4 of the West House, with the decoration that covered its walls. Archive of Cl. Palyvou.

37. Fragment of a wall-painting from Room 4 of the West House.

first, while the existence of a second is conjectured both from the flight of the staircase that continues above the first floor and from the volume of rubble around the building. A stone column base near the centre of the large Room 3, to the left of the staircase, confirms the existence of a central column to support the floor of the second floor or the roof, if there was no second floor. A large window, over three metres wide (fig. 27), admitted abundant light into this room, which seems to have been a weaving workshop, judging by the hundreds of loomweights found in one corner. From Room 3 there was access to Room 5 in the northwest corner, the exterior walls of which were broken by *polyparathyra* (multiple windows) and the interior walls by doors and cupboards. The southwest corner of the building was occupied by the L-shaped Room 4 (figs 36, 37) and the unique toilet 4a. In Room 6, finally, in the northeast corner of the building, were found hundreds of small vessels that seem to have been the equipment for feeding a large number of individuals (engaged in weaving activities?).

One feature that more than any other proclaims the urban character of the city was the decoration of these buildings with wall-painted compositions. No building has so far been discovered that does not have at least one room adorned with wall-paintings. It is as though the new city had been transformed into a gigantic atelier, where patrons and artists competed to flaunt their social status, in the case of the former, and their artistic talent, in the case of the latter. The wide variety of subjects could also be interpreted as the result of competition amongst the much-travelled, worldly seafarers of Akrotiri – especially the paintings depicting exotic landscapes with animals

38

38. Flotilla. Part of the miniature frieze on the south wall of Room 5 of the West House. Ships and their crews return from a voyage and approach a city on the coast, where a warm reception seems to be awaiting them. The free treatment of the subject and the great attention to detail are both impressive.

39. Gold figurine of an ibex, as found in its box, on top of the rubble from the earthquake.

40. Gold ibex figurine from fig. 39.

and plants unknown in an Aegean environment (fig. 38). Competition of this kind appears to be without precedent in the entire Aegean world.

The gold figurine of an ibex (figs 39, 40), kept securely in its case, was found placed on the carefully arranged rubble from the earthquake. The fact that the inhabitants did not take it with them – they probably looked on it as a sacred symbol, possibly of a deity they worshipped – may indicate that they deliberately left it behind to protect their city.

The city of Akrotiri was destroyed precisely at the height of its prosperity. A massive earthquake caused major damage to the buildings and, as always, the population of the city presumably fled to the countryside and temporary shelter. After the earthquake subsided and they had recovered from the first shock, the inhabitants of the city began at once to organise their life anew. Their first concern was presumably to rescue any victims. This is possibly the reason that the archaeologist's

39

40

spade has not located human skeletons at any point of the city. The victims, if there were any, had been removed by the rescue teams, for the reasons mentioned above. Immediately after this, the effort began to retrieve from the ruins not only foodstuffs, but also any household equipment that would be useful in organising life in the temporary encampment. Hastily arranged furniture and utensils, often with their burnt contents – barley, pulses, fish, etc. – were found almost everywhere in the settlement (fig. 41). Alongside the attempt to rescue material property, work began on the reconstruction of the city. Heaps of selected stones and piles of earth were separated out for reuse by the teams clearing the ruins.

And while the work was proceeding at a feverish pace, the volcano erupted (fig. 42). A thin layer of pumice, only 2-2.5 cm. thick, covered the entire island, sealing in all human activity. This thin rain of pumice took the work teams by surprise and they were obliged to abandon the city and what they had saved up to that point. This may account for the absence of human skeletons beneath the volcanic matter. There followed a series of eruptions, and the pumice that was heaped up around the crater of the volcano was as much as six metres thick, while on the periphery, inside the settlement, it was no more than about a metre. The following phases of the eruption were more violent and stronger. The entire island was buried by the products of the eruption in a shroud that took the form of a layer of fine dust about sixty metres thick around the crater and 6-8 metres at Akrotiri. The inhabitants of the city and the entire island in general probably did not have time to abandon it and must lie buried deep in the area of their temporary encampment.

This terrible tragedy that befell the Therans of the Bronze Age proved to be a blessing for modern scientific investigation. Thanks to the eruption of the volcano the evidence for Aegean society at the beginning of the Late Bronze Age is excellently preserved, making it possible to achieve a very accurate, credible picture of that society. The dating of the eruption on the basis of the archaeological finds to about the middle of the 17th century BC provides valuable evidence for volcanologists studying the history of the Thera volcano. Finally, the dispersal of the volcanic ash to various points of the planet enables meteorologists to study the meteorological phenomena of the time.

41. Almost everywhere in the settlement, hastily arranged vessels, often together with their charred contents, such as barley, pulses, etc., were found on the rubble from the earthquake.

42. The island of Santorini and the volcano. Engraving from the Illustrated London News *(1842-1885).*

41

42

Stella Drougou

Vergina
On the tracks of the Macedonian kings

One hot afternoon in October 1977, in Vergina, a small village in Imathia, Macedonia, the iron teeth of the monstrous yellow excavator crushed the soft, earthen body of Megali Toumba (Great Tumulus). The layers of sand and red earth disintegrated, raising a cloud of dust. The large, man-made hill continually changed its shape, the shape that had for years dominated the houses of the village on which it set its stamp (fig. 1). Years earlier, in the 1950s, pines had been planted on its slopes, possibly to hide the wounds left by the Greek Civil War. This had created a small grove in which children played.

The earth was quickly removed and clouded our eyes with dust as we waited for a chance to seize the coveted message of an ancient time. Sand and red earth clung to our skin and the heat tormented us. The driver of the excavator, Stergios Zervas, jumped down. "That's enough for today," he said, and looked at us meaningfully. "Tomorrow I may have something to show you." At once, it was as though a fresh breeze blew and dispersed our pessimism. We didn't have great expectations any longer, because so many days' work had failed to yield any tangible results. We had to be patient. The year before, in 1976, Manolis Andronikos had advanced the hypothesis that the ancient city at Vergina was Aigai, the ancient capital of the Macedonians. If this was correct, then at some point, sooner or later, we should find important monuments. If there was any truth in this theory, then the existence of the huge tumulus could naturally not be a matter of chance. Despite all this, the soil resisted us with its silence and its volume.

Stergios didn't usually say very much. He was very good at his job. He knew at any point in time what was happening beneath the iron teeth of his machine. That's why Professor Andronikos liked him, causing a little jealousy amongst the young archaeologists and colleagues.

Next morning, the excavation resumed, with the machines working again. Manolis Andronikos was on the site early, as usual (fig. 14). The afternoon was not yet upon us when suddenly everything fell quiet. The digging machine stopped working. The workmen and archaeologists gathered in the

1. The village of Vergina was dominated Megali Toumba, a large man-made hill. It was bare and treeless until a pine grove was created in the 1950s.

middle of the huge trench that had been opened up on the south edge of the tumulus, facing the centre. Soon, the surface of a wall appeared. This was the first building remains in Megali Toumba. During the rest of the day these remains increased in number and, as cleaning proceeded, began to take form. The possibility that we were dealing with more than one monument gradually became a certainty. It was October 11, 1977.

Over the next few days, excavation confirmed our first observations. In the long, deep trench, two corners of poros walls emerged, the first features of two fine buildings: an underground 'Heroön' and a large cist grave built of poros, which we later called the Grave of "Persephone." A few metres to the north, we could already see the brick wall that we would recognise a few days later as the superstructure of a large Macedonian tomb.

About one year had passed since Professor Andronikos, having found fragments of grave stelai and other remains of destroyed tombs in the earth of Megali Toumba (fig. 4), had reverted to the old

2. Reconstruction drawing of the hunting scene in the Tomb of Philip (drawing by G. Miltsakakis).

3. The facade of the large unrobbed Macedonian tomb (the Tomb of Philip) offered a simple, yet at the same time distinctive picture. In place of a pediment is a frieze with a wall-painting of the hunt. The lower part was dominated by a large marble door flanked by two Doric columns.

2

3

4. *Fragments of the grave stelai that had probably been sacked by the Gauls were placed in the deposits of the Megali Toumba. The best-preserved stele, known as the 'Madonna of Vergina', has the form of a small temple and is one of the finest examples of painting in the 3rd c. BC. Vergina, Shelter for the Protection of the Royal Tombs.*

5. *Aerial photograph of part of the archaeological site of Vergina. At the right is the palace, in the centre can be seen the theatre of Aigai in which Philip II was murdered, and at the bottom left, next to the road, is the sanctuary of Eukleia.*

4

view held by the British historian N.G.L. Hammond, that the ancient city at Vergina should be identified with the ancient capital, Aigai, for which he now had strong archaeological evidence. Much debate had taken place in the intervening period, and there had been great tension in the preparations and period of waiting. The likelihood that the statements of Plutarch and the ideas of the historians would prove to be accurate opened the way for a new interpretation not only of the monuments of Vergina, but also for much of the archaeological record of Macedonia. The well-known ancient palace at Vergina, first brought to light in the 19th century by the French archaeologist L. Heuzey (figs 5-10), and the large cemetery excavated in the 1950s by Manolis Andronikos, probably belonged to the old headquarters of the Temenids, the royal family of Macedonia. All these thoughts and hypotheses attended the beginning of the 1977 excavations season. The financial support of the Aristotle University of Thessaloniki gave a substantial fillip to the archaeological work. And the

5

6

7

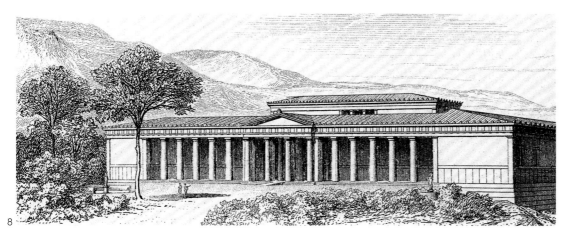

8

9

6-10. The French archaeologist and traveller Léon Heuzey came to the area in the middle of the 19th century and admired the visible remains of the palace on the hill of Ayia Triada, near Palatitsia. He returned in 1861 and conducted a short excavation. His colleague, the architect Henri Daumet, accurately and sensitively drew the architectural members and the ruins of the one resplendent building. (L. Heuzey-H. Daumet, Mission Archéologique Macédoine, *Paris 1876). The importance of the palace is evident from the superb architectural members and reconstructions (second half of the 4th c. BC). The drawing in fig. 6 is of the ruins of the cemetery church of Ayia Triada, which was built on the ancient building remains.*

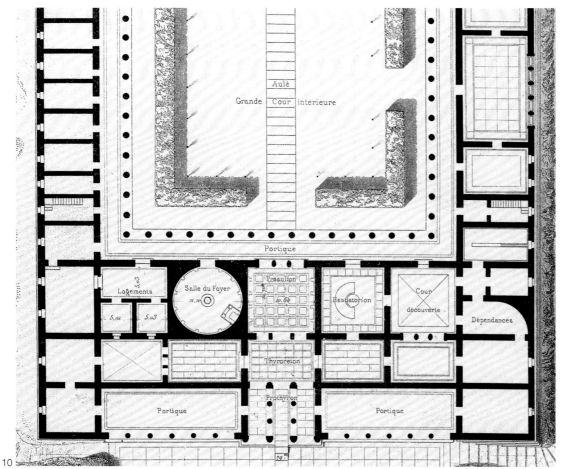

10

11

11. Manolis Andronikos in front of the Macedonian Tomb of Rhomaios, a monumental tomb excavated and studied by his teacher, Konstantinos Rhomaios.

12. Konstantinos Romaios, professor of Archaeology at the Aristotle University of Thessaloniki and the first excavator of Vergina in the 20th century (1938-1940), explains the excavation to his students, one of whom is Manolis Andronikos himself. Next to him, the old custodian Pankratis Pavlidis looks on.

13. Manolis Andronikos, Chrysoula Saatsoglou-Paliadeli and Stella Drougou in the village during a local festival.

excavation of Megali Toumba resumed for one more year. At this point, in the middle of October, the first building remains made it clear that the beginning of a thread of a great and unexpected discovery was unwinding. But nobody could imagine what would come to light in the immediate future, and in the years that were to follow.

The cleaning continued, particularly of the brick wall. On its top surface, clay vases, either complete or in fragments, began to come to light, the first 'reading' of which pointed to the years after 350 BC. These broken clay vases weighed on our minds and opened up some strange paths. In reality, these cheap finds were bringing to us the first messages from ancient times. It was curious: we hadn't seen the monument, yet we were certain that it could be dated to the 4th century BC, more specifically to the early decades after 350 BC. But we still didn't suspect what the excavation held in store.

The rhythm of the work changed, the programme was reorganised, and at the same time, the

12

13

needs increased. There was no more peace and quiet, and we got less and less sleep. The earth disappeared rapidly from the monument. From the wall that we first saw, we moved on to the upper cornice of a large wall-painting that adorned the facade of the tomb, as was clear from the narrow strip of its surface that we uncovered (fig. 15). While Manolis Andronikos was doing his best to bring to Vergina the conservators needed for the wall-painting, the excavation slowly approached the marble doorway of the tomb. This stood in situ, intact and closed. By now there seemed to be a great chance that the tomb had not been robbed. It was even more certain that the building that was gradually emerging before our eyes was a large Macedonian tomb with a magnificent, lavishly adorned facade. Above a zone with a dark-blue triglyphs, undecorated metopes, and a cornice lavishly adorned with mouldings and palmettes, there was, instead of a pediment, a large frieze, about 1.18 m. high, and 5.56 m. long with a superb wall-painting. We could not yet see the full extent of this, but it was certainly a wonderful piece of work and a rare find. The professor said repeatedly

14

that even if the tomb proved to have been robbed, this large ancient painting would recompense us completely for our efforts (figs 2, 3).

The excavation continued as the October days dwindled in number. The closed, untouched marble door in the facade of the tomb, and the volume of earth that covered even its large barrel vault, made the work difficult. The condition of the other, west, end of this barrel-vaulted roof had to be established. If it was intact, as was suggested by the undisturbed deposits, then the monument had probably been preserved unharmed and unrobbed.

We all concentrated on the large deposits of the barrel vault, which we calculated to be ten metres long. As the curved ridge of the vault appeared a little at a time, day by day, the excavation work became more difficult. Hundreds of burnt objects, fragments of iron weapons or of bronze vessels, clay vases and small pieces of burnt ivory came to light amongst disintegrated bricks. It became clear that they had come from

14. The excavator, Professor Manolis Andronikos, on the site of the excavation of Megali Toumba.

15. From the very first days after the emergence of the monuments, protection measures were immediate and rapid. Temporary shelters covered the parts of the tombs that came to light (1977).

15

16

16-20. *The poros cist Grave of 'Persephone' was found looted (1977). Nevertheless, it concealed a great treasure, the superb wall-paintings narrating the myth of the abduction of Perephone by Hades, the king of the underworld, the lamentation of her mother, and the three Fates. Manolis Andronikos attributed the work to the painter Nikomachos (middle of the 4th c. BC). Austere lines, rich colours on large surfaces, and a strong expression of the ethos of the figures are the hallmarks of this great painting in the Tomb of Persephone.*

the large pyre on which the tomb's occupant had been cremated. The cremation had taken place elsewhere, not on the barrel vault. A large number and wide variety of items had been cast on the fire. However, we had still not found the body to which all these funeral honours had been paid. The clay vases, both broken and whole, were of no great value, though they were precious to us, since they confirmed our initial chronological assessment.

The atmosphere on the excavation had by now become one of 'warfare', as the small group of archaeologists and workmen fought against time and the impending winter. At the same time as we cleaned the barrel vault of the large Macedonian tomb, we proceeded to uncover two more monuments nearby. All that survived of the underground 'Heroön' were the foundations and a number of fragments of its marble superstructure.

The large poros cist grave found between the 'Heroön' and the large Macedonian tomb had been plundered and was full of earth. When this was removed, however, it became clear that this was an important find. Three of the four walls of the tomb were lavishly decorated on the inside with fine wall-paintings (figs 16-20). A few colours, red, violet, yellow, and large bold lines enchanted our eyes. The grief of Demeter and the abduction-marriage of Persephone, legends sung in paint, had, through their grandeur, transformed the confined tomb into a large open space. We were entranced by what we saw before us, and even more impressed, as we proceeded, by the discovery of the large wall-paintings on the facade of the neighbouring Macedonian tomb. The subject of this was a great

17

21. A difficult moment, and an even more difficult decision for the scholar and excavator. The great tomb was unrobbed. The sealed capsule of ancient time had to reveal its secrets, concealed in the hermetically sealed underground building. Soon ancient and modern time would acquire continuity and the scholar would become part of it (November 1977).

22. Model of the Tomb of Philip, with its parts clearly distinguished.

and challenging one. In the evenings, there were endless discussions about the painting. The professor was profoundly pleased and impressed by this great artwork of antiquity. The most important, practical side of the excavation, however, did not leave much room for calm or relaxed discussion, and there was always some question that had to be left until later.

The large deposits of earth above the barrel vault of the Macedonian tomb were rapidly removed and the west end was clearly outlined. The hard plaster covering the barrel vault extended beyond the stones to the earth that filled the large trench of the building. All this was undisturbed, and showed once again that the tomb was probably unplundered. If things were as they seemed at this point in time, the excavation was becoming a very difficult, urgent task. Manolis Andronikos carefully studied the new data. He had to make decisions based on what he saw and on a great unknown behind the ancient walls.

Calmly and pragmatically, he continued to take the necessary steps to assemble the specialist conservators, photographers and craftsmen at Vergina. The stone-worker from Corfu, Spyros Kardamis, and his sons were already working on the excavation, as were the conservators Yiorgos Michailidis and his wife, Eleni, and Yiorgos Konstantinidis. The heads of conservation, Photis Zachariou and T. Margaritof, had just arrived from Athens, as had Spyros Tsavdaroglou, Andronikos's friend and photographer, who was to capture everything that came to light with his lens. Chrysoula Saatsoglou-Paliadeli, Kostas Pavlidis, Barba-Yiorgis Stephanidis, the undersigned, and a few excavation workmen toiled constantly, aware that we were approaching a culmination, the enormous final act of the drama. Over the last days we had the company of Oly Andronikou, whose calming presence brought us a little peace and sweetness.

It was 7 November 1977, the eve of the feast of the archangels Michael and Gabriel. The area of the west side of the Macedonian tomb had been cleaned and the final observations were being made of the entire barrel vault. It was now certain that the barrel vaulting of the tomb had not been violated at any point. At our evening gathering for dinner there was no longer much appetite for talking. Weariness, and even more so the thought of the work to be done next day, reduced us to few words. It was certain that the professor would take the decisive step towards the interior of the tomb. And this, of course, was the most difficult task of the excavation.

November 8, the feast of the Archangels. In the early afternoon the professor gathered us all together at the rear, west, side of the tomb. Around and above us stood a few people from the village who had heard what was happening, and one or two colleagues and friends, the ephor Maria Siganidou, and the then prefect of Imathia, Mr Theodosiou. Mastro-Kardamis cut a piece of the plaster and the last poros block of the vault that it covered. The silence made the tension even greater. Manolis Andronikos followed the work closely and decided on the next step. At that moment, none of us could help the responsible archaeologist in his work, except possibly the craftsman, who carefully handled and cut the stone (fig. 21).

A rectangular hole was formed in the blocks of poros at the top of the narrow side of the barrel vault. The breeze rushed impatiently from outside into the unknown dark room and time began its game before we even realised it (figs 23, 24). Manolis Andronikos thrust his head down into the hole and lit the interior of the tomb with a torch. He got up almost at once. "It's empty!" he said. Our blood turned cold, because we'd allowed our hopes to run free since the morning. No-one spoke, as we saw the professor's face set. He tried again, and bent even further into the hole, and over the vertical wall. Then we heard him describing a number of objects in a few words, as though he were dictating, in a slow voice. We breathed again, though at the same time we realised that it was something serious. Manolis Andronikos stood up again. He looked at us intently; his face was serious but he seemed to be lit by an imperceptible ecstasy. He shouted to us to approach and see for ourselves the "unknown site." At the same time, he gestured to us to be quiet. As he wrote later in his *Chronicle of Vergina,* he thought that for us younger archaeologists this was a special event and it was worth recording it on our consciousness. And he was right!

To the eyes of the observer, the large, dark room seemed enormous (fig. 22). I was in front and

23. The stone in the barrel vault of the tomb was cut. The informal entrance to the interior of the tomb was ready. The excavator is already inside; his archaeologist colleagues, the valuable craftsmen and a few friends are around, full of the agony of the next step (November 1977).

24. The rear (west) side of the tomb. An informal entrance was created in the intact barrel vault, for the scholars, for knowledge and for time (November 1977).

25. Most of the bronze vases and the bronze shield cover were gathered together in a corner of the tomb. On the floor around them are the remains of other grave offerings.

26. Small ivory head from the decoration of the funerary couch. Portrait of Philip II. Vergina, Shelter for the Protection of the Royal Tombs.

27. Behind and next to the marble door of the main chamber were found two bronze greaves, the gold gorytos (bow and arrow case) and alabastra.

looking down, just behind the double marble door. There was nothing in front of it on the floor; this is what the professor first saw, and explains his disappointment. Guided by the large pool of light from the torch, the eye moved anxiously through the darkness. Just behind, and up to the walls, the floor was covered with a thick layer of material. From above, we could at once make out metal vessels, silver and bronze objects (figs 25, 27-30). In the middle of the west side there was a large stone cube covered with straw and other materials. Our eyes tried to retain all the details of the picture. We were silent, trying to keep calm and be useful. This great game of time had left us amazed. Ancient time, trapped in the underground building, the time of the burial of some unknown man, opened up before our eyes and connected with our own time. The act of burial had now been completed by us, and there began an act defined by our own time, by today, and by science.

The professor and the conservators looked for a way down into the interior of the tomb. The ladder had to rest on a free part of the floor. It had to be confirmed that the building was safe. This was done, and soon the professor went down into the tomb and made his observations. When he came back up, he briefly described to us what he had seen, gave us our assignments, and the craftsmen made the iron ladder secure.

In the early afternoon, the photographer, Spyros Tsavdaroglou, began his work. He was to be the first to record what the archaeologist's eyes had seen, and much more, in hundreds of photographs, fighting a real battle against time, which had begun to smite the monument again. He worked for twenty-four hours without stopping and left. When he told us that the photography session had gone well, work continued with the task of making measured drawings of the burial chamber, carried out by the architect Yiannis Kiayias.

29

28

Two days later, two of us archaeologists, Chrysoula Saatsoglou-Paliadeli and myself, went down inside the tomb to record its contents and make the necessary observations (fig. 13). The humidity level was over 80%. The silver vessels and the relief figures on them made a great impression on us. Objects made of organic material still kept their shape, wonderful weapons, vessels and furniture, all of them signs of great wealth and luxury (figs 25-30). The first hours we were in there, we had the impression that someone was watching behind our backs, that we had disturbed someone, but later the needs of the work brought us back and we worked without break until the early evening. Dozens of boxes to package and protect the objects had been assembled in the old brick storeroom on the excavation next to the tombs. We stayed up late at nights with the watchmen,

30

28-30. Most of the silver tableware and drinking vessels had been piled up on the floor on the north side of the chamber of the large tomb. Vergina, Shelter for the Protection of the Royal Tombs.

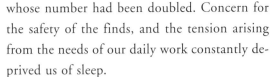

whose number had been doubled. Concern for the safety of the finds, and the tension arising from the needs of our daily work constantly deprived us of sleep.

News of the discovery had already gone around the world, but the reverberations only reached Vergina and ourselves when some journalist appeared, or one of our friends or colleagues.

As we worked in the tomb, our eyes wandered from one corner to the other, captured the images of the objects, and wandered off again. Every now and then, however, they dwelt on the large stone cube. What could this heavy object mean? The professor said nothing, and attended assiduously to the excavation and the finds. A few days later, he called upon us once more to go down into the large underground room. The chief custodian, Kostas Pavlidis, and the conser-

vator Sideris, were with us. The two men moved the slab covering the stone cube. Next to them stood the professor and ourselves. In a cut cavity was a decorated gold box, a gold casket, with a large star on its lid (fig. 36). We stood speechless and amazed. Inside the casket were the burnt bones of the deceased and a large gold oak-wreath (fig. 35). We took a deep breath and then went up out of the tomb for a while and closed it behind us. We were numb, as though returning from a great storm. Now things seem to us lie beyond the bounds of scientific investigation. For the first time since the burial of this body, we, the first people after the last relatives, would have to move this ancient casket containing the bones of the 'dear departed'.

35

We returned to the tomb. Inside it we made a small, light box of wooden planks, and placed the gold casket in it. The professor went up to the surface with the box, put it in his car, and drove off quickly to Thessaloniki. At the exit from the village, army and police vehicles were waiting to escort him to the Thessaloniki Museum. All of this took only a very short time, but this time belonged neither to the excavation nor to research. As the professor was leaving with the wooden box holding the casket, it was as though, after so many centuries, he was continuing the burial process with the exhumation. Whoever he was, the deceased was a man who lived in the distant past, and it had fallen to us who had chanced upon his grave to care for him.

The brief moment of time occupied by this great act soon came to an end, and we returned to our work. But this thought, this experience, was inscribed in our minds forever. There was still much to be done. In the evening, Chrysoula and I, now back at home, exhausted, looked at each other, wondering if everything that had happened was real. However, all this created a new, difficult

36

31-34. In the antechamber of the large Macedonian Tomb of Philip there was another gold casket protected in the cavity of a stone cube (fig. 33). It concealed the bones of a young woman wrapped in a gold-woven cloth with large floral motifs (figs 32, 34). The contents of the casket were completed by a precious diadem (fig. 31). Vergina, Shelter for the Protection of the Royal Tombs.

35. The heavy gold wreath of oak leaves and acorns was placed on the carefully washed bones of the deceased in a gold casket in the large Tomb of Philip. Vergina, Shelter for the Protection of the Royal Tombs.

36. The gold casket found in the main chamber of the tomb has impressive ornamentation, arranged in a strict, 'classical' composition. Vergina, Shelter for the Protection of the Royal Tombs.

37

situation, and would later open up a great debate, and, above all, would yield a wealth of material for the understanding of the history of ancient Macedonia. The debate had already begun about the identity of the dead body in the large Macedonian tomb, with its rich offerings, impressive weapons and furniture. From the very beginning, we had assigned the monument to the first decades after 350 BC. It was certain that a long, difficult adventure was beginning for archaeological investigation, and not simply for the interpretation of the find. For now, however, the pressing issues were the preservation, conservation and enhancement of so many valuable artworks and artefacts. It is true that much has happened, both at that time and in the thirty years of the excavation since then: the picture of the ancient city of Aigai at Vergina has become clearer, with its palace, sanctuaries, theatre and agora. Other important funerary monuments now attest to continuous occupation of the lower slopes of the northeast Pierian mountains from the 10th century BC onwards down to Roman times.

In 1978, another large unrobbed Macedonian tomb was uncovered in Megali Toumba: the 'Tomb of the Prince', which dates from the last quarter of the 4th century BC (figs 37-39). In the 1980s, the ancient theatre, agora, with the sanctuary of Eukleia and its fine sculptures, and many Archaic and Classical tombs were discovered. In 1990, the excavation of the Metroon began, and in the decade down to the year 2000, other important tombs came to light. The investigation of the site of Vergina is still ongoing, and its monuments are gradually being published. Most importantly, however, it is being demonstrated that the city was historically alive, following the impressive course of Macedonia as a whole, as became clear later from the finds of all periods, which provide important evidence and knowledge. The data assembled from the excavation enabled Manolis Andronikos and other archaeologists and researchers to form a picture of a great historical figure, King Philip II, father of Alexander the Great. Manolis Andronikos's bold suggestion sparked off a great debate that is still raging today with the same feverish intensity. Many of the ideas that have come to the fore have caused not only turmoil, but sometimes confusion as well, but no find and no persuasive argument, has so far emerged to overturn Manolis Andronikos's original suggestion.

39

For those who were present at this excavation in Megali Toumba and the events of autumn 1977, the experience was unique, and the lesson complex. The intense effort, the experience of time, the significance of events at that point, multiplied for all of us the value of the finds. The role played by all those who helped to carry through the project was enormous. One realised the value of people mainly on special days like this. Today visitors circulate amongst the monuments and dozens of books and articles have been written about them – which is a huge gain. Time has changed the form of the things that came to light on those days in November 1977. The protective roof, the showcases, the lights, the custodians, the visitors – all these are indispensable, important elements of our own time, the present time (figs 40, 41). Vergina was also the starting point for a large chapter on ancient Macedonia, bringing inestimable benefit. For those of us who were there, it is something more. It is time experienced, a legend that we actually lived through.

40

George Ch. Chourmouziadis, Marina Sophronidou

Dispilio near Kastoria
The prehistoric lake settlement

The interest in excavating the lake settlements of Greece was evinced as early as the beginning of the 20th century, though public references to ancient sites of this nature had been made even earlier. In 1897, for example, Spyridon Lambros made the following pronouncement in a lecture delivered in the Parnassos Hall and published in issue 2510 (1900) of the newspaper *Asty*:

"In this prehistoric period, people built huts in lakes, so that they would be more securely defended. There are no remains of this kind in Greece. Use was probably made of houses of this kind, however [...] In some of the Thessalian lakes, particularly Lake Boibeis, there are unclear, indistinct traces of this nature."

This interest derived not only from well-founded hypotheses that similar settlements existed in some of the lakes of Greece, to which, moreover, Herodotus makes reference in book V of his *History*, but also on the major systematic excavations that began in Switzerland in 1854. At Obermeilen on the Lake of Zurich these revealed a large number of piles that formed the building material for such

1. Panoramic view of the reconstruction of the prehistoric lake settlement at Dispilio from the west. The reconstruction was based on the excavation finds and a study by A. Chourmouziadou. Courtesy of the Prefectorial Administration of Kastoria.

2. Reconstruction of the prehistoric lake settlement at Dispilio from the northwest. Courtesy of the Prefectorial Administration of Kastoria.

prehistoric installations. Similar events served as the starting point for later excavations in other countries in the area of the Alps. All this forms the context for the interest shown by Greek archaeology. And 'Greek interest' in this kind of excavation also emerges from the following report in issue 3404 (1900) of *Asty*:

"The ephor of Antiquities Mr. Tsountas will probably leave today for Italy, in order to study the lake dwellings there, since it is likely that in Greece, too, in ancient times, there were similar dwellings, and that excavations will be conducted in some places."

It may be assumed, then, that Chr. Tsountas's visit to Italy in 1900 to study lake settlements in that country is evidence for the readiness of the Greek state to finance the investigation of lake settlements in Greece. There is no evidence, however, as to whether Tsountas ever made this visit to Italy, nor whether the Archaeological Society continued to show interest in organising a systematic excavation of one of the lake settlements. Possibly this is because at about the same period Tsountas undertook the excavation of the prehistoric settlements at Sesklo and Dimini, or because finds from lake settlements, and prehistoric sites in general, did not possess the monumentality that at that period in particular was the main requirement for archaeological investigation. This does not mean, of course, that there were not those who held opposing views: as early as 1874, for example, A.R. Rangavis regarded the Neolithic tools in the Bournias collection as the first link in a chain that ended in the masterpieces of Pheidias and Praxiteles.

A. KERAMOPOULLOS AND DISPILIO

Over forty years were to pass, however, before the first such excavation was conducted, as a trial, on a lake settlement in Greece – at Dispilio, which lies on the western shore of Lake Orestis, 8 kilometres south of Kastoria. It was the direct result of field research by A. Keramopoullos in Western Macedonia, which he explored systematically from as early as 1930, initially with the aim of locating the homeland of the ancient Macedonians. Judging by the articles published in the local press of the time, as in the newspaper *Kastoria* on 28 August 1938, Keramopoullos's research was greeted with great enthusiasm. Not, of course, because journalists and others appreciated the scientific importance of these investigations. They were moved simply by the fact that there were 'antiquities' in their region, which demonstrated their ancient origins, and even more so the possibility that objects would come to light that would make these origins more concrete, more real.

"Very important finds," wrote *Kastoria* "have been made by the wise professor of the University and President of the Academy, Mr. Ant. Keramopoullos. At Dispilio, he has found prehistoric lake dwellings borne on piles [...] These piles supported floors and wooden huts, forming a unified township." To confirm the accuracy of this information, it also published a telegram sent by A. Keramopoullos to the Ministry of Education and Culture: "On the southern shore of Lake Kastoris were found two lake settlements supported on piles. Using a small boat we collected twenty stone tools and sherds of handmade vases near the village of Dispilio." Keramopoullos did not, of course, confine himself to the announcing his finds by telegram. In *PAE* 1938 he gave full descriptions of the conditions of the excavation, which lasted a few days, and of the first finds. Particularly the piles and the 33 stone tools. Keramopoullos, however, who realised the great importance of the finds from Dispilio, returned to the area in 1940 and conducted a second excavation at "Nisi." This site had already been known to the bibliography since at least 1913, on account of the fortification wall enclosing it, which dated from the prehistoric period. Of this second excavation, A. Keramopoullos wrote: "[...] I excavated down to the bed of the neighbouring part of the lake, and at the bottom I found piles and stone tools as in the adjacent lake settlement." And he described the deposits that he excavated as earth brought there by the later occupants of the site, who also constructed the fortification walls of historical times. This 'description' of a Greek lake settlement was, of course, belied by later systematic archaeological excavations. It would be a historical error, however, to fail to recognise that the first hasty archaeological excavations at Dispilio, and the eloquent texts describing them are amongst the greatest moments of archaeological investigation in Greece. Not because they brought to light splendid, monumental finds, on a par with those of the Mycenaean period or other historical periods of ancient Greece, but because they provide important information about a measured, tranquil culture. A culture whose individual features do not give rise to exclamations of wonder, but which certainly reveal the pangs of man's struggle to survive, as impressed in stone, bone and clay. In materials, that is, which are to be found in one way or another throughout the history of Greece.

THE MODERN ARCHAEOLOGICAL EXCAVATIONS

Almost forty years elapsed between the report of Chr . Tsountas's visit to Italy (which we cannot be sure took place) to study the excavation methods for lake settlements, and the trial excavation by A. Keramopoullos at "Nisi," Dispilio in 1940. And fifty-two more years were to pass before the

3. The site of "Nisi," where the Aristotle University of Thessaloniki is excavating the prehistoric lake settlement of Dispilio.

3

4, 5. The east sector of the excavation at Dispilio, showing the piles of the Neolithic houses and the attempt to conserve them in situ.

6, 7. Sections of the stone enclosure wall that closed off the settlement on the north and west side.

beginning of the modern systematic excavations by the Aristotle University of Thessaloniki, which are still ongoing (2006). This investigation commenced in 1992 with four trial trenches in the eastern part of "Nisi," and was resumed in 1993 as a systematic excavation, involving its extension horizontally in space. It should be noted from the outset that the excavation at Dispilio not only has to deal with the unprecedented conditions that are a feature of the deposits of a lake settlement, but also involves a constant struggle against the water of the lake, since every time the level rises, the trenches fill with water and the excavation programme changes.

The excavation of Dispilio, which was so long in starting, not only had to deal with the objective conditions of the site. It had to answer from the outset, and in a specific manner, the difficult question as to what its objective was. Was it to confirm the enthusiasm of Keramopoullos and all those who from the very first believed that the piles of Dispilio concealed an enchanting secret? Or simply to assemble yet another collection of prehistoric artefacts? A large or small number of broken

8

9

8, 9. The east and west sectors of the
excavation, seen from the photography tower.

vases, a few stone or bone tools, and a handful of clay figurines? No... From the outset of the excavation, the decision was taken to study first of all the age of the settlement and its history. That is, to locate those elements that would provide evidence for its foundation and those that would lead to a conclusion as to when the settlement was abandoned and ceased to exist. On the basis of the relative chronology, derived from study of the pottery and confirmed by radiocarbon dating, it was ascertained that the first settlers at "Nisi" established themselves there about 7500 years before the present, and stayed on the same site for over 3000 years. This means that Dispilio was continuously inhabited from the Middle Neolithic period to the beginning of the Bronze Age.

With reference to the elements that were characteristic of this occupation and formed its individual components, three cultural phases may be distinguished on the basis of a study of the stratigraphy. These involve internal settlement events whose form is defined over time by the relationship of the settlement to the lake and consequently to the productive activities of the occupants dictated by this relationship. Part of the settlement, however, may conceivably have been occupied a little earlier than this. This theory is

10-12. The west sector of the excavations, where an attempt is being made to conserve the clay structures of the Late Neolithic period and protect them in situ.

supported by a few examples of pottery that are at present the object of systematic study. Now that the excavation has advanced and it is possible to assess the full depth of the deposits and the character of the finds, the impression is increasingly strong that there was continuity of life at the settlement, with intervals of abandonment, whose causes are still to be traced beyond the end of the Neolithic period. This impression was particularly strengthened by the three trenches sunk at the south end of the site where, in addition to a few post-holes and certain indefinable structures, a number of bronze objects also came to light (a small axe and a needle), and a large quantity of pottery characteristic of the period, such as kantharoid vases etc.

Questions do not stop at the age of a prehistoric settlement, of course. Particular attention was paid to the study of the internal organisation of the settlement: to the spatial distribution of functions and their relationship to the lake. This was achieved by uncovering a large area of the site. A study of this kind, of course, does not confine itself solely to the proper 'reading' of the prehistoric lake settlement at Dispilio. The site forms an archaeological sample that may (and this, at least is a basic objective of the archaeological excavation) provide significant information useful to the systematic study and interpretation of the methods of organisation and development of life in the Neolithic period in Greece in general, under the influence of a significant environmental factor such as the water of a large, rich lake, which would certainly be one of the basic sources of food for the inhabitants of the settlement. A study of a water culture!

So far over 2000 m2 have been excavated. A large number of vertical piles and horizontal timbers

have been discovered preserved in very good condition, thus making it possible to study with some confidence the way in which the prehistoric occupants of Dispilio processed the timber they cut from the neighbouring forests of the period and used them to erect their huts or to make other ancillary structures. Traces of destruction also came to light which, in their silence, provide arguments for conclusions relating to the inhabitants of the settlement.

It might therefore be said, in a very general and distinctly descriptive manner, that prehistoric Dispilio is a typical, relatively dense lake installation built on stilts. The archaeological record suggests that the relationship between the settlement and the lake changed over time. During the final Neolithic, for example, the usable space of the settlement contracted and was confined to the south part of the site, at the highest point of the tumulus created by earlier manmade deposits. The nature of the destruction level is also significant: in it were found structural elements made

13. Students of archaeology being trained in the uncovering of wooden finds during the excavation at Dispilio.

14. Clay object with incised 'communication signs'.

15. The post-holes in which were fixed the wooden posts that were the basic building materials in lake settlements.

of clay and straw, and post-holes defining areas of household industrial activity, as well as seven ovens. In the same area, though at a higher level, four burials were excavated, two of them child burials, and four vases were found bearing traces of fire, which were probably connected with some form of burial practice. One of these vases is decorated and may be securely dated to the final period of the Neolithic.

Nowadays, the view is generally held that the study of a prehistoric culture does not end with the determination of its date and a description of the areas in which it left its remains. The study of its economy is also of great importance: study, that is of the ways in which the fisherman, farmers and stock-raisers of that period 'exploited' the natural environment, learned its secrets and ultimately compelled it to be friendly towards them, learned how to live in it and to be at once its creator and its creature. The study of the economy of the prehistoric farmers and stock-raisers of Dispilio, along with the study of their 'technological' experience, was based on careful analysis of the large number of tools, clay vessels (figs 16-18) and food remains, which fall into the categories familiar from the Neolithic period. The tools are made of local stone, bone, horn and clay. There were also, of course, tools that came from distant regions, made of obsidian, or artefacts made from the seashell Spondylus gaederopus, demonstrating that Dispilio was part of a network of settlements with which it communicated and exchanged products and ideas on how to struggle for survival.

A large number of vases have also been restored at Dispilio, representing a wide variety of shapes (figs 16-18). On the basis of these shapes, we may speak of cooking pots and food vessels, vessels relating to ideological practices, and storage vessels, that is, pithoi (phot). These last are of great importance for the study of the economy of the settlement, since they are associated with surplus production. In some years, not only would the crop suffice for their daily consumption, but there would also be something extra. This surplus crop had either to be stored to prevent it from spoiling, so that it could be consumed later, in times of scarcity, or to be exchanged for other products that were in surplus with other people. It was precisely this need that led to the making of the first pithoi. At first, these were made whenever there was a surplus and the storage jars were needed. Later, however, the surplus was not fortuitous, but deliberately produced. And it was on this act of expediency that the creation of the market was based. So much for the pithoi of Dispilio!

As regards cooking, it has been established on the basis of the variety of shapes discovered that there

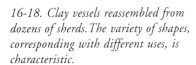

16-18. Clay vessels reassembled from dozens of sherds. The variety of shapes, corresponding with different uses, is characteristic.

16

17

18

was a choice between different ways of preparing food, and also a choice of foods for consumption. This last emerged from food remains, carbonised fruit, the bones of domestic and wild animals, and finds connected with the fishing activities of the settlement (fig. 22).

The life and activities of people who lived in a prehistoric settlement located next to a lake for thousands of years is not restricted to the tasks relating to the site and the economy. Ideas about various things occurred to those who engaged in these tasks, as they devised, made and used artefacts. Ideas about things that are easy and readily explained without much effort, and also about things that do not seem logical and are not easy to explain. All these ideas formed the

19. Neolithic jewellery from Dispilio, made of various materials.

20. Neolithic male figurine from Dispilio.

21. Finds with incised decoration that probably had a 'semiological' character.

22. Fishing tools and finds connected with weaving.

belief-system of the prehistoric lake people. An idea, of course, cannot be excavated, but it is possible to establish the way in which it is reflected in specific categories of finds, such as jewellery (fig. 19), figurines (fig. 20), the decorative motifs on vases, and a small ensemble of funerary objects, to which reference has already been made. From Dispilio a very important collection of such small finds has been assembled, made of materials of various origins. An important place in this collection is occupied by three 'musical instruments' made of bone and clay. There is also a fragment of worked wood, on the surface of which are incised horizontal and vertical signs, some of them recalling the signs of the Linear A script, and also clay and bone objects

with similar incised signs (fig. 21), all of which are attributed to activities connected with the 'ideological' life of the occupants of the settlement: that is, activities not directly related either to the organisation of space or to the economy.

Finally, it should be noted that one basic element in the strategic aims of the exploration of Dispilio was that the excavation, and above all its conclusions, whether final or not, should not remain an isolated event. As an integral part of a collective research project, the archaeological information needed to be transformed into specific historical discourse. To be transformed, that is, into public property through the publication of the results of the excavation: of the archaeological material

23

24

25

yielded by the excavation, systematically studied and assigned to individual functional groups (space, economy, technology, ideology), in order to be invested with its historical and above all its social significance and transformed into cultural information. Part of this objective has been achieved by the creation of the Eco-museum. This involves the reconstruction of part of the settlement, consisting of eight huts made and equipped with the materials that emerged during the excavation (figs 23-27). A further aspect of it is the construction of the Excavation Park, which is now in hand, and the submitting of the museological study for the foundation and operation of a specialised museum. And all that, the studies and interpretations, impressions and descriptions, dreams and disappointments will still be only a beginning, however many years pass. The study of a water culture is not easily relinquished.

26

23-27. Details of Neolithic huts built on platforms supported on piles, which were reconstructed in the lake.

27

Great moments in marine archaeology

Susan Womer Katzev

The *Ancient Ship of Kyrenia,*
beneath Cyprus seas

We glided thirty meters down, hovering over the most beautiful sight of our lifetimes (pp. 284-285). Here, surrounded by rippling eelgrass, a mound of graceful amphoras emerged from the otherwise flat seascape. This was the tombstone of what would become known worldwide as the *Kyrenia Ship.* Guiding my husband Michael Katzev and me from the boat above was Andreas Cariolou of Kyrenia, Cyprus (fig. 2). In his home town midway along the island's northern coast, Andreas was known as a citrus farmer, town councilman and respected diving instructor whose passion for the depths had led him to make his own equipment when news of the aqualung first emerged. He had found the wreck by chance two years earlier while diving for sponges. Once we explained the seriousness of our work as archaeologists, he generously guided us to the site, and in return we named the future excavation to honor his town. That is the story of just the first discovery. There would be so many to follow that our excavation findings will fill two large scientific volumes.

2

1. *An underwater telephone booth is lowered from the diving barge.*

2. *Andreas Cariolou, discoverer of the wreck.*

3. *Claude Duthuit holds a metal detector above the untouched wreck site.*

1

3

One thing was certain, the flat silty bottom off Kyrenia offered perfect oxygen-free conditions for preserving the wooden architecture of the ship that contained these amphoras. Our first clue to its age came from Dr. Virginia Grace, respected amphora expert at the Athenian Agora. She judged the jars in the mound as being made on Rhodes in the last quarter of the 4th century BC – just after the death of Alexander the Great.

Two summers of excavation were kindly granted by the Cyprus Department of Antiquities in 1968 and 1969. Under my husband's direction an international team of over 54 specialists anchored a barge over the wreck (fig. 1), divided the site into three-meter squares of plastic piping on legs, then labeled each artifact as it was exposed (fig. 5), and mapped the site using stereo photography, manual triangulations (fig. 6) and a system of moveable vertical rods running across the hull. The excavators' hands fanned debris into underwater vacuum pipes that carried it off the site. Carefully we peeled away layers of cargo, dining wares, tools and ship's rigging to finally come down upon the site's true treasure – the intact hull (some 75% of its representative timbers preserved) of a Greek merchant ship (fig. 7). We would later learn that it was built around 320

4. David Owen saws the starboard hull into sections to be raised intact. The port side was dismantled piece by piece.

5. Architect Laina Swiny attaches a numbered label to one of the Rhodian amphoras.

6. To 'triangulate' a small object, a diver manually measures its position from three corners of the plastic grid square.

7. The hull, seen from the bow, separated along the keel into two sections after years on the seabed. The well-preserved mast step is at the photo's centre.

9

8. *The ship's wood was held in fresh water pools for cleaning and to leach out the sea salts.*

9. *Netia Piercy traces details of a plank onto clear mylar. This process, repeated hundred of times, recorded the dimensions of the ship's timber before treatment.*

10. *Wood dowling joins fragments of the ribs (known as 'frames') together in their original curvature. From the left to the right are: Excavation Director Michael Katzev, Robin Piercy and J. Richard Steffy.*

to 310 BC and sank off Kyrenia sometime between 295 and 285 BC in the turbulent years when Alexander's generals fought each other to carve his empire into their own kingdoms.

The exposed hull, freed of the weight of its 384 amphoras, 29 millstones from Nisyros, and 230 kilos of ballast now lay exposed, split in two halves along the keel. After recording the wood in several different ways we dismantled the hull first in sections, then piece by piece. Over the next five years we coddled six thousand pieces of the ship in fresh water (fig. 8), drew (fig. 9) and photographed each surface and then preserved the timbers in a hot, water-soluble wax, poly-ethylene glycol, known as PEG (fig. 11).

While final cleaning of the waxen wood was revealing adze and saw marks, ship reconstructor J. Richard Steffy designed a flexible wood scaffold on which he began to reassemble the treated timbers. Using stainless steel rods to pin the ship together, he was able to match up the original joins to reshape the hull (figs 10, 12-14). This has become the principle used today to reconstruct

11. Ship timbers are lifted out of treatment regularly to see if they are absorbing the wax preservative well. Some pieces took six months to reach 100% saturation.

12. Originally locked edge to edge by mortise and tenon joins, the ship's wax-filled planks are now pinned in place for final exhibition using stainless steel rods.

13. Ship reconstructor J. Richard Steffy positions a piece of planking along the ship's better-preserved port side.

13

ancient ships. Consider that a ship's hull is like a piece of sculpture, its planks and ribs constantly curving and twisting to achieve its final contours. When a hull sinks and becomes waterlogged, the timbers will soften and relax. To find their earlier contours, you need only to rebend those flattened timbers to join where they were originally connected, and the ancient hull shape will be revealed. Steffy pioneered this idea with the *Kyrenia Ship*. Five years after her raising, the reassembled ship (fig. 15) went on exhibit atop permanent scaffolding in a handsome vaulted gallery of Kyrenia's crusader castle.

The men who built the *Kyrenia Ship* worked in a long tradition exactly the opposite of ours. Today we form a skeleton of ribs bolted to the keel and then wrap sawn, steamed planks around those ribs. This saves money. But in antiquity when labor, timber and time were plentiful, shipbuilding involved sculpture. The builders of the ship built up nearly her entire outer shell of pine planks before an internal rib ever went in place (fig. 16). To do this, they adze-carved each plank to its proper curve along the 14 meter long hull, wasting as much as 70% of the original wood, and locked the planks together edge to edge with nearly 4,000 oak tenons set into 8,000 mortise cuttings spaced every 12 cm. Pegs locked these links in place so tightly that, when the ship was launched and its planks swelled, no caulking was needed. Lastly the builders carved ribs to fit inside the shell and drove long copper spikes from outside and clenched them down on each rib's inner face, thus stiffening the hull even more (fig. 17).

The ship, so superbly built, sailed the eastern Mediterranean over a long trading life of perhaps 15-25 years, an estimate supported by the fact that there are signs of many repairs. Not long before she sank, she underwent a massive overhaul in an attempt to keep her watertight. A thin wood veneer was added outside her worm-riddled bow planks. A break in the keel was repaired. Then the entire outer hull was coated in pitch, and an armour of lead sheathing padded with reed-like matting was nailed on in overlapping sheets. The captain and owner no doubt expected the investment would pay off in many years' more service.

We suspect the captain and crew homeported on Rhodes where most of the ship's cabin pottery was made. In fact, finds within the ship tell us quite a lot about their lives. Their black-glazed

14. Ship reconstructor J. Richard Steffy adjusts a flexible wood scaffold to the ship's original shape using the ribs, called 'frames'.

15. The Kyrenia Ship, *her two halves now rejoined, shows a remarkable state of preservation despite sinking 2300 years ago.*

14

15

16. *A faithful replica of the ship named* Kyrenia II *begins to take shape at Psaros yard in Perama, Greece, in 1985, sponsored by the Hellenic Institute for the Preservation of Nautical Tradition, Harry Tzalas President.*

17. *The internal ribs are added to* Kyrenia II *late in the construction. Copper nails clenched over their tops act like staples.*

18. *A later replica of the Kyrenia, known as the* Kerynia Liberty, *was constructed in the modern frame-first method, but to the same dimensions as the original. Here, its square sail is adjusted.*

pottery numbered four oil jugs, four identical drinking cups, four bowls, plates and salt dishes, four wine pitchers (fig. 22) and four wooden spoons, telling us that a captain and three sailors lived in the confined space of the ship's 14 meter length and 4.2 meter width. A short foredeck held at least two wood anchors, their stocks filled with lead. The space below had barely room for one or two men to curl up. Topside, a casting net for fishing at day's end was drying on a rail. Sets of crockery found to either side probably hung there in baskets – one for each sailor. At the stern was a much deeper deck where crew and captain took turns steering with two long tillers attached to quarter rudders either side. One rudder blade survived. From this afterdeck the crew could adjust the single square sail. Below their feet was an ample, closed cabin accessed by a hatch, where valuables, ship's equipment and foodstuffs stayed out of the weather, and where the captain stored personal gear.

Between the fore and aft decks the hold was completely open to receive cargo. We believe the sailors moved across this space on two beams that spanned the hull and that they went fore and aft on narrow catwalks running along the sides at deck level. For the three crewmen comforts were few. In the last voyage, as no doubt in most runs, the hold was completely full. Deep down were the millstones (fig. 20) to supply bakers with replacements, now serving also as ballast with beach stones packed in around them. On top, were multiple layers of 320 tall and 28 short Rhodian amphoras (fig. 21), all lined with pitch and, we believe, filled with wine. In the forward mix and in the stern, 28 bulbous jars from Samos contained almonds and possibly onions or garlic.

19. The Kerynia Liberty *was built at the Avgousti yard by the Kyrenia Chrysocava Cultural Foundation and launched in Limassol, Cyprus, in 2001.*

19

No evidence of fabric survives, but considering summer sun on the amphoras and nighttime dews, we feel confident that heavy tarpaulins of linen fabric or sewn skins covered the hold, just as broad linen sails powered the ship. Sailors, we are told, worked nude but needed protection from the dew and chill that settles on the sea after sunset. Sheltering in coves most nights, cloaks and skins would offer some comfort as they slept on decks or atop the amphora cargo.

For the captain life was considerably better. He had the option of sleeping on the afterdeck or in his cabin below where we found an interesting array of goods. A cargo of iron ingots (fig. 25) was packed with reeds, possibly in a wooden crate over which lay a spare sail complete with the lead brail rings which guided ropes to raise and lower it. A marble basin on a pedestal that looks like a classical bird-bath and is commonly found on shipwrecks, seems to have been brought topside and assembled on deck or dockside for religious ceremonies asking or giving thanks for safe passage. Eleven knuckle-bones could be for gaming, but more probably served for divination of such unknowns as weather, wind and unfriendly encounters. Special to the captain were a bronze ladle with a duck finial, an inkwell, proving that he was literate and kept records, a possible 'private' amphora of wine marked EY and an unusual 'fishplate' for eating tidbits of raw fish with sauce in the centre, on whose base he inscribed the first three letters of his name, EYΠ (fig. 24).

20. While removing an amphora, diver David Owen walks upon millstones quarried on the island of Nisyros. The stones lay in three rows centered over the keel, also serving to ballast the ship.

21. Modern replicas of the Rhodian amphoras loaded on Kerynia Liberty recreate the cargo of the ancient ship before sinking.

As the cargo of iron ingots disintegrated in the cabin, a concretion formed around it, encapsulating rope, a bronze fish hook, a wood bowdrill, lids for small vessels in copper and lead and the tiny larva of a common housefly, amazingly preserved, Even remnants of foods such as grapes, pistachios, millet, olives, almonds, figs, filberts, pomegranate and garlic survived. Found elsewhere in the wreckage casserole pots, a copper cauldron and two portable grills, but no discernable shipboard hearth, combine to tell us that the men cooked on shore most nights, probably anchoring in a quiet cove and rowing there in a small boat normally towed from the stern. Fish caught by line while sailing or in the two casting nets would be grilled on the beach or combined with millet and spices for a stew that could survive several days of open ocean sailing if kept cool in the cabin.

What was the fate of our four sailors as their ship sank with a full load of more than 17 tons of cargo in the autumn, after the millet and almond harvest (fig. 23), some 2300 years ago? The coast was clear of natural hazards off the ancient town of Kyrenia. A few objects from Cyprus tell us that our 'venerable lady' had been here before. Her trade items suggest a regular circuit between Samos, Rhodes, Nisyros and Kos, then east to Cyprus and the Levant, with possible forays to

Egypt and back. Whether she had entered the Hellenistic port of Kyrenia on this journey we cannot know. But the circumstances of her sinking offer several scenarios. We already know that she was old and weak and heavily laden. In a sudden storm, the captain would point north away from the dangerous shoreline, trying to ride it out. This is the direction in which she sank. After doing experiments loading a modern replica with all the recreated cargo, we conclude that, unless the original ship was higher than we have evidence for, she was overloaded by modern standards. If her old, patched seams opened up again, captain and crew would have to let her go, seeing her becoming swamped by waves as they rowed ashore.

A more dramatic possibility came to light when my husband Michael Katzev made rubber castings of concreted iron objects found in the seabed cavity after the hull was raised. They turned out to be eight javelin heads (fig. 26), possibly carried on board for protection. Several of their molds contained the ship's lead sheathing, telling us that they lay in contact with the outer hull. One tip was bent at right angles, as if stuck into the hull when it sank, becoming bent when the ship rolled over onto her port side. Were these javelins stuck into the hull from an attack?

Despite her full cargo and ample kitchen and dining wares, there are some things curiously missing from the ship. Balance scales and sets of weights for weighing cargo are absent. Only

22. The crew's cabin pottery was made on Rhodes. Upper left, hands hold a wine measure, one of four found in the ship.

23. Nearly 10,000 almonds were found concentrated at the bow and stern. Their autumn harvest time tells the season of the ship's sinking.

24. Perhaps the captain himself inscribed the beginning of his name on the base of the 'fishplate'.

25

seven bronze coins of small denominations remain…two from the cabin, the others amongst the clusters of weights from casting nets carried in the bow. Our current theory is that these coins, polished up, might have been 'sparklers' used to attract fish to the nets. In any case, they do not represent the captain's purse of valuable coinage needed on such a merchant venture. That is missing. So too are any personal belongings of the crew except for four bone eyelets and two tiny bronze beads. Over a ton of cargo is missing from the bow, possibly perishables, possibly looted goods.

Something sinister is also on board. Inside the hold we found a lead 'curse tablet' folded inside an envelope of lead and pierced through by a clenched copper spike (fig. 27). Such tablets from Greek and Roman times were usually inscribed by a professional spellmaker with a curse to bring

26

27

harm to one's enemy. They are found planted deep in graves or thrown down wells, and they speak of binding the victims down, making them unable to function. Inside our tablet (fig. 28) there was no writing, but there were two pieces of string, perhaps to symbolize binding the old ship down.

In the years of her sinking around 295-285 BC Ptolemy and Demetrius were still at war and Ptolemy had just won Cyprus. Independent Rhodians sucessfully resisted Demetrius' year-long seige of 305/4 BC and favored Ptolemy for their lucrative grain trade with Egypt. The Rhodian fleet patrolled its own coasts for pirates, but Demetrius had declared a policy of rewarding pirates who could intercept trade in and out of Rhodes. Far away, on the north coast of Cyprus where small coves east of Kyrenia offered shelter to fast-rowing bandits, it is easy to imagine a group of opportunistic pirates spotting the old, leaking ship, heavily laden with Rhodian amphoras, approaching or

28

departing the harbor. Swiftly overpowering her, they might have hurled javelins into the hull to pull alongside, then taken off valuables and the ultimate prize of all, her sailors who could be sold in slave markets or ransomed back to their families.

With the old hull not worth towing away, a ramming or scuttling chop would bring water streaming in. I picture an illiterate pirate captain incanting a spell over the curse tablet he has brought with him. Driving the copper spike through it into a crossbeam, he invokes the underworld to drag the old ship down and conceal his ancient crime.

Old age, overloading and now piracy all compete to explain why the ship went down. We have put the pieces together as best we can for now. Perhaps through future technologies the riddle of the ship's sinking can be solved, becoming a next great moment in Greek archaeology. For, in the end, we have come to care about the ship's four mariners who spent years of their lives in close quarters, mending their sails, sleeping on cargo, steering by the stars, fearfully invoking their gods, and yet dining with fine crockery, savoring their wine and committing their lives to the *Ancient Ship of Kyrenia*.

29

25. *Loaves of hammered iron called 'billets', nearly 100% pure, were being carried protected from the elements in the ship's aft cabin.*

26. *The tips of small spears or javelins lay underneath the hull and were found once the ship was raised.*

27. *Before its unfolding, the lead curse tablet was inside this envelope, also of lead. A copper spike was driven through it and clenched down.*

28. *There is no inscription on the lead curse tablet, just two pieces of white string.*

29. *The helmsman of* Kerynia Liberty *steers with two great oars known as 'quarter rudders'.*

I would like to thank the following institutions that have supported our work:
The Cyprus Department of Antiquities, Oberlin College, the Hellenic Institute for the Preservation of Nautical Tradition, the Institute of Nautical Archaeology and the University Museum of the University of Pennsylvania.
Our financial sponsors were: the Cook Foundation, Cyprus Mines Corporation, the National Geographic Society, the National Endowment for the Humanities, UNESCO, the Dietrich, Ford , Houghton-Carpenter and Louise Taft Semple Foundations, and generous individual donors.

S.W.K.

Harry E. Tzalas

The *Kyrenia II*
An attempt in experimental archaeology

In the summer of 1981 after an attentive study and evaluation of what was up to then known on the *Ancient Ship of Kyrenia*, I decided to approach the excavator of this unique shipwreck, the late Professor Michael Katzev (fig. 4) and Mrs. Susan Womer Katzev, coordinator of the project.

So I started discussing the possibilities of obtaining their cooperation for the construction, in Perama, near Piraeus, of a full-scale replica of the *Ancient Ship of Kyrenia*. Before envisaging that proposal, I had repeatedly met with Mr. Manolis Psaros to ascertain the feasibility of such a project. Psaros is a leading boat-builder in Perama, whose ancestors had for generations built wooden crafts on the island of Symi.

I tried over lengthy discussions to assess if the project I had in mind was feasible and if Manolis Psaros was willing to embark on such a construction. His hesitations had to do mainly with the shell-first method of construction. After showing him the documentary film that narrated in detail the story of the discovery, the raising, the conservation and the final reassembly of the ancient hull, Manolis agreed, reluctantly at first, to give it a try. To my assurance that hulls were built differently in antiquity, that the planking came first and the frames later, Manolis's father, Mastro Georgis, a man in his late 80s, the most respected boat-builder in Greece, reacted by dismissing this possibility. As far as he was concerned, it was a crazy theory and his son should not endanger the family's reputation by attempting the impossible. And then what about this rocked keel? And the lack of

1

1. *The* Kyrenia II *is now a permanent exhibit at the 'Thalassa' Museum, Aghia Napa, Cyprus. Courtesy of Municipality of Aghia Napa.*

2. *On her long experimental voyages to Cyprus and back to Greece, the* Kyrenia II *encountered various weather conditions, from flat calm to nearly gale-force winds.*

caulking! Manolis's approach was more inquisitive: "If the archaeologists say that this is the way ships were built in antiquity, then I am ready to take on this challenge." Those were his words.

What had decided me to propose a shell-first construction, something that had not been attempted up to then on a full scale for perhaps 1500 years, was the fact that the *Ancient Ship of Kyrenia* had preserved enough of its hull timber. Nearly the 75% of the hull, including the keel, extended parts of the planking and of the frames, as well as pieces of the stem and sternposts and other structural details had been preserved. The assembly followed the intricate method of mortise and tenon joints. Save the Roman ships of Nemi, which had unfortunately been destroyed at the end of the Second World War, there was no other hull of an ancient sea-going vessel so well preserved to compare with that of the *Ship of Kyrenia*.

The documentary film I had viewed, again and again, showed the attempt made by the American scholars to better understand the construction of the ship by building a full-scale mid-section of the hull and then trying to learn more about how such a ship would sail by constructing a much-reduced replica. This strengthened my belief that a 1/1 duplication would not only help better our understanding of the intricate and little investigated method of 'shell-first' construction, but could also result in obtaining a working replica, which would generate, in turn, a multifold program in experimental archaeology. Besides 'confirming' experimentally that a ship could be built shell-first, I hoped that we would benefit in our understanding of how an ancient ship, so unlike the traditional Aegean caïques in its structural details, steering mechanism, and rig, would perform with its square sail.

3. The 'shell-first' technique of building a boat: Roman shipwright completing a boat. Frames are placed after the hull has been completed. Late 2nd c. AD funerary relief in the Archaeological Museum of Ravenna.

The *Kyrenia II* project presented various difficulties, not only on a technical level related to the construction itself, but also regarding its financing and other logistical considerations. What may have taken three or four months for the ancient shipwright to build necessitated nearly three years for Michalis Oikonomou, the master-builder, and his assistants. Going through my diary and notes, I see that I spent during the construction of that ship 307 days at Manolis Psaros's yard. The ship was finally launched in June 1984.

Old Mastro Georgis Psaros had predicted that the hull would sink because of the water that would infiltrate through the non-caulked seams. In his words, one could expect the planks of a small dinghy to swell and close tightly together but not those of a 50ft hull. Unfortunately, the old shipwright died a few months before the launching and did not experience the near sinking of the hull. In fact, the water did rush through the openings in the strakes and seams and soon filled the hull up to the main wale. But a day later, after the water was pumped out, she remained high and dry because the wood had swelled and the seams had closed.

In 1984 and 1985, the ship undertook a round of sea trials, which were continued in September 1986 and in the spring of 1987 with two long experimental voyages to Cyprus and back to Piraeus, Greece (figs 2, 5). Selecting the crew and planning the itineraries for the voyages from Piraeus to Cyprus and back was a major responsibility. The discovery of the ancient ship and the construction of the replica had made the *Kyrenia II* a mythical sea craft right from her launching. Every Greek champion sailor, not to mention those athletes who had won or participated in the Olympic Games, felt entitled to the supreme honor of being recruited as crew. Likewise every island of the Aegean, claiming a history of seamanship counted by millennia of years, considered that the *Kyrenia II* should call at least at one of its ports. The Aegean is scattered with hundreds of islands and the maritime route to Cyprus has since immemorial times seen gods and heroes steering ships.

So the crew was selected not only bearing in mind their great sailing experience but mainly because of their ability of going back in time and forgetting as much as possible, the innovations brought to navigation during the last 2300 years.

I remember that to the question: "how will you use the square sail?," the answer: "I will reef it and use it as a triangular sail" was sufficient to get the candidate disqualified. As to the course, I had to compromise and the voyage to Cyprus allowed for some ceremonial calls while the return itinerary with a full – Cypriot – crew, duplicated as close as possible a sea voyage of ancient times.

The construction, the lengthy sea trials and voyages of the *Kyrenia II* proved to be greatly beneficial for our better understanding of how a shell-first hull is built and how such as ship can sail with the use of a square sail, steered by two lateral oars.

It was proved, beyond any doubt, that a ship can be built by assembling first the planks of its hull and then, after the body is completed, to add the frames, as buttresses to the action of the sea.

This method of construction, present on every ship found in the Mediterranean from Prehistorical

4. Michael L. Katzev and J. Richard Steffy, the American scholars who collaborated in the Kyrenia II *project, standing in front of the completed hull.*

times until the Late Roman antiquity (fig. 3), results in a very sturdy construction. The *Kyrenia II* sailed very well under different directions of wind and conditions of the sea. The average speed varied from 2 to 6 knots. She has proved her seaworthiness, with a remarkable ability to sail into the wind.

It should however be stressed that, besides the scientific aspects of this project of "Archaeology by Experiment," the *Kyrenia II* project can be described as a multifold project, which was beneficial in various other fields.

Like most programs in experimental nautical archaeology, the *Kyrenia II* was an 'expensive' attempt, not so much in its financial cost – a lot of voluntary work was offered – but in that a multitude of people specialized in various skills invested enormous time and effort. The coordination of the construction and of the trial voyages involved an incredible amount of administrative work. The list of contributors range from the Minister of Culture of Greece, the late Melina Mercouri, to shipwrights, apprentices, caulkers, smiths, riggers, naval architects, archaeologists, historians, draftsmen, ship modelers, captains and sailors, plus a host of others – a list too long to enumerate in the limited space of an article.

I will mention only that, to safely escort the ship and keep a detailed record of the voyage to and from Cyprus, the Hellenic Navy made available a minesweeper and the Merchant Marine Ministry a 195-ft three-mast for the stretch of Piraeus to Rhodes. From Rhodes to Paphos, Cyprus, *Kyrenia II* was escorted by a destroyer of the Hellenic Navy and, on her return voyage, she was again escorted by the same destroyer, the *Aegeon*, and a 165-ft tugboat, the *Hellas*, graciously placed at the disposal of the project by a Greek ship-owner.

Because this project owed so much to so many, I thought that it would be good that *Kyrenia II* benefit a variety of persons. Of course, the ship should primarily serve her original, scientific purpose: experimental nautical archaeology. Nonetheless, during the 17 years that followed the end of her experimental voyages, she was assigned other tasks, which will be briefly enumerated.

Her role as a goodwill ambassador, aiming to promote the idea of nautical archaeology by experiment, saw the ship transported on the decks of large merchant vessels across oceans and seas. *Kyrenia II* was exhibited at the Mystic Seaport Museum in Connecticut, in New York (fig. 6), Nara, the old Japanese capital, for the Silk Road Exhibition, Seville for the World Fair, Hamburg for its 700 years commemoration and ten different Greek towns.

Thirty years after her launch, the *Kyrenia II* deserved a 'retirement'. The high standards of my expectation for the construction of a modern museum were met by the D. Pierides Foundation and the Municipality of Aghia Napa, Cyprus (fig. 1). She is a permanent exhibit in the 'Thalassa' Museum that will be equipped with a specialized library and archives dedicated to marine archaeology with the establishment of a centre focused on the promotion of experimental nautical archaeology.

5. Sailing with a light breeze in the central Aegean.

6. New York, July 4, 1996. Against the silhouette of the skyscrapers, the Kyrenia II *is ready to set sail and represent Greece at the great parade of ships for the Centennial of the Statue of Liberty celebrations. Courtesy of Melina Merkouri Foundation.*

5

6

George F. Bass

Uluburun
A Bronze Age shipwreck

Without doubt it was a royal cargo. And an exceptional one, at that. We can only guess how its loss, toward the end of the 14th century BC, affected the history of some unknown Aegean kingdom. The varied cargo included ten tons of copper and one ton of tin, the perfect ratio for making eleven tons of bronze, could have equipped an entire army with weapons had they reached port. Instead, the ship that carried this invaluable freight crashed against a rocky cape known today as Uluburun, on the south-west Turkish coast, and sank onto a steeply sloping seabed 41 m (135 ft) to 61m (200 ft) deep.

The labor involved in amassing such a cargo in the century of King Tut was staggering. The copper, alone, required the mining of at least a hundred tons of ore on the island of Cyprus. The tin, possibly from Afghanistan, not only was mined, smelted, and cast into four-handled ingots, it was then transported overland by donkey caravan to the Syro-Palestinian coast of the Mediterranean Sea. Hunters probably obtained both elephant and hippopotamus ivory from animals that still lived wild along that

1. The white vessel on the right of Uluburun ("Great Cape") is moored directly above the Bronze Age shipwreck.

2. Divers carry a tray of copper ingots from the wreck to the surface, buoying it with an air-filled lifting bag.

1

2

coast. Meanwhile, woodsmen in tropical Africa cut logs of what the Egyptians called ebony and sent them by an unknown route to eventually end up on the ship, along with Baltic amber from northern Europe, bitumen from Mesopotamia, a sword from Italy, and a royal or priestly scepter-head from the west coast of the Black Sea. What an incredible international effort!

Half a ton of terebinth resin, burned as incense in ancient religious rites, was carried in the ship's hold in about a hundred Canaanite jars (figs 9, 17). The resin's source near the Dead Sea was shown by land snails from that region that had been trapped in the resin. The ship's protective deity, a gold-clad goddess (fig. 20), was also Canaanite, as were intact pieces of gold and silver jewelry. And the ship's twenty-four stone anchors (fig. 3), of a type made and used only in the eastern Mediterranean, can be considered Canaanite. Careful sieving of the jars' contents showed that the ship also carried spices from the East.

Although the ship and its crew were of Near Eastern origin, there were two Greeks on board, Mycenaean

3. Resting between the rows of 354 copper ingots were most of the 24 large stone anchors carried on board.

4. Claire Peachy reinforces a corroded and fragile copper ingot with a layer of plaster of Paris over a fast-setting epoxy before raising it from the wreck.

Greeks of high status as revealed by their glass necklaces, their bronze swords, their stone seals, and the ceramic tableware they used. Can we doubt that they were envoys accompanying the cargo to a destination on Crete or on the Greek mainland?

The cargo, and part of the cedar hull that carried it, lay untouched on the seabed until 1982, when they were stumbled upon by sponge-diver Mehmet Çakır, who described the flat, four-handled copper ingots he saw as "metal biscuits with ears." His captain recognized these as Late Bronze Age ingots that archaeologists from the Institute of Nautical Archaeology (INA) were hoping to find. INA had been conducting annual shipwreck surveys along the Turkish coast, often interviewing sponge-divers and drawing picture of what the sponge divers might recognize, including such ingots. The captain advised Mehmet Çakır to report his find, which led to an INA underwater excavation between 1984 and 1994. The excavation required 22,500 dives by an international team, including graduate students from America, Turkey, Greece, Japan, Belgium, Germany, and France, enrolled in the Nautical Archaeology Program at Texas A&M University, where INA is based. Up to 35 people lived together for three to five months each year in a camp built (fig. 7) on the face of the cliff against which the ancient ship was dashed. Diving was conducted from INA's 20-meter vessel *Virazon* (fig. 8), moored directly above the wreck, just offshore. I directed the first summer excavation campaign,

*5. The position of every artifact was
carefully plotted on a site plan by means
of measurements taken by meter-tapes from
fixed points placed around the wreck.*

6. *Nearly 200 glass ingots, the earliest known, were among the raw materials carried by the ship. Some imitated lapis lazuli and others imitated turquoise.*

7. *The camp, disassembled and rebuilt annually, in which the excavation team lived for three to five months every year for eleven years.*

8. Virazon, *the Institute of Nautical Archaeology's 20-meter research vessel, was moored over the wreck as a platform from which all diving took place between 1984 and 1994.*

9. *Nicolle Hirschfeld carries a Canaanite jar across a row of copper ingots. To avoid stirring up sediment, divers normally removed their fins when on the wreck.*

and then turned the directorship of the excavation over to one of the students, Cemal Pulak, who is now an associate professor in the Texas A&M program.

Before removing any of the artifacts, excavators, as on land, mapped the site with care. Measurements were taken with meter tapes and plumb bobs (fig. 5), but stereophotography also played a role. Most of the cargo was covered by sediment, which we removed with nearly vertical suction pipes called airlifts (fig. 13). We carried the heaviest artifacts up the slope to land in a metal tray partly buoyed by an air-filled bag (fig. 2).

It was the deepest underwater project of any kind ever undertaken with normal scuba equipment, but INA put safety before all else. Extremely rare cases of decompression sickness (bends) were treated in a recompression chamber on *Virazon*. A physician was always on hand. Special diving tables for the project were devised by Duke University. And on the seabed we set up two "underwater tele-

phone booths" (fig. 12), air-filled acrylic hemispheres into which divers could retreat, dry from their chests up, in case of equipment failure at the great depths in which they worked.

INA calculates that it spends two years on conservation and library research for every month it dives, and this holds true with the Uluburun shipwreck. A team of INA conservators still works year-round more than a decade after the last dives were made, dealing with twenty tons of pottery, stone, copper, tin, gold, silver, lead, glass, faience, shell, wood and other materials, while Cemal Pulak, with colleagues and students, toils diligently to interpret and publish what was found, conserved, and then recorded by both drawings and photographs.

9

Meanwhile, tourists can see, in the Museum of Underwater Archaeology in Bodrum, Turkey, a film of the excavation, a full-scale replica of the ship and its cargo (fig. 25), and a displayed sample of the actual artifacts:

The oldest known "book" (an ivory-hinged boxwood diptych with originally waxed writing surfaces). The oldest known glass ingots (fig. 11). The oldest known tin ingots (fig. 10). The largest collection of gold and silver Canaanite jewelry from any archaeological site (figs 14, 22, 23). The only known gold scarab of Egypt's famed Queen Nefertiti (part of a hoard of scrap gold; the ship sank after her reign) (figs 15, 24). The largest sets of Bronze Age weights, including some shaped like animals: lions, bulls, cows, ducks, frogs, and even a house fly (fig. 16). Faience drinking cups in the shape of ram's heads. Ostrich eggshells made into fancy canteens by the insertion of glass or metal spouts, now missing. Musical instruments (finger cymbals, a hippopotamus tooth carved in imitation of a ram's horn trumpet, and tortoise carapaces that served as sound boxes for lutes). Weapons (swords, daggers, spears, and arrows). Tools. Perhaps the finest Canaanite statuette seen in modern times. The list goes on.

Archaeologists, of course, love to claim "the first," "the oldest," "the only" example of anything, showing that their work is providing new and unique glimpses into the past. Visitors to the museum thrill to see them. But the true value of the ship that sank around 1300 BC off Uluburun ("Great Cape") on the southwest coast of Asia Minor is what it has told us about the early history of the Aegean.

10

11

10. The earliest tin ingot ever seen is raised from the wreck. Before the excavation ended, a ton of pure tin in ingot form had been found.

11. One of the cobalt-blue glass ingots cast to imitate more valuable lapis lazuli.

I had a personal interest in excavating this Late Bronze Age ship, for I began my career as an underwater archaeologist, while I was still a graduate student at the University of Pennsylvania in 1960, by excavating the cargo of another Late Bronze Age ship, a ship that sank around 1200 BC off Cape Gelidonya, the very next cape to the east of Uluburun. It was a modest vessel from which we raised about a ton of pure copper from Cyprus, in the form of 34 four-handled flat ingots, and dozens of broken bronze Cypriot agricultural tools. In addition, we found a white substance, the consistency of toothpaste, that proved to be remnants of tin ingots. In other words, we had the ingredients, copper and tin, for making new bronze, as well as scrap bronze intended to be recycled into new bronze implements.

During the course of excavating the Cape Gelidonya shipwreck, and for months afterward, I assumed that it was Mycenaean, or Bronze Age Greek, for it was believed by virtually all 20th-century preclassical archaeologists and ancient historians that the Mycenaeans held a monopoly on maritime commerce in the eastern Mediterranean, and that Semitic seafarers, merchants, and metal smiths did not begin their expansion in the Mediterranean before Phoenicians first set sail in

12. The "underwater telephone booth," an air-filled hemisphere of clear plastic, served as a safety refuge for any diver experiencing equipment problems 50 m. deep.

13. The author removes sediment by hand from a large jar, allowing the airlift to carry the sediment up into the current 20 m. above his head.

14. The ship carried the largest collection of Canaanite gold and silver jewelry ever excavated from a single site; the largest piece is this gold medallion.

15. The wreck yielded the only known gold scarab of Egypt's famed Queen Nefertiti; the form of her name suggests that she was co-regent of Egypt with her husband, Akhenaten.

the later Iron Age. Indeed, the main reason so many scholars date the composition of the *Odyssey* to the 8th century BC is Homer's frequent mention in it of Phoenician seafarers.

I was surprised, therefore, to conclude from personal possessions such as seals, stone mortars, pan-balance weights, and a terra-cotta lamp that the Cape Gelidonya ship was Near Eastern in origin, probably Canaanite – at least proto-Phoenician. This showed that at least one Near Eastern ship approached the Aegean in the Late Bronze Age. But a single ship does not rewrite history.

The importance of the Cape Gelidonya excavation was that it led me to re-examine Egyptian tomb paintings, which showed that Egyptians associated the typical four-handled ingots with tribute from Syria. Indeed, the only scenes of foreign ships reaching Egypt at that time depict Syrian vessels, including one that carried copper ingots. The Cape Gelidonya excavation also prompted me to look again at clay tablets sent to Egypt by Near Eastern rulers. On the tablets, written in cuneiform, are lists of tribute, including copper and other raw materials, sent to the pharaoh by these rulers. Nowhere do Mycenaeans appear, in either the paintings or the tablets.

It seemed clear that there was a Near Eastern element in the maritime activity between Greece, Cyprus, and the Syro-Palestinian coast. Why had it not been recognized earlier?

The theory of a Mycenaean monopoly on sea trade in the eastern Mediterranean during the Late Bronze Age was based on the large amounts of Mycenaean pottery found in Egypt, Cyprus, and Syro-Palestine, for similar amounts of Near Eastern goods were not found by archaeologists in Greece. In my publication of the Cape Gelidonya wreck, however, I pointed out that surely goods equal in value to the Mycenaean pottery reached Greece from the Near East, but that they must have left no traces in the archaeological record. What could these invisible goods be? Raw materials, I suggested, such as copper, tin, ivory, gold, and food stuffs. But I could not prove it.

Now we have evidence of a ship that was bearing tons of such raw materials toward the Aegean. If the ship had not sunk, we might never have suspected the existence of these materials, for had they reached port, they would have been quickly transformed by craftsmen into objects typical of the culture that imported them. Tin ingots, for example, had not been found on land, yet such ingots must have been widely traded at a time when bronze was the metal of choice.

Although the ship lost at Uluburun carried more than a dozen hippopotamus teeth, they were unsuspected, for few such teeth have been found on land, because in antiquity they were carved into figurines that archaeologists simply assumed were of elephant ivory.

Glass ingots are virtually unknown from terrestrial excavations, yet the nearly 200 on the Uluburun ship suggest that they, too, were widely traded. In fact, Robert Brill of the Corning Museum of Glass has shown that the Uluburun ingots are chemically identical to the glass in Egyptian vases and Mycenaean necklaces of the period, suggesting a single source for blue glass in the eastern Mediterranean and Aegean. Cakes of blue material shown in Egyptian tomb paintings are identified in hieroglyphics either as lapis lazuli and turquoise, or as "genuine" lapis lazuli and turquoise. Because of the Uluburun discovery, Egyptologists now assume that unless the word "genuine" appears, it is glass imitations that are depicted.

People often ask me what was my most exciting discovery. I doubt that they believe me when I say that my most exciting discoveries are made in the library, sometimes months or even years after finding an

16. The smallest of a set of bronze pan-balance weights was in the form of a house fly.

17. Conservator Claire Peachy inspects one of approximately a hundred Canaanite jars found on the wreck.

actual artifact. Of course to find a gold scarab is exciting. But to learn later that it is a scarab of Egypt's famed Queen Nefertiti is even more exciting. And then to learn that this is the only gold scarab ever found of such a well-known historical personage is breathtakingly exciting. The ultimate thrill, however, comes when some Egyptologists say that they suspect from the form of her name on the scarab that Nefertiti was co-regent of Egypt with her heretical, monotheistic husband, the Pharaoh Akhenaten. For that is rewriting history.

18-24. Artifacts from the wreck include: the ivory figurine of a female acrobat with her feet on her head (18); a gold pendant of a nude fertility goddess holding gazelles in her hands (19); a partly gold-clad bronze figurine of a goddess, perhaps the ship's protective deity (20); an ivory cosmetics box shaped like a duck with movable wings (21); two Canaanite gold pendants (22, 23); and the gold Nefertiti scarab (24).

25. A full-scale replica of the ship in the Museum of Underwater Archaeology in Bodrum, Turkey.

Masterpieces of Greek sculpture
see the light of day

Aliki Samara-Kauffmann

The Aphrodite of Melos

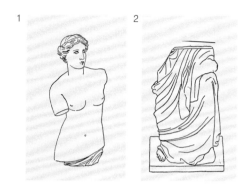

1, 2. Rough sketch of the two parts of the statue of Aphrodite, drawn by the French officer Olivier Voutier, 1820 (photo. Louvre Museum, Department of Greek, Etruscan and Roman Antiquities).

3. The statue of the Aphrodite of Melos in the stable of the villager who discovered it. Anonymous drawing, 1820. From the Great Greek Encyclopaedia, *vol. 6, p. 358.*

4. The Aphrodite of Melos. Parian marble. Height 2.04 m. Late Hellenistic period, 130-110 BC. Paris, Louvre Museum, no. Ma 399 (photo. Louvre, RMN).

From the time of the discovery of the Aphrodite of Melos to the present day, much has been written both about the story of the discovery and about the statue itself, by people competent and sometimes, less competent to do so: eyewitnesses of the event, later commentators, philologists, archaeologists and art historians – most of them French, though also Greeks and authors of other nationalities. The frequently controversial texts concerning the finding of the statue are so many that it has been said "*more ink has been spilt over it than blood for Helen of Troy.*"

The discovery of the statue on the island of Melos and its subsequent removal to France are to be seen in the context of the general policy of antiquities-hunting pursued by Europeans with the aim of filling the newly founded museums of that period. The French acquired the Aphrodite of Melos at the beginning of the 19th century, when the Greeks were preparing for their struggle against Ottoman rule. Specifically, in February 1820, the Melian villager Kentrotas, while digging on his land in the village of Kastro, near the ancient theatre, found the famous sculpture by chance.

The first to offer a description of the event were eyewitnesses to the discovery, sailors from the French fleet, which was sailing to Melos at the time. Of them, we may single out the officer Olivier Voutier, who, indeed, helped Kentrotas to bring the statue to the surface and then even made a rough sketch of it (figs 1, 2).

"*A villager was removing stones from the ruins of a small church buried by earth. Seeing him stop and stare at the bottom of the hole, I went up to him. He had uncovered the upper part of a statue in very good condition. I offered to pay him his wages if he agreed to carry on searching. And in fact, he soon found the lower part of the statue, but it didn't fit. After searching carefully, he found the central piece [...].*"

The first article in Greek about the discovery of the statue, though much later (1892), is also interesting. It was written by Photios Dimitriadis and published in the journal *Parnassos*: "*In the month of February of the year 1820, a villager on the island of Melos, while digging to level a field, found fragments of marble, which he took to belong to a buried building [...] Upon resuming the work with greater zeal, in the hope of finding more abundant material of this nature, he soon came upon a cella, at a depth of seven or eight feet beneath the surface. The cella, contained the statue, but it was, unfortunately, shattered. This unexpected find was the famous Aphrodite of Melos, which is now proudly housed in the Louvre [...]*"

The 'adventures' of the Aphrodite of Melos from the time she left the Aegean island until her arrival on the banks of the Seine are known from many varied and often confused literary sources. They may be summarised as follows:

When the French ambassador at the Sublime Porte, the Marquess de Riviére, was informed about the unexpected find, he suspected that it might be of importance and sent the diplomatic secretary Comte de Marcellus to the spot to settle the matter. Meanwhile, the local notables persuaded

LA *VENUS DE MILO* EST TRANSBORDÉE
DU NAVIRE *LE GALAXIDI* A BORD DE
LA GOÉLETTE *L'ESTAFETTE*.

5

Kentrotas to sell them the statue of Aphrodite, which had been hidden in a stable until then (fig. 3). Regulations in force at the time required that any find be handed over to the dragoman, in this case the Phanariot Prince Nikolaos Mourouzis. It was loaded on a ship leaving Galaxidi, heading for Constantinople. After this turn of events, the French diplomat de Marcellus managed to secure the purchase, arguing that his compatriots had priority and taking advantage of the situation. After this, as A. Miliarakis writes, citing a document of the year 1822 written by one of his ancestors, an eyewitness: "*There was some dispute as to whether the statue was taken by the French from Melos by peaceful means and through friendly mutual agreement reached between the*

5. Depiction of the top part of the statue being transported by the Greek ship Galaxidi *to the French schooner* L'Estafette. *The scene was played out in the harbour of Milos a few days after the discovery of the statue. From J.P. Alaux,* La Vénus de Milo et Olivier Voutier *(1939).*

6. Map of the south-east Mediterranean showing the travels of the Aphrodite from 25 May to November 1820 on the French ships L'Estafette *and* La Lionne. *From J.P. Alaux,* La Vénus de Milo et Olivier Voutier *(1939).*

6

Melians and her recipients, or by force and under the threat of the cannon of the French warship."
Despite the controversy, the famous sculpture was transferred to the French ship (fig. 5). N. Mourouzis, representing the strong Greek objections to this act of archaeological plundering, ordered the notables to be punished by a fine and a beating. Several years later, in 1856, de Marcellus recalled this unique moment in his book *Reminiscences of the East*: "*The same evening, the statue came into my possession and I took her at once, to the ship. When I finally saw the Aphrodite I had just acquired. I recited verses of Homer to her and admired those curves and that bearing.*"
On 25 March 1820, after a long tour of the eastern Mediterranean the French warship *L'Estafette* approached the harbour of Smyrna bearing its precious cargo (fig. 6). This journey

was described by de Marcellus: "*I carried my acquisition successively to Rhodes, Cyprus, Sidon, and Alexandria, where it was admired by many European travellers [...]*".

In Smyrna the statue was transferred to the transport ship *La Lionne*, which called at Constantinople in October 1820, took on board the French ambassador himself, and reached its final destination of Toulon in December of the same year. The only port of call on this last voyage was the island of Melos again, where the French explored the site in the vain hope of finding the arms of the statue.

In February 1821, almost one year after her discovery, the Aphrodite of Melos arrived in Paris along with de Riviere, who at once presented it to King Louis XVIII. A few days later, the French monarch was to present it in turn to the newly founded Louvre Museum. There, officials, academicians and art historians unanimously expressed their wonder, but disagreed as to the restoration of the sculpture and the ideal place for it in the Museum. Initially, partly restored (these restorations would soon be removed), the Aphrodite was placed at various points in the Museum, finally occupying a display room in a conspicuous position (fig. 4), from where it has been moved on four occasions: during the course of three wars, the Franco-Prussian War of 1870-1871, and the First and Second World Wars (fig. 7), it was moved for its own safety; the fourth and final occasion was in 1964, when it travelled to Japan on the occasion of the Olympic Games as

7

an ambassador of ancient Greek art and as the most representative treasure in the Museum.

After its return it was set once more in its former position. An emblematic figure of Classical beauty, Aphrodite moves ordinary visitors and famous men of letters, at the same time drawing the attention of international scholarship.

Though there are numerous books and articles devoted to this authentic example of ancient Greek sculpture, the experts are still not agreed about the statue type – that is, whether she was alone, leaning against a pillar, or was accompanied by Eros or Ares, and what object she held, a mirror, a wreath, or an apple, her attribute and the prize won by her beauty. According to recent investigations, Aphrodite, with her imposing carriage and the harmonious lines of her noble face, is probably connected, like other works from Melos, with a Hellenistic Rhodian sculpture workshop and dates from between 130 and 110 BC.

7. The Aphrodite of Melos in a wooden box, in which it was placed to transfer it to a safe location during the Second World War (photo. Louvre Museum, Department of Greek, Etruscan and Roman Antiquities).

The Aphrodite of Melos, the eternal muse of poets, was described in the 19th century as "beauty deified" (Chateaubriand), a "dream in stone" (Baudelaire), and as a "marble shrine, dressed in power and brilliance" (Leconte de Lisle). In contrast with the perhaps grandiloquent French poetic invocations, the verses of Georgios Drosini, inspired in 1921 by the centenary of the transportation of the statue to France, express simply the poet's profound nostalgia when presented with the unique ancient Greek masterpiece:

What if they have enthroned you / in some mouldering palace on dry land, my queen. / Your marble, without sun and without freshness, / yearns for the crystal salt of the Aegean.(From the collection *Alkyonides*).

Aliki Samara-Kauffmann

The Victory of Samothrace

The story of the discovery of the Victory of Samothrace is like a novel. It is connected with the life of Charles Champoiseau (1830-1909), French ambassador in the late 19th century in Adrianople, then under Turkish suzerainty. Like most diplomats of his time, Champoiseau was very interested in archaeology.

In 1862, he wrote a letter to the French authorities in which he asked to be assigned the mission of excavating on the island of Samothrace, which he had already visited. At the same time, he describes the condition of the island: "*Everywhere one sees hundreds of columns and marble capitals, which show that the site, now covered by evergreen plane trees and oleanders was once covered by temples. There is no doubt that serious excavations would bring to light art and precious objects.*"

Finally, in March 1863, equipped with labourers from Adrianople, Champoiseau investigated the ancient city, in search of "precious and rare objects." In the very first days the Greek workers uncovered the torso of a female statue at a depth of a few metres just above the ruins. They announced to Champoiseau, as he himself recorded in his report, word for word and in Greek, "Sir, we've found a woman!" In his enthusiasm at the unexpected find, he hastened to inform the French ambassador at Constantinople: "*Just today, as I dug, I found a statue of winged Victory of colossal dimensions. Unfortunately I found neither the head nor the arms. However, the part that survives, from the breast to the legs, is in a very good state of preservation. It exhibits very delicate workmanship the like of which I have never before encountered, neither in the reliefs of the temple of wingless Victory, nor in the Caryatids of the Erechtheion. The drapery of the garment is exquisite, with the thin fabric clinging to the flesh. Everything in it seems, without exaggeration, perfect.*" Subsequently, many marble fragments from the body and wings of the sculpture were discovered, as well as a number of other pieces, which were very substantial and made of grey marble. Champoiseau regarded the latter as the remains of a funerary monument and, on account of their bulk, left them behind on the island, planning to transport them later.

According to the French archives, the 'fragments' from Samothrace travelled via Constantinople and Piraeus to the port of Toulon, but thanks to the French bureaucracy did not arrive at the Louvre until May 1864. Immediately, skilled expert technicians devoted themselves to the delicate task of reassembling the pieces, and from this process the outstanding female statue was born. On display since 1866 in one of the Museum's exhibition halls on the ground floor, it was to be the subject of general admiration (fig. 3). Meanwhile, Champoiseau, on assignment in Italy, continued to yearn nostalgically for Samothrace and attempted in vain to procure fresh funding to reinvestigate the island. In 1873 and 1875, during two official missions, Austrian archaeologists headed by A. Hauser and A. Conze, located many buildings of the ancient city and the sanctuary, as well as the place where the Victory was found. At the same time they studied the restoration of the entire monument, in connection with the substantial pieces from the old French excavations which, according to them, depicted the prow of a ship that formed the base of the statue. Conze, indeed, states that in a chance meeting with Champoiseau on the ship to Adrianople, he informed him of the above studies. This brought home to the French diplomat the question of Austrian rivalry and also provided him

1. The Victory of Samothrace on its pedestal (Parian marble and Rhodian marble). Height 3.28 m. Rhodian workshop. About 190 BC. Paris, Louvre Museum, Ma 2369 (photo. Louvre, RMN).

2. Plaster copy of the statue of the Victory of Samothrace, placed as a trial on its original base, which had the shape of ship's prow (around 1880; photo made available by Marianne Hamiaux).

with the perfect arguments by which finally to secure the mission he sought. With lightning speed by the standards of the day, and despite all the technical difficulties, he loaded twenty-nine of his 'celebrated stones' on a ship for France in July 1879.

As soon as the new pieces reached the Louvre and the team of conservationists and marble-technicians assembled them experimentally together with the plaster cast of the statue in the Museum courtyard (fig. 2), the result was striking and it was decided to reassemble the entire monument. The torso was reconstructed, the wings were added and restored (the left wing is entirely a restoration), and when the statue was placed on its prow-shaped base, the sculpture was more than 3 metres high and weighed over a thousand kilos.

In 1884, the sculpture, in its new imposing form, was put on display in the ideal space designed especially for it at the top of the most monumental staircase in the Louvre. A few years later, in 1892, the indefatigable Champoiseau, still longing for Samothrace, exploited the glory he had acquired from his important find and returned once more to the island, hoping that he would find the arms and head of the statue. Instead, he brought back a box containing some marble fragments of the wings and garment of the Victory, which were kept in the Museum storerooms.

From the end of the 19th century to the present, this "heaven-sent ethereal woman who became a sculpture," an eternal source of inspiration for modern literature and art, has remained in her conspicuous position, indifferent to the various rearrangements of the Museum. The only exception was the period of the Second World War, when she was transported, for her safety, along with other Greek antiquities, to central France (fig. 4 and 5). After her return in 1945, which was looked upon as symbolizing the restoration of national freedom, she was reinstated in the same distinguished place, where her triumphant silhouette would impress and move millions of visitors.

Finally, the French archaeologist Jean Charbonneaux, Director of the Greek department of the Louvre in the 1950s, excavated a trial trench on Samothrace, in cooperation with the American School of Classical Studies, which has been responsible for archaeological excavations on the island from that time to the present day, and had the good fortune to uncover the palm of the right hand of the Victory. This new fragment, and two fingers found earlier by the Austrians, were presented as a permanent loan to the Louvre and have since then been on display opposite the famous sculpture.

3

4

5

This gigantic figure, made of white Parian marble, dominated the highest part of the sanctuary of the Kabeiroi on Samothrace and gave the impression that she was flying and sailing at one and the same time. With wings still spread as if in descent (fig. 1), Victory barely touches the prow-shaped base on which she was placed, perhaps recalling a victorious naval encounter, probably the victory won by the Rhodians against the fleet of Antiochos at Side and Myonnesos in 190 and 189 BC. She is a work of a Rhodian or Asia Minor workshop and belongs to the mature phase of Hellenistic sculpture at the beginning of the 2nd century BC. Representative of Rhodian baroque, this style is characterised by the dramatic intensity of the drapery, which billows in the wind with strong chiaroscuro effects, and found its culminating expression in the decoration of the famous Pergamon altar.

3. The Victory of Samothrace in the Louvre Museum, before its wings were placed in position (1866-1880; photo. Louvre, Department of Greek, Etruscan and Roman Antiquities).

4, 5. The Victory, placed in a wooden frame, is taken away from the Louvre Museum for safe-keeping during the Second World War (photo. Louvre, Department of Modern Sculpture).

Acknowledgement

I would like to express my grateful thanks to Alain Pasquier, director of the Department of Greek, Etruscan and Roman Antiquities of the Louvre, who offered me every facility so that I could in turn write a few lines in Greek on the two famous statues. I would also like to thank Marianne Hamiaux, scientific collaborator in the Department of Greek, Etruscan and Roman Antiquities of the Louvre and author of many studies on the Victory of Samothrace, for the valuable information she has supplied.

Georgios Steinhauer

The Piraeus bronze statues

The four bronze statues that are now the pride of the Piraeus Museum are amongst the very few – no more than fifty – works of large-scale sculpture in which the spirit of ancient Greek art is still preserved with its original clarity. Forty-five years later, the day of their discovery still remains fresh in the memory of an entire generation of Piraeus. This was the point in time that saw the crystallisation of growing expectations for the promotion and regeneration of the city.

It was a warm summer morning, Saturday – still a work day at the time – 18 July 1959, and the Hydrex Company was digging in order to lay pipes at the intersection of Georgiou I and Philonos Streets, near the north-west corner of the Tinaneios Garden. Suddenly, at a depth of about 1.50 m., just below the asphalt, the pneumatic drill hit a hard object – the hand of a bronze kouros that seemed to be greeting the dawning of a new day for archaeology in Piraeus (fig. 2). Dimitrios Kalantonis, the only custodian of the small local, hitherto unknown, Museum was at once informed, and he in turn telephoned (those were different days – more direct and more effective) the Director of the Archaeological Service, the late Yiannis Papadimitriou, who rushed to the site with his then curator, Efthymios Mastrokostas. An excavation was then carried out by a special team of the Archaeological Service under the supervision of Mastrokostas, amidst general enthusiasm that was not diminished by the heatwave and the crowd that jostled around the trench, as the surprises of the new finds succeeded each other in rapid succession.

Finally, in the early evening, after seven hours of excavation, two larger than life-size bronze statues were removed to the Museum – the Archaic Apollo and the large Artemis dating from the 4th century, along with a complete marble herm in the type of the Hermes of Alkamenes. News of the find spread rapidly. On the very same afternoon, Pavlos Dedidakis, the Mayor of Piraeus, G. Boyiatzis, from the Ministry of Education and Culture, and Dim. Alibrantis, the Deputy Minister of Economic Affairs, came to see it, while the Prime Minister, Konstantinos Karamanlis, accompanied by the Minister of Shipping, Georgios Andrianopoulos, himself from Piraeus, came down the following afternoon, and a few days later – in a notable escalation – King Paul himself and Crown Prince Constantine paid a visit.

The excavations continued at the same pace, and for a week the entire city revolved around the small trench in the middle of the main street. Another surprise came at the end of the week, on Saturday 25 July: after the discovery of a bronze shield the day before, a second herm was found, then the marble statuette of the eastern Artemis Kindyas, a bronze tragic mask, and finally, embracing each other, the larger than life-size bronze statue of Athena and a second – this time smaller – bronze statue of Artemis (fig. 3).

At this point the difficulties began – the conservation problems, and above all the problems of recognition, dating and identification, which, by a strange (but not fortuitous) coincidence attend all the great finds. The splendour of the discovery overshadowed the find itself, as often happens. So great was the enthusiasm, such the focus on the magic moment, that only the journalists, those capturers of the instant, managed to preserve some of its details. Apart from references in the archaeological journals to Papadimitriou's lecture the following year, and the publications by Miltiadis Paraskevaidis in *Kathimerini* and the foreign press, the archives of the Archaeological Service are silent. No daybooks have been found, nor drawings, and not even photographs, apart from those in the newspapers. Even the excellent state of preservation of the statues was compromised when they suffered irreparable damage due to neglect, particularly in the case of the Athena, which was abandoned without notice for a long time on the damp floor of the Piraeus Museum. (I remember it there myself, as a child.)

Where did these statues originally belong? All that we know is that they were found arranged in groups (not piled up by chance) at a depth of 0.85-1.50 m. in a space measuring 5.70 x 2.30 m. in the south corner of a room with thick (0.65 m.) walls, which is thought to have been square. A small trial trench

in the north part of the room, which continued under the tramlines, revealed that it had probably been completely destroyed. At this point we enter the realm of hypothesis as to the date, manner and reason for the concealment of the finds, and endless debate on their origins, date and style.

From the way in which they had been 'packed' and the place they were found, a short distance from Akti Miaouli and about 160 m. from the head of the main harbour, it seemed clear at first that they had been stored in a stoa in the harbour with a view to being taken off to Italy. The discovery "near the statues" of a coin of King Mithridates VI the Eupator, issued in 87/86 BC, left no doubt as to the connection between the assembling of the statues and a state of war: either as a

1. The Piraeus Apollo, possibly the earliest surviving large-scale bronze sculpture, differs from the archetypal kouros in that the positions of the legs are reversed and the torso and head are slightly turned towards the raised hand holding the bowl. A new spirit informs the epiphany of the god, calling the adorant, and also the modern visitor, to a new life. Piraeus, Archaeological Museum.

2. Apollo, who can just be seen beneath the hermaic stele, was the first of the bronzes to come to light. At the right, still covered by earth, can be seen the legs of the large Artemis. Archive of the Archaeological Society at Athens.

result of the plundering of the sanctuaries of Piraeus after the city was captured by Sulla in 86 BC, or – more probably, since this would solve the problem of their subsequent abandonment – as a precautionary measure to protect them in the face of the impending Roman attack, during which they were buried. In this case, either the statues were from sanctuaries in Piraeus (sanctuary of Zeus Soter and Athena Soteira, sanctuary of Artemis Mounichia) and on the coast (sanctuary of Apollo Zoster), or from Delos, as G. Dontas suggested, noting the triple presence of Artemis. They may have been part of the treasure of Apollo (the sacred funds) which Mithridates' general sent to Athens after the capture of the island in 88 BC. If the latter hypothesis is valid, it gives rise to hope of many more finds from the area.

There are, however, less dramatic interpretations of the find. Despite the short distance from the harbour, it is now certain that the room in which the sculptures were found did not belong to the well-known stoas of the Emporion, traces of which have been found partly submerged in the sea (the level of which has risen since that time). The ancient crossroads, and the banquet room of a Classical house that had been uncovered slightly earlier in the basement of the adjacent church of Ayia Triada, demonstrate that this area was outside the harbour

3. Rare amateur photograph of the discovery of the statues of Athena and Artemis, which had been stored embracing each other, in order to save space. Archive of the Archaeological Society at Athens.

4. The small Artemis. The goddess's column-slim girlish body, hidden beneath the dense drapery, is emphasised by the tapering of the body and the successive horizontal divisions of the highly girt peplos. Together with the small head, the hair in a top-knot, it acquires an unexpected youthful unsteadiness as the figure turns towards the relaxed right leg. Piraeus, Archaeological Museum.

5. On the back of the small Artemis, the careful coiffure was unaffected by the corrosion that destroyed the delicate facial features of the young huntress. How the quiver, held on her left, was supported is an enigma. Piraeus, Archaeological Museum.

6. The statue of the large Artemis reflects a different conception of the goddess, that of a serious young woman, in which her role as huntress is indicated only by the position of the fingers holding the bow and arrow, and the quiver on her back. The statue is attributed to the sculptor Euphranor on the basis of similarities with the Apollo Patroos in the Agora. Piraeus, Archaeological Museum.

6

zone, inside the city. On the other hand, the archaeological levels, disturbed by modern interventions, and the many building phases of the site (of which Papadimitriou speaks) from the 5th century BC to the Roman – though not Late Roman – period cannot easily be reconciled with the hypothesis that the statues were interred at an early date (they would have been found or destroyed in the meantime), much less with the recent interpretation of the site as a Late Hellenistic classicising workshop. Even less convincing is the theory that the storage area was destroyed by a great fire that followed the capture of Piraeus in 86 BC. This would be expected to have extended to the site and, with the high temperatures created, would have affected the statues irrevocably: on the contrary, however, they are excellently preserved (apart from the little Artemis, which is eroded by water). The question of the reason for the concealment thus remains open, as does that of the date, which could theoretically be any point in time between the 1st century BC and the 3rd century AD, when the city was finally destroyed by the Herulians.

The identification – and dating – of the statues followed a parallel course. The early enthusiastic hypotheses, arguing that they originated from and therefore should be kept in Piraeus, sought to identify them with the cult statues of the sanctuary of Zeus Soter (Athena Soteira – in the drapery of whose peplos some similarity has been detected with the Eirene of Kephisodotos – and Zeus Soter, a hypothetical kouros-Zeus) and of Artemis Mounichia. These were succeeded by

7, 8. The larger than life-size Piraeus Athena, which was certainly a cult statue, is a distant memory of the majestic Parthenos of Pheidas, just as the Athens of Lykourgos was a memory of that of Perikles. An oblique overfall and an oblique aegis emphasise the swaying movement and carry the eye to the right, where the attention focuses on the hand holding the Victory, while the left hand, with the spear, rests lightly on the shield. The overfall, ignoring the existence of the helmet, is raised behind to cover the head, as was the custom, though here its only purpose is to reveal the back, making the swaying motion of the figure more evident. Piraeus, Archaeological Museum.

academically more sober theories. Golden-haired Apollo has been recognised in the statue of the kouros (fig. 1). The ethos of the god is evident in the tilt of the head and the way in which he holds the phiale and the bow. It is a powerful Archaising piece of the early 5th century BC, as is clear from the contrast between the Archaic shape of the face and the dry torso, and the different modelling and relaxed stance of the superb legs. These, in essence, bear the weight of the figure, transforming the tension of the Archaic stance into an elevation of the entire, splendid body. The god's image culminates in the long, narrow face, with pronounced axes, crowned by two pairs of curls. The Piraeus Apollo is a forerunner, in terms of ethos and stance, of Pheidias's Kassel Apollo.

The female statues of the 4th century, such as the large Artemis (fig. 6), are different, more human. Thanks to certain details, such as the quiver on her back and the characteristic position of the fingers of the archer-goddess, she finally revealed herself – though with some difficulty since for a long time she suffered (and caused scholars to suffer), as Sappho, Telesilla or, at one point, as the Muse

Melpomene. The reason for this was not so much certain similarities with sculptures by Silanion, as the different plastic conception of the goddess from the usual type of the young, almost boyish huntress. The height and modelling of the robust female body and drapery, and the rather theatrical frontality and the over-emphasis on the contrast in the figure, call to mind the work of the sculptor and painter Euphranor, the main representative of the classicising trend which, about the middle of the 4th century BC, sought to return to more robust, earthy figures, such as his Theseus, "who was raised on meat, not roses, like that of Parrhasios."

The larger than life-size Athena (figs 7, 8) must be considered later in date. It was undoubtedly a cult statue, which, however, lacks the majesty of the Pheidian model and the robust nature of the statues of the time of the Eirene of Kephisodotos or the classicising works of Euphranor, two sculptors to whom this statue has been attributed in the past. In place of the dynamic juxtaposition of the folds of the garments found in those figures, as clear as the fluting of a column, the movement and drapery of the Athena are characterised by a lack of dynamism which, in the relatively small face, descends to a sugary sentimentality.

The noble origins of the statues are attested, quite apart from any other arguments, by the power of their presence – this despite the fact that some, arguing from insubstantial details, have sought in them the features of a classicising workshop of the 1st century BC that produced (bronze and marble!) copies. In the statue of the divine kouros can be seen the ethos of Apollo, just as the youthful flame of Artemis radiates from the robust kore of Piraeus, and her deer-like nature is imprinted on the slender figure of the other, little Artemis (figs 4, 5). And in the mild, yet at the same time majestic Athena do we not recognise at once the descendant of the Pheidian statue of Athena Parthenos and the ancestor of the benevolent Virgin (= Parthenos) Mary? The proof of the antiquity of the find, however, is provided by the shield, which has recently been restored from thousands of fragments, kept all these years in the National Archaeological Museum of Athens. Essentially, these fragments form the double (inner and outer) facing of the wooden shield, dating from the end of the 5th century BC, the exterior of which is adorned by a representation of a Classical four-horse chariot in a border of a laurel wreath.

Today, after half a century, the Piraeus find is still essentially unpublished despite a number of articles on details. However, the power exuded by the statues themselves, and the now legendary story of their discovery, has inspired the efforts of the people of Piraeus to create the modern Archaeological Museum of Piraeus.

8

Evangelos Ch. Kakavoyiannis

Memories of Phrasikleia

O n 18 May 1972, two ancient marble statues were discovered at Merenda, near Markopoulo in Attica, an area densely planted with olives, figs and vines that was once occupied by the ancient *deme* of Myrrhinous. One of the statues depicts the *kore* Phrasikleia and the other, a *kouros*, "her brother," as it was called by the locals when they saw them emerging "alive" from the earth that had lovingly protected them for so many centuries. Both date from the Archaic period, just after the middle of the 6th century BC. The statues had been carefully placed side by side, almost in contact with other, in a shallow pit dug especially for the purpose. The discovery was unexpected and considered to be of outstanding archaeological significance, since similar statues of this period – especially virtually intact – were not a common find.

The following day the find was given great publicity by the entire Athenian press, with extensive descriptions, pictures and commentaries. From their presentation, however, the readers formed the impression that the antiquities had come to light more or less by chance. The truth was very different: the statues were not found during digging for some municipal or private project, but as the result of a systematic, relatively long-term excavation by the Second Ephorate of Prehistoric and Classical Antiquities.

In December 1967, during mechanical ploughing of the property owned in this area by Spyros Panayiotou, an inhabitant of Markopoulo, vases were retrieved from tombs dating from the Geometric and Archaic periods. The owner of the land, a true lover of the ancient world, at once informed the Archaeological Service, and its then head, Dimitrios Lazaridis, immediately carried out a systematic excavation. This soon established the existence of an important cemetery with tombs containing superb offerings and dating from the Geometric, Archaic and Classical periods.

Nevertheless this excavation was not brought to completion, since Lazaridis was dismissed from the Archaeological Service during the political persecutions that followed the imposition of the dictatorship in Greece on 21 April 1967. Lazaridis, however, published a short article that appeared in the journal *Archaiologika Analekta ex Athinon*, mainly in order to report the discovery of these outstanding finds. The Panayiotou property was a rectangular plot 19 m. wide, and only the east half

1. The excavator, Evangelos Kakavoyiannis (left), and the then Head of the Second Ephorate of Antiquities, Efthymios Mastrokostas (centre), carefully removing the earth that had covered the kouros of Merenda and Phrasikleia for centuries. Athens, Epigraphical Museum, Archive of Efth. Mastrokostas.

of it had been investigated by Lazaridis. After the first tombs were explored, the Second Ephorate of Antiquities forbade any further cultivation of the property until the excavation had been completed. Since this represented a considerable loss to the owner, he complained to the Ministry and requested that either the excavation should be resumed, so as to decide the fate of his property, or that it be expropriated immediately, so that he could receive compensation. Yielding to this pressure, the Second Ephorate of Antiquities resumed the excavation under the direction of its then head, Andreas Vavritsas. The new excavation lasted until 1969, during which time roughly the central part of the property was investigated, producing equally impressive finds, mainly of Geometric and Archaic date.

Vavritsas was succeeded as Ephor of the Second Ephorate of Antiquities by Efthymios Mastrokostas. The new Ephor also acceded to Sp. Panayiotou's request that the investigation of his property should continue and be brought to a conclusion and, like his two predecessors, attempted to resolve this

2-4. The two statues once adorned the tombs of members of a rich family of Myrrhinous and were buried in the pit in which they were found, probably by the relatives of the dead, to protect them either from the Persian invaders or from possible political rivals. In fig. 4, next to the feet of the statues, can be seen the lead dowel that secured the kore to its pedestal. This was a find of crucial importance in associating the statue with the inscribed base of Phrasikleia, which had been discovered earlier built into a nearby church. Athens, Epigraphical Museum, Archive of Efth. Mastrokostas.

outstanding matter. The new excavation began on 28 February 1972 and was extended to the west part of the property, which had not been investigated so far. Mastrokostas assigned the supervision of the excavation to the undersigned, who was at that time employed as a Scientific Assistant in the Second Ephorate of Antiquities.

This new excavation season on the Panayiotou property, like the previous ones, produced a wealth of finds, amongst which were the most important of the entire excavation. At the south, the Panayiotou property bordered that of Georgios Chasiotis, which was planted with olive trees. During the investigation of the area near the boundary between the two properties, at about the middle of the area that had been explored on the Panayiotou plot, we noticed that the deposits contained a considerable scattering of chips of Parian marble. This gave rise to the hypothesis that somewhere nearby there might well be a – probably Archaic – sculpture, from which the fragments might have come. It was clear, of course, that in order to find it, we would have to extend the investigation to the Chasiotis property. On the basis of these hypotheses, I reported my thinking to Mastrokostas and asked him for permission to extend the excavation a little into the Chasiotis property; however, under the pressure of the great burden of excavation obligations incumbent on the Second Ephorate of Antiquities, and possibly in order to avoid entering another property, he didn't want to open another "front" and refused my request.

After this, the excavation of the Panayiotou plot continued without further distractions. We continued, however, to find chips of marble in the deposits along the boundary between the two properties, and, despite the risk of making a nuisance of myself, I repeated my request to be allowed to extend the investigation into the Chasiotis property a number of times to the Ephor. On each occasion, however, I received a negative answer, on the basis of the same – well founded, of course – arguments. Ultimately, in my efforts to change his mind, and because I realised that in fact he also basically wanted to extend the excavation, I modified my request and asked to be allowed, after I had completed the investigation of the Panayiotou property, simply to open a small trial trench which would occupy our modest excavation team for only one day. Mastrokostas agreed to this suggestion. It should be noted at this point that my insistence on extending the excavation was not due to any certainty that there were major finds in this area, nor to intuition: I was simply convinced that the number and quality of the finds from the excavation on the Panayiotou property demanded that the full potential of the excavation there should be realised.

A short time later, the excavation on the Panayiotou plot was completed and the day had finally arrived on which the trench I had requested would be dug on the Chasiotis property. We began by tracing a

5. A fine, moving epigram is carved on the front of Phrasikleia's pedestal: Σῆμα Φρασικλείας· / κόρη κεκλήσομαι / αἰεὶ ἀντὶ γάμου / παρὰ θεῶν τοῦτο / λαχοῦσ' ὄνομα. "Grave of Phrasikleia. I shall ever be called maiden (kore), the gods allotting me this title in place of marriage." Athens, National Archaeological Museum.

5

notional "corridor" 1 m. wide, running east-west, from which we removed the deposits. After a short time and at a depth of only 0.40 m. below the ground surface, we were astonished, delighted and moved to see emerging the right leg, followed by the entire side, of a marble kouros which was lying in an almost supine position. All the signs were that the kouros was preserved intact. We immediately set about revealing it systematically. As the work of removing the earth covering it progressed, we realised with even greater astonishment that the marble statue of a kore, also intact, wearing garments with fine colours and embroideries, had been placed parallel to the kouros as its eternal companion. The statue, which was as beautiful as a blossoming myrtle from its native land, was preserved together with its plinth, next to which the lead dowel was also preserved intact.

Our first concern after the discovery of the two statues was naturally to inform the Ephor at once. For this purpose, and also in order to receive instructions on how to protect the finds, I went to Markopoulo and phoned Athens. Fortunately I found him in his office straight away and announced with delight that a kouros had been found about two hours earlier in our trial trench. Mastrokostas found it hard to believe that as soon as we had started we had really come upon so important a find, especially one whose existence had long been thought probable. He said to me, almost severely: "Vangeli, cut out the jokes, I'm busy." I tried to explain that we really had found a kouros and that

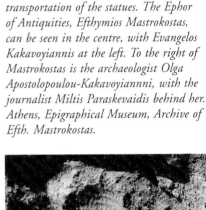

6. Scenes from the raising and transportation of the statues. The Ephor of Antiquities, Efthymios Mastrokostas, can be seen in the centre, with Evangelos Kakavoyiannis at the left. To the right of Mastrokostas is the archaeologist Olga Apostolopoulou-Kakavoyiannni, with the journalist Miltis Paraskevaidis behind her. Athens, Epigraphical Museum, Archive of Efth. Mastrokostas.

he had to come to Merenda at once, or at least tell me what we should do next. Either because he didn't believe that we actually had made the find, or perhaps because he wanted to rule out the slightest chance of it being a well-meant practical joke, the Ephor replied: "Do what you like." "And what should I do about the kore?" I asked, whereupon he exclaimed: "Tell me, where did you see the kore?" He was beginning to get angry – and rightly so. In order to prevent any possible misunderstanding, I described in detail how we had found the kouros and the kore in the trial trench; and I also asked him to come to Merenda as soon as possible.

Less than two hours later he arrived, accompanied by the art photographer N. Kondos, a few members of the foreign archaeological schools in Athens, including Eugene Vanderpool, and journalists, such as M. Paraskevaidis. The removal of the statues from the place where they had been found would have to be documented as fully as possible. Since this could not be completed within the day, the entire excavation team spent the night on the site to protect the finds, because antiquities theft had always been rife in the Mesogeia. Our work was resumed next day, and the statues were taken to the Brauron Museum for temporary safekeeping.

7. This exceptionally fine photograph, showing the imprint in the soil left by the coiffure and part of the back of the kouros, captures in a spare, yet eloquent, manner the fleeting nature of the unique moment of archaeological discovery. Athens, Epigraphical Museum, Archive of Efth. Mastrokostas.

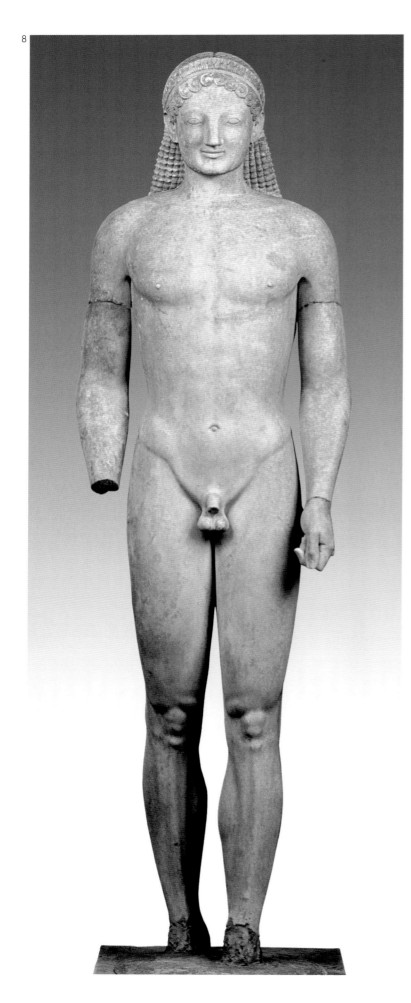

Before our investigation had even begun, we knew that an inscribed statue base, then in the Epigraphic Museum in Athens, had been found built into the nearby church of the Panayia a short distance to the south of the Panayiotou property. On it was carved a fine epigram which, in addition to giving the name of the kore, Phrasikleia, also stated that the statue was the work of the sculptor Ariston of Paros. Ariston was also known from the bases of other signed, but now lost, works by him. As soon as we saw the dazzling kore smiling, bathed once more in the light of the Attic sun, we wondered at once, though with guarded optimism, whether what we saw before us was indeed the statue of Phrasikleia, the work of Ariston of Paros, according to the epigram. As it in fact quickly proved to be. Next day, the Ephor took the lead dowel found next to the plinth of the statue to the Epigraphic Museum and placed it in the socket on the inscribed base, and it fitted perfectly. The excavation on the adjoining properties of Sp. Panayiotou and G. Chasiotis yielded truly glorious fruit: in addition to the other important finds, it provided us with two masterpieces of large-scale sculpture. These now adorn the Archaic sculpture wing of the National Archaeological Museum in Athens, where they stand side by side, probably as a reminder that they were found together. Phrasikleia is one of the few surviving Archaic sculptures for which we know beyond doubt the name of the sculptor. From this point of view, this statue and the kouros found along with it, are of value not only in themselves, but because they open up new possibilities of identifying a number of preserved works by hitherto unknown artists, and of studying the development of Archaic sculpture in general.

8-11. The kouros of Merenda (height 1.89 m., ca. 540-530 BC) and Phrasikleia (height 1.79 m., ca. 550-540 BC). Athens, National Archaeological Museum.

10

11

Helmut Kyrieleis

The large kouros of Samos

1. The picture seen by the archaeologists and workmen after the initial cleaning around the colossal sculpture: the kouros face down in the earth, just as it fell in ancient times.

It was a routine excavation. Its purpose was to clarify a topographical problem connected with the Sacred Way in the Heraion on Samos. No-one imagined that morning in September 1980 that we were about to experience a truly significant excavation event. During the removal of an archaeological level from a deposit of Late Antiquity, we uncovered, quite unexpectedly, the left shoulder and part of the hair of a very large Archaic marble statue. As we went on to remove the earth layer by layer, the torso of a colossal kouros gradually emerged (fig. 1). The tension and emotions of those hours, as the delicate plasticity of this majestic figure came ever more clearly to light, will never be forgotten by all those who were present.

What made the torso a unique discovery, however, was the colossal size of the work; as restored, it is

almost 5 metres tall – about 2 metres taller than the large kouros from Sounion, for example. As soon as it was raised from the excavation trench (fig. 2), and while it was being transported to the Samos Museum, the gigantic size of the sculpture created enormous problems for us.

Since the Archaeological Museum on Samos was too small, and did not have room for all the finds, the construction of an extension to house the Archaic sculptures from the Heraion had already begun in 1979, funded by the Volkswagenwerk foundation. However, the rooms of the new building that had already been designed now proved to be too low to receive the colossal figure of the kouros: naturally enough, no-one had taken into account a find of this nature. A solution to this problem was found in the notion of setting the floor of one of the rooms 1.5 m. deeper than planned. If the kouros had been discovered six months later, it would have been impossible to put it on display in the Museum. The torso was transferred to the Museum building under construction before its walls were constructed. Later, the colossus would not have passed through the door. During its setting in place in the Muse-

2. The colossal sculpture is lifted from the ground. Despite the passage of the centuries, the lifting system used is not very different from that used by the Archaic sculptor to erect the statue.

2

um, a difficult and technically demanding task, under the direction of the conservator Silvano Bertolin, a few fragments of the figure found earlier were added to it, such as the left thigh with the votive inscription of Ische (fig. 3), the right lower leg, and the left forearm. In 1984, work had progressed to the extent that the statue on display in the museum now stood free for virtually its full height (figs 5, 6). The story does not end here, however. Despite the majesty of the preserved figure, the fact that the head was missing deprived it of a definitive feature. Naturally, no-one even dreamed that the head of the statue would be found, since almost all the heads are missing from the sculptures of the Heraion. Nevertheless, since the other pieces belonging to the kouros had been found near the torso, we began a small, supplementary excavation on the Sacred Way in autumn 1984. And then a

small miracle occurred: as early as the second day of the excavation, one of the workmen struck a large piece of marble with his spade, immediately below the surface. When we turned it over, there appeared before us, in the sunlight, the smiling face of the large kouros (fig. 4). It is rare, indeed, that the secret wishes of an excavator are unexpectedly realised in this way. The face was preserved except for the nose, which had broken away vertically from the rest of the head, but it was not badly damaged and was fitted piece by piece on to the neck of the torso. It was only when the face was added to the standing figure that it became apparent for the first time just how much the colossus had lacked in life and expressive power.

The enormous figure of the youth, the ambitious masterpiece of a Samian artist of the early 6th century BC, has been almost completely reconstructed, and now stands in all its imposing size and astonishing beauty before visitors to the Samos Museum (figs 5, 6).

3. The left thigh of the statue is carved with a votive inscription.

4. The head of the kouros sees the light once more, revealing a resplendent Archaic face.

5, 6. Visitors feel a sense of awe at the sight of the enormous sculpture, which dominates not only by virtue of its size, but also through the clarity of the flesh. Most of the great sanctuaries of the Archaic period were adorned with sculptures like this, dedicated by wealthy families of the early city-states of ancient Greece. Samos, Archaeological Museum.

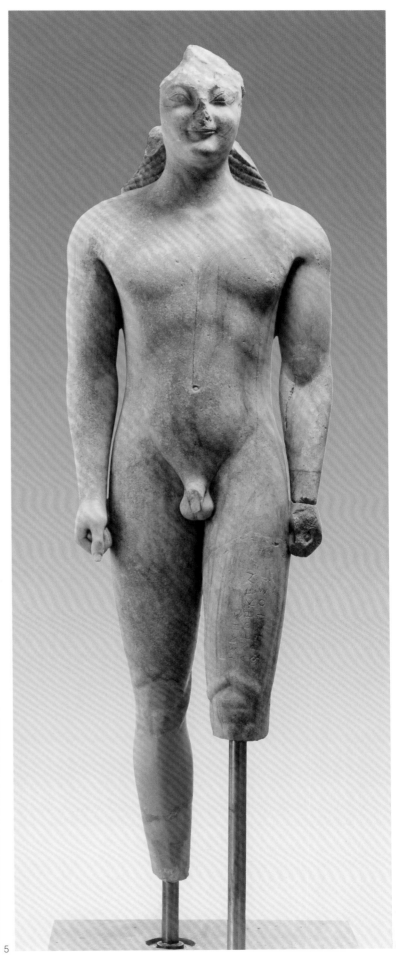

Harry E. Tzalas

Bronze statues from the depths of the sea

The commencement of the seizure and expatriation of Classical and Hellenistic artworks was marked by the capture, destruction and looting of Corinth (146 BC), Thebes, Chalkis and other Greek cities, by the Roman general Mummius in the middle of the 2nd century BC. Their artworks were carried off to the Italian peninsula, particularly to Rome.

The sculptures served as models for Roman artists, illustrating the perfection of the Greek sense of moderation and unsurpassable beauty. The emperors and officials did not confine themselves to commissioning copies of Greek originals from the 5th and 4th century BC: they wanted the originals. In order to adorn the palaces and villas, masterpieces from Greece and from Greek cities in Asia Minor found their way to Ostia, the port of Rome. Some of the works included in this inexhaustible treasure were transferred, after AD 330, to Constantinople, the New Rome, capital of the Eastern Roman Empire. Nevertheless sea travel involved many hazards even for the large merchantmen of the period: many were wrecked and their precious cargoes lost at the bottom of the Mediterranean. Long before 1832, when the first bronze statue (the Apollo of Piombino) was found in the sea, bronze limbs from statues were being pulled up in fishermen's nets, along with amphoras. These finds were very 'annoying', since they were so heavy that they tore the nets. The amphoras were smashed with crowbars to let the water out, while any solid, but useless items were thrown back into the sea. Anything made of bronze was cut up into pieces, regardless of whether it was a work of art, enabling the fishermen to make a small profit from the scrap value. Fabulous treasures have probably been lost due to this practice, while, for the same reason, the first large bronze statues pulled up in fishermen's nets or found by sponge-divers were retrieved in a large number of pieces. The simple fishermen or divers, unaware of the value of the finds, did not hesitate to make their task easier by breaking off arms, legs, or heads and bringing them up separately from the bottom of the sea.

Nowadays, everyone seems to be aware of the importance of these finds. For a bronze statue to be retrieved in good condition, however, at least three conditions need to be met, in which chance plays a large part: first, the captain of the ancient ship carrying the cargo has to be unlucky; second the ship has to founder at a spot where it won't be dragged along and broken up by the tackle of a fishing trawler, and third, it has to be discovered by a conscientious diver who doesn't damage it in an attempt to exploit it commercially.

In this article, I shall recount some of the exceptional stories surrounding the discovery and retrieval of nineteen bronze statues, all regarded as masterpieces.

Very little is known of the discovery of the Apollo of Piombino (figs 1, 2). It is reported that in 1832, fishermen, pulling in their nets in the bay of Baretti, near Cape Piombino to the south of Livorno in Tuscany, drew in a fine bronze statue depicting Apollo. It is without doubt an original

of late Archaic Greek art, preceding 480 BC. It is smaller than life size, being 1.15 m. tall, and is now on display in the Louvre.

Similarly, very little is known of another statue of the Early Classical period, found at Kreusis in Boeotia, in the Corinthian Gulf. It was given the name Poseidon of Livadostra (fig. 3) from the location on the coast where it was found in 1897. It is 1.18 m. tall, has both arms missing from the shoulder, as well as both eyes, which were inlaid. It is now on display in the National Archaeological Museum, Athens, and seems to have been

1, 2. The Apollo of Piombino, a masterpiece of the Late Archaic period (ca. 480 BC), is the first statue to have been retrieved from the depths of the sea, in 1832. Paris, Louvre Museum.

3

found in very poor condition, judging by the extent of the conservation work on it.

It is an original dating from about 460 BC, which certainly depicts Poseidon, since it bears a votive inscription to the god of the sea.

The Antikythera Shipwreck is a landmark in marine archaeology, though this was a chance find. The bottom of the sea was explored for the first time by sponge-divers, and the retrieval of the bronze statues was not a matter of their being caught in nets, as had previously been the case.

It was 1900, and two small sponge-diving boats were returning to the island of Symi from Benghazi. They encountered very bad weather and in an attempt to seek shelter from the raging storm, they put in at Pinakakia on Antikythera (fig. 4). The rock formation above and below sea level in this area is steep, so they anchored and waited for the weather to improve. In order not to waste the day, the captain and owner of the sponge-diving boat, Dimitrios Kondos, asked one of the divers, Ilias Stadiatis, to make a dive and see if there were any sponges. The depth was 30 fathoms, or over 50 metres.

A century earlier in 1802, on Kythera, Lord Elgin's representative had sought the help of sponge-divers to retrieve 17 crates containing masterpieces from the Parthenon. They had gone down when the ship transporting them to England, the *Mentor*, had foundered. Free divers had carried out the search, at that time, while Kondos's men wore primitive diving apparatus. Stadiatis disappeared under water. Suddenly, the rope went taut. Merkourios, the sailor tending

3. In 1897, an original Archaic statue of Poseidon (ca. 460 BC) was found in the shallows off the coast of Livadostra, ancient Kreusis, in the Corinthian Gulf. Although mutilated, with both arms missing as well as part of the right leg, it remains one of the important sculptures in the National Archaeological Museum of Athens.

the line that monitored the dive, was worried. The diver had been in the sea for less than two minutes. Why was he beginning his ascent so soon? Had he encountered a large shark? Was his suit letting in water? They brought him up, and as they were taking off the helmet of his diving apparatus, they heard him stammering breathlessly: "horses, men, naked people …" The young diver had chanced on one of the most important shipwrecks of ancient times, fully loaded with artworks. The captain now went down to see for himself and was in no doubt that the find was important, but he had no idea as to how they were going to benefit from it. In order to convince some would-be purchaser, he broke the arm off a bronze statue as evidence for the find.

The captain hastily raised the anchor and set a course for Symi. Kondos tried to put his thoughts in order. It was not the first time that local divers had chanced on an ancient shipwreck. They usually found large broken 'pitchers', but in this instance, they were dealing with an unusual cargo. Broken, badly damaged statues, in a difficult location, crushed by stone boulders. The captain and his crew were preoccupied by the question of how they could reap some financial reward from their discovery. What were the broken statues worth? Where and to whom could they sell them? They approached a teacher from the island, A. Oikonomou, who agreed to act as intermediary and arrange a meeting with the Greek Minister of Education, Spyridon Stais. When he examined the bronze arm, Stais immediately realised the value of the find and proceeded to try to reach an agreement with Captain Kondos and his divers.

The negotiations were tough. It did not escape the minister's attention that Kondos and his men were the only ones who knew the exact position of the wreck, and more importantly, only sponge-divers were capable of working at the bottom of the sea in order to retrieve the finds. He was also aware of the enormous dangers they would face (fig. 5). Kondos, too, certainly realised that he was only in a position to exploit his discovery if he cooperated with the Greek government. Only the minister could make a suitably equipped naval vessel available to bring up the ancient cargo.

An agreement was finally reached. The first attempts to raise the statues took place in midwinter, during December 1901, thus revealing how eager Stais was to bring the enterprise to a close as soon as possible. The details of this first organised survey of an ancient shipwreck are recorded in the diary of Emmanuel Lykoudis, legal consultant to the Ministry of Education.

As one reads Lykoudis's diary, one is astounded at the unacceptable manner in which the survey was carried out. A diver lost his life in the presence of representatives of the Greek state, and some large-

scale ancient works of art slipped out of the inadequate lifting crane available and fell to the seabed, perhaps lost forever. Despite repeated efforts made during recent decades, two involving the research vessel *Calypso*, captained by Jacques-Yves Cousteau, very few additional finds have bean retrieved. Without going into further detail about the poorly organised 'underwater archaeological investigation' from the decks of the Navy vessel *Mykalis*, it must be said that two bronze masterpieces of Hellenistic art emerged from the seabed: the well-known Youth of Antikythera (figs 6, 8), which dates from 340-330 BC and is probably by Euphranor, and a head from a large male statue thought to be the portrait of an unknown philosopher and dating from 240 BC (fig. 7). Parts of other bronze statues were found with them.

The Antikythera Mechanism is an important find. It is a unique instrument which a century after its discovery continues to raise many questions for scholars (figs 9–13). It was initially thought to be an astrolabe. Thanks to the inscriptions on it, however, which have recently been deciphered,

4. A unique photograph of 1900 showing two small sponge-diving boats at Pinakakia, Antikythera. The Antikythera Shipwreck has entered history as the first organised underwater archaeological survey, despite the primitive and non-scientific means used. From P. Throckmorton (ed.), History from the Sea, Shipwrecks and Archaeology *(1987).*

5. Cumbersome diving apparatus was used by sponge-divers from Symi who, at the risk of their lives, located and retrieved the finds of the Antikythera Shipwreck. From P. Throckmorton (ed.), History from the Sea, Shipwrecks and Archaeology *(1987).*

6. The restoration of the superb Hellenistic statue known as the Youth of Antikythera was an achievement for the Greek restorers, bearing in mind that it was carried out a century ago. Archive of National Archaeological Museum.

7. The head of a mature man, known as the Antikythera Philosopher, belonged to a large statue of the Hellenistic period (240 BC). Despite repeated attempts, the body was never found. Athens, National Archaeological Museum.

8. It is thought that the Youth of Antikythera was probably the work of the great sculptor Euphranor and dates from 340-330 BC. Visitors to the Museum wonder what the young man once held in his outstretched right hand. Athens, National Archaeological Museum.

6

7

it has been shown – *inter alia* – that the indicators at the back of the mechanism moved on spiral grooves, not on concentric circles. The inscription on fragment E is clear: the spiral is divided into 235 sections. These sections corresponded to 235 lunar months (fig. 13). According to the inscription on fragment 19, a second spiral had 223 subdivisions (fig. 11). It is thus clear that the mechanism was used – *inter alia* – to predict the movements and eclipses of the sun and moon. It was therefore a very complex mechanism, for which the word astrolabe is hardly appropriate. It might be described as the first astronomical calculator known to mankind. As early as the time that the statues were retrieved, a date of about 85-80 BC was proposed for the shipwreck. A recent study of the coins found on the ship, published by Dr. Mando Oikonomidou, confirms the date (*terminus ante quem* of 70-60 BC), and also indicates the probable port of the ship's departure and its cargo for this fateful voyage. Almost all the coins were issued by Pergamon, which vindicated those who suggested that the statues had been looted from this important Greek centre in Asia Minor. All the finds are now kept in the National Archaeological Museum of Athens.

The Marathon Boy is another chance find retrieved from the sea (figs 14, 15). Very little is known of the circumstances under which this very important work of art was found, other than that it was entangled in fishing nets in the shallows of the bay of Marathon in 1925.

In contrast with other finds, the arms and legs of which were broken off during their recovery, it is one of the few bronze statues found intact in the sea. Despite repeated attempts to locate the wreck of the ship that had transported the statue – Cousteau investigated the area for this purpose in 1975 – neither the wreck nor traces of any other finds have been discovered.

The Marathon Boy is probably an original from the workshop of Praxiteles dating from 340-300 BC. It is 1.30 m. tall but the arms are not the originals; for some unknown reason, they were replaced in ancient times. It is now in the National Archaeological Museum of Athens.

9. *Two of the fragments of the Antikythera Mechanism. These are the largest and best known of the total of 82 fragments of the Mechanism that have been found. Athens, National Archaeological Museum.*

10. *The interior of fragment A, from a picture (section) taken by a radiography device weighing 8 tonnes that was brought to Greece from Britain in autumn 2005 specially to study the Antikythera Mechanism. Courtesy of* The Antikythera Mechanism Research Project.

11. *Fragment 19 as seen through the special Hewlett-Packard PTM system. Courtesy of* The Antikythera Mechanism Research Project.

12. *Reconstruction of the Antikythera Mechanism (front part) resulting from the recent investigation by the Antikythera Mechanism Study Group. Small spheres representing the sun and moon can be seen, as well as the signs of the zodiac and the months of the Egyptian calendar. Courtesy of* The Antikythera Mechanism Research Project.

13. *Radiograph of an inscription, the larger part of which is on the interior of fragment E. The text, which was read for the first time by the Antikythera Mechanism Study Group, is a kind of 'instruction manual' for the mechanism. Courtesy of* The Antikythera Mechanism Research Project.

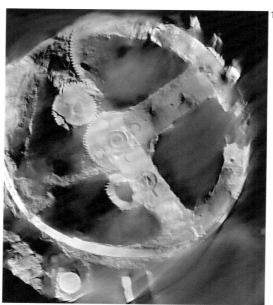

In the case of the Artemision Shipwreck, there exist all the elements of the plot of an exciting thriller: the attempted but ultimately unsuccessful smuggling of antiquities, the involvement of a high-ranking civil servant, together with the participation of fishermen, divers and archaeologists. An additional element that lends suspense to this drama is the discovery of pieces of the ancient works of art, separated by a decade and 13 nautical miles. I had the exceptional good fortune, 25 years ago, to meet a seaman, who played a leading role in the events and who, despite being 83 years old when I interviewed him, remembered everything in the greatest detail (fig. 17). A fisherman from the age of twelve, like his father and grandfather before him, Captain Parisis was born in 1898 in Asia Minor. He left Çesme for Chios with his family because of the pogrom of 1914. From Chios he went on to Volos and from there to Pefki in north Euboea.

14. The Marathon Boy is one of the few bronze statues that were preserved intact at the bottom of the sea for over 2000 years. It is probably an original work from the workshop of Praxiteles (340-300 BC). This early photograph of the find at the National Archaeological Museum shows the statue before its restoration. Archive of National Archaeological Museum.

15. Many interpretations have been proposed for the position of the arms of this exquisite statue of a youth found by fishermen in 1925 and brought to light from the sea at the bay of Marathon. Athens, National Archaeological Museum.

I checked Captain Parisis's account, comparing it with that of the archaeologist Nikos Bertos, who had undertaken to supervise the investigation, as well as with the details that emerged from cross-questioning by the police: everything was consistent. But Parisis supplied some additional evidence: he had noted the exact location at which the large statue of Zeus was raised: "I have the exact position, I took the bearings on the shore…" The old mariner did not ask for any reward. He did, however, confirm that, after the discovery of the large statue and half the horse, two more heavy statues became entangled in the nets of their caïque, but, unfortunately, they slipped out as the boat departed.

I refer to my notes, made in 1981, and the cassette recording on which the voice of the veteran of the sea is captured: "It was April 1926 when we got the god out of the sea … we were all expecting it to be a goddess, they were saying that it was Artemis. But what goddess, I shouted … look here …" and Captain Parisis's amused chuckle can be heard.

It all began when fishermen from Skiathos caught a heavy bronze arm in their nets: it was the left arm of the statue of Zeus of Artemision, now in the National Archaeological Museum of Athens (figs 16, 18, 19). They kept the find from the port authorities, but the news spread amongst the other fishermen, and when they passed over the spot, they searched the area with great care. Eventually the statue was caught in the nets of a trawler owned by one Markos Tsakoumakos, Parisis's uncle. Since, he reports, they did not have the means to raise the heavy statue, they brought a diver

16. The head of the life-size statue of Zeus of Artemision. The attention to the details of the hair, the beauty of the curls, the harmonious flow of the beard, and the serene majesty of the face, all converge to render a truly Olympian god. Athens, National Archaeological Museum.

17. In the year 1981, the author of this article interviewed the last survivor of the fishermen who found the Artemision Shipwreck. Captain Parisis was then 83 years old but remembered everything in great detail.

18. A unique photo taken during the restoration of the statue of Zeus of Artemision, one of the most beautiful statues of ancient Greek art. Archive of National Archaeological Museum.

19. With a serene expression in the eyes and the body of an athlete, the father of the gods hurls a thunderbolt. The statue, an original bronze by a great sculptor, dates from about 460 BC. Athens, National Archaeological Museum.

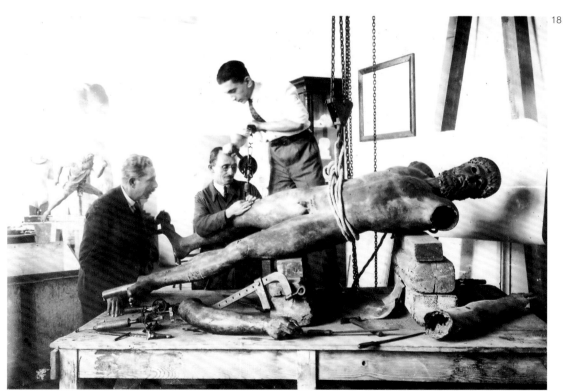

19

20. Mutilated, with the right leg missing, the Jockey was retrieved in fishermen's nets off Cape Artemision.

21, 22. With its pronounced negroid features, the restored statue of the Jockey waits to ride again the horse that was found in two separate parts, dragged up by the nets of fishing trawlers in the waters of northern Euboea. It is an original statue group dating from about 140 BC. Archive of National Archaeological Museum.

from Trikeri, whose name was Lalaios. At this point, the seabed lay at a depth of over 45 metres. They promised him they would divide anything they found fifty-fifty. A man called Deliyiannis also appeared on the scene. He had spent time in America and insisted he knew an Italian antiquities dealer. He also promised that he would make sure they received millions.

However, the resting place of the statue was very muddy, and a number of divers were required to retrieve it, with Lalaios digging all around to free it. As luck would have it, one Gogos, a retired army captain, became suspicious as he saw the two boats anchored at the same location and divers repeatedly emerging from the sea. He informed the president of the nearby village, who in turn told the police and the local magistrate, and just as they were joyfully preparing to heave up the anchor

20

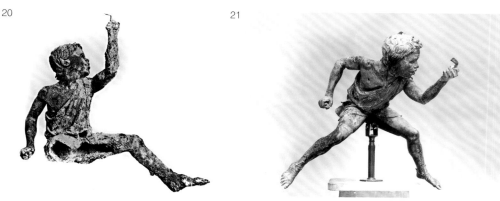

21

and leave with the truncated masterpiece, they were caught red-handed.

Parisis's laugh could be heard again. "They took us all to court, but the judge let us all go free, on the following rationale: if you had acted lawfully and reported the find, you would have received a reward of one million drachmas; your punishment is that you won't receive anything." And Poseidon, as Parisis named the statue, was loaded on to a cart at Pefki and taken to the National Archaeological Museum. The task of conservation was laborious, but rewarding. The two arms were replaced in position and the god once more acquired his majestic stance. The statue is thought to have probably been the work of Kalamis and dates from about 460 BC. It is 2.09 m. tall and the arm span is 2.10 m.

22

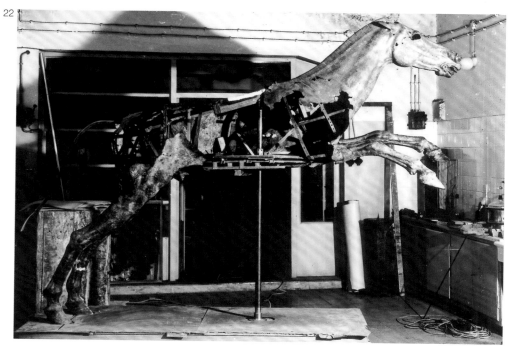

As one reads the report of N. Bertos, one gains the impression that the authorities were negligent, they allowed a full year to pass before they organised an investigation of the site of the shipwreck. Eventually, with five divers and a Navy ship, the *Pleias*, they found a millstone and a large number of other irregularly shaped stones that had been used as ballast, along with broken ancient pottery, some intact amphoras, and the front half of a horse with its young jockey (figs 20-23).

The divers, searching for a statue of the goddess Artemis, were greatly disappointed when they realised they had found part of a horse. Delikonstantis, the head diver, shouted: "What a waste of time. We've worked all these days for a lousy horse!"

For many years it was thought that the Jockey was too small to belong to the same statue group. Nine years were to pass before the other part of the horse was found by chance in 1937 near Oraioi and associated with the horse and rider. Today the young Jockey has found his huge horse once more and they 'gallop' lightly in a gallery at the National Archaeological Museum. The group dates from about 140 BC.

Jacques-Yves Cousteau searched the area sporadically in 1959 and 1975, and since 1980 the Ephorate of Underwater Antiquities has continued using modern sonar equipment, though without any

23. *Ridden by the young Jockey, the restored horse is in full gallop. It is thought that the ship that sunk off the coast of Cape Artemision may still yield more of the masterpieces it was carrying. Athens, National Archaeological Museum.*

23

positive results. Cape Artemision continues to guard its secrets, but the day may come when other finds are discovered, hopefully in fishermen's nets, or with the aid of constantly improving technology.

As we see from the above, all the finds yielded by the sea are accompanied by extraordinary stories. The story about the recovery of the Autostephanoumenos in the J. Paul Getty Museum at Malibu (statue of an athlete crowning himself by placing a wreath on his own head) deserves the description of the most extraordinary (fig. 24). In 1961, two fishermen from Fano in the northern Adriatic Sea were pulling their nets in the area of Numana and hauled up one of the finest statues of post-Classical Greek art. The fishermen had no way of knowing that this statue might be a very rare original by Lysippos. The preserved height of the young athlete is 1.51 m.

If one adds the length of the legs, which are missing from the thighs down, it is probably a life-size portrait statue of a victorious athlete, possibly an Olympic champion. The experts date the Autostephanoumenos after 340 BC, during the years when the sculptor of Sikyon went to the court of Philip II in Macedonia.

On 13 September 1964, Denis Fanquerle explored the bed of the river Hérault with a team of divers from the Agde Marine Archaeological Research Group. As an archaeologist, he was aware that the name Agde is derived from the Greek word *agathe* ([good] fortune). Fortune smiled on him when, on the muddy river bed, at a depth of 6 m., he discovered a smaller than life-size bronze statue of a youth: the Youth of Agde (fig. 26). Both arms were missing below the elbows, as were both feet. After persistent efforts, the left foot was found six months later, 600 m. away from the statue, beneath 1.5 m. of silt deposits. Other ancient objects, such as millstones, two stone anchors and a large number of small finds which cannot, with any certainty, be attributed to the same shipwreck were also found. The statue, which was kept in storage in the Louvre for fifteen years and is now on display once more in the Agde Museum, has a preserved height of 1.33 m., but the bronze surface is unfortunately in a poor state of preservation. The interest in this statue is primarily concerned with the head, which, according to experts, fol-

24. The Autostephanoumenos in the J. Paul Getty Museum in Malibu, USA, is believed to be an original created after 340 BC by Lysippos. It probably represents a victorious athlete. Malibu, J. Paul Getty Museum.

25. The head of the mature bearded man known as the Philosopher of Porticello is probably one of the earliest Greek portraits (about 420-410 BC). Reggio di Calabria, National Museum.

26. Mutilated and heavily corroded because of its lengthy immersion in the waters of the Hérault estuary, the Youth of Agde recalls the statue of Doryphoros Alexander attributed to Lysippos. Agde, Musée de l'Éphèbe.

24

lows the models established by portraits of Alexander the Great. It is thought to be a work from the school of Lysippos influenced by the Doryphoros (Spear-bearing) Alexander by the great master. It dates from the 2nd century BC and probably depicts a young prince of the Seleucid dynasty or one of the other rulers of the Late Hellenistic period, who were partial to having themselves portrayed with the features of the great Macedonian.

The head known as the Porticello Philosopher (fig. 25) is an outstanding work of art, and it was found in 1969.

It is not a conventional statue of a god or hero, but one of the earliest surviving portraits from the ancient Greek world. It is dated to 420-410 BC, earlier according to some scholars, and is thought to have come from an Attic workshop. It depicts a mature man with noble features, a luxuriant beard and carefully groomed hair. Only the head is preserved, which is 0.40 m. high and it is kept in the National Museum of Reggio di Calabria.

The circumstances under which this masterpiece was found, are further evidence for the way in which unique works of art disappear following

25

26

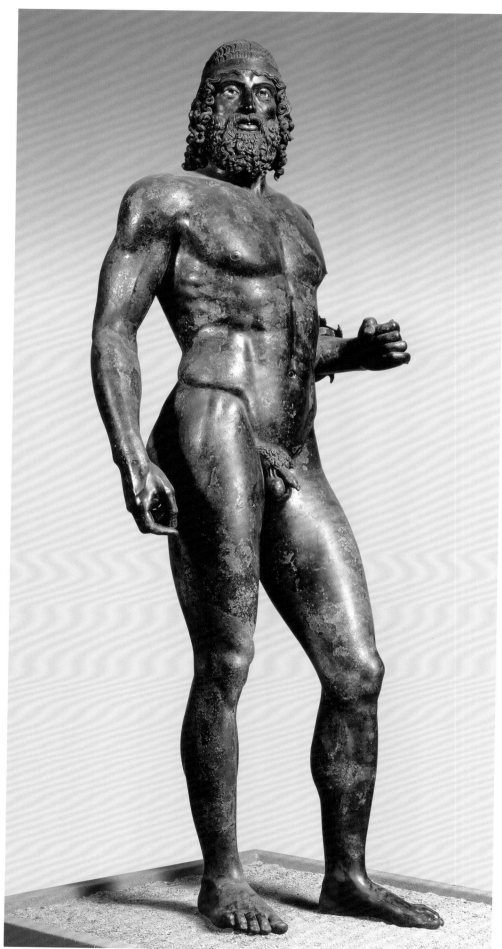

their discovery by unscrupulous 'searchers' of the depths, attracted by the now legendary sums of money private collectors as well as museums, are prepared to pay to acquire them.

When fishermen and amateur divers looted the Porticello shipwreck in 1961, it was not the first act of vandalism against it. It was readily accessible at a depth of only 20 m. in the straits of Messina, and the larger part of its cargo had already been dispersed.

The ship wrecked at Porticello was about 15 m. long and appears to have sunk in about 400 BC. It is believed that the amphoras and statues were being carried together and that the date of the amphoras provides the date at which the cargo was being transported. The question arises of how to account for the transportation of ancient statues from Greece to Italy in 400 BC. It is possible that the statues and amphoras were transported on separate vessels at different times and that, by coincidence, they sank at the same point. (The site of the finds, near the Villa San Giovanni, is renowned for its dangerous currents.) If this was the case, the ship carrying the statues probably went down much later than 400 BC.

For scholars of early Classical sculpture, the Warriors of Riace are, together with the Zeus of Artemision, the supreme works of this period. That they are originals dating from about 460 BC is beyond doubt. They are thought to be the work of Pheidias, and a variety of Greek sanctuaries have been advanced as their provenance, the most probable being the sanctuary at Delphi. They were possibly removed from it during Sulla's raid in 86 BC.

Both statues are larger than life size: A, is 2.05 m. tall and B, 1.97 m. They were found complete and in a very good state of preservation (figs 27, 28). The shields they were holding have been lost, with only the sockets in the arms that held them in place surviving. The weapons they held in their right hands are also missing. Warrior B wore a helmet, which is also lost.

The two statues were found by Stefano Mariottini, an amateur diver, at Cape Riace in southeast Calabria, Italy, at a depth of only 7 m., and

27

28

27, 28. *The Warriors of Riace (A: fig. 27, B: fig. 28) are, with the Zeus of Artemision, the most magnificent bronzes of the Early Classical period (ca.460 BC). Reggio di Calabria, National Museum.*

300 metres off shore. Mariottini at once informed the authorities and a few days later, together with divers from the Messina police and in the presence of archaeologists, he raised the statues from the seabed.

Both the inlaid eyes were still preserved in statue A, while the right eye was missing from B. Certain points of the mouth, the lips and teeth are made of copper and silver, as are the nipples on the breast; this was to distinguish them by colour from the bronze.

The question that immediately arises is how was it possible they had not been found earlier in such an accessible location. Popular theory was that it was likely the statues were found in different locations and were being transported aboard a ship by illicit antiquities dealers, when something unexpected apparently occurred and they hurriedly dumped them in the sea to avoid arrest.

Whatever the mystery behind their final retrieval from the sea, good fortune rescued and presented us with two masterpieces of ancient Greek art, which now adorn a special gallery in the National Museum of Reggio di Calabria.

We have very little information about the discovery of the upper part of a very fine statue of the Roman emperor Augustus (fig. 29). It was found on 12 March 1979 by the fisherman V. Mazarakis in his nets and was handed over to the port authorities of Kymi. The precise location of its recovery is not certain, since he was fishing between Ai-Stratis and the east coast of Euboea, covering a distance of over 60 nautical miles.

The preserved height of the statue is 1.23 m. The great Roman emperor is depicted on horseback, but the horse and the entire lower part of the body are missing. The statue is a bronze of a very high quality that was probably made in one of the great Greek workshops, which continued to produce in Roman times. It was probably executed about 10 BC, and is now on display in the National Archaeological Museum of Athens.

In theory, the rest of the statue and the horse are still at the bottom of the sea in the central Aegean, waiting for fortune to decide to bring them to light, as in the case of the Artemision find.

In the case of the Youth in the Smyrna Museum (fig. 30), all that is known is that it was found about fifteen years ago in the nets of Turkish fishermen near the coast of Aeolian Kyme in Asia Minor. It is a very fine bronze statue depicting a victor in a foot race. Its right arm is missing. It is probably an original work of the Hellenistic period. In the Museum catalogue it is listed as the Athlete of Foça, and is still unpublished.

In 1996, Dr Don Frey of the Institute of Nautical Archaeology at Texas A & M University carried out an underwater survey using Side Scan Sonar in an attempt to

29

locate the position of the wreck. Under the guidance of Necati Beytorum, the captain of a Turkish trawler, who had found the arm of a larger than life-size bronze statue in the same region, he investigated likely areas. The records of the instrument possibly point to an ancient shipwreck, but the American archaeologists were unable to dive, because of the great depths involved. They intend to return with a remotely operated vehicle for a further survey.

The discovery of the Apoxyomenos (athlete scraping his body with strigil) of Vele Orjule (figs 31-36) in Croatia, like the Warriors of Riace, marks one of those rare moments in underwater archaeology when the prerequisites stated above exist and ensure the retrieval of a complete, outstanding work of art.

It was 12 July 1997 when the Belgian diver René Wouten, on holiday in Istria, decided to take advantage of the wonderful weather by diving in the channel between two islets, Vele Orjule and Kosjak. At a depth of 42 metres, he had to turn on a powerful torch to light his way. The sight that met his eyes made his hair stand on end and he came up to the surface visibly shaken. A full-length statue, lying down, half buried in the sand, covered by sponges and other marine organisms, looked to him like a lifeless body. His curiosity, however, impelled him to

30. The bronze statue found in the Aegean sea, near the coast of Aeolian Kyme, probably depicts the winner of a foot-race. It dates from the Hellenistic period. Smyrna, Archaeological Museum.

31-33. Complete, with only the head separated from the body, a superb copy of the Apoxyomenos of Lysippos lay on the sandy sea bottom.

31

32

34. The statue from Vele Orjule (in Croatia) was conserved in Florence, in the same laboratory in which the Warriors of Riace were conserved. The picture shows three successive phases of the process of cleaning the head.

35, 36. It was first thought that the Apoxyomenos of Vele Orjule was an original by Lysippos. However, new studies have revealed that it is in fact a copy made in Roman times. Zadar, Archaeological Museum. (All the photographs were kindly provided by Dr. Iasen Messic, Deputy Minister of Culture of Croatia, who presented the Apoxyomenos at the 9th International Symposium on Ship Construction in Antiquity, held at Ayia Napa, Cyprus, in 2005).

33

dive down again, and after careful examination he became aware that he had come across a complete bronze statue. Hands, legs, and head … nothing was missing: but when he touched the head, he realised that it had become separated from the body when the neck had struck a large rock as it fell.

Wouten went at once to the port authorities and reported the find. It was brought up in April 1999. Although a careful search of the seabed was conducted, there was no sign of the wrecked ship. The fine bronze statue of Vele Orjule is 1.92 m. tall and is kept in the Zadar Museum (figs 34-36). It is undoubtedly a great work – a Roman copy influenced by Lysippos's Apoxyomenos.

The years 1996 and 1997 were lucky for the Greek Ephorate of Underwater Antiquities. Two fishermen in the Dodecanese handed in the stat-

34

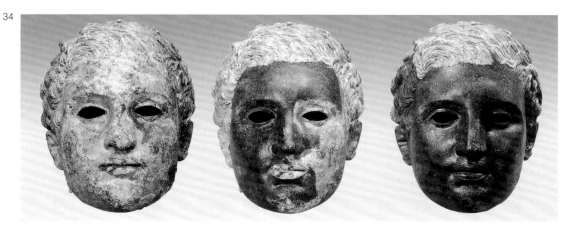

37, 38. Fishermen in the vicinity of
Kalymnos raised in their nets the head
of a male bronze statue wearing the causia,
a typical Macedonian hat (left). This is an
original from the Hellenistic period. This
find is exhibited in the Fortress of Pylos.
In the same waters, fishermen also caught
a life-size female statue in their nets (right).
This find is still unpublished. Athens,
National Archaeological Museum.

39, 40. The life-size statue of a young male
figure, as it is temporarily known, was
clandestinely retrieved from Greek waters.
Thanks to the combined efforts of Greek
and German authorities, the statue was
repatriated and is now on display in the
National Archaeological Museum
of Athens. It is the work of an artist
of the Early Roman Imperial period
and it probably depicts a nude athlete.

ue known as the Kalymnos Kore and the head of a Macedonian. Both were fished up in nets in the waters off Kalymnos.

The Kore has just been put on display, at the beginning of June 2005, in a room in the National Archaeological Museum of Athens, while the 'Macedonian' has for six years been displayed with other artefacts retrieved from the sea in a room in the Fortress of Pylos, the headquarters of the Centre for Underwater Archaeological Research of the Ministry of Culture (figs 37, 38). Both are important works, probably originals dating from the Hellenistic period. Did they belong to the same cargo? Were they on their way from Pergamon? These questions will forever remain unanswered.

We come now to the last of the large-scale bronzes guarded by the sea for about 2000 years. This is a full-length statue of a young male figure, as it is temporarily known (figs 39, 40). It depicts a young nude athlete; both of the arms are missing from the shoulder and the left leg from below the knee. The eyes were inlaid and have been lost. The total height of the statue is 1.41 m. It is dated somewhere in the Early Roman Imperial period (1st century BC – 1st century AD), and the influence of the school of Polykleitos is evident.

In this case, too, we have an interesting scenario. Precisely when and in what circumstance the statue was retrieved from the waters of the Ionian Sea is not known. At the trial held in 1998, the antique smugglers asserted that it was found in international waters between Greece and Albania, while the Greek officials countered that it was discovered in the Bay of Preveza. The statue was apparently smuggled out of Greece a long time ago and, after remaining in the display rooms of an

37

38

antiquities dealer in Basel for several years, it was taken to Saarbrücken in Germany, where it was confiscated. It was repatriated to Greece in 2002. This beautiful statue was displayed in the National Archaeological Museum of Athens in the exhibition "Agon" during the 2004 Olympic Games in Athens. It was published provisionally in the catalogue of this exhibition by Dr. Rosa Proskynitopoulou, the head of the Bronze Collection of the National Archaeological Museum, whose definitive publication is awaited with great interest. We now surface after diving countless times at fourteen different places in the Mediterranean, from which good fortune has ensured that nineteen fine works of ancient Greek sculpture have been retrieved. This list will certainly grow longer, for many masterpieces patiently wait to be brought to the surface to see the light of day once more.

39

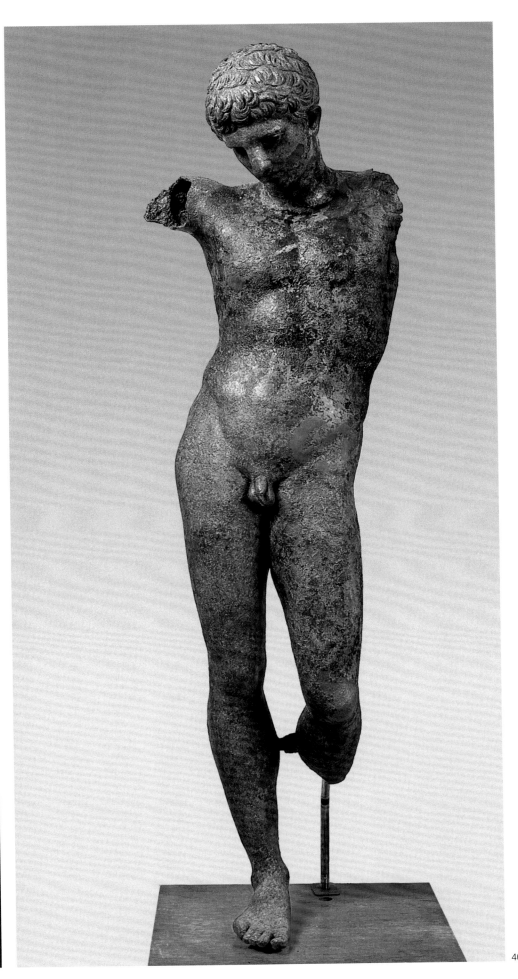

40

Bibliography

ABBREVIATIONS

AAA Archaiologika Analekta ex Athinon
AΔ Archaeological Deltion
AEMΘ Archaiologiko Ergo sti Makedonia kai Thraki
BCH Bulletin de Correspondance Hellénique

THE STAGES OF GREEK ARCHAEOLOGY

*Rangavis A. R., Συνοπτικὴ ἔκθεσις τῆς τύχης τῶν ἀρχαίων μνημείων εἰς τὴν Ἑλλάδα κατὰ τὰ τελευταῖα ἔτη, Ἀρχαιολογικὴ Ἐφημερὶς 1837 (τεῦχ. Ὀκτωβρίου πρῶτο), 5-13.

*Kastorchis E., Ἱστορικὴ ἔκθεσις τῶν πράξεων τῆς ἐν Ἀθήναις Ἀρχαιολογικῆς Ἑταιρείας, Athens 1879.

Kavvadias P., Συλλογὴ ἀρχαιολογικῶν νόμων, διαταγμάτων καὶ ἐγκυκλίων, Athens 1892 (and 1905).

Legrand Ph.-E., Biographie de Louis-François-Sébastien Fauvel, Revue Archéologique 30, 1897, 41-66, 185-201, 385-404; 31, 1897, 94-103, 185-223.

*Kavvadias P., Ἱστορία τῆς Ἀρχαιολογικῆς Ἑταιρείας, Athens 1900.

*Gennadios J., Ὁ Λόρδος Ἔλγιν καὶ οἱ πρὸ αὐτοῦ ἀνὰ τὴν Ἑλλάδα καὶ τὰς Ἀθήνας ἰδίως ἀρχαιολογήσαντες ἐπιδρομεῖς, Athens 1930, 1997².

*Chatzis A. Ch., Περὶ τοῦ ἀληθοῦς ἱδρυτοῦ τῆς Ἀρχαιολογικῆς Ἑταιρείας, Πρακτικὰ Ἀρχαιολογικῆς Ἑταιρείας 1930, 35-51.

*Economou G., Λεύκωμα τῆς ἑκατονταετηρίδος τῆς ἐν Ἀθήναις Ἀρχαιολογικῆς Ἑταιρείας 1837-1937, Athens 1937.

Protopsaltis Emm. G., Ὁ Γεώργιος Χριστιανὸς Gropius καὶ ἡ δρᾶσις αὐτοῦ ἐν Ἑλλάδι, Athens 1947.

Pharmakidis G. Al., Ὁ ζωγράφος Ἀθανάσιος Ἰατρίδης, 1799-1860, Athens 1960.

Manis J. E., Ἀνδρέας Μουστοξύδης 1785-1860, Athens 1960.

Panagiotopoulos B. P., Βαρῶνος Κωνσταντῖνος Μπέλιος, ἕνας ὁμογενὴς στὴν Ἀθήνα τοῦ 1836, Ἐποχές 17, 1964, 78-92. Reprinted in: Σταθμοὶ πρὸς τὴ νέα ἑλληνικὴ κοινωνία, special edition of the magazine Ἐποχές, Athens 1965, 194, 220.

*Protopsaltis Emm. G., Ἱστορικὰ ἔγγραφα περὶ ἀρχαιοτήτων καὶ λοιπῶν μνημείων τῆς ἱστορίας κατὰ τοὺς χρόνους τῆς Ἐπαναστάσεως καὶ τοῦ Καποδίστρια, Athens 1967.

*Kalogeropoulou A. G. - Prouni-Philip M., Ἀρχαιολογικὴ Ἐφημερίς, Εὑρετήριον πρώτης καὶ δευτέρας περιόδου 1837-1874, Athens 1973.

Protopsaltis Emm. G., Στοιχεῖα περὶ τῆς γαλλικῆς ἐπιστημονικῆς ἀποστολῆς εἰς Πελοπόννησον καὶ τοῦ ἔργου αὐτῆς, Ἐπιστημονικὴ Ἐπετηρὶς Φιλοσοφικῆς Σχολῆς Παν. Ἀθηνῶν ΚΔ΄, 1973-1974, 228-247.

Maurer G. L., Ὁ Ἑλληνικὸς Λαός (transl.: Olga Robakis), Athens 1976. For the antiquities: 545-552.

Ross L., Ἀναμνήσεις καὶ ἀνταποκρίσεις ἀπὸ τὴν Ἑλλάδα 1832-1833 (transl.: A. Spiliou), Athens 1976.

Kokkou A., Ἡ μέριμνα γιὰ τὶς ἀρχαιότητες στὴν Ἑλλάδα καὶ τὰ πρῶτα μουσεῖα, Athens 1977.

Petrakos V. Ch., Δοκίμιο γιὰ τὴν ἀρχαιολογικὴ νομοθεσία, Athens 1982.

Giotopoulou-Sisilianou E., Ἡ Φιλόμουσος Ἑταιρία καὶ οἱ ἑλληνικὲς ἀρχαιότητες, in: Ἀμητὸς στὴ μνήμη Φώτη Ἀποστολόπουλου, Athens 1984, 191-253.

*Petrakos V. Ch., Ἡ ἐν Ἀθήναις Ἀρχαιολογικὴ Ἑταιρεία. Ἡ ἱστορία τῶν 150 χρόνων της, 1837-1987, Athens 1987.

*—, Ἰδεογραφία τῆς ἐν Ἀθήναις Ἀρχαιολογικῆς Ἑταιρείας, Ἀρχαιολογικὴ Ἐφημερίς 1987, 25-197.

—, Τὰ πρῶτα χρόνια τῆς ἑλληνικῆς ἀρχαιολογίας, Ἀρχαιολογία, 26, 1988, 90-99.

Velianitis T. Th., Ἡ Φιλόμουσος Ἑταιρεία τῶν Ἀθηνῶν, Athens 1993.

Simopoulos K., Ἡ λεηλασία καὶ καταστροφὴ τῶν ἑλληνικῶν ἀρχαιοτήτων, Athens 1993.

*Petrakos V. Ch., Ἡ περιπέτεια τῆς ἑλληνικῆς ἀρχαιολογίας στὸν βίο τοῦ Χρήστου Καρούζου, Athens 1995.

*—, Οἱ ἑλληνικὲς ἀναστηλώσεις (ed.: B. Ch. Petrakos), Ὁ Μέντωρ 37, 1996, 1-186.

*—, Δημήτριος Ἰ. Κοντῆς (1910-1975), Ὁ Μέντωρ 43, 1997, 41-70.

*—, Ἰωάννης Κ. Παπαδημητρίου, in the volume Ἔπαινος Ἰωάννου Κ. Παπαδημητρίου, Athens 1997, 9-51.

*—, Ἡ ἑλληνικὴ ἀρχαιολογία κατὰ τὰ χρόνια τοῦ Κυριακοῦ Σ. Πιττάκη, Ὁ Μέντωρ 47, 1998, 74-112.

*—, Ἡ ἀνασκαφὴ τοῦ Κεραμεικοῦ ἀπὸ τὴν Ἀρχαιολογικὴ Ἑταιρεία, Ὁ Μέντωρ 48, 1998, 117-207.

*Mallouchou-Tufano F., Ἡ ἀναστήλωση τῶν ἀρχαίων μνημείων στὴ νεώτερη Ἑλλάδα (1834-1939), Athens 1998.

*Petrakos V. Ch., Ἡ ἐν Ἀθήναις Ἀρχαιολογικὴ Ἑταιρεία 1837- 1999, Athens 1999.

Badima-Fountoulaki O., Κλεάνθης, 1802-1862, Athens 2001.

Petrakos V. Ch., Οἱ Ἕλληνες τοῦ '21 καὶ τὰ μνημεῖα, Πρακτικὰ Ἀκαδημίας Ἀθηνῶν 2001, 265-282.

*—, Ἡ ἀπαρχὴ τῆς ἑλληνικῆς ἀρχαιολογίας καὶ ἡ ἵδρυση τῆς Ἀρχαιολογικῆς Ἑταιρείας, Ὁ Μέντωρ 73, 2004, 109-222.

Ministry of Culture, Ξένες Ἀρχαιολογικὲς Σχολὲς στὴν Ἑλλάδα, 160 χρόνια, Athens 2005.

Note: The asterisk indicates that the work is a publication of the Archaeological Society of Athens.

THE VICISSITUDES OF THE ATHENIAN ACROPOLIS IN THE 19TH CENTURY.
FROM CASTLE TO MONUMENT

Efstratiadis P., Ἡμερολόγιον Ὑπηρεσίας (in the archives of the Archaeological Society of Athens).

Rangavis A. R., Ἀπομνημονεύματα, 1-2, Athens 1895.

Kavvadias P. - Kawerau G., Η ανασκαφή της Ακροπόλεως από του 1885 μέχρι του 1890, Athens 1907.

Neezer Ch., Τα πρώτα έτη της ιδρύσεως του Ελληνικού κράτους, Athens 1963.

Ross L., Αναμνήσεις και ανταποκρίσεις από την Ελλάδα (1832-1833) (transl.: A. Spiliou), Athens 1976.

Kokkou A., Η μέριμνα για τις αρχαιότητες στην Ελλάδα και τα πρώτα μουσεία, Athens 1977.

Petrakos V. Ch., Ιδεογραφία της εν Αθήναις Αρχαιολογικής Εταιρείας, Αρχαιολογική Εφημερίς 1987, 25-197.

Mallouchou-Tufano F., Η αναστήλωση των αρχαίων μνημείων στη νεώτερη Ελλάδα (1834-1939), Athens 1998.

Papageorgiou-Venetas Al., O Leo von Klenze στην Ελλάδα, Athens 2000.

Petropoulou E., O «μέγας πρίων» των Προπυλαίων, Ενημερωτικές Ειδήσεις από την αναστήλωση των μνημείων της Ακρόπολης, July 3, 2003, 22-23.

Petrakos V. Ch., Η απαρχή της ελληνικής αρχαιολογίας και η ίδρυση της Αρχαιολογικής Εταιρείας, Ο Μέντωρ 73, Decemeber 2004, 109-222.

KERAMEIKOS I.
THE DISCOVERY OF THE ANCIENT CEMETERY

EXCAVATION SERIES

Various authors, Kerameikos. Ergebnisse der Ausgrabungen, vol. 1-17, Berlin, Munich 1939-2005.

OTHER LITERATURE

Knigge U., Der Kerameikos von Athen. Führung durch Ausgrabung und Geschichte, Athens 1988.

Niemeier W.-D., Der Kuros vom Heiligen Tor, Mainz 2002.

Stroszeck J. - Hallof K., Eine neue Schauspielerstele vom Kerameikos, Mitteilungen des Deutschen Archäologischen Instituts in Athen, vol. 117, 2002, 115-131, pl. IV and 18-21.

Stroszeck J., ΗΟΡΟΣ ΚΕΡΑΜΕΙΚΟΥ. Zu den Grenzsteinen des Kerameikos in Athen, in: Polis. Studi interdisciplinari sul mondo antico, vol. 1, 2003, 53-83.

KERAMEIKOS II.
THE ARCHAIC SCULPTURES OF THE SACRED GATE, SPRING 2002

Gabelmann H., Studien zum frühgriechischen Löwenbild, Berlin 1965.

Richter G. M., Kouroi, Archaic Greek Youths, 3rd edition, New York 1970.

Mertens-Horn M., Studien zu griechischen Löwenbildern, Mitteilungen des Deutschen Archäologischen Institutes, Römische Abteilung 93, 1986, 1-61.

Martini W., Die archaische Plastik der Griechen, Darmstadt 1990.

Ridgway B. S., The Archaic Style of Greek Sculpture, 2nd edition, Chicago 1993.

Kyrieleis H., Der grosse Kuros von Samos, Samos X, Bonn 1996.

Bol P. C. (ed.), Die Geschichte der antiken Bildhauerkunst I: Frühgriechische Plastik, Mainz 2002.

Neimeier W.-D., Der Kuros vom Heiligen Tor, Mainz 2002.

DELOS.
THE EXCAVATION OF THE SACRED ISLAND OF APOLLO

Délos. Île sacrée et ville cosmopolite, published by L'École française d'Athènes and coordinated by Ph. Bruneau, M. Brunet, A. Farnoux et J.-Ch. Moretti, Paris 1996.

Guide de Délos, Coll. Sites et Monuments 1, L'École française d' Athènes, Paris 2005. [The fourth edition of this work, a remarkable synopsis of Delian archaeology, was originally written by Philippe Bruneau and Jean Ducat, and was later revised by the younger generations of archaeologists that took over the excavations on the island.]

Sculptures déliennes, Coll. Sites et Monuments 16, L' École française d'Athènes, Paris 1996, published under the direction of J. Marcadé.

Zaphiropoulou Ph., Δήλος, Μνημεία και Μουσείο, Athens 1983. [Translated into many languages.]

—, Δήλος, Μαρτυρίες από τα μουσειακά εκθέματα, Athens 1998.

Chatzidakis P. I., Δήλος, Eurobank-Ergasias Bank Publ., Athens 2003.

Of the many books on the general history of Delos, special mention may be made of the following:

Bruneau Ph., Recherches sur les cultes de Délos à l'époque hellénistique et à l'époque impériale, Bibliothèque des Écoles françaises d'Athènes et de Rome, vol. 217, 1970.

Roussel P., Délos, colonie athénienne, Bibliothèque des Écoles françaises d'Athènes et de Rome, vol. 111, 1916 (revised and expanded edition: 1987).

Vial Cl., Délos indépendante, BCH Suppl. 10, 1984.

Of the many articles on Delos, special mention may be made of the following: BCH Suppl. 1, 1973, Études déliennes présentées à l'occasion du centième anniversaire des fouilles de l'École française à Délos (1973). Recently, all the articles of Philippe Bruneau that refer to Delos were collected and published in BCH Suppl. 47, 2006 under the title: Études d'archéologie délienne (1000 p.).

The French School at Athens has published the results of the excavations on Delos in a series entitled Exploration archéologique de Délos. The first volume appeared in 1909 and the series now numbers 41 titles, all devoted to the excavations on the island under the direction of the French School.

OLYMPIA.
EXCAVATIONS AND DISCOVERIES
AT THE GREAT SANCTUARY

The results of the German excavations at Olympia in the 19th century are published in the series:

Curtius E. - Adler Fr. (eds), Olympia - Die Ergebnisse der vom Deutschen Reich veranstalteten Ausgrabungen, vol. I-V, Berlin 1890-1897.

The results of the excavations since 1937 are published in two series:

Bericht über die Ausgrabungen in Olympia, vol. I-XII, Berlin 1937- 2003.

Olympische Forschungen, vol. I-XXXI, Berlin 1944-2006.

Of the extensive modern bibliography on Olympia, special mention may be made of the following:

Herrmann H.-V., Olympia - Heiligtum und Wettkampfstätte, Munich 1972.

Mallwitz A., Olympia und seine Bauten, Munich 1972.

Kyrieleis H. (ed.), Olympia 1875-2000, 125 Jahre Deutsche Ausgrabungen, Mainz 2002.

Valavanis P., Games and Sanctuaries in Ancient Greece, Kapon ed., Athens 2004.

SCHLIEMANN AND HOMER'S
"MYCENAE RICH IN GOLD"

Schliemann H., Mykenae, Leipzig 1878.

—, Ilios, Leipzig 1881.

—, Troja, Leipzig 1884.

Steffen B., Karten von Mykenai, Berlin 1884.

Schliemann H., Tiryns, Leipzig 1886.

Tsountas Chr., Ανασκαφαί Μυκηνών του 1886, Πρακτικά της εν Αθήναις Αρχαιολογικής Εταιρείας 1886.

—, Αρχαιότητες εκ Μυκηνών, Αρχαιολογική Εφημερίς 1887, 155-172.

—, Ανασκαφαί Τάφων εν Μυκήναις, Αρχαιολογική Εφημερίς 1889, 120-180.

—, Μυκήναι και Μυκηναϊκός Πολιτισμός, Athens 1893.

Tsountas Chr. - Manatt J. I., The Mycenaean Age, London 1897.

Karo G., Die Schachtgräber von Mykenai, Munich 1930.

Wace A. J. B., Chamber Tombs at Mycenae, Oxford 1932.

—, Mycenae. An Archaeological History and Guide, Princeton N.J. 1949.

Blegen C. W. et al., Troy I, II, III, IV, Princeton 1950-58.

Mylonas G. E., Ancient Mycenae. The Capital City of Agamemnon, Princeton N. J. 1957.

—, Η Ακρόπολις των Μυκηνών, Αρχαιολογική Εφημερίς 1958, 153-207.

—, Η Ακρόπολις των Μυκηνών, Οι περίβολοι, αι Πύλαι και αι Άνοδοι, Αρχαιολογική Εφημερίς 1962, 1-199.

—, Mycenae and The Mycenaean Age, Princeton N. J. 1966.

—, Το Θρησκευτικόν Κέντρον των Μυκηνών, Πραγματείαι της Ακαδημίας Αθηνών, 1972.

—, Ο Ταφικός Κύκλος Β των Μυκηνών, Βιβλιοθήκη της εν Αθήναις Αρχαιολογικής Εταιρείας 73, Athens 1973.

Marinatos Sp. - Hirmer M., Kreta, Thera und das mykenische Hellas, Munich 1973.

Mylonas G. E., Πολύχρυσοι Μυκήναι, Athens 1983.

Iakovidis Sp., Late Helladic Citadels, Leiden 1983.

Sakellariou A., Οι Θαλαμωτοί Τάφοι των Μυκηνών, Paris 1985.

French E. B., Mycenae, Agamemnon's Capital, Tempus Publishing Ltd, 2002.

Iakovidis Sp. - French E. et al., Archaeological Atlas of Mycenae, Archaeological Society at Athens Library 229, Athens 2003.

Iakovidis Sp., Ανασκαφή Μυκηνών Ι. Η βορειοδυτική συνοικία, Βιβλιοθήκη της εν Αθήναις Αρχαιολογικής Εταιρείας 244, Athens 2006.

DELPHI.
THE EXCAVATION OF THE GREAT ORACULAR CENTRE

Of the hundreds of monographs on Delphi, special mention may be made of La redécouverte de Delphes, Paris 1992, an important collection of studies published to celebrate the 100th anniversary of the French excavations at Delphi.

The following two guides are strongly recommended:

Guide de Delphes. Le musée. Coll. Sites et Monuments VI, École française d'Athènes, Paris 1991.

Bommelaer J.-Fr., Guide de Delphes. Le site. Coll. Sites et Monuments VII, École française d'Athènes, Paris 1991. - A new revised and expanded edition is under release.

Of the numerous guidebooks published in many languages, special mention may be made of those by V. Chr. Petrakos (1971), P. Amandry (1984) and V. Pentazos and M. Sarla (1985). Of the major works, the following are of special importance:

Amandry P., La mantique apollinienne à Delphes, Bibliothèque des Écoles françaises d' Athénes et de Rome, vol. 170, Paris 1950.

Roux G., Delphes, son oracle et ses dieux, Paris 1976.

The French School at Athens has published the results of the excavations in a series entitled Fouilles de Delphes. [Volume II: Studies of the topography and architecture; vol. III: epigraphy; vol. IV: sculpture; vol. V: various finds (bronzes, ceramics etc.)]. A new publication of the inscriptions, organised by subject, is currently in progress under the title Le corpus des inscriptions de Delphes. Four volumes of this work have already appeared.

KNOSSOS.
THE DISCOVERY OF THE MINOAN PALACE

Details of the work of the British School at Athens at Knossos, including a 'virtual tour' of the palace and other monuments including the Roman Villa Dionysos can be found at the website of the main British research establishment in Greece:

http://www.bsa.gla.ac.uk/

The NESTOR website is a searchable database of most publications (including articles) connected with the prehistory of the Aegean region: http://classics.uc.edu/nestor/

GENERAL SURVEYS OF PREHISTORIC CRETAN ARCHAEOLOGY AND GUIDES

Pendlebury J. D. S., The Archaeology of Crete, London 1939.

Alexiou S., Minoan Civilization, Herakleion 1969.

Graham J. W., The Palaces of Minoan Crete, Princeton 1969.

Hood S., The Minoans, London 1971.

Sakellarakis I. A., Herakleion Museum. Pictorial Guide, Athens 1982.

Myers J. W. and E. E. - Cadogan G., The Aerial Atlas of Ancient Crete, London 1992.

Driessen J. - Macdonald C. F., The Troubled Island. Minoan Crete before and after the Santorini Eruption, Liège 1997.

Sakellarakis I. and E., Archanes: Minoan Crete in a New Light, Athens 1997.

Vasilakis A., Knossos - Mythology, History, Guide to the Archaeological Site, Athens 1998.

Huxley D., Cretan Quests. British Explorers, Excavators and Historians, London 2000.

THE PALACE, TOWN AND CEMETERIES

Evans A. J., The Prehistoric Tombs of Knossos (Archaeologia 59), London 1906.

—, The Palace of Minos, vol. 1-4 and Index, London 1921-1936.

Pendlebury J. D. S., A Handbook to the Palace of Minos, London 1954.

Hood M. S. F. - Smyth D., Archaeological Survey of the Knossos Area, London 1981.

Popham M. R., The Unexplored Mansion at Knossos, British School at Athens, Supplementary vol. 17, London 1984.

Hood M. S. F. - Taylor W., The Bronze Age Palace at Knossos: Plans and Sections, British School at Athens, Supplementary vol. 13, London 1987.

MacGillivray J. A., Knossos: Pottery Groups of the Old Palace Period, British School at Athens Studies 5, London 1998.

Panagiotaki M., The Central Palace Sanctuary at Knossos, British School at Athens, Supplementary vol. 31, London 1999.

Hatzaki E., Knossos: The Little Palace, British School at Athens, Supplementary volume, London (on press).

Macdonald C. F. - Knappett C. J., Knossos: Protopalatial Deposits in Early Magazine A and the South-West Houses, London (on press).

Hatzaki E., Knossos: The Temple Tomb, British School at Athens, Supplementary volume, London (forthcoming).

KNOSSOS AND MINOAN PALACES IN GENERAL, COLLECTED ESSAYS AND CONFERENCES

Hägg R. - Marinatos N., The Function of the Minoan Palaces, Stockholm 1987.

Evely D. - Hughes-Brock H. - Momigliano N. (eds), Knossos. A Labyrinth of Prehistory, London 1994.

Evely D. - Lemos I. S. - Sherratt S. (eds), Minotaur and Centaur, Oxford 1996.

Hamilakis Y. (ed.), Labyrinth Revisited: Rethinking 'Minoan' Archaeology, Oxford 2002.

Driessen J. - Schoep I. - Laffineur R., Monuments of Minos. Rethinking the Minoan Palaces (Aegaeum 23), Liège 2002.

Cadogan G. - Hatzaki E. - Vasilakis A. (eds), Knossos: Palace, City, State. Proceedings of the Conference in Herakleion organised by the British School at Athens and the 23rd Ephoreia of Prehistoric and Classical Antiquities of Herakleion, in November 2000, for the Centenary of Sir Arthur Evans's Excavations at Knossos, British School at Athens Studies 12, London 2004. (Received after the completion of this book).

SIR ARTHUR EVANS, DUNCAN MACKENZIE AND KNOSSOS

Evans J., Time and Chance: The Story of Arthur Evans and his Forebears, London 1943.

Powell D., The Villa Ariadne, London 1973.

Farnoux A., Cnossos. L'archéologie d'un rêve, Gallimard, Paris 1993.

Brown A., Arthur Evans and the Palace of Minos, Oxford 1994.

Hood R., Faces of Archaeology in Greece, Oxford 1998.

Momigliano N., Duncan Mackenzie: a Cautious Canny Highlander and the Palace of Minos at Knossos, London 1999.

MacGillivray J. A., Minotaur: Sir Arthur Evans and the Archaeology of the Minoan Myth, London 2000.

HISTORIC KNOSSOS

Coldstream J. N., Knossos. The Sanctuary of Demeter, British School at Athens, Supplementary vol. 8, Oxford 1973.

Sandars I. F., Roman Crete: an Archaeological Survey and Gazetteer of Late Hellenistic, Roman and Early Byzantine Crete, Warminster 1982.

Cavanagh W. G. - Curtis M. (eds), Post-Minoan Crete. Proceedings of the First Colloquium on Post-Minoan Crete held by the British School at Athens and the Institute of Archaeology, University College, London, 10-11 November 1995, British School at Athens Studies 2, London 1998.

SESKLO AND DIMINI.
THE PREHISTORIC CITADELS

Tsountas Chr., Αι προϊστορικαί ακροπόλεις Διμηνίου και Σέσκλου, Athens 1908.

Tringham R., Hunters, Fishers and Farmers in Eastern Europe 6000-3000 BC, London 1971.

Theocharis D., Νεολιθική Ελλάς, Athens 1973.

Chourmouziadis G., Το Νεολιθικό Διμήνι, Volos, Greece 1979.

Papathanasopoulos G., *Neolithic Civilization*, Athens 1981.

Sophronidou M., Les premières fouilles préhistoriques dans le monde Égéen d'après la presse grecque de l'époque, *Mythos, La préhistoire égéenne du XIXe au XXIe siècle après J.-C., Actes de la table ronde internationale d'Athènes (21-23 Novembre 2002)*, éd. Pascal Darcque, M. Fotiadis, O. Polychronopoulou, BCH Supplément 46, École française d' Athènes 2006, 209-221.

POLIOCHNI ON LEMNOS.
THE EARLIEST CITY IN EUROPE

Bernabò Brea L., *Poliochni. Città preistorica nell'isola di Lemnos*, I, Rome 1964.

—, *Poliochni. Città preistorica nell'isola di Lemnos*, II, Rome 1976.

Benvenuti A. G., *Η Πολιόχνη και το νησί της Λήμνου ανάμεσα στην αρχαιολογία και τη μυθολογία*, Athens 1993.

Greco E. – Benvenuti A. G., *Scavando nel passato. 120 anni di archeologia italiana in Grecia*, Athens 2005.

Tiné S. – Traverso A., *Πολιόχνη. Η αρχαιότερη πόλη της Ευρώπης*, Athens 2005.

THE ATHENIAN AGORA.
ENCOUNTER WITH THE FIRST DEMOCRACY

For the history of the excavations in the Athenian Agora, see:

Lord L. E., *A History of the American School of Classical Studies at Athens, 1882-1942*, Cambridge Mass. 1947.

Merrit L. S., *History of the American School of Classical Studies at Athens, 1939-1980*, Princeton NJ 1984.

Mauzy C. A., *Agora Excavations 1931-2006. A Pictorial History*, Athens 2006.

The excavation results are published in the series: *The Athenian Agora* I-XXXI (1953-1998).

The series *Picturebooks* I-XXXIV (1958-1998) is also very useful.

General guidebooks to the excavations and monuments:

McK. Camp II J., *The Athenian Agora Guide*, Athens 1990.

—, *The Athenian Agora, A Short Guide to the Excavations*, Athens 2003.

—, *The Athenian Agora. Excavations in the heart of the classical Athens*, London 1998.

Christopoulou B. - Choremi-Spetsieri A., *Αρχαία Αγορά της Αθήνας - Άρειος Πάγος*, Association of Friends of the Acropolis, Athens 2004.

Saraga N., *Μουσείο Αρχαίας Αγοράς. Σύντομο ιστορικό και περιήγηση*, Association of Friends of the Acropolis, Athens 2004.

THE "ROYAL" TOMBS AT SALAMIS IN CYPRUS

Karageorghis V., *Excavations in the Necropolis of Salamis*, vol. I, Nicosia 1969.

—, *Salamis. Recent discoveries in Cyprus*, London 1970.

—, *Salamis. Die zyprische Metropole des Altertums*, Bergisch Gladbach 1970.

—, *Excavations in the Necropolis of Salamis*, vol. II, Nicosia 1970.

—, *Excavations in the Necropolis of Salamis*, vol. III, Nicosia 1973 and 1974.

—, *Salamina di Cipro. Omerica, Ellenistica e Romana*, Rome 1974.

—, *Excavations in the Necropolis of Salamis*, vol. IV, Nicosia 1978.

—, *Excavating at Salamis in Cyprus, 1952-1974*, The A. G. Leventis Foundation/Kapon ed., Athens 1999.

—, *Early Cyprus: Crossroads of the Mediterranean*, The J. Paul Getty Museum, Los Angeles 2002.

AKROTIRI ON THERA.
THE EXCAVATION OF A BURIED CITY

Marinatos Sp., The volcanic destruction of Minoan Crete, *Antiquity* XIII, 1939, 425-439.

—, *Excavations at Thera*, vol. I-VII, Athens 1967-1976.

Page D., *The Santorini Volcano and the Destruction of Minoan Crete*, Society for the promotion of Hellenic Studies, Suppl. Paper 12, London 1970.

Pomerance L., The final collapse of Thera, *Studies in Mediterranean Archaeology* 26, 1970.

Marinatos S., *Treasures of Thera*, Commercial Bank of Greece, Athens 1972.

—, *Kreta, Thera und das Mykenische Hellas*, Munich 1973.

Doumas Chr., *The Wall-Paintings of Thera*, The Thera Foundation - Petros M. Nomikos, Athens 1978-1980.

Doumas Chr. (ed.), *Thera and the Aegean World, Proceedings of the Second International Scientific Congress, Santorini, Greece, August 1978*, vol. I and II, Thera Foundation, London 1980.

Doumas Chr., *Thera: Pompeii of the Ancient Aegean*, Thames and Hudson, London 1984.

Morgan L., *The Miniature Wall Paintings of Thera*, Cambridge University Press 1988.

Hardy D. A. - Doumas Chr. - Sakellarakis J. A. - Warren P. M. (eds), *Thera and the Aegean World* III, Proceedings of the Third International Congress, Santorini, Greece, 3-9 September 1989, vol. 1, Thera Foundation, London 1990.

Doumas Chr., *Santorini: A Guide to the Island and its Archaeological Treasures*, Ekdotike Athinon, Athens 1992.

Sherratt S. (ed.), *Proceedings of the First International Symposium: The Wall Paintings of Thera*, The Thera Foundation - Petros M. Nomikos, Athens 1999.

VERGINA.
ON THE TRACKS OF THE MACEDONIAN KINGS

Andronikos M., Οι βασιλικοί τάφοι της Μ. Τούμπας, *ΑΑΑ* Χ, 1977 (1978), 1 ff.

—, *Ελληνική Κιβωτός*, Athens 1984.

Saatsoglou-Paliadeli Chr., *Τα επιτάφια μνημεία από τη Μεγάλη Τούμπα της Βεργίνας*, Salonica 1984.

Faklaris P., Περιτραχήλιο, *ΑΔ* 40, 1985, 1-16.

—, Ιπποσκευές από τη Βεργίνα, *ΑΔ* 41, 1986, 1-58.

Drougou S., Το χρυσούφαντο ύφασμα της Βεργίνας, πρώτες παρατηρήσεις, *Αμητός, τιμητικός τόμος για τον καθηγητή Μ. Ανδρόνικο*, Salonica 1987, 304 ff.

Faklaris P., Ταφή πρώιμης εποχής σιδήρου στη Βεργίνα, *Αμητός, τιμητικός τόμος για τον καθηγητή Μ. Ανδρόνικο*, Salonica 1987, 304 ff.

Drougou S., *ΑΕΜΘ* 1-16, 1987-2003 (excavation activity).

Saatsoglou-Paliadeli Chr., *ΑΕΜΘ* 1-16, 1987-2004 (excavation activity).

Andronikos M., *Βεργίνα. Οι βασιλικοί τάφοι και άλλες αρχαιότητες*, Athens 1992².

—, *Ελληνικός Θησαυρός*, Athens 1993.

Dimakopoulos G., *Κελύφη προστασίας εν είδει τύμβου*, Athens 1993.

Andronikos M., *Βεργίνα ΙΙ. Ο τάφος της Περσεφόνης*, Athens 1994.

Drougou S. - Saatsoglou-Paliadeli Chr. - Faklaris P. et al., *Βεργίνα, Η Μεγάλη Τούμπα*, Salonica 1994.

Andronikos M., *Το Χρονικό της Βεργίνας*, Athens 1997.

Drougou S. - Saatsoglou-Paliadeli Chr., *Βεργίνα. Περιδιαβάζοντας τον αρχαιολογικό χώρο*, Athens 1999.

Saatsoglou-Paliadeli Chr., *Ο τάφος του Φιλίππου. Η τοιχογραφία με το κυνήγι*, Athens 2004.

Drougou S., *Βεργίνα. Η Κεραμική από τη Μ. Τούμπα*, Athens 2005.

Drougou S. - Saatsoglou-Paliadeli Chr., *Βεργίνα. Ο τόπος και η ιστορία του*, Athens 2006.

DISPILIO NEAR KASTORIA.
THE PREHISTORIC LAKE SETTLEMENT

Keramopoullos A., Μακεδονία Προϊστορική, *Αρχαιολογική Εφημερίς* 1927-1928, 210-218.

—, Ανασκαφαί και έρευναι εν τη Άνω Μακεδονία, *Αρχαιολογική Εφημερίς* 1932, 48-133.

—, Μακεδονικά εγχωρίου κατασκευής λίθινα εργαλεία, *Αρχαιολογική Εφημερίς* 1937, part Α΄, 367-373.

—, Έρευναι εν τη Δυτική Μακεδονία, *Πρακτικά της εν Αθήναις Αρχαιολογικής Εταιρείας* 1938, 53-66.

—, Ανασκαφή εν Καστορία, *Πρακτικά της εν Αθήναις Αρχαιολογικής Εταιρείας* 1940, 22-23.

Makaronas Ch., Ανασκαφαί, έρευναι και τυχαία ευρήματα εν Μακεδονία και Θράκη κατά τα έτη 1940-1950, *Μακεδονικά* ΙΙ, 1953, Χρονικά Αρχαιολογικά, 590-672 (Western Macedonia); 637-646, 645 (Dispilio).

Marinatos Sp., Ο Λιμναίος συνοικισμός Καστοριάς, *ΑΑΑ* 1968, 162-166.

Moutsopoulos N., Λιμναίοι οικισμοί, *Επετηρίδα της Πολυτεχνικής Σχολής ΑΠΘ*, Salonica 1974, 280-330.

Chourmouziadis G. Ch. (ed.), *Δισπηλιό 7500 χρόνια μετά*, University Studio Press, Salonica 2002.

THE *ANCIENT SHIP OF KYRENIA*,
BENEATH CYPRUS SEAS

Ormerod H. A., *Piracy in the Ancient World*, Chicago 1967.

Katzev M. L., Resurrecting the Oldest Known Greek Ship, *National Geographic*, June 1970, 840-857.

Katzev M. L. - Katzev S. W., Last Harbor for the Oldest Ship, *National Geographic*, November 1974, 618-625.

Berthold R. M., *Rhodes in the Hellenistic Age*, Ithaca and London 1984.

Steffy J. R., The Kyrenia Ship: An Interim Report on its Hull Construction, *American Journal of Archaeology* 89, 1985, Centennial Issue, 71-101.

Katzev M. L. - Katzev S. W., Kyrenia II, *INA Newsletter* 13, no. 3, November 1986, 1-11.

Katzev M. L., Voyage of Kyrenia II, *INA Newsletter* 16, no. 1, March 1989, 4-10.

Steffy J. R., *Wooden Shipbuilding and the Interpretation of Shipwrecks*, College Station, Texas 1994, 42-59.

THE *KYRENIA II*.
AN ATTEMPT IN EXPERIMENTAL ARCHAEOLOGY

Tzalas H., The Construction of a Replica of an Ancient Ship, *Science in Archaeology, Proceedings of a meeting held at the British School at Athens, January 1985, Fitch Laboratory Occasional Paper 2*, Athens 1986.

Katzev M. L. - Katzev S. W., Kyrenia II, Building the Replica of an Ancient Greek Merchantman, *Proceedings of the 1st Symposium on Ship Construction in Antiquity, Piraeus 1985*, Tropis I, Athens 1989.

Katzev M. L., An Analysis of the Experimental Voyages of Kyrenia II, *Proceedings of the 2nd International Symposium on Ship Construction in Antiquity, Delphi 1987*, Tropis II, Athens 1990.

Tzalas H., Kyrenia II in the fresco of Panaghia Pedoula church Cyprus: A comparison with ancient ship iconography, *Proceedings of the 2nd International Symposium on Ship Construction in Antiquity, Delphi 1987*, Tropis II, Athens 1990.

Steffy J. R., *Wooden Shipbuilding and the Interpretation of Shipwrecks*, College Station, Texas 1994.

Tzalas H., Η ναυτική πειραματική αρχαιολογία και οι ελάχιστες προϋποθέσεις για ένα δόκιμο πείραμα, *Αρχαία Ελληνική Τεχνολογία, 2ο Διεθνές Συνέδριο Αρχαίας Ελληνικής Τεχνολογίας*, Athens 2006.

ULUBURUN.
A BRONZE AGE SHIPWRECK

Bass G. F., Cape Gelidonya: A Bronze Age Shipwreck, *Transactions of the American Philosophical Society* 57, no. 8, Philadelphia 1967.

—, *Archaeology Beneath the Sea*, New York 1975, 1-59.

—, A Bronze Age Shipwreck at Ulu Burun (Ka): 1984 Campaign, *American Journal of Archaeology* 90, 1986, 269-296.

—, Oldest Known Shipwreck Reveals Splendors of the Bronze Age, *National Geographic Magazine* 172 no. 6, December 1987, 692-733.

Pulak C., The Bronze Age Shipwreck at Ulu Burun, Turkey: 1985 Campaign, *American Journal of Archaeology* 92, 1988, 1-37.

Bass G. F. - Pulak C. - Collon - Weinstein J., The Bronze Age Shipwreck at Ulu Burun: 1986 Campaign, *American Journal of Archaeology* 93, 1989, 1-29.

Bass G.F., Beneath the Wine Dark Sea: Nautical Archaeology and the Phoenicians of the Odyssey, in: J. Coleman and C. Walz (eds), *Greeks and Barbarians: Essays on the Interactions between Greeks and Non-Greeks in Antiquity and the Consequences for Eurocentrism*, Ithaca NY 1997, 71-101.

Pulak C., Shipwreck: Recovering 3,000-Year-Old Cargo, *Archaeology Odyssey* 2, no. 4, 1999: Sept./Oct., 18-29.

—, The Balance Weights from the Late Bronze Age Shipwreck at Uluburun, in: *Metals Make the World Go Round*, Oxford 2000, 247-266.

—, The Cargo of Copper and Tin Ingots from the Late Bronze Age Shipwreck at Uluburun, in: Ünsal Yalçin (ed.), *International Symposium 'Anatolian Metal I'*, (Der Anschnitt, Bochum, Beiheft 13, 2000), 137-57.

—, Evidence from the Uluburun Shipwreck for Cypriot Trade with the Aegean and Beyond, in: L. Bonfante and V. Karageorghis (eds), *Italy and Cyprus in Antiquity, 1500-450 BC*, Nicosia 2001, 13-60.

—, The Uluburun Hull Remains, in: H.E. Tzalas (ed.), *Tropis VII. Proceedings of the 7th International Symposium on Ship Construction in Antiquity (27-31 August, Pylos)*, Athens 2002, 615-636.

—, Discovering a Royal Ship from the Age of King Tut: Uluburun, Turkey, in: G. F. Bass (ed.), *Beneath the Seven Seas: Adventures with the Institute of Nautical Archaeology*, London and New York 2005, 34-47.

THE APHRODITE OF MELOS

Gaitanos G. Th., *Πραγματεία περί της Αφροδίτης της Μήλου*, Athens 1928.

Alaux J. P., *La Vénus de Milo et Olivier Voutier*, Paris 1939.

Bracken C. Ph., *Antiquities Acquired*, London 1975.

Pasquier A., *La Vénus de Milo et les Aphrodites du Louvre*, Paris 1985.

Stoneman R., *Land of Lost Gods. The Search for Classical Greece*, London 1987.

Chalkoutsakis G. M., *Η ιστορία της Αφροδίτης της Μήλου*, Athens 1988.

Etienne R. & F., *La Grèce antique, archéologie d'une découverte*, Paris 1990.

D'Urville D., *Marcellus et Voutier, Enlèvemen de Vénus*, Paris 1994.

Tolias G., *Ο πυρετός των μαρμάρων*, Athens 1996.

Hamiaux M., *Les sculptures grecques du Musée du Louvre II. Le période hellénistique (IIIe - Ier siècle av. J.C.)*, Paris 1998, 41-44.

Trianti Is., Ελληνιστικά αγάλματα της Μήλου, in: O. Palagia (ed.) *Regional Schools of Helenistic Sculpture, Proceedings of an International Conference held at the American School of Classical Studies. March 15-17, 1996*, Oxford 1998.

Samara-Kauffmann A., *Greek Antiquities in the Louvre Museum*, Athens 2002.

THE VICTORY OF SAMOTHRACE

Champoiseau Ch., La Victoire de Samothrace, *Revue Archéologique* 1880, 11-17.

Conze A. - Hauser A. - Benndorf O., *Neue archaeologische Untersuchungen auf Samothrake*, Vienna 1880.

Matsas D. - Bakirtzis A., *Σαμοθράκη. Μικρός πολιτισμικός οδηγός, Ανατολική Μακεδονία και Θράκη* 1998.

Hamiaux M., *Les sculptures grecques du Musée du Louvre II. Le période hellénistique (IIIe - Ier siècle av. J.C.)*, Paris 1998, 27-40.

Hamiaux M., La Victoire de Samothrace: découverte et restauration, *Journal des Savants*, Jan.-June 2001, 153-223.

Samara-Kauffmann A., *Greek Antiquities in the Louvre Museum*, Athens 2002.

Hamiaux M., La Victoire de Samothrace: étude technique de la statue, *Monuments Piot* 83, 2004, 61-129.

Hamiaux M., La Victoire de Samothrace: construction de la base et reconstitution, *Monuments Piot* 85, 2006, 5-60.

THE PIRAEUS BRONZE STATUES

GENERAL

Eckstein F., Τα χάλκινα του Πειραιά, *Επετηρίς Φιλοσοφικής Σχολής ΑΠΦ* 15, 1976, 35-50.

APOLLO

Kontoleon N., Zur archaischen Bonzestatue aus dem Piraeus, *Opus Nobile, Festschrift U. Jantzen*, Wiesbaden 1969, 91 ff.

Richter G., *Kouroi³*, 1970, no. 159 bis.

Wallenstein K., *Korinthische Plastik des 7. und 6 Jahrhunderts vor Christus*, Bonn 1971, 163 ff.

Dontas G., Archaische und klassische griechische Plastik, *Akten des internationalen Kolloquiums vom 22-25. April 1985*, Mainz, 1986, I, 181-192.

Fuchs W., *Die Skulptur der Griechen*, Munich, 1993, 42.

THE GREAT ARTEMIS

Dontas G., La grande Artemis du Pirée: une œuvre d' Euphranor, *Antike Kunst* 25, 1987, 15-34.

ATHENA

Schefold K., Die Athene des Piraeus, *Antike Kunst* 14, 1971, 37 ff.

Waywell G. B., Athena Mattei, *Annual of the British School at Athens* 66, 1971, 373 ff.

Palagia O., *Euphranor*, Leiden 1980.

ATTRIBUTION TO A NEOATTIC WORKSHOP

Fuchs M., *In doc etiam genere Graeciae nihil cedamus: Studien zur Romanisierumg der späthellenistischen Kunst im 1. Jh. V. Chr.*, Mainz 1999.

ARTEMIS KINDYAS

Jucker I., Artemis Kindyas, *Gestalt und Geschichte, Festschrift Karl Schefold* (=*Antike Kunst*, Beiheft 4, 1967), 133 ff.

MEMORIES OF PHRASIKLEIA

Lazaridis D., Μυρρινούς (Μερέντα), *AAA* I, 1968, 31 ff.

Vavritsas A., Ανασκαφή γεωμετρικού νεκροταφείου Μερέντας, *ΑΔ* 25, 1970, Χρονικά, 127-129.

Kontoleon N. M., *Aspects de la Grèce préclassique*, Paris 1970, 53 ff.

Mastrokostas E., Η κόρη Φρασίκλεια Αριστίωνος του Παρίου και κούρος μαρμάρινος ανεκαλύφθησαν εν Μυρρινούντι, *AAA* V, 1972, 298-324.

Kontoleon N. M., Περί το σήμα της Φρασικλείας (Απολογία μιας ερμηνείας), *Αρχαιολογική Εφημερίς*, 1974, 1-12.

Vivliodetis E. P., *Ο Δήμος του Μυρρινούντος. Η οργάνωση και η ιστορία ενός δήμου της Αττικής*, Athens 1997 (Ph.D. Thesis, University of Athens, Philosophical School, Department of Archaeology and History of Art) [in press].

Kaltsas N., *Sculpture in the National Archaeological Museum, Athens*, Los Angeles 2002, 48-49.

—, Die Kore und der Kuros aus Myrrhinus, *Antike Plastik* 28, 2002, 7-26, pl. 1.

Kakavoyiannis E. Ch., Ο Δήμος Μυρρινούς και οι αρχαιολογικές έρευνες στον νέο Ιππόδρομο και το Ολυμπιακό Ιππικό Κέντρο στην Μερέντα Μαρκοπούλου, in: Kakavoyianni O. (ed.), *Αρχαιολογικές έρευνες στην Μερέντα Μαρκοπούλου*, Athens 2003, 9, figs 1-2.

Karakasi K., *Archaische Koren*, Munich 2004, 122-124, pl. 236-237.

THE LARGE KOUROS OF SAMOS

Kyrieleis H., Der Kuros von Samos. Das Abenteuer, ein Meisterwerk archaischer Kunst ins Museum zu bringen, *Archäologie in Deutschland*, Heft 1/1988, 18-23.

—, Der grosse Kuros von Samos, *Samos X*, Mainz 1996.

BRONZE STATUES
FROM THE DEPTHS OF THE SEA

BIBLIOGRAPHY ABOUT SHIPWRECKS AND BRONZE STATUES

Frost H., *Under the Mediterranean, Marine Antiquities*, Routledge and Kegan Paul, London 1963.

Rackl H.-W., *Archäologie unter Wasser, ein Tatsachenbericht*, Vienna-Heidelberg 1964.

Throckmorton P., *Diving for Treasure*, Thames and Hudson, London 1965.

—, *Shipwrecks and Archaeology: The Unharvested Sea*, Boston 1969.

Rackl H.-W., *Βουτιά στα Περασμένα, Υποβρύχια Αρχαιολογία*, (Greek translation with many additions); it contains an appendix about the underwater archaeology in Greece written by Ch. Kritzas, Gutenberg ed., Athens 1978.

Boardman J., *Greek Sculpture. The Classical Period*, London 1985.

Throckmorton P. (ed.), *History from the Sea, Shipwrecks and Archaeology*, Mitchell Beazley., London 1987, 14-23.

Boardman J., *Greek Sculpture. The Late Classical Period*, Thames and Hudson, London 1995.

Dellaporta K., Αρχαία Ναυάγια, in: *Ελλάδα της Θάλασσας*, Melissa ed., Athens 2004, 146-153.

BIBLIOGRAPHY ON THE CIRCUMSTANCES OF DISCOVERY

Svoronos J., Ο θησαυρός των Αντικυθήρων, in: *Το εν Αθήναις Εθνικό Μουσείο*, Athens 1903.

Lykoudis Emm. St., Ημερολόγιο της έρευνας στα Αντικύθηρα, *Σελίδες: Ποικίλα*, Βιβλιοπωλείον της Εστίας, Athens 1920.

Bertos N., *Αρχαιολογικό Δελτίο*, Appendix to vol. 10, 1926, 86-95.

Charbonneaux J., *La sculpture grecque au Musée du Louvre*, Paris 1964.

Pasquier A., *Le Louvre: Les antiquités grecques*, Paris.

Gallet de Santerre M. H., Informations Archéologiques, *Gallia* 24, 1926, fasc. 1, Paris 1966, 462-464.

Foti G., *Il Museo Nazionale di Reggio Calabria*, Naples 1972.

—, *I bronzi di Riace*, Istituto Geografico De Agostini, Novara 1981.

Busignani Al., *Gli Eroi di Riace*, Sansoni Editore, Florence 1981.

Sabbione Cl., Il ritrovamento di Porticello, *I bronzi di Riace*, Istituto Geografico De Agostini, Novara 1981, 36-37.

Rolley Cl., *Les Bronzes Grecs*, Office du Livre, Fribourg 1983.

Touloupa E., Das Bronze Reiters Tandbild des Augustus aus dem nordägäischen Meer, *Mitteilungen des Deutschen Archäologisches Institut, Athenische Abteilung*, Band 101, 1986, 185-205.

Charbonneaux J., *Œuvres d'Art les Bronzes Antiques, Musée d'Archéologie Sous-marine d'Agde (Catalogue)*, 1987, 86-88.

Lattanzi El. (ed.), *Il Museo Nazionale di Reggio Calabria*, Rome 1987.

Mattusch C. E., *Greek Bronze Statuary*, Ithaca and London 1988.

Moreno P., *Lissippo, L' Arte e la Fortuna*, Fabbri Edizioni, Rome 1995.

Podany J. - Scott D., The Getty Victorious Youth Reconsidered: Initial Report on the Scientific and Technical Reexamination, *From the Parts to the Whole: Acta of the 13th International Bronze Congress held at Cambridge, Massachusetts 1996*.

Mattusch C. C., *The Victorious Youth*, The J. Paul Getty Museum, Los Angeles 1997.

Pruneti P., Il bronzo della Croazia, *Archeologia Viva*, N. 76 n.s., Florence 1999, 48-61.

Rolley Cl., *La sculpture Grecque 2, la période classique*, Les manuels d'Art et d' Archéologie Antique, Paris 1999.

Viacava A., *L' atleta di Fano*, L' ERMA di Bretschneider, Rome 1999.

Mattusch C. C. et al., *From the Parts to the Whole* I, Portsmouth, R.I. 2000, 178-191.

Oikonomidou M., Νομισματικός «θησαυρός» Αντικυθήρων, «Καλλίστευμα», Μελέτες, προς τιμήν Όλγας Τζάχου-Αλεξανδρή, Athens 2001, 541-544.

Lugand M. - Bernond L., Agde et le Bassin de Thau, *Carte Archéologique de la Gaule* 34/2, Paris 2001, 402-403.

Stenuit M.-E., The Apoxyomenos of Vele Orjule, A Greek Bronze Statue discovered off Croatia, *MINERVA* 13, Sept.-Oct. 2002, 4-44.

Rolley Cl., Les Bronzes Grecques et Romaines: Recherches recentes, *Revue Archéologique*, 2003, 331-359.

Hemingway S., *The Horse and the Jockey of Artemission*, Berkeley 2004.

Proskynitopoulou R., article in: *Agon*, Kapon ed., Athens 2004, 101-103.

Biographical notes

GEORGE F. BASS

Distinguished professor emeritus at Texas A&M University, he has conducted shipwreck excavations and underwater surveys, mostly off the Turkish coast, since 1960. A native of Columbia, South Carolina, he obtained an M.A. in Near Eastern Archaeology from the Johns Hopkins University in 1955, followed by two years at the American School of Classical Studies at Athens, Greece, and two years in the U.S. Army, mostly in Korea. In 1964 he received a doctorate in Classical Archaeology from the University of Pennsylvania, where he remained as a faculty member until he resigned an associate professorship in 1973 to found the Institute of Nautical Archaeology (INA), which affiliated with Texas A&M University in 1976. He has written or edited seven books and over a hundred articles, five in *National Geographic*. He has been awarded the Archaeological Institute of America's Gold Medal for Distinguished Archaeological Achievement, an Explorers Club Lowell Thomas Award, a National Geographic Society La Gorce Gold Medal and the Society's Centennial Award, the J.C. Harrington Medal from The Society for Historical Archaeology, and honorary doctorates by Boghaziçi University in Istanbul and the University of Liverpool. In 2002 President George W. Bush presented him with the National Medal of Science.

ALBERTO G. BENVENUTI

He was born in Florence in 1944. He studied at Florence University and received the diploma in Classical Philology (with a thesis on subjects connected with Prehistoric Archaeology). He received a Masters degree in Cultural Anthropology at Stanford University, California. After a competition, he was appointed head of the Library of the Italian Archaeological School at Athens, of which he has been general secretary since 2000. He has taken part in excavations in Italy and Greece and has also attended numerous international conferences. He is the author of many studies, mainly on the archaeology, architecture and prehistoric topography of the Italian peninsula and the Aegean. He is a member of the Istituto Italiano di Archeologia Sperimentale (Genoa), the Society for Roman Studies (Athens), the Society for the Study of Ancient Greek Technology (Athens), the Archaeological Society (Athens), and the German Archaeological Institute (Berlin).

GEORGE CH. CHOURMOUZIADIS

He studied at the Aristotle University of Thessaloniki from 1953 to 1958. From 1965 to 1981 he served in the Ephorate of Antiquities of Thessaloniki. In 1973 he was awarded a doctorate in the Philosophical School of Thessaloniki University. In 1981 he was appointed to the chair of Prehistory in the Philosophical School of this same university. In 1983 he was appointed dean of the school and in 1985 vice-chancellor of the university.

He specialises in the Neolithic period and has excavated many prehistoric sites in Thessaly and Macedonia. He has published numerous articles and books, edits the journal *Anthropologika*, and is closely involved with museology. Since 1992 he has directed the excavations at the prehistoric lake settlement at Dispilio, Kastoria.

CHRISTOS DOUMAS

Professor emeritus of Archaeology at Athens University, where he taught Aegean archaeology from 1980 to 2000. He was born in 1933 in Patras, where he completed his basic schooling. He studied theology, history and archaeology at Athens University and from 1960 to 1980 was Curator or Ephor of Antiquities in the Hellenic Archaeological Service, having served in turn in the North Aegean islands, Attica, the Cyclades, the Athenian Acropolis and the Dodecanese. He also served as Ephor of the Prehistoric Collection of the National Archaeological Museum of Athens, and Director of Antiquities and Director of Conservation in the Hellenic Ministry of Culture. He was assistant and colleague of professor Sp. Marinatos on the excavations at Akrotiri on Thera (1968-1973) and, after Marinatos's death, succeeded him as director (1975 to present).

His service duties on the Aegean islands gave him the opportunity to familiarise himself with their cultures, to the study of which he has devoted the larger part of his scientific research, as is attested by his numerous books and academic articles.

He has taught at various universities in Europe, the USA and Japan and has been elected member of many scientific associations, including the Archaeological Society of Athens, the Society of Antiquaries in London and the Academia Europaea. The Hellenic Republic has awarded him the title of Commander of the Order of the Phoenix.

STELLA DROUGOU

She was born in Thessaloniki. She studied Archaeology in the Philosophical School of the Aristotle University of Thessaloniki and at the Universities of Würzburg and Heidelberg in Germany. She is professor of Classical Archaeology at Thessaloniki University. She has taken part in the excavation of Vergina from 1976 to the present, and was director of it from 1992-2002. She was a member of the scientific committee for the Organisation of Scientific Meetings on Hellenistic Pottery (1986-2006). Her published work is mainly on ancient pottery and vase-painting, though also on other subjects: Stella Drougou, I. Touratsoglou, Λαξευτοί τάφοι της Βέροιας (1980). S. Drougou, Πέλλα. Οι πήλινοι λύχνοι (1995). S. Drougou, Das antike Theater von Vergina, *AM* 112, 1997, 281-305. S. Drougou, Frieden und Krieg, *AM* 115, 2000, 147ff. S. Drougou, Βεργίνα. Μ. Τούμπα. Τα πήλινα αγγεία (2005), and others.

SPYROS IAKOVIDIS

Born in Athens in 1923. 1940: enrolled in the Philosophical School of Athens University. 1944: enlisted with the National Groups of Greek Guerrillas under N. Zervas in 1944. 1946: graduated in Archaeology from Athens University. 1962: received a Ph.D. from the same university. 1952-1954: curator of antiquities. He has taught Archaeology at the Universities of Athens (1970-1974), Marburg (1976-1977), Heidelberg (1977) and the University of Pennsylvania (1979-1991). Member of the Institute for Advanced Study at Princeton, USA (1977-1978). Excavations: Athens area, Perati, Eleusis, Pylos, Thera, Glas, and Mycenae. Director of the excavations at Mycenae since 1988. Books: *Η Μυκηναϊκή Ακρόπολις των Αθηνών* (1962), *Περατή* (1969-1970), *Αι Μυκηναϊκαί Ακροπόλεις* (1973), *Vormykenische und Mykenische Wehrbauten* (1977), *Ιστορία του Ελληνικού Έθνους*, vol. I (Ekdotike Athenon SA, 1970, three chapters), *Late Helladic Citadels on Mainland Greece* (1988), *Γλας I* (1989), *Γλας II* (1998), *Gla and the Kopais* (2001), *The Mycenaean Acropolis of Athens* (English transl. 2006), *Ανασκαφές Μυκηνών*, I, *Η Βορειοδυτική Συνοικία* (2006). Contributor to the *Ägäische Bronzezeit* (1987), contributor to and editor of the *Archaeological Atlas of Mycenae* (2003). Articles and excavation reports published in Greek and foreign academic journals, lectures at universities, museums and academic organisations in Greece, Germany, USA, Austria, Britain, Belgium, Canada, Cyprus, Ireland, Spain, Israel, Australia, and Switzerland. Participant in about 70 academic conferences in Greece and abroad (1971-2003). Member of the Archaeological Society at Athens, the Greek Historical and Ethnological Society, and five British, American, French and German academic bodies. Honorary member of the Society of Antiquaries of London, regular member of the Athens Academy, foreign member of the Lincei Academy (Rome), and honorary member of the Austrian Academy of Sciences (Vienna). Honorary doctorate in Archaeology from Dickinson College, Pennsylvania, USA. Distinctions: Medallion of the Greek Resistance, Grand Commander of the Order of the Phoenix, Grand Commander of the Order Stella della Solidarietà Italiana.

EVANGELOS CH. KAKAVOYIANNIS

He was born in 1938 and studied in the Philosophical School of Athens University, graduating from the Department of Archaeology and History. He later received a doctorate from the same university for his study *Μέταλλα Εργάσιμα και Συγκεχωρημένα*, which dealt with the organisation of the exploitation of the mineral wealth of Laureotike by the Athenian State. He has worked in the Archaeological Service for many years, in various Ephorates of Prehistoric and Classical Antiquities. During this time he has carried out excavations in many places, including Rhodes, Edessa, Velestino, Glyka Nera in Attica, and above all Laureotike, where he has systematically investigated the ancient mines at all periods. He has participated in various academic conferences and has published his work in Greek and foreign journals.

VASSOS KARAGEORGHIS

He was born in Trikomo, Cyprus, in 1929. He studied Classics at London University, where he submitted his doctoral dissertation in 1957. He served as Director of the Antiquities Department of Cyprus from 1963 to 1989, and was professor of Archaeology at the University of Cyprus from 1992 to 1996. He is a member or corresponding member of seven European Academies and has been awarded honorary doctorates at eight universities in Europe and Canada. He has written over ninety books and more than 425 articles on the archaeology of Cyprus and the Mediterranean. He has been awarded the Onassis Prize and the Prize of Cavalli d'Oro di San Marco. He was Visiting Fellow at Merton College and All Souls College (Oxford University) and Visiting Professor at the Institute for Advanced Study at Princeton (USA); he is now Honorary Fellow of Merton College (Oxford University). He serves as a member of the Board of Directors of the A.G. Leventis Foundation and holds the post of the Director of the Anastasios G. Leventis Foundation (Cyprus).

SUSAN WOMER KATZEV

Trained as a sculptor, she was schooled at Swarthmore College, the Boston Museum School and Tyler School of Fine Arts. While working as an artist on Roman and Early Byzantine shipwrecks at Yassi Ada, Turkey, she met her future husband Michael L. Katzev, then at the American School of Classical Studies, Athens. Through his directorship of the *Kyrenia Ship* excavation, she served as draftsman, photographer, film director and script writer for their Cyprus Broadcasting Corporation documentary, *With Captain, Sailors Three: the Ancient Ship of Kyrenia*. Since Michael Katzev's death in 2001, she has worked to bring his studies to final publication by the Texas A&M University Press, adding practical experiments, use of virtual reality, and the insights of numerous specialists whose writings will detail the journey of understanding from the survey of 1967 to the present.

HELMUT KYRIELEIS

He was born in Hamburg in 1938. From 1959 to 1965 he studied Classical Archaeology, Ancient History and Classical Philology at the Universities of Freiburg, Tübingen and Marburg. In 1965 he received his doctorate from the University of Marburg. From 1967 to 1972 he was Assistant in the Department of Classical Archaeology at the University of Bonn. In 1972 he was appointed professor in the same university. From 1972 to 1974 he was Director of the German Archaeological Institute of Berlin, and from 1975 to 1988 Director of the German Archaeo-

logical Institute in Athens. From 1976 to 1984 he directed the excavations at the Samian Heraion and from 1985 to 2000 the excavations at Olympia. From 1988 to 2003 he was president of the German Archaeological Institute. In the years 1991-2005 he was honorary professor in the Free University of Berlin, honorary doctor of the University of Athens, foreign member of Athens Academy, foreign member of the Academy of Georgia at Tbilisi, honorary member of the Society of Antiquaries, London, honorary member of the American Institute of Archaeology, and honorary member of the Council of the Archaeological Society at Athens.

COLIN F. MACDONALD

Born in 1957 in Edinburgh, Scotland, he was educated in Newcastle and Edinburgh and gained his doctorate at Christ Church, Oxford in 1985. His first excavation was with Prof. Henri de Lumley at the Lower Palaeolithic cave site of La Caune de l'Arago in south-west France. In Greece, from 1977 onwards, he was trained in excavation in Attica, Crete and Cyprus by John Ellis Jones, Hector Catling, Peter Warren, Hugh Sackett, Gerald Cadogan and Sinclair Hood. In 1988, he was appointed Archaeological Research Assistant to archaeological scientists under Noel Gale at Oxford University. From 1990-1999, he was Curator at Knossos for the British School at Athens, during which time he directed excavations near the palace and in the town of Knossos, as well as assisting the 23rd Ephorate of Antiquities. He now lives in Athens and continues his work at Knossos, Palaikastro (Siteia) and Maroni (Cyprus). He is the author of three books – *Knossos* (Folio Society 2005), *The Troubled Island: Minoan Crete before and after the Santorini Eruption* (Liège 1997), the latter with Jan Driessen, Professor of Archaeology at Louvain la Neuve, Belgium, and *Knossos: Protopalatial Deposits in Early Magazine A and the South-west Houses* (London 2007, *in press*), with Carl Knappett, Lecturer in Archaeology at the University of Exeter, England. He has also participated in numerous documentaries about Minoan Crete broadcast on ET1, Kriti TV, the Discovery and History Channels (USA), BBC2 and Channel 4 (UK).

FANI MALLOUCHOU-TUFANO

She studied Archaeology in the Philosophical School of Athens University. She specialised in the restoration of monuments at the International Centre for the Study of the Preservation and the Restoration of Cultural Property (ICCROM) in Rome and the Scuola di Perfezionamento per lo Studio ed il Restauro dei Monumenti of the School of Architecture of the University La Sapienza of Rome. She holds a doctorate from the Philosophical School of Athens University.

Since 1976 she has worked on the restoration of the Acropolis Monuments, and is head of the Documentation Office of the Acropolis Restoration Service in the Ministry of Culture. Since 2000, she has also taught courses in preservation history and cultural management

in the Interdepartmental Post-Graduate Programme on Monument's Protection at the National Technical University of Athens and in the Department of Archaeology and Art History in the Philosophical School of Athens University. She is a member of the Archaeological Society at Athens, the Historical and Ethnological Society of Greece, vice-president of the Council for Architectural Heritage of the Elliniki Etaireia for the Protection of the Environment and the Cultural Heritage and general secretary of the Association of Friends of the Acropolis.

Her academic research is mainly devoted to the history of monuments in Greece after the foundation of the modern Greek state. The subject of her doctoral dissertation was the history of the restoration of ancient monuments from the foundation of the modern Greek state to the Second World War. It was published in 1998 by the Archaeological Society at Athens and in 1999 received an award from the Athens Academy as 'a fundamental reference work on the modern history of the monuments of Greece'.

DOMINIQUE MULLIEZ

He was born in 1952 in Roubaix, France. From 1979 to 1984 he was a member of the French School at Athens. After this he worked as *maître de conferences* in Greek language and literature in Reims University (1985-1995) and then as professor of Greek Language at Lille University. Since 1979, he has found himself torn between two places. At Delphi, he is charged with the publication of a critical study of the manumission inscriptions carved on the walls and monuments in the sanctuary of Apollo. Also, in collaboration with two colleagues, he is preparing a selection of inscriptions from Delphi, accompanied by translations and comments. On Thasos, he and two colleagues have excavated a public area at the heart of the ancient city. The excavation of this complex made it possible to revise the history of Thasos from the Archaic period to Early Christian times. Since January 2002, he has been Director of the French School at Athens.

WOLF-DIETRICH NIEMEIER

He was born in 1947 and studied Classical Archaeology at the Universities of Göttingen, Mannheim and Heidelberg from 1968 until his graduation in 1976. From 1976 to 1979 he was an academic collaborator at the Academy of Sciences in Mainz, from 1979 to 1982 an assistant at Marburg University, from 1983 to 1986 a scientific collaborator at the German Archaeological Institute in Athens, from 1986 to 1991 professor at Freiburg University, and from 1991 to 2001 professor at Heidelberg University. Since 2001 he has been Director of the German Archaeological Institute in Athens and Director of the excavation of the Kerameikos. In 2002 he was awarded an honorary doctorate by the University of Liège. His most important excavations, other than that of the Kerameikos in Athens, are early Miletos (Ionia), Tel Kabri (Israel), the sanctuary at Kalapodi (Lokris) and, in the near future, the Samian Heraion. He has published 10 monographs and over 80 articles, has taken part in 40 international conferences, and has given numerous lectures in Greek universities as well as in other European countries, Turkey, Israel, the United States, Canada and Australia.

VASILEIOS PETRAKOS

He was born in 1932 in Piraeus and studied History and Archaeology in Athens, Lyon and Paris. In 1959 he was appointed to the Archaeological Service and served as Curator and Ephor of Antiquities in Sparta, Euboea, Mytilini, Delphi, Patras and Attica, and at the National Archaeological Museum of Athens. Since 1988 he has been General Secretary of the Archaeological Society of Athens. In 1996 he was named Correspondant of the Académie des Belles-Lettres of the Institut de France, and in 1998 he was elected a foreign member of the same Academy. In 1999 he was elected a member of the Athens Academy.

ALIKI SAMARA-KAUFFMANN

She is a scientific collaborator in the Department of Greek, Etruscan and Roman Antiquities of the Louvre. She studied History and Archaeology at Athens University and at the Sorbonne in Paris, where she defended her doctoral dissertation on the subject of the Geometric pottery in the Louvre. Her thesis was published in two volumes by the Académie des Inscriptione et Belles-Lettres: *Corpus Vasorum Antiquorum, France fasc. 25. Louvre 16, Céramique géometrique attique* (Paris 1972) and *Corpus Vasorum Antiquorum, France fasc. 27. Louvre 18, Ceramique géometrique non attique* (Paris 1976). In the 1970s she was assistant to the professor and academician Pierre Devambez, director of the Department of Greco-Roman Antiquities of the Louvre. She has participated in international archaeology conferences and has published articles on vase-painting and iconography in French and Greek academic journals. A researcher at the French National Research Centre (CNRS) and member of the team working on the *Iconographic Lexicon of Classical Mythology* (*LIMC*), she has written a large number of entries for this lexicon, and recently contributed to the international publication *Thesaurus Cultus et Rituum Antiquorum* (*ThesCRA*). Since 1989 she has been a member of the Archaeological Society at Athens. In 2001, she published the first study in Greek devoted to the Greek antiquities of the Louvre Museum, entitled *Greek Antiquities in the Louvre*. This book was translated into English in 2002.

MARINA SOPHRONIDOU

She was raised in Kalabaki, Drama. In 1991 she graduated from the Department of History and Archaeology of the Aristotle University of Thessaloniki in Archaeology. She followed the Post-graduate Programme in the same department from 1992 to 1995. In 1997 enrolled in the second cycle of the Post-graduate Programme in order to work on her doctoral dissertation on Archaeo-

logical News in Newspapers, which she defended in January 2003. She held a Greek state scholarship for 2003-2004 to carry out post-doctoral research into Pottery Vessels from the Neolithic Lake Settlement at Dispilio, Kastoria. She has participated in several excavation programmes, mainly in northern Greece, and since 1993 has been a permanent member of the research group of the Dispilio excavations. Since 2004 she has participated as main researcher in the scientific coordination of the Information Society programme "Digitisation and Filing of Archaeological Publications in the Daily Press and Periodicals from the period 1831-1932 and Developing Website".

She has read papers at various Greek and international conferences and published articles on the pottery of Dispilio.

GEORGIOS STEINHAUER

He was born in Piraeus and studied History and Archaeology at Athens University. In 1970 he was appointed to the Ephorate of Prehistoric and Classical Antiquities of Lakonia-Arkadia, of which he was Director from 1971 to 1979. From 1980 to 2003 he served in the Second Ephorate of Prehistoric and Classical Antiquities for Attica (as Ephor from 1994) and from 2004 to 2005 with the new Ephorate of Antiquities of Piraeus. He oversaw the redisplaying of finds in the Museums of Piraeus, Aigina, Marathon, Lavrio, and at the new airport of Athens. He was director of the excavations for the new airport, for the Attiki Odos (Athens orbital motorway) and the Olympic facilities, of the restoration of the Gate of Eëtioneia in Piraeus, and (as President of the appropriate scientific committee of the Hellenic Ministry of Culture) the enhancement and unification of the archaeological sites at Marathon. His doctoral dissertation was on Roman Sparta, and he is the author of about thirty articles, devoted mainly to epigraphy, history and topography, which have appeared in Greek and foreign scientific journals, as well as books on War in Ancient Times (2000), Antiquities (2001) and the Archaeological Museum of Piraeus (2001). For three years (1991-1994) he taught Ancient History and Epigraphy at the University of Crete.

JUTTA STROSZECK

She was born in Donauwoerth, Germany. She graduated from the Gymnasium there in 1980, having studied Latin and Greek. In the years 1980-1991 she studied Classical Archaeology, History of Byzantine Art, and Musical Sciences at the Universities of Erlangen, Göttingen and Berlin (FU). In 1986 she received a Master of Arts with a thesis on 7th century BC find contexts from southern Etruria. In 1991 she defended her doctoral dissertation on the production of lion sarcophagi at Rome in the Imperial period. In 1991-1992 she received a scholarship from the German Archaeological Institute to travel for one year visiting the important Classical sites around the Mediterranean. In 1992-1993 she was appointed to a research post at the University of Marburg and also

made numerous research trips to Italy and Greece. Since 1994 she has been working permanently at the German Archaeological Institute in Athens, and since 1995 has been field director of the Kerameikos excavation. Her academic interests include Greek state burials and war monuments; 'street archaeology'; and the building, function and use of ancient streets; and pastoral cults from ancient times to the present.

HARRY E. TZALAS

He was born in Alexandria. From 1956 to 1959 he lived in Brazil where he first became acquainted with the traditional boatbuilding techniques of the Amazon River. Later he established himself in Greece and, from 1966 to 1970, led a program centered on the revival of traditional boatbuilding on the island of Simi. He also researched similarities and differences in construction between ancient and traditional sea crafts of the Eastern Mediterranean.

In 1981 he established the Hellenic Institute for the Preservation of Nautical Tradition and a year later started a program in experimental archaeology, in cooperation with the Institute of Nautical Archaeology at Texas A&M University, for the construction of a full-scale replica of the *Ancient Ship of Kyrenia*.

A few years later he led another program in experimental archaeology aiming at researching the obsidian transportation by papyrus raft in Mesolithic times.

He also participated in the project for the construction of the Athenian Trireme *Olympias* led by late Professor John Morrison and John Coates.

Since 1985 he has organised nine international conferences on Ship Construction in Antiquity.

In 1997, he formed the Hellenic Institute of Ancient and Mediaeval Alexandrian Studies and is the director of the underwater surveys carried out regularly since then in Alexandria.

He has participated in numerous Greek and international conferences, presenting papers on marine archaeology, experimental archaeology and the topography of ancient Alexandria.

PANOS VALAVANIS

He was born in 1954. He studied Archaeology in Athens (1972-1977) and in Würzburg, Germany (1985-1986), being lucky to have as teachers V. Lambrinoudakis, P. Themelis, M. Tiverios and E. Simon. He is professor of Classical Archaeology at Athens University, where he has taught since 1981.

His doctoral dissertation and the majority of his books and articles deal with ancient Greek pottery and iconography, the architecture and topography of Athens and Attica, ancient athletics, and ancient Greek technology. He has taken part in many excavations and has given papers at many Greek and international conferences. He has written 15 books, including archaeological guides and books for the general public, as well as books for teachers and students.

Sources of illustrations

Kapon ed. / G. Giannelos: p. 10 ▪ Kapon ed. / M. Kapon: p. 12 ▪ Kapon ed. / P. Katertziadis: p. 15.

THE STAGES OF GREEK ARCHAEOLOGY: Archaeological Society at Athens: figs 1–6, 8–10 ▪ Archive of the newspaper 'Kathimerini': fig. 7.

GREAT MOMENTS IN GREEK ARCHAEOLOGY
N. Daniilidis: pp. 34–35.

THE VICISSITUDES OF THE ATHENIAN ACROPOLIS IN THE 19TH CENTURY. FROM CASTLE TO MONUMENT: Kapon ed. / G. Maravelias: figs 1, 33, 34 ▪ National Historical Museum (Athens): figs 4, 10, 16, 17, 29 ▪ Archaeological Society at Athens: figs 11, 12, 25, 28 ▪ Museum of the City of Athens (Vouros-Eutaxias Foundation): fig. 3 ▪ Pushkin Museum (Moscow): figs 5, 6 ▪ Statens Museum for Kunst (Copenhagen): fig. 7 ▪ German Archaeological Institute (Athens): figs 14, 30 ▪ Kunstakademiets Bibliotek (Copenhagen): fig. 13 ▪ Det kongelige Bibiotek (Copenhagen): fig. 20 ▪ Committee for the Conservation of the Acropolis Monuments (Athens): figs 18, 19; Committee for the Conservation of the Acropolis Monuments (Athens) / S. Mavrommatis: fig. 36, 38. ▪ Th. Theodorou Collection (Athens): figs 21, 26 ▪ Dietmar Siegert Collection (Munich): fig. 22 ▪ N. Catsimpoolas Collection (Boston): fig. 23 ▪ P. Venieris Collection (Athens): fig. 35 ▪ Studio, N. Kontos: fig. 37 ▪ 1st Ephorate of Prehistoric and Classical Antiquities: fig. 32.

Mallouchou-Tufano F., *Η αναστήλωση των αρχαίων μνημείων στη νεώτερη Ελλάδα (1834–1939)* (1998): figs 2, 8, 9, 15.
Papageorgiou-Venetas A., *The Athenian Walk and the Historic Site of Athens* (2004): fig. 24.
The Illustrated London News (1842–1885): figs 27, 31.

KERAMEIKOS I. THE DISCOVERY OF THE ANCIENT CEMETERY: German Archaeological Institute (Athens): figs 2, 3, 5, 7, 8, 15–19, 21, 23, 24, 26; German Archaeological Institute (Athens) / V. Scheunert: fig. 27; German Archaeological Institute (Athens) / V. Scheunert & R. Posamentir: fig. 28 ▪ Kapon ed. / G. Maravelias: figs 4, 9, 11, 12, 25; Kapon ed. / K. Tsiriggakis: fig. 1; Kapon ed. / G. Fafalis: figs 10, 22, 29–31 ▪ Archaeological Receipts Fund (Athens): fig. 20 ▪ 3rd Ephorate of Prehistoric and Classical Antiquities: figs 6, 13 ▪ N. Daniilidis: fig. 32.

The Graphic (1869–1885): fig. 14.

KERAMEIKOS II. THE ARCHAIC SCULPTURES OF THE SACRED GATE, SPRING 2002: German Archaeological Institute (Athens) / W.-D. Niemeier: figs 2–6; German Archaeological Institute (Athens): figs 9, 10 ▪ Archaeological Museum of Kerameikos (Athens) / G. Maravelias: fig. 7 ▪ Kapon ed. / M. Kapon: fig. 1; Kapon ed. / G. Maravelias: figs 8, 11, 12–14.

DELOS. THE EXCAVATION OF THE SACRED ISLAND OF APOLLO: Kapon ed. / G. Maravelias: figs 1, 3, 4, 11, 16, 23, 38; Kapon ed. / Chr. Iosifidis – G. Moutevellis: fig. 22; Kapon ed. / M. Kapon: figs 27, 29–32, 35 ▪ N. Daniilidis: figs 2, 28 ▪ French School of Athens: figs 6, 7, 9, 10, 14, 15, 17–20, 24–26, 36, 39 ▪ Archaeological Receipts Fund (Athens): figs 12, 13, 33, 34, 40 ▪ D. Mulliez: fig. 37 ▪ GEOMET Ltd / G. Vozikis: fig. 21.

Chatzidakis P.I., *Δήλος* (2003): figs 5, 8.

OLYMPIA. EXCAVATIONS AND DISCOVERIES AT THE GREAT SANCTUARY: National Historical Museum (Athens): figs 1, 2 ▪ German Archaeological Institute (Athens): figs 3–5, 19, 20, 22–24, 26, 27; German Archaeological Institute (Athens) / Romaides Bros.: figs 32, 35 ▪ Kapon ed. / M. Kapon: figs 8–9, 38, 39; Kapon ed. / G. Kitsios: figs 11, 12; Kapon ed. / G. Fafalis: figs 6, 7 ▪ Archaeological Receipts Fund (Athens): figs 13–18, 25, 28–31, 33, 34 ▪ École Nationale Supérieure des Beaux-Arts (Paris): fig. 21 ▪ G. Giannelos: figs 36, 37.

SCHLIEMANN AND HOMER'S "MYCENAE RICH IN GOLD": Archaeological Society at Athens: figs 1, 26, 39 ▪ Kapon ed.: figs 3, 7; Kapon ed. / M. Kapon: fig. 16; Kapon ed. / M. Skiadaresis: figs 21, 23; Kapon ed. / G. Fafalis: figs 17, 25, 32 ▪ National Historical Museum (Athens): figs 2, 11–13, 34–36 ▪ Staaliche Museen zu Berlin – Preußischer Kulturbesitz, Museum für Vor- und Frühgeschichte: fig. 6 ▪ N. Daniilidis: fig. 14 ▪ National Archaeological Museum (Athens): figs 27, 30, 37.

The Illustrated London News (1842–1885): figs 9, 10, 15.
Bacon E., *The Great Archaeologists* (1976): fig 8.
Aslanis I. (ed.), *Τροία. Ανασκαφές και ευρήματα του Ερρίκου Σλήμαν* (1985): figs. 4, 5.
The Graphic (1869-1885): fig. 38.
Demakopoulou K. (ed.), *The Mycenaean World. Five Centuries of Early Greek Culture 1600–1100 BC* (1988): figs 18, 24.
Demakopoulou K. (ed.), *Τροία, Μυκήνες, Τίρυνς, Ορχομενός. Εκατό χρόνια από το θάνατο του Ερρίκου Σλήμαν* (1990): figs 19, 20, 22, 29, 31, 33.
Chourmouziadis G.Ch., *The Gold of the World* (1998): fig. 40.

DELPHI. THE EXCAVATION OF THE GREAT ORACULAR CENTRE: National Historical Museum (Athens): fig. 3 ▪ Archaeological Receipts Fund (Athens): figs 23, 26, 32, 37, 38 ▪ École Nationale Supérieure des Beaux-Arts (Paris): figs 2, 18, 19, 22 ▪ French School of Athens: figs 4, 5, 7, 8, 10–17, 20, 21, 24, 25, 27, 30, 33, 34, 39–42, 44, 46 (drawing by K. Iliakis) ▪ Kapon ed.: fig. 6; Kapon ed. / M. Kapon: fig. 45; Kapon ed. / G. Maravelias: figs 3, 35, 36; Kapon ed. / G. Fafalis: figs 28, 29, 31 ▪ D. Mulliez: figs 4, 43 ▪ N. Daniilidis: fig. 47 ▪ G. Kouroupis: fig. 48.

Δελφοί. Αναζητώντας το χαμένο Ιερό. École française d'Athènes (1992): figs 1, 9.

KNOSSOS. THE DISCOVERY OF THE MINOAN PALACE: RMN / Apeiron: fig. 1 ▪ N. Daniilidis: figs 2, 46 ▪ Numismatic Museum (Athens): fig. 3 ▪ C.F. Macdonald: figs 4, 9, 12, 13, 26, 29, 30, 32, 33, 37, 38, 40, 44, 47, 48, 55 ▪ Kapon ed.: fig. 44 ▪ The Ashmolean Museum of Art and Archaeology (Oxford): figs 6–8, 10, 14, 18, 19, 23–25, 27, 28, 35, 36, 54 ▪ Archaeological Receipts Fund (Athens): fig. 43 ▪ Archaeological Museum of Herakleion (Crete): figs 22, 31, 41, 42, 45, 53; Archaeological Museum of Herakleion (Crete) / I. Papadakis: figs 11, 17 ▪ G. Giannelos: fig. 34 ▪ E. Attali: fig. 49 ▪ S. Paton: fig. 50 ▪ Institute for Aegean Prehistory Study Center for East Crete / Chr. Papanikolopoulos: fig. 51 ▪ Corpus der minoischen und mykenischen Siegel (Marburg) / I. Pini: figs 15, 16.

Chourmouziadis G.Ch., *The Gold of the World* (1998): figs 20, 21, 52.
Bacon E., *The Great Archaeologists* (1976): figs 5, 39.

SESKLO AND DIMINI. THE PREHISTORIC CITADELS: Kapon ed. / D. Benetos: fig. 12; Kapon ed. / M. Kapon: fig. 14; Kapon ed.: fig. 16; Kapon ed. / M. Skiadaresis: fig. 22 ▪ Drawing by M. Korres: figs 8, 9, 13.

Papathanasopoulos G., *Neolithic and Cycladic Civilization. National Archaeological Museum* (1981) / A. Levidis: fig. 1.
Tsountas Chr., *Αι πρϊστορικαί ακροπόλεις Διμηνίου και Σέσκλου* (1908): figs 2–6.
Η Νεολιθική Συλλογή του Αρχαιολογικού Μουσείου Βόλου, European Program Raphaël Eu.Ne.Cu. (2001): figs 7–11, 15, 17, 18–21, 23, 24.
Hourmouziadis G. – Asimakopoulou-Atzaka P. – Makris K.A., *Magnesia. The Story of a Civilization* (1982): figs 16, 17.

POLIOCHNI ON LEMNOS. THE EARLIEST CITY IN EUROPE: National Archaeological Museum (Athens): fig. 1 ▪ Kapon ed. / Chr. Iosifidis – G. Moutevellis: figs 5, 7 ▪ Italian Archaeological School at Athens: figs 2–4, 6, 8.

THE ATHENIAN AGORA. ENCOUNTER WITH THE FIRST DEMOCRACY: A.S. Mailis Collection (Athens): fig. 1 ▪ The American School of Classical Studies at Athens, Archives of the Agora Excavations / C.A. Mauzy: fig. 3–12, 14–21, 23–29, 31–33 ▪ German Archaeological Institute (Athens): figs 7–9 ▪ A. Kokkou: fig. 22 ▪ Kapon ed. / G. Kouroupis: fig. 2; Kapon ed. / R. Kapon: fig. 34.

Papageorgiou-Venetas A., *The Athenian Walk and the Historic Site of Athens* (2004): fig. 13.
Athens in Prehistory and Antiquity. Exhibition on Architecture and City Planing. 15th century B.C.–6th century A.D. (1987): fig. 30.

THE "ROYAL" TOMBS AT SALAMIS IN CYPRUS:
Karageorghis V., *Excavating at Salamis in Cyprus 1952-1974* (1999): figs 1–21, 26–39.
Karageorghis V., *Early Cyprus: Crossroads of the Mediterranean* (2002): figs 22–25.

AKROTIRI ON THERA. THE EXCAVATION OF A BURIED CITY: Archives of the Excavations at Akrotiri (Thera): figs 2, 4–10, 12, 18–27, 30, 31, 39, 40, 41 ▪ German Archaeological Institute (Athens): fig. 3 ▪ N. Fintikakis: fig. 15 ▪ 21st Ephorate of Prehistoric and Classical Antiquitites: figs 16, 17 ▪ Cl. Palyvou: figs 34–36 ▪ Kapon ed. / Chr. Iosifidis – G. Moutevellis: figs 11, 13, 14, 38.

The Illustrated London News (1842–1885): fig. 42.
Doumas Chr., *The Wall-Paintings of Thera* (1992): figs 1, 28, 32, 33, 37.

VERGINA. ON THE TRACKS OF THE MACEDONIAN KINGS: Aristotle University of Thessaloniki, Archives of the Excavations at Vergina: figs 1–5, 11, 12, 14–15, 40; Aristotle University of Thessaloniki, Archives of the Excavations at Vergina / Sp. Tsavdaroglou: figs 16–20, 25, 27, 28, 33, 34, 37, 38 ▪ St. Drougou: figs 13, 21, 23, 24 ▪ Heuzey L. – Daumet Ch.H., *Mission Archéologique Macédoine* (1876) / Kapon ed. / G. Maravelias: figs 6–10; Kapon ed. / M. Skiadaresis: figs 22, 26, 29, 30, 32; Kapon ed. / S. Mavrommatis: figs 31, 35, 36, 39 ▪ Archaeological Receipts Fund (Athens): fig. 41.

DISPILIO NEAR KASTORIA. THE PREHISTORIC LAKE SETTLEMENT: Prefectorial Administration of Kastoria: figs 1–3 ▪ Kapon ed. / M. Kapon: figs 10, 23–27 ▪ Archives of the Excavations at Dispilio: figs 4–9, 15.

Chourmouziadis G.Ch., *Ανασκαφής εγκόλπιον* (2006) / F. Yfantidis: figs 11–14, 16–22.

GREAT MOMENTS IN MARINE ARCHAEOLOGY
M.L. Katzev: pp. 284–285.

THE ANCIENT SHIP OF KYRENIA, BENEATH CYPRUS SEAS: S. Womer Katzev: figs 1, 4, 9–19, 21–29 ▪ J. Veltri: figs 2, 5, 7, 20 ▪ M.L. Katzev: fig. 3 ▪ B. Dunn: fig. 6 ▪ D. Owen: fig. 8.

THE KYRENIA II. AN ATTEMPT IN EXPERIMENTAL ARCHAEOLOGY: Municipality of Aghia Napa (Cyprus): fig. 1 ▪ S. Womer Katzev: fig. 4 ▪ H.E. Tzalas / Y. Vichos: figs 2, 5 ▪ Melina Merkouri Foundation (Athens): fig. 6.

Spathari E., *Sailing through Time. The Ship in Greek Art* (1995): fig. 3.

ULUBURUN. A BRONZE AGE SHIPWRECK: Institute of Nautical Archaeology / D.A. Frey: figs 1–25.

MASTERPIECES OF GREEK SCULPTURE SEE THE LIGHT OF DAY
RMN / Apeiron: pp. 316–317.

THE APHRODITE OF MELOS: Louvre Museum, Department of Greek, Etruscan and Roman Antiquities: figs 1, 2 ▪ RMN / Apeiron: fig. 4 ▪ Documentation Histoire du Louvre / Archives Aulanier: fig. 7.

Μεγάλη Ελληνική Εγκυκλοπαίδεια (Great Greek Encyclopaedia), vol. 6, p. 358: fig. 3.
Alaux J.P., *La Vénus de Milo et Olivier Voutier* (1939): figs 5, 6.

THE VICTORY OF SAMOTHRACE: RMN / Apeiron: fig. 1 ▪ Documentation Histoire du Louvre Reproduction: P. Philibert / Archives Aulanier: figs 2, 4, 5 ▪ Louvre Museum, Department of Greek, Etruscan and Roman Antiquities: fig. 3.

THE PIRAEUS BRONZE STATUES: Kapon ed. / S. Mavrommatis: figs 1, 4–8 ▪ Archaeological Society at Athens: figs 2, 3.

MEMORIES OF PHRASIKLEIA: Epigraphical Museum, Archive of Efth. Mastrokostas (Athens): figs 1–3, 6, 7 ▪ Kapon ed. / N. Kontos: fig. 4; Kapon ed. / Chr. Iosifidis – G. Moutevellis: figs 10, 11 ▪ National Archaeological Museum (Athens): fig. 5 ▪ Archaeological Receipts Fund (Athens): figs 8, 9.

THE LARGE KOUROS OF SAMOS: H. Kyrieleis: figs 1, 2, 4, 5 ▪ German Archaeological Institute (Athens): figs 3, 6.

BRONZE STATUES FROM THE DEPTHS OF THE SEA: RMN / Apeiron: figs 1, 2, 26 ▪ National Archaeological Museum (Athens): figs 6, 14, 18, 21, 22, 39 ▪ The Antikythera Mechanism Research Project: figs 10–13 ▪ H.E. Tzalas: figs 17, 20 ▪ The J. Paul Getty Museum (Malibu): fig. 24 ▪ National Museum of Reggio di Calabria / L. Pediccini: fig. 28 ▪ Archaeological Museum of Smyrna (Izmir, Turkey): fig. 30 ▪ Kapon ed. / D. Benetos: figs 3, 16; Kapon ed. / G. Fafalis: figs 7–9, 15, 23, 24, 29 ▪ Archaeological Receipts Fund (Athens): fig. 19 ▪ Scala Instituto Fotografico Editoriale SPA: fig. 27 ▪ Jasen Messic, Ministry of Culture of Croatia: figs 35, 36 ▪ Ephorate of Underwater Antiquities: figs 37, 38.

Throckmorton P. (ed.), *History from the Sea, Shipwrecks and Archaeology* (1987): figs 4, 5.
Bourbon F. – Durando F. (ed.), *I Greci in Italia. Civiltà e arte della Magna Grecia* (2004): fig. 25.
Karnišl. et al., *Hrvatski Apoksiomen – The Croatian Apoxyomenos: Archaelogy Museum, Zagreb May 18–September 17, 2006* (2006): figs 31–34.
Valavanis P., *Games and Sanctuaries in Ancient Greece* (2004): fig. 40.

Glossary

adyton: Literally, "a place not to be entered"; a small inner shrine sometimes placed at the back of a temple cella.

aegis: A goatskin fringed with snakes worn by Athena; protection, auspices, sponsorship.

agora: Marketplace; but more than stalls and shops—the central civic area of a Greek city.

ajouré: Pierced or perforated metalwork.

akroterion/akroteria: Ornament or sculpture placed on the apex or corners of a gabled roof; an ornament similarly placed (as on the prow of a galley).

alabastron/alabastra: An ancient Greek or Roman jar for oils, ointments, or perfumes, having a flattened lip with narrow orifice and an elongated body rounded at the bottom.

amphora: Large two-handled lidded jar for wine or oil storage.

anastylosis: To prop with pillars; the reconstruction of a monument from fallen parts.

anthemion/anthemia: Ornament consisting of floral or foliated forms arranged in a radiating cluster but always flat (as in relief sculpture or in painting).

archaeobotany: The study of plant remains from archaeological sites. Also known as palaeoethnobotany.

archaeoentomology: The study of insect remains from archaeological sites.

archaeoicthyology: The study of fish remains from archaeological sites.

archaeomalacology: The study of mollusks as they relate to archaeological sites.

archaeozoology: The study of animal remains from archaeological sites. The remains primarily consist of the hard parts of the body, such as bones, teeth, and shells. Such remains represent the food refuse of ancient populations, as well as the use of animals for transportation, decoration, or pets.

archon basileus: An office of civic and priestly scope, one of the oldest and most honored in Athens.

cavea: The tiered semicircular seating space of an ancient theater.

cella: The principal room of a temple.

cenotaph: A tomb or monument erected in honor of a person whose body is elsewhere.

crepis: A genus of herbs (family Compositae).

dedication (i.e, monuments/votive gifts): A devoting or setting aside for a particular purpose; rite of dedicating to a divine being or to a sacred use; solemn appropriation.

deme: A village or district, used to organize Athenian citizens into topographical units.

dromos: Literally, racecourse, course, or public walkway; the passageway into an ancient Egyptian or Mycenaean subterranean tomb.

drum (architecture): Any of the cylindrical blocks that form the shaft of a column; a round wall or structure that supports a dome.

ephebe: Adolescent boy; from the fourth century BC, used of members of a military training college in Athens.

epistyle: Architrave; the beam resting directly on the tops of the columns or between a column and another structure.

euergetai: An act of individual beneficence, most frequently the embellishment of a town with new public buildings.

exedra: A room for conversation, usually open like a portico and furnished with seats; a large, open, outdoor nearly semicircular seat or bench with a solid back.

frieze: The part of an entablature that is between the architrave and the cornice; a sculptured or richly ornamented band, as on a building or a piece of furniture.

gorytos: A bow case for a Scythian bow.

guilloche motif: A continuous scroll pattern formed by two or more bands twisted one within the other to form a plait; the interstices are usually filled with rosettes or semispheres.

hathoric: Of or relating to Hathor or to a column surmounted by her image.

Heraion: Temple dedicated to Hera, the most famous of which is in Argos.

herm: Quadrangular stone pillar that functioned as a boundary marker; originally topped with a head of Hermes, later with that of other figures.

heroön, heroon: Building or place consecrated to a hero.

hydria: Three-handled jar, used for carrying water.

kantharos/kantharoi: Wine cup with two vertical handles and a deep, footed bowl. Often associated with Dionysos or Herakles.

kore/korai: "Young girl" or "maiden"; a statue type from the Archaic period of a modestly dressed female.

kosmetai: Annually chosen magistrates who were responsible for the city gymnasia. They came from prominent Athenian families and usually held other civic offices later in life.

Kouros/kouroi: "Young man"; usually denotes generic Archaic statue-type of a nude male.

krater: Capacious open-mouthed vessel used for mixing wine with water. Large examples hold around 45 liters (10 gallons). Volute, kalyx, column, and bell shapes are subdivisions.

Kylix/kylikes: Wine cup; wide and shallow in shape, with two horizontal handles and a stemmed foot.

megaron/megara: The great central hall of an ancient Mycenaean house, usually containing a central hearth; cella.

metope: Rectangular panel inserted between triglyphs of a building in the Doric order; together they form its frieze.

Metroön: The name given to a building dedicated to a mother goddess, Cybele, Rhea, or Demeter, in ancient Greece.

naiskos/naiskoi: Diminutive of the Greek naos, or temple.

odeion: A small roofed theater, in contrast to theaters in the open air.

omphalos: "Navel"; used of the center of a geographical area, and most famously as a title of Delphi (celebrated by a domed stone in the shape of a navel).

ostrakon/ostraka: Potsherd; a chip or shard of limestone or pottery used as a writing tablet.

palaistra/palaistrai: Literally, "wrestling school"; often a separate precinct, or else the area of a gymnasium complex set aside specifically for wrestling.

peplos/peploi: Long, sleeveless woolen robe, worn pinned at the shoulders and belted; the normal apparel of Greek women.

peribolos: Wall surrounding a holy area.

pithos/pithoi: Large terracotta storage vessel.

polemarchos: Literally, "master of war"; military officer in ancient Greece.

poros: A coarse limestone found in the Peloponnese and extensively used as building material by the ancient Greeks.

potsherd: A pottery fragment usually unearthed as an archaeological relic.

pyrtanis/pyrtaneis: The executive committee of the ancient Greek senate.

Pyxis/pyxides: Small lidded box for cosmetics or jewelry.

Rhyton/rhyta: Drinking horn.

skyphos/skyphoi: Drinking cup with two small handles.

Stele/stelai: Upright stone slab, often used as a gravestone or to carry an inscription.

stereobate: Base or substructure of a building.

stoa: Colonnade or portico.

stratigraphy: Arrangement of depositional layers and their sequence. In archaeology, the superposition of layers of refuse, foundations of buildings, and the like, determine their sequences.

thalassocracy: Maritime supremacy.

tholos: Circular building or tomb.

tholos tomb: A "beehive tomb"; a round, chamber tomb common throughout the Mycenaean world.

trierarchs: The ancient Athenian plan whereby individual citizens furnished and maintained triremes as a civic duty.

trireme: A ship with three banks of oars, used in naval warfare.

triglyphs: Panel with three vertical grooves, or bars, alternating with metopes in a Doric frieze on a building.

tumulus: An artificial hillock or mound (as over a grave); especially an ancient grave.

Index

Note: Page numbers in italics indicate illustrations.

Boeckh, August, 19, 20, 21, 22–23, 23
book, oldest known, 312
Bötticher, Adolf, 103
Bottos, tomb of, at Cyrene, 123
bouleuterion
    at Agora of Athens, 205, 207, 219
    at Poliochni on Lemnos, 197, 198, 200
Boundroukas, Tasos, 72
Bousquet, Jean, 153
boxer, head of (sculpture), 104, 105
Boxing Boys (wall-painting), 242
Boyiatzis, G., 326
Brauron, sanctuary of Artemis at, 30
Brauroneion, 52–53
Brea, Luigi Bernab_, 198
Brill, Robert, 314
British School of Archaeology, 18, 27
Brønsted, P. O., 138
bronze cauldrons
    at Mycenae, 129
    at Olympia, 106
    at Salamis, 225, 226, 232
bronze plaque at Olympia, 114–15, 115
bronze statues
    retrieved from the sea, 342–63
    at Olympia, 104–7, 114, 114
    at Piraeus, 16, 30, 326–31, 327–31
Brouskari, Maria, 32
Bruce, Thomas (Lord Elgin), 19
Brueckner, Alfred, 60–66, 65
Buchon, Jean Alexandre, 42
Buda, Giovanni, 151
bull motif
    at Akrotiri, 247
    at Delphi, 152
    at Kerameikos, 62–63
    at Knossos, 175, 175
    at Mycenae, 128, 128–29
Bullard, M., 91, 95
Buondelmonti, Christopher, 78
Burnouf, Émile, 21
Byzantine Museum, 32

C

Cakir, Mehmet, 308
Calf-Bearer (sculpture), 48, 49
Calvert, Frank, 120–21
Camp, J. McK, 219
Camp-stool Fresco, at Knossos, 176
Canaanite finds, in shipwreck, 308, 311, 312, 313, 314, 315
Canadian Archaeological Institute, 30
Cape Gelidonya shipwreck, 312–13
Capps, Ed., 206
Cariolou, Andreas, 286, 286
Caryatids, 38, 43, 44, 46
casket, at Vergina, 268, 268–69, 269
Cassandra, tomb of, 118, 123–24
catalogues, museum, 31–32
Cave of the Dragon, 84, 84–85
Cayeux, L., 95
cemetery. See also tombs
    at Kerameikos, 22, 58–69, 72–77
    at Knossos, 180–82
    at Rhenia, 98
    at Tanagra, 22
Centaurs, battle with (sculpture), 107
Central Court, at Knossos, 159, 162
Central Service, 18
Centre for Underwater Archaeological Research, 362
Chairon, 65
Chalkotheke, 52–53
Chamonard, J., 87, 91, 92

Champoiseau, Charles, 322–25
Chancel Screen, House of the, 170, 172
Chandler, Richard, 102
Charbonneaux, Jean, 325
chariot(s), at Salamis, 226–28, 230, 231, 232, 233
Chariot of the Rhodians, base of, 154
chariot race (sculpture), 107
Charioteer of Delphi (sculpture), 147–49, 148, 149, 153
Chase, Th., 136
Chasiotis, Georgios, 334
Chasiotis property, 334–37
Childe, G., 187–88
Christie, Agatha, 210
cistern of Inopos, 92, 96
citadel of Mycenae, 24, 118, 119, 122
clay tablets, at Knossos, 164–65, 165, 171, 182–83
Cleopatra, House of, 92, 93
Clinton, Kevin, 26
Clytemnestra, tomb of, 118, 124, 130, 131
Cockerell, C. R., 82
coins
    of Ancient Ship of Kyrenia, 297–98
    of Antikythera Shipwreck, 346
    of Knossos, 158, 160
    of Mithridates VI, at Piraeus, 327
Colonnades, Hall of the, 168, 169–71, 170
Colossus of the Naxians, 80, 81, 82
Constantine (Greek crown prince), 326
Convert, Henri
    at Delos, 80, 85, 87, 88–89, 96, 99
    at Delphi, 141–42, 142
Conze, Alexander, 60, 322–24
copper ingots, 306, 307, 308, 308, 311, 312–13
Corinth, 22, 32
Corinthian helmet, at Olympia, 113, 113
Corpus Inscriptionum Graecarum, 19, 22–23
Corridor of the Bays, at Knossos, 167, 168
Courby, F., 87, 92
Cousteau, Jacques-Yves, 345, 346
Couve, L., 85, 142
Crimean War, 18
Cup-bearer (wall-painting), 176
curse tablet, 298, 298
Curtius, Ernst, 19, 24, 103, 137
Cyclades, Bronze Age phases of, 243–44
Cyclopean walls, 52
Cyriaco of Ancona, 134

D

Dancing Women (column), 150, 150, 151
Danish Institute, 30
Daumet, Henri, 259
Daux, Georges, 154
Daveluy, Amédée, 21
daybooks
    of Acropolis of Athens, 50–51
    of Agora of Athens, 211
    of Delphi, 149–50, 151, 153
death masks, 127, 129, 129, 130
Decree 191, 18
Dedidakis, Pavlos, 326
Delian House, 93
Deliveris, Kriton, 216
Della Seta, Alessandro, 29, 196–97
Delos, 78–99
    aerial photographs of, 79, 98–99
    comparison with Delphi, 78, 86, 91, 138
    first excavations of, 80–83
    first French excavations of, 84–86
    foreign travellers to, 80–83
    great excavation of, 26, 87–98
    mapping of, 78, 78–80, 85, 95, 97, 98
    mosaics at, 94, 95, 95

museum of, 32
    plundering of, 22, 82–83
    purification of, 22
    wall-paintings at, 92, 95
Delphi, 134–57
    comparison with Delos, 78, 86, 91, 138
    copies and photographs of, 151
    daybook of, 149–50, 151, 153
    discovery of, 134–36
    early exploration of, 137–38
    expropriation of site, 138–41
    great excavation of, 28, 140–43, 141–56
    later excavations of, 153–56
    museum of, 32, 153, 153
    negotiations over, 139–41
    panoramic view of, 156–57
    rail system at, 141–43, 142–44
    restoration of, 154, 154–56
    stratigraphy of, 150–51
Delphic Hymn to Apollo, 144, 144–47, 151
Deltion Archaeologikon (bulletin), 27–28
Demangel, Robert, 153
Demeter, grief of (wall-painting), 262, 262–64, 263
Demetria and Pamphile, grave relief of, 61
Demetrios Poliorketes, 235
Demetrius, 298
Demos, sanctuary of, 205
Demosthenes (statue), 218
Description of Greece (Pausanias), 100–102
Dexileos, grave of, 22, 58, 62, 62–63, 63
diadems
    at Mycenae, 126–27, 129
    at Vergina, 268, 269
Diadoumenos, 86, 86
Diffusionism, 187–88
digital photos, of Kerameikos, 68, 69
Dikaios, P., 221–22, 222
Dikili Tas, 31
Dimini, 184–95, 274
    excavation of, 26, 28–29, 184, 185–88, 186, 187
    finds at, 189–95, 193–95
    houses at, 192, 192
    reconstruction drawing of, 188
Dimitriadis, Athan., 23
Dimitriadis, Photios, 318
Dimitsas, Margaritas G., 32
Diodorus, 235
Dion, 31
Dionysios of Kollytos, grave of, 62–63
Dionysos, House of, 91, 94
Dionysos, Theatre of, 22
Dionysos mosaics
    at Delos, 94, 95
    at Knossos, 180, 181
Dipylon Artist, 76–77
Dipylon Gate, 66, 69, 74
Dipylon Head, 66, 66, 72, 74–77, 76
Dispilio, 272–82
    clay vessels at, 280, 280
    communication of, 279, 281, 281–82
    economy of, 280, 280–81, 281
    figurines at, 281, 281
    jewellery at, 281, 281
    Keramopoullos's excavation of, 274–75
    modern excavations of, 275–79, 275–82
    reconstruction of, 272, 273, 282, 282, 283
Dodecanese, annexation of, 18, 30
Dodona, oracular tablets at, 32
Doll, Christian, 180
dolphin motif, 94, 246, 247
Dontas, G., 328
D'Ooge, Martin L., 26
Doric capital at Kerameikos, 73, 73–74

Dörpfeld, Wilhelm, 23, 52, 103, 107, 131, 205
Doryphoros (Spear-Bearing) Alexander (statue), 354–55
Double Axes, Hall of, 166, 167–71, 169, 171
Doublet, G., 85
Drama, 30
dromos, at Salamis, 221, 221–22
Drosini, Georgis, 321
Drosinos, V., 131
Drosinos's Treasure, 131
Drougou, Stella, 260
Dugas, Ch., 87, 92–95
Dumont, Albert, 21, 85
Dürrbach, F., 85–88, 91
Dutch Institute, 30
Duthuit, Claude, 286

E

Edessa, 31
Efendi, Osman, 36
Efstratiadis, Panayiotis, 23, 27, 48–51
Eirene of Kephisodotos, 331
Eleusis, 26, 32, 33
Elgin, Lord (Thomas Bruce), 19
Elgin Collection, 49
Emporion, stoas of, 328
Ephemeris Archaeologiki (journal), 17, 20–21, 23, 26–27, 29, 30
Ephesos, 30
Ephors, 20, 23
Epidaurus, 25, 32
Epirus, 30
Erechtheion, 38, 39, 43, 43, 44, 53, 54
Etruscans, 196
Eukleia, sanctuary of, 258, 270
Eumenus, stoa of, 22, 24
Euphranor, 329, 331, 345
Eurymedon, tomb of, 118, 123–24
Evangelidis, D., 32
Evans, Sir Arthur, 29, 131, 158–83, 161, 183, 244
experimental archaeology, 300–304

F

Fauvel, L. S., 22, 82
figurines
    at Akrotiri, 244, 245, 254, 254
    at Dispilio, 281, 281
    at Mycenae, 122–23, 124–25, 126
    at Olympia, 106–7
    at Sesklo and Dimini, 194, 195
Finnish Institute, 30
First International Conference on Archaeology, 16, 29
Fisherman (wall-painting), 242
fishing, at Dispilio, 281, 281
fishplate, in shipwreck, 296, 297
Florimond, Joseph (Duke of Loubat), 87, 87, 92, 98
Flotilla (wall-painting), 254
Fonseca, G. Simoes da, 95
Ford Foundation, 219
foreign gods, sanctuary of, at Delos, 85–86, 92
Fortress of Pylos, 362
Foucart, Paul, 21, 137–41
Fougères, G., 85
Fougères, M., 85–86
fountain of Minos, at Delos, 92
Fourni, House at, 98
Frangos, Dimos, 138–39
Frankish Tower
    demolition of, 24–25, 48, 48–50
    in fortified castle, 36–37
Frantz, Alison, 217
Franz, Johannes, 19
Frederica (Greek queen), 218, 218
French Archaeological School of Athens, 18, 21

at Delos, 26, 78, 84–98
at Delphi, 78, 137–51
Frey, Don, 358–59
Furtwängler, Adolf, 103, 107

G

Gabriel, A., 87, 92
Gaertringen, Hiller von, 238
Gandar, Eugène, 137
Gardner, E. A., 27
General Ephor, 20
Geometric period
    art of, 107
    cemetery at Kerameikos, 66–67, 67
Georgian Institute of Athens, 30
German Archaeological Institute, 18, 23
    at Agora of Athens, 205
    at Kerameikos, 60–69, 62–65
    at Olympia, 24, 26, 102–3, 115
Giants, stoa of, 204, 204, 205
Gjerstad, Einar, 222
glass ingots, 310, 312, 312, 314
gold, Mycenaen, 118–32. See also Mycenae
gold casket, at Vergina, 268, 268–69, 269
gold-clad goddess, in shipwreck, 308, 315
gold grave offerings, at Mycenae, 126–29, 126–31
gold rings
    at Knossos, 182, 183
    at Mycenae, 128, 129
gold scarab, of Queen Nefertiti, 312, 313, 314, 315
golden fleece, 200
Goodwin, William Watson, 26
Gortyn, Law Code of, 161
Goudi Rising, 29
Grace, Virginia, 288
Graces, at Agora of Athens, 205
Grand Staircase, at Knossos, 167–69, 168, 169
Grave Circle at Mycenae, 24, 119, 123–25, 123–31
Great Altar, at Delphi, 144
Greek archaeology. See also specific sites and findings
    beginnings of, 19
    first great moment of, 20
    stages of, 18–33
    tourism and, 33
Greek Ephorate of Underwater Antiquities, 360–62
Greek War of Independence, 19
grill supports, Neolithic, 191
Griswold, E., 218
Gropius, George Christian, 22
Guigniaut, Joseph, 137
gymnasium
    at Delphi, 151, 153–54, 154, 155
    at Salamis, 220, 220

H

Hadrian, stoa of, 32
Hadrian statue, 180, 180, 182
Halbherr, Frederico, 29, 161
Halos, at Delphi, 144
Hammond, N. G. L., 257–58
Hansen, Christian, 40
Hatzfeld, J., 87, 92–95
Hatzidakis, Joseph, 161
Hauser, A., 322
Haussoullier, Bernard, 138, 144, 160
Hauvette, A., 85
Heberdey, Rudolf, 28
Hegeso, funerary monument of, 63
"Hekatompedon," 52–53
Hephaistos, temple of, 32, 217–18
Hera, temple of, at Olympia, 105
Heraion
    at Olympia, 102, 115
    at Samos, 338, 340

Herakles, twelve labors of (sculpture), 107, 107
Hérault estuary, statue from, 354–55, 355
Hermaistai, Agora of, 90–91
Hermes, House of, 94, 98
Hermes of Praxiteles (statue), 105–6, 106
Herodes Atticus, odeion of, 22
Herodotus, 272
Heroön, at Vergina, 257, 262
Hess, A. H., 65
Heuzey, L., 258, 259
hieromnemon, of Thessalians, 144
Hirschfeld, Gustav, 103
Hirschfeld, Nicolle, 311
History of Ancient Greek Art (Tsountas), 29
History of Greek Art (Kavvadias), 29
Hogarth, D. G., 27
Holleaux, M., 89–90, 92, 96
Holy Apostles, church of the, 216–17, 217
Holy Trinity, church of the, 58, 60
Homer
    and burial customs at Salamis, 224, 230–33
    and Schliemann, 118–32
Homolle, Théophile
    as director of French School, 21
    at Delos, 81, 85–88, 95–96, 99
    at Delphi, 141–42, 142, 151, 154
horses, in tombs at Salamis, 224, 224, 226–28, 230, 231, 232
Hymn to Apollo, Delphic, 144, 144–47, 151

I

Iakovidis, Spyros, 24
ibex figurine, at Akrotiri, 254, 254
Idrisi, Abou Abdallah Mouhammed Al, 78
Ikonomos, Georgis, 17, 32
incense-burner, from Delphi, 152
Inopos, cistern of, 92, 96
inscriptions
    publication of, 19, 22–23, 32
    at Agora of Athens, 207
    at Attica, 22–23
    at Delphi, 137, 137
    at Eleusis, 26
    at Kerameikos, 58, 60, 65, 65, 68, 69
    at Knossos, 161
    at Macedonia, 30, 32
    at Merenda, 335–37, 337
    at Olympia, 104, 105, 105, 111, 111
    at Piraeus, 20
    at Samos, 339–40, 340
Institute of Nautical Archaeology (INA), 308–10, 310
Institution of the Poseidoniastai, 90, 91
Ionic column at Kerameikos, 73, 73–74, 77, 77
Irish Institute of Hellenic Studies, 30
iron ingots, 296, 298
Isopata cemetery, 182
Isopata gold ring, 182, 183
Italian Archaeological School, 29, 196–98
ivory
    bed, at Salamis, 226, 229
    head, at Vergina, 266
    throne, at Salamis, 225–26, 227, 228
    in shipwreck, 306–8, 314

J

J. Paul Getty Museum, 353–54, 354
Jacquemin, Anne, 150
Jardé, A., 91
Jason and the Argonauts, 200
javelin heads, in shipwreck, 297, 298
Jebb, Richard, 27
jewellery
    at Dispilio, 281, 281

Rachel Misdrachi-Kapon, *Artistic Designer*

Moses Kapon, *Artistic Consultant*

Dora Dialeti-Komini, Zeta Livieratou, George Diamantis, *Copy Editors*

Eleni Valma, Matina Vroulou, Ioannis Alekou *DTP*

Stelios Anastasiou, Gogo Trikerioti, Michalis Janetakis, *Processor of Illustrations*

D. Plessas, Michailides Brothers, Toxo, *Colour separations*

Printed by Escalina M. EPE

Bound by Moutsis Brothers

Printed on Garda-P, 150 gsm